The Economics of Biodiversity
Conservation in Sub-Saharan Africa

The Economics of Biodiversity Conservation in Sub-Saharan Africa

Mending the Ark

Edited by

Charles Perrings

Professor of Environmental Economics and Environmental Management, University of York, UK

Edward Elgar

Cheltenham, UK • Northampton, MA, USA

Published by
Edward Elgar Publishing Limited
Glensanda House
Montpellier Parade
Cheltenham
Glos GL50 1UA
UK

Edward Elgar Publishing, Inc.
136 West Street
Suite 202
Northampton
Massachusetts 01060
USA

A catalogue record for this book is available from the British Library

Library of Congress Cataloguing in Publication Data

The economics of biodiversity conservation in Sub-Saharan Africa/
    edited by Charles Perrings.
        1. Biological diversity conservation — Economic aspects — Africa,
        Sub-Saharan. I. Perrings, Charles.
    QH77. A43E36 1999
    338.4 '333.9516' 0967 — dc21
                                                                    99–22821
                                                                        CIP

ISBN 1 84064 150 9

Printed and bound in Great Britain by Bookcraft (Bath) Ltd.

Contents

Figures

Tables

Appendices

Acronyms and Abbreviations

ADB	Agricultural Development Bank
ASIP	Agricultural Sector Investment Project
AT&P	African Timber and Plywood Company
CAMPFIRE	Communal Areas Management Program for Indigenous Resources
CARE(K)	Canadian and American Relief Everywhere (Kenya)
CDM	Consolidated Diamond Mines
CEPA	Centre for Economic Policy Analysis
CIDA	Canadian International Development Agency
CITES	Convention on International Trade in Endangered Species of Wild Fauna and Flora
CMB	Cocoa Marketing Board
COCOBOD	Cocoa Board
CPUE	Catch per unit effort
CRS	Catholic Relief Services
CSD	Cocoa Services Department
DAES	Department of Agricultural Extension Services
DANIDA	Danish International Development Agency
DARD	Department of Agriculture and Rural Development
DEVPOL	Statement of Development Policies, Malawi
DREA	Department of Research and Environmental Affairs
EAP	Economically Active Population
ECGI	Export Credits Guarantee Department, UK
EENESA	Environmental Economics Network of Eastern and Southern Africa
EI	Economic Index
EKC	Environmental Kuznets Curve
EPC	Export Promotion Council
ERP	Economic Recovery Programme
EU	European Union
FAO	Food and Agriculture Organization of the United Nations
FD	Forestry Department, Ghana
FMU	Forest Management Units

FOB	Free on Board
FPIB	Forest Products Inspection Bureau
FRMP	Forest Resource Management Project
GATT	General Agreement on Tariffs and Trade
GBA	Global Biodiversity Assessment
GDP	Gross Domestic Product
GFDC	Ghana Food Distribution Corporation
GHI	Genetic Heat Index
GIPC	Ghana Investment Promotion Centre
GMP	Guaranteed Minimum Prices
GRN	Government of the Republic of Namibia
GTMB	Ghana Timber Marketing Board
GTZ	German Agency for Technical Cooperation
HVP	Hadejia Valley Project
IBRD	International Bank for Reconstruction and Development – World Bank
ICBP	International Council for Bird Preservation
ICDPs	Integrated Conservation and Development Projects
IDA	International Development Association
IFAD	International Fund for Agricultural Development
IIED	International Institute for Environment and Development
IMF	International Monetary Fund
IPI	Integrated Poverty Index
ISSER	Institute of Statistical, Social and Economic Research
ITCZ	Inter Tropical Convergence Zone
ITTO	International Tropical Timber Organization
IUCN	The International Union for Conservation of Nature and Natural Resources
kJ	Kilojoules
KRIP	Kano River Irrigation Project
Ksh	Kenyan Shillings
KWS	Kenya Wildlife Service
LSU	Livestock Unit
MEATCO	Meat Corporation
MET	Ministry of Environment and Tourism
MFR	Marsabit Forest Reserve
MK	Malawi Kwacha
MLF	Ministry of Lands and Forestry, Ghana
MNCPB	Marsabit National Cereals and Produce Board
MSY	Maximum Sustainable Yield
MTADP	Medium Term Agricultural Development Programme
NAEP	National Agricultural Extension Project

NAFTA	North American Free Trade Area
NARS	National Agricultural Research System
NARSP	National Agricultural Research Strategic Plan
NEAP	Malawi National Environment Action Plan
NCCK	National Christian Council of Kenya
NGO	Non-governmental organization
ODA	Overseas Development Agency
OECD	Organization for Economic Co-operation and Development
OFI	Oxford Forestry Institute
OLS	Ordinary Least Squares
PBC	Produce Buying Company
PPMED	Policy Planning, Monitoring and Evaluation Department
PWCs	Protection Working Circles
RBDAs	River Basin Development Authorities
SAP	Structural Adjustment Programme
SG2000	Sasakawa Global 2000
TDR	Transferable Development Right
TEDB	Timber Export Development Board
THF	Tropical High Forest
TRADA	Timber Research and Development Association
TVA	Tenessee Valley Authority
UK	United Kingdom
UN	United Nations
UNCED	United Nations Conference on Environment and Development
UNDP	United Nations Development Programme
UNEP	United Nations Environment Programme
WCED	World Commission on Environment and Development
WCMC	World Conservation Monitoring Centre, UK

Contributors

Gayatri Acharya is a Research Associate at the School of Forestry and Environmental Studies, Yale University

Adano Wario Roba is completing a doctorate in environmental economics at the University of York

Edward B. Barbier is a Reader in Environmental Economics at the University of York

James K. Benhin is completing a doctorate at the University of York and is a research associate on a CIFOR project on the economics of deforestation in West Africa

Omu Kakujaha-Matundu is a Senior Lecturer in Economics at the University of Namibia

Victor Kasulo is completing a doctorate in environmental economics at the University of York on leave of absence from the Ministry of Economic Planning and Development, Malawi

Jon Lovett is a Lecturer in Environmental Management at the University of York

Charles Perrings is Professor of Environmental Economics and Environmental Management at the University of York

Preamble

This volume reports research undertaken with the support of a grant from the Department of Environment, Transport and the Regions under the Darwin Initiative. The research had three main objectives: (i) training of African researchers in the ecology and economics of biodiversity loss; (ii) research into the causes and consequences of biodiversity loss in Sub-Saharan Africa; and (iii) the development of recommendations for:

- the development of national strategies, plans or programmes for the conservation and sustainable use of biological diversity (called for under Article 6 of the Convention on Biological Diversity);
- the adoption of economically and socially sound measures that act as incentives for the conservation and sustainable use of the components of biodiversity (called for under Article 11 of the Convention); and
- for semi-arid or arid lands, the integration of strategies called for under both Biodiversity and Desertification Conventions.

The volume reports the research undertaken to meet the second of these goals, and the recommendations that flow from that research to meet the third goal.

The approach adopted is based on case studies. This reflects the view, expressed in the *Global Biodiversity Assessment* (V. Heywood (ed.), Cambridge: Cambridge University Press, 1995), that the primary costs of biodiversity loss stem not so much from the loss of genetic information through the global extinction of species – important though that is – as from the loss of ecosystem productivity, functioning and resilience. That is, the deletion of species at the local level can have the effect of reducing the capacity of local ecosystems to support human activities and local life support services. This makes biodiversity loss as much a local as a global problem.

Since the Convention on Biological Diversity starts from the premise that individual countries have sovereignty over the biological resources that fall within their territorial boundaries, the extent to which they meet the aims of the Convention will depend on how they weight the local costs and benefits of biodiversity loss. The research reported here considers that problem: the local costs and benefits of biodiversity loss in a selection of Sub-Saharan African countries. The countries have been chosen so as to offer a representative sample of Sub-Saharan African ecosystems. These include wetlands (Nigeria), freshwater lakes (Malawi), tropical forests (Ghana), montane forests (Kenya), and semi-arid savannas (Namibia).

A second feature of the approach is that it is based on economic principles. That is, biodiversity use is treated as a resource allocation problem. It reflects the view that for any given ecosystem there is an 'optimum level' of biodiversity which depends not only on the biogeophysical characteristics of that system, but also on the preferences of people who depend on that system, the technology available to them, and the variability of the natural and economic environments in which they work.

A common feature of the studies reported in this volume is that they ask what benefits resource users forgo when they take actions that lead to a reduction in biodiversity. This is not a question about tourists' willingness to pay to view or hunt large mammals. It is a question about the direct and indirect gains to African householders, foresters, fishermen and farmers of biodiversity conservation. It is seldom the case that it will be optimal for resource users to preserve everything, but it is almost always the case that too many species are being driven to local extinction, or are being depleted beyond the point where they can support the provision of valued goods and services. In many cases this is the unintended consequence of development policies, or policies on land tenure, agricultural or forest pricing and the like. In such cases a strategy for biodiversity conservation may centre on the removal or modification of policies that have such an effect. In other cases it will depend on the introduction or extension of land use restrictions – through the designation of protected areas or the limitation of resource use rights. Just what the components of a strategy should be is very case-specific, as these studies show.

The authors of the case studies have benefited from the advice of senior research associates in Africa (Agyapong Gyekye of the University of Venda and Chris Mupimpila of the University of Zambia) and at the University of York (Ed Barbier and Jon Lovett). They have also benefited from feedback offered at review workshops in Harare and Nairobi. In this connection the support of the African Economic Research Consortium (AERC) and, in particular, of William Lyakurwa, is gratefully acknowledged. The Nairobi workshop was organized by the AERC, and brought together researchers in the field, non-governmental organizations and administrators to review the preliminary results of the work. Feedback from the workshop has been particularly useful in preparation of the final draft.

Finally, development and extension of the project to consider the role of economic incentives in biodiversity conservation in Sub-Saharan Africa has been made possible by a grant from the MacArthur Foundation. Given the relatively low priority accorded to environmental economics in the region, the expansion of the Foundation's environmental programme in Africa is to be welcomed.

Charles Perrings
York
September 1998

1. The Biodiversity Convention and biodiversity loss in Sub-Saharan Africa

Charles Perrings

1.1 INTRODUCTION

The Convention on Biological Diversity came into force on 29 December 1993 as a concrete expression of global concern over the problem of biodiversity loss. As a framework document it comprises a set of goals rather than a set of precise obligations. Moreover, it allows the Contracting Parties very wide discretion as to how they choose to interpret those goals, and how they seek to achieve them. Under the Convention, the Contracting Parties are required to develop national strategies, programmes or action plans for the conservation and sustainable use of biodiversity, but the form and content of those strategies, programmes or plans is left open. Indeed, the Convention makes a point of asserting sovereign rights over biodiversity within the territories of the Contracting Parties. Although this is qualified by references to the responsibilities that states have to others, given that biodiversity is a common concern, the Contracting Parties can choose the level of protection to be offered depending on their view of the problem.

It follows that implementation of the Convention will depend on national perceptions of how and where the loss of biodiversity imposes costs on society. In the five years since the Convention came into force there has been considerable scientific analysis of the economic causes and consequences of biodiversity loss (Perrings et al., 1994, 1995; Heywood, 1995; Pearce and Moran, 1994). But the Contracting Parties have been left to assess for themselves both the nature of the national biodiversity problem, how it maps into the goals of the Convention, and what the elements of a biodiversity policy should be. The programme of research reported in this volume is designed to assist that process. It identifies the causes and consequences of biodiversity loss in specific countries and specific ecosystems. It also discusses methods for formulating and analysing the loss of biodiversity, and options for its conservation.

The findings of the studies reported here reflect the idea that there is an 'optimal' level of biodiversity associated with different land uses. Biodiversity conservation does not imply the preservation of all species in all places. It does imply the protection of those species needed to deliver the goods and services on which people may depend, and over the range of environmental conditions that people may experience. The studies reported here also reflect the idea that the main benefits of biodiversity accrue to users of particular ecosystems – they are local rather than global. In both respects the work is evidence of the changing perception of the importance of biodiversity reported in the Global Biodiversity Assessment (GBA) (Heywood, 1995). Although the GBA discussed the state of the art on *ex situ* and *in situ* preservation of biodiversity, it also reported the growing perception among both ecologists and economists that the value of biodiversity lies first and foremost in its role in the production of directly or indirectly useful goods and services.

On the economic side, the problem is that while many private benefits of biodiversity loss are captured in market prices, many of its social costs are not. Markets for foods and fibres drive specialization in agriculture, forestry and fisheries but do not generally signal the costs to society of private land conversion and agricultural specialization. The GBA provides evidence for a change in perception of the nature and measurement of these costs. It reported that the main value of biodiversity derives from the role of a combination of species in supporting specific ecological services. But they also include some that are much less familiar. Biodiversity in tropical forests has historically been valued through: (a) the direct use values of timber and other products including medicinal plants, and (b) economic activities that depend on forests such as hunting, fishing, recreation and tourism. Increasingly, however, it is also being valued through its role in habitat provision, soil conservation, soil productivity, water supply, water storage and flood control.

On the ecological side, the GBA showed that the cost of such ecosystem services are mediated by particular combinations of species. The species that support ecological processes under one set of environmental conditions may be different from the set that is important under a different set of conditions. One implication of specialization in agroecosystems, for example, is a tighter and tighter control regime. The smaller the diversity of cultivated species, the greater the expenditure on pesticides, fertilizers, irrigation and so on.

This last point is considered in more detail in the next section. What is most important is that biodiversity loss matters everywhere not just in megadiversity zones. Indeed, species deletion may impose much higher costs in species-poor systems than in species-rich systems. It may impose higher costs in heavily impacted or managed systems than in slightly impacted or natural systems. This questions the importance accorded to the designation of protected areas in megadiversity zones. It implies that the analysis of the costs of biodiversity loss, and the development of appropriate institutions and incentives, is primarily a local exercise. Hence the focus of the volume is on case studies drawn from a range of ecosystem types and a range of countries. While this chapter provides an overview of the biodiversity problem in Sub-Saharan Africa, its main purpose is to give a context for the case studies that follow in Parts I and II.

1.2 THE ROLE OF BIODIVERSITY

Biodiversity is generally analysed at three different levels – genetic, species and ecosystem (or community). Biodiversity at the ecosystem or community level represents the highest level of aggregation and consists of the differences between systems or communities in terms of spatial scale, structure and function. Biodiversity at the species level consists of differences between species and their interactions with their environment. Biodiversity at the genetic level consists only of differences in the genetic information species contain. Each of these concepts of diversity therefore implies some measure of difference or 'distance' between the elements of a set (Weitzman, 1995). The relevant measure of distance depends on what aspect of biodiversity matters.

The GBA (Heywood, 1995) marked, as has already been indicated, something of a watershed in the science of biodiversity in that it identified a discernible shift in the consensus about where the most important costs of biodiversity lie. The main value of biodiversity is thought to lie in the role of combinations of species supporting different ecosystem services: watershed protection and the mitigation of floods and droughts, waste assimilation, detoxification and decomposition, microclimatic stabilization and the purification of air and water, the generation and renewal of soil and its fertility, the pollination of crops and other vegetation, the control of agricultural pests, the dispersal of seeds and the transport of nutrients (Daily, 1997). Within this set of ecosystem services, however, there has also been a change in emphasis. For example, the point has already been made that biodiversity in forests is generally valued through the marketed goods and services obtained from forests: timber, medicinal plants, hunting, tourism, fishing and the like. But there is now a tendency to add the non-marketed service of, for example, carbon sequestration, wastershed protection, water supply, water storage, flood control and soil conservation.

Each of these services is mediated by particular combinations of species. More importantly, the species that support a given ecosystem service under one set of environmental conditions may be different from the species that support the same service under a different set of conditions. The mix of species in an ecosystem enables that system both to provide a flow of ecosystem services under given environmental conditions, and to maintain that flow if environmental conditions change. The Global Biodiversity Assessment was not the first document to report such findings (see Perrings et al., 1994; 1995). But it was the first document to report them as consensus findings. What this implies is that the diversity of species is valued for what it enables species to do – for the services it enables species to deliver.

In any agro-pastoral system, economic productivity ultimately depends on photosynthetic activity, and this depends on the mix of species available to exploit spatial and temporal variation in environmental conditions. Much of Sub-Saharan Africa has a markedly seasonal climate, and is also subject to a high degree of interannual variation (Nicholson, 1994; Tucker et al., 1991). Maintaining the biodiversity required to cope with this variation is a primary aim of biodiversity conservation. Figure 1.1 shows variation in a measure of photosynthetic activity, the Normalized Difference Vegetation Index, in Sub-Saharan Africa at different times during the year. Although there is a great deal of difference over the year, it is moderated by the existence of species adapted to the differing conditions. Native vegetation has evolved to be adapted to climatic fluctuations and responds to both short-term changes, and longer climatic cycles such as those generated by the orbital changes which are responsible for ice ages.[1]

Consider the geographical incidence of the main causes of soil degradation in Africa – overgrazing of rangelands, agriculture, over-exploitation of savanna vegetation and deforestation. These are illustrated in Figure 1.2. The first three map very closely onto those areas subject to the greatest fluctuation in photosynthetic activity during the year: the Sahel and the Horn of Africa, East, and South Central Africa.

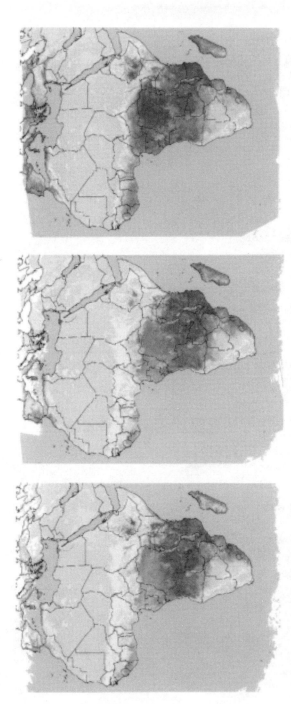

Dekad 1 – January, average 1982-93   Dekad 6 – February, average 1982-93   Dekad 12 – April, average 1982-93

Note: This is derived from the National Oceanic and Atmospheric Administration satellites and processed by the Global Inventory Monitoring and Modelling Studies at the National Aeronautics and Space Administration in the USA. The data are ten-year means and the six images are 60 days apart to cover annual variation. Darker areas have higher levels of photosynthetic activity.

Source: ADDS web site http://edcintl.cr.usgs.gov/.

Figure 1.1   Normalized Difference Vegetation Index for Africa

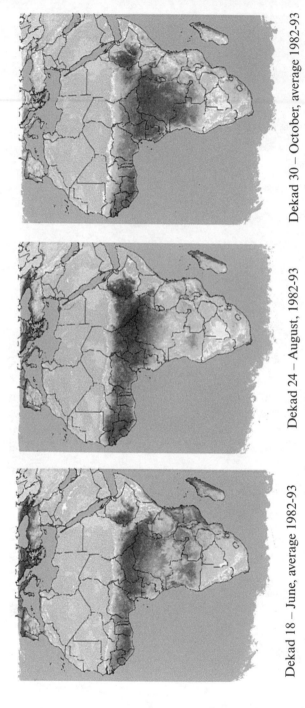

Dekad 18 – June, average 1982-93   Dekad 24 – August, 1982-93   Dekad 30 – October, average 1982-93

Figure 1.1 continued

a. Areas affected by overgrazing

b. Areas affected by agricultural activities

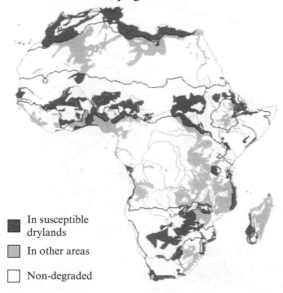

■ In susceptible
   drylands

▨ In other areas

□ Non-degraded

Source: UNEP (1997) *Global Environment Outlook 1997*, Oxford: Oxford University Press.

Figure 1.2   Sources of soil degradation in Sub-Saharan Africa

c. Areas affected by overexploitation of vegetation

d. Areas affected by deforestation

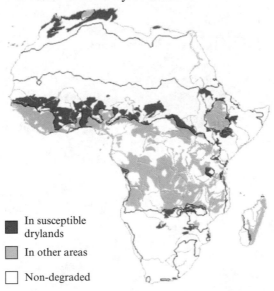

■ In susceptible drylands

▨ In other areas

□ Non-degraded

Figure 1.2   continued

The functional diversity of species is used by ecologists to refer to two rather different things: the diversity of the ecological functions mediated by different species, and the diversity of species mediating a given ecological function (Schindler, 1990a). The second of these concerns the number of species supporting the provision of ecosystem services. Consider the problem of rangeland degradation. A major feature of semi-arid rangelands in Africa is the large variation in fodder production in response to fluctuations in rainfall. This may vary five-fold or more from one year to the next (Barnes, 1979). Grazing patterns in Eastern and Southern Africa have typically led to two major changes in the diversity of rangeland vegetation. The first is the loss of perennial grasses and their replacement by annuals, which vary far more in response to fluctuations in rainfall. The second involves a reduction in the phenological diversity of the grass sward, an ecological mechanism to counteract interannual variation in production. In systems that are not subject to grazing pressure there tend to be approximately even amounts of early-, mid- and late-season growing grasses. This means that there is about the same amount of grass able to respond to rainfall whenever it occurs in the season (Walker, 1988). However, where there is heavy grazing pressure the loss of early-season palatable species implies a relative increase in the later growing species (Silva, 1987). It follows that in years dominated by early-season rains, production will be lower in heavily grazed as opposed to lightly grazed systems. The interannual variation in fodder production will also be higher. A study of the Serengeti grasslands, for instance, showed that communities which have least interannual variation in fodder production also have more species contribution to biomass (McNaughton, 1985).

Semi-arid rangelands with rapid species responses to variation in environmental conditions tend to be more resilient to – better able to maintain primary production over – variations in seasonal and interannual rainfall. The mechanism, in this case, is the effect of grazing pressure on the patchiness of rangeland: the relative size and structure of erosion and deposition surfaces. Increasing patchiness exaggerates the response of the system to climatic shocks or events. If the rangeland becomes more sensitive to environmental fluctuations, then it is said to lose resilience. In other words, the smaller the event needed to force a change in flow of ecosystem services, the lower the resilience of that system. Rising grazing pressure frequently has the effect of lowering the resilience of rangelands (Perrings and Walker, 1995; 1997).

Loss of resilience induced by the loss of grass species will show up in lower weight gains of livestock. It will therefore have an economic value determined by the change in the value of output under the new conditions. More generally, the value of the functional diversity of species depends on the value of all of the ecosystem services provided by those species. Since this is conditioned by the state of nature it follows that the value depends on the range of environmental conditions over which the system may have to operate. It is worth adding that environmental conditions in this context means more than rainfall and temperature. A change in world prices for agricultural commodities is just as much a change in environmental conditions as a change in rainfall or temperature. Just as the phenological diversity of grasslands can maintain primary productivity despite seasonal variation in rainfall, so can it maintain the condition of livestock to meet seasonal variation in stock prices.

The example of semi-arid rangelands illustrates the role of biodiversity in maintaining ecosystem services over a certain range of environmental conditions – the rainfall cycle, for example. But even in this example, the loss of some species turns out to be much more significant than the loss of others. There is considerable empirical evidence that loss of some species has minimal effect on the provision of ecosystem services, while loss of others can trigger a fundamental change in ecosystem type – causing grassland to switch to shrubby semi-desert, for instance (Walker et al., 1969). There are, however, not enough long-term studies to show whether loss of seemingly less important or 'redundant' species involves slower more subtle shifts in ecosystem structure or function, or whether they may become important if there is a fundamental change in environmental conditions.

The resilience of ecosystems – their capacity to function when subject to stress or shock – depends on the species which support the critical structuring processes of those systems over different environmental conditions. Some species are particularly important under existing environmental conditions, but this does not mean that all other species are redundant. Species that are 'passengers' in one set of environmental conditions may have a key structuring role to play in other sets of environmental conditions (Holling et al., 1995). Indeed, this is one reason why at least some ecologists argue that resilience is an increasing function of biodiversity. While there is insufficient evidence to judge this, it is intuitive that in the management of ecological systems there may be trade-offs between the benefits from the commercial exploitation of individual species and the provision of a wider array of ecosystem services. The one favours either simplification or modification of the system to increase output of the valuable species, the other favours maintenance of the set of species that will protect the flow of ecosystem services.

Individual biological resources are valuable for many reasons including their importance as sources of food or fibre, their pharmacological properties, their totemic or aesthetic value or because of their capacity to add value to other species through breeding or genetic manipulation. Biodiversity matters partly because of the value of individual species, but also because of the role of the mix of species in supporting ecosystem services over a range of environmental conditions. Many of the most important problems in the conservation of biodiversity worldwide stem from the fact that the private resource users tend to focus on the value of individual species in consumption of production and to neglect the value of the mix of species in supporting ecosystem services. Because resource users are either unaware of the trade-offs, or because they are encouraged to ignore them, the mix of species attracts less weight than do individual species.

Another source of difficulty is the fact that, as we have seen, even though any ecosystem contains hundreds to thousands of interacting species the system tends to be driven by a small number (Holling, 1992). The deletion of some species seems to have minimal effect on the functioning of many ecosystems, even though the deletion of others triggers a fundamental transformations from one ecosystem type to another. If resource users perceive species to be redundant in this sense they will have little incentive to conserve them. The property of ecosystems that is most relevant to the sustainability of economic development is their resilience: the capacity to respond positively and creatively to external stress and shocks. Biodiversity is important from this perspective because of its role in preserving ecosystem resilience by underwriting the provision of key ecosystem functions over a range of environmental conditions (Holling et al., 1995).

1.3 THE PROXIMATE CAUSES OF BIODIVERSITY LOSS IN SUB-SAHARAN AFRICA

There are four processes that lie behind current concern over biodiversity loss in Sub-Saharan Africa.

- The first is the destruction and fragmentation of habitat associated with the expansion of mining, forestry and agriculture. Habitat fragmentation and loss in areas of high endemism are considered to be the major cause of species extinction worldwide. Mackinnon and Mackinnon (1986) estimated that 65 per cent of the 'original' ecosystems in Sub-Saharan Africa have been subject to major disturbance through human activity. This represents ecosystems converted to economic use. Much more of the land area is, however, impacted or indirectly affected by economic activity. Indeed, it is no longer useful to describe any of the world's habitats as 'undis-turbed'. The main proximate cause of species loss is therefore better described as habitat disturbance, the effect of disturbance depend-ing on its nature and location (Heywood, 1995). Nevertheless, habitat conversion remains one of the main rationales for biodiver-sity conservation through the designation of protected areas.

- The second is a persistent tendency towards the degradation of arable and grazing lands that is closely related with changes in bio-diversity. During the 1970s, successive reports noted the coincidence between deepening poverty and accelerating environmental degrada-tion in Sub-Saharan Africa. The problem was particularly severe in the countries of the Sudano-Sahelian region, but was also causing concern in Lesotho and the countries straddling the high plateau from Botswana to Kenya (United Nations Conference on Desertification, 1977). The main proximate causes were thought to be livestock densities in arid and semi-arid rangelands that were unsustainably high given the variance in climatic conditions, and fallow periods in arable areas that were unsustainably low. Both were referred to by the generic term desertification: desertification being defined to include 'reduced productivity of desired plants, undesirable alterations in biomass and the diversity of micro- and macro-fauna and flora, accelerated soil deterioration, and increased hazards for human occupancy' (Dregne, 1983). Hence desertifica-tion is first and foremost a problem of biodiversity loss in managed systems. Biodiversity conservation in such systems implies a change in the information and incentives offered to resource managers.
- The third is the controlled and uncontrolled introduction of species. Most introductions in Sub-Saharan Africa have been more or less controlled imports to support agriculture and, more particu-larly, fisheries. An important subset of introductions are, however, entirely uncontrolled. These include a range of pests and pathogens that affect the health of human and non-human species alike. Although only a small proportion of introduced species establish themselves and spread, and although not all invasive species are undesirable, the Global Biodiversity Assessment concludes that the evidence overwhelmingly supports the view that invasives have neg-ative effects on both species and genetic diversity at local and global levels (Heywood, 1995; see also Williamson, 1996). These effects include the deletion of indigenous species through preda-tion, browsing or competition; genetic alteration of indigenous species through hybridization; and the alteration of ecosystem structure and function including biogeochemical, hydrological and

nutrient cycles, soil erosion and other geomorphological processes (Macdonald et al., 1989; Ramakrishnan and Vitousek, 1989). Traditionally, invasives have been addressed through controls on the movement of goods and people.

- The fourth is the harvesting and hunting of individual wild species, and particularly of individual wild fauna. In Sub-Saharan Africa this is primarily seen as a problem involving large mammals hunted either (a) for ivory, horn, skin products or trophies or (b) to protect livestock or crops. The most often cited examples are elephant and rhinoceros. Elephants have been hunted over the whole of their range for both purposes: to protect crops and (indirectly) livestock, and for the various products they yield. The popular perception is that the main threat to the viability of remaining elephant populations is illegal hunting (poaching) to meet international demand for ivory products, and the main solution is thought to lie in restrictions on the trade in those products. International trade in wild fauna and flora is regulated under the Convention on International Trade in Endangered Species of Wild Fauna and Flora (CITES) to which 122 countries are signatory. Endangered species are listed in Appendix I of the convention, and trade in such species is banned. A second group of species, listed in Appendix II, may be traded providing that the trade has not been shown to threaten the species in the wild. As a mechanism for biodiversity conservation trade bans are, however, highly controversial. Indeed, the trade ban on ivory products has been strongly contested as a conservation device by the countries of Southern Africa (Barbier et al., 1990; Barbier, Burgess and Folke, 1994).

These processes represent the proximate causes of biodiversity loss. The evidence on each of them is patchy at best, but there is nevertheless enough to indicate the relative importance of each to the problem.

Habitat Loss

Estimation of the extent of habitat destruction or fragmentation in any region is complicated by lack of hard data. Most global assessments use simple proxies that are consistent with remote sensing techniques, of which land cover is the most popular (World Resources Institute, 1994). Such techniques are, however, not capable of capturing more subtle changes, such as forest thinning or conversion of natural to plantation forest and so on. The estimates of habitat loss in Sub-Saharan Africa due to Mackinnon and Mackinnon (1986) are based on identification of an area of 'original' wildlife habitat (total area) and an area 'remaining' for wildlife, the difference being taken to measure the loss of habitat. The results are recorded in Table 1.1.

Table 1.1   Estimates of habitat conversion in Sub-Saharan Africa

	Original wildlife habitat (1000km^2)	Amount remaining (1000km^2)	Habitat loss (%)		Original wildlife habitat (1000km^2)	Amount remaining (1000km^2)	Habitat loss (%)
Angola	1247	761	39	Malawi	94	40	57
Botswana	585	258	56	Mali	754	158	79
Burkina Faso	273	55	80	Mauritania	389	74	81
Burundi	26	4	86	Mozambique	783	37	57
Cameroon	469	192	59	Namibia	823	444	46
CAR	623	274	56	Niger	566	128	77
Chad	721	173	76	Nigeria	920	230	75
Congo	342	172	49	Rwanda	25	3	87
Côte d'Ivoire	318	67	79	Senegal	196	35	82
Djibouti	22	11	49	Sierra Leone	72	11	85
Eq. Guinea	26	13	51	Somalia	638	376	41
Ethiopia	101	30	70	South Africa	1237	531	57
Gabon	267	174	35	Sudan	1703	511	70
Gambia	11	1	89	Swaziland	17	8	56
Ghana	230	46	80	Tanzania	886	505	43
Guinea	246	74	70	Togo	56	19	66
Guinea-Bissau	36	8	78	Uganda	193	43	78
Kenya	570	296	48	Zaire (Congo)	2336	1051	55
Lesotho	30	10	68	Zambia	752	534	29
Liberia	111	14	87	Zimbabwe	390	171	56
Madagascar	595	149	75				

Source: Heywood (1995) from Mackinnon and Mackinnon (1986).

The measure is, however, crude. It captures major changes in land cover, but fails to capture less destructive changes in land use. In most cases, human activities are designed to exploit the system concerned by selecting for certain species (that have properties which make them useful or desirable) and against others (typically predators or competitors). This generally has the effect of simplifying the system concerned, but it does not prevent it from being a habitat for some wild species.

Agricultural activities that eliminate pests or pathogens may still allow habitats for species whose presence contributes to or at least does not detract from the value of output. Indeed, agricultural policies are increasingly being geared towards the promotion of habitats for wildlife within arable or grazing areas.

Nevertheless, land use change on this scale necessarily has implications for the diversity of species. What those implications are depends on the habitat and the way it is affected. Habitat destruction may result in the rapid decline of species, while habitat fragmentation may have the same effect but take much longer. For instance, fragmentation can convert a continuous population structure into a metapopulation structure, with each local population reduced to the point where its probability of survival falls to zero (Heywood, 1995). It can also lead to undesirable edge effects. The destruction of tropical forests, for example, typically involves both the isolation of fragments of previously contiguous habitat, and edge effects in the moving boundary zone between forested and non-forested areas (Skole and Tucker, 1993).

Table 1.2 reports deforestation by region in the decade of the 1980s. It shows that the highest rates of forest loss occurred in West Africa, while the lowest rates occurred in Central Africa. This does not necessarily imply that rates of biodiversity loss are higher in West Africa than in Central Africa. But it is at least one indicator that the role of habitat conversion in the problem may be more important in West Africa than in Central Africa. To put this in perspective, however, the annual rate of forest loss in the countries where forest clearance was most rapid – Ghana and Togo – was still only between 1.3 and 1.4 per cent. This is low compared to other regions

Table 1.2   Forest resources and deforestation in Sub-Saharan Africa, 1980–90

	Extent of natural forest (1000 ha)		Annual deforestation (1981–1990)	
	1980	1990	(1000 ha)	(%)
West Sahelian Africa	43 720	40 768	295	0.7
East Sahelian Africa	71 395	65 450	595	0.8
West Africa	61 520	55 607	591	1.0
Central Africa	215 503	204 112	1 140	0.5
Tropical Southern Africa	159 322	145 868	1 345	0.8
Insular Africa	17 128	15 782	135	0.8

Source: The World Resources Institute (1994).

where the forest stock is more depleted. For example, Costa Rica, El Salvador, Honduras and Paraguay were all converting remaining forests at more than 2 per cent a year, while Bangladesh, Pakistan, Thailand and the Philippines were converting what is left of their forest resources at 2.9 to 3.0 per cent a year.

Desertification

Desertification is primarily an agricultural problem. An analysis of the causes of soil degradation in Africa over the whole of the post-war period finds the main factors to be overgrazing and crop production. Some 73 per cent of degradation is due to pastoral and arable practices, while only 14 per cent is due to the conversion of land (World Resources Institute, 1992). On rangelands the immediate cause of the problem is increasing herd sizes without concomitant changes in either the area of the range or animal husbandry and range management regimes. On arable lands, overcultivation under existing pest management, tillage, fertilization and fallow regimes is an important part of the problem. But there has been some growth in the area under cultivation. Between the mid-1960s and the early 1990s, whereas the land committed to livestock remained roughly constant, the land committed to arable agiculture grew at 0.7 per cent a year.

To put some more detail on the process, Table 1.3 reports changes in land use and agricultural production for selected countries in Sub-Saharan Africa in the same period. The most striking features of the changes are (a) the declining per capita output in a majority of the countries recorded, (b) increasing levels of grazing pressure indicated by changes in cattle, sheep and goat stocks relative to grazing lands, again in a majority of the countries, and (c) positive rates of deforestation in all but one country (South Africa). Both (a) and (b) are indirect evidence of the processes described as desertification, although the evidence suggests that the extent of the problem is very different in the case of rangelands, rain-fed and irrigated arable areas. It is estimated that some 74 per cent of rangelands, and 61 per cent of rain-fed arable lands are 'moderately', 'severely' or 'very severely' desertified, whereas only 18 per cent of irrigated lands fall into this category (Tolba et al., 1992).

The nature of land degradation is different in each case. In irrigated lands, for example, the problems centre on salinization and alkalinization. Worldwide, annual losses due to these causes are now running at about 1.5 million ha. In Africa, 18 per cent of all irrigated lands are considered to be degraded. In rain-fed croplands the dominant manifestation of land degradation is soil erosion and the loss of soil organisms, which account for at least 3.5 million ha annually worldwide. In Africa, 61 per cent of

Table 1.3   *Agricultural production and change in land use during the 1980s in selected countries in Sub-Saharan Africa*

	Index of aggregate agricultural production 1988–90 (1979–81 = 100)	Index of per capita agricultural production 1988–90 (1979–81 = 100)	Cropland: percentage change between 1987–89 and 1977–79	Permanent pasture: percentage change between 1987–89 and 1977–79	Forest and woodland: percentage change between 1987–89 and 1977–79	Cattle: percentage change since 1978–80	Sheep and goats: percentage change since 1978–80
Botswana	110	79	1	0	–0.9	–13	199
Burkina Faso	146	116	27.5	0	–8.2	5	88
Chad	124	100	2.3	0	–5.8	–2	–9
Ethiopia	104	84	1	–1.1	–3.5	10	3
Kenya	146	105	6.8	0	–7.8	27	11
Mali	130	100	1.8	0	–4.1	–3	–10
Mauritania	113	89	1.4	0	–2.2	7	–2
Namibia	123	93	1	0	–1.6	–23	14
Niger	108	80	13	4	–22.1	12	15
Somalia	135	99	4.8	0	–1.1	29	26
South Africa	107	88	–1.3	–0.1	8.8	–13	–1
Sudan	100	76	0.9	0	–6.2	19	18
Tanzania	122	88	2.2	0	–2.8	5	43

Sources: World Resources Institute, (1992); World Bank (1996).

rain-fed croplands is considered to be degraded – a greater proportion than in any other region. In rangelands the problem is both much more severe and much more extensive. One estimate of the global annual cost of the desertification of arable and rangelands puts forgone income from rain-fed agriculture at US$8.2 billion, compared with $US23.3 billion from rangelands (Tolba et al., 1992). Just under 75 per cent of all rangelands in Africa (and all rangelands worldwide) are considered to be degraded (Biswas, 1994).

To understand the connection with biodiversity loss we need to understand just what the process of land degradation implies. Consider the case of rangelands. Increasing grazing pressure implies a reduction in the proportion of palatable grasses and an increase in both unpalatable grasses and woody plants, an important effect of which is to change the role of fire. In many savanna rangelands, woody plants are controlled by a combination of periodic fire and the capacity of the grass layer to suppress woody seedlings (Knoop and Walker, 1985). In such cases an increase in grazing pressure both raises the probability that woody seedlings will successfully establish, and reduces the effectiveness of fire as a control. Once established, the growth of woody plants generates positive feedback effects. Reduced grass cover means that more water passes through to the sub-soil, taking nutrients with it and enhancing the competitive ability of plants which have more of their roots in deeper layers. In addition, reduced fuel load reduces the incidence of fire and hence the main control on the establishment of woody plants. The net effect is that the rangeland may be transformed from one state (characterized by one mix of species, and one level of productivity) to another state (characterized by another mix of species, and another level of productivity).

Invasives

There is little systematic data on the problem of invasives in Sub-Saharan Africa, or on its implications for the loss of biodiversity. Although the weight of evidence worldwide suggests that invasives have generally negative effects on both species and genetic diversity, the set of case studies of the problem in Africa do not all point in the same direction. Part of the reason for this is that not all ecosystems are equally affected by invasives. Typically, mixed island systems have higher numbers of invasives proportionate to the total species diversity than do continental biomes. Moreover, xeric environments in continental biornes – warm deserts and semi-deserts, tropical dry forests and woodlands – typically have few invasives, and there is no known example of a terrestrial continental species driven to extinction by invasives (Heywood, 1995). This said, there is certainly evidence of considerable ecological disruption due to invasives. The *fynbos* and *karoo* systems in South Africa, for example, have both suffered a very substantial reduction in local diversity as a result of the introduction of exotic trees and shrubs. In addition, it is estimated that a little over 6 per cent of the 237 threatened terrestrial fauna in Sub-Saharan Africa have been placed at risk by invasives: a figure which rises to 25 per cent for reptiles (Macdonald et al., 1989).

Most of the evidence for the impact of invasives in Sub-Saharan Africa comes from freshwater aquatic systems, and is somewhat mixed. Some invasive aquatic plants such as *Salvinia molesta* and *Eichhornia crassipes* are almost universally damaging in their effects, but the impact of fish introductions is less clear. Some 50 fish species have been introduced into Sub-Saharan African lakes, both to create fisheries and to feed on macrophytes. Judged in terms of their capacity to meet growing demand for protein the introductions of both the Nile Perch, *Lates niloticus*, and the Lake Tanganyika Sardine, *Limnothrissa miodon*, have been extremely successful. But both have also had an effect on the biodiversity of the lakes to which they were introduced.

The introduction of the Nile Perch into Lake Victoria, for example, is linked with the loss of some 200 of the estimated 300 endemic cichlid species. Similar declines have been recorded in other lakes where the fish has been introduced. As in Lake Victoria, Lakes Kyoga and Nabugabo are now dominated by two introduced species, *Lates niloticus* and *Oreochromis niloticus*, and one native, *Rastrineobola argentea* (Ogutu-Ohwayo, 1995). While it may be that other factors are involved in the disappearance of cichlids in the lakes – fishing pressure and environmental change among them (Bundy and Pitcher, 1995) – the introduction of the Nile Perch has been at least partly responsible for a very significant decline in the diversity of these lake ecosystems.

The introduction of the Tanganyika Sardine into Lake Kariba and Lake Kivu has had less dramatic ecological consequences than the introduction of the Nile Perch into Lake Victoria, but it has not been at all neutral. The sardine, a pelagic zooplanktivorous fish, has had less of an impact on other fish species (Karenge and Kolding, 1995), but has had a profound effect on the plankton community. It is argued, for example, that it has severely reduced populations of larger zooplankton and has led to the disappearance of the lake fly *Chaoborus* from Kariba (Marshall, 1995).

Fish introductions to control pests have also had ecological effects, sometimes profound, but these have tended to excite less concern. For example, the introduction of *Tilapia grahami* into Lake Nakuru as a form of mosquito control in the 1960s has transformed the lake ecosystem from one of very low diversity – essentially flamingoes and two species of algae – to one that includes at least 30 species of fish-eating birds (Heywood, 1995).

Hunting and Harvesting

While hunting has led to the extinction of many endemic species on islands there are no documented cases of terrestrial species hunted to extinction in continental Sub-Saharan Africa, but there are innumerable examples of species eradicated from particular parts of their range; species whose ranges have been dramatically reduced; species whose abundance has fallen to the point where they are 'endangered'; and species that survive only through active conservation programmes and protection regimes IUCN, 1994). The dramatic decline in the black rhinoceros, for example, is due almost solely to illegal hunting stimulated by demand for its horn (for its medicinal properties). Its survival, similarly, is due almost solely to the efforts that have been made to conserve it (Cumming et al., 1990).

Many other species threatened by hunting or harvesting over parts of their range are exploited to satisfy purely local demand. Nearly 70 per cent of the population in Sub-Saharan Africa is rural, and relies on wild living resources for a substantial part of their needs. Almost all rural domestic energy requirements and a high proportion of urban domestic energy requirements are met from wild harvested timber, which threatens both the exploited species – particularly specialist species – and the habitat to which they contribute. Wild living resources that have been put under strain by the hunting and harvesting activities of local communities include both flora and fauna.

So far as lakes and rivers are concerned, it has already been noted that one view of the loss of so many endemic cichlid species in Lake Victoria is that the impact of the Nile Perch was exaggerated by the effects of over-fishing (Bundy and Pitcher, 1995). A similar phenomenon has been observed in Lake Malawi even though there have been no introductions to that lake. Turner, Tweddle and Makwinja (1995) note that increasing fishing pressure and changes in fishing technology in Lake Malombe and Lake Malawi south of Boadzulu Island has had a significant effect on community structures, involving a reduction in diversity and an increase in the relative abundance of smaller species. He argues that if the same patterns were to extend to other areas of the lake, species extinctions might well become inevitable. The reason for this is that many endemic species have highly restricted distributions within the lake. As in Lake Victoria, the species thought to be most at risk are demersal and pelagic haplochromine cichlids that are susceptible to small-meshed unselective fishing gear.

1.4   THE UNDERLYING CAUSES OF BIODIVERSITY LOSS

The diagnosis of the underlying causes of biodiversity loss from economists has tended to focus on the role of institutions/property rights and policy in distorting the operation of commodity markets in general, and agricultural commodity markets in particular (Swanson, 1995). There is a wide range of rights conferred by law or custom on the users of natural resources and these vary from country to country, and from resource to resource. Land rights include private ownership, leasehold, state ownership, regulated access common property together with open access common property. While the last of these is most frequently cited as an underlying cause of the overexploitation of resources, all are implicated to some degree. The implicit subsidy on agricultural land offered by traditional (common or communal) land tenure systems is an important source of bias. So is the weakening of social control over access to the resource base as rural institutions and property rights have been redefined in the development process (Githinji and Perrings, 1992). But even where there are private or leasehold rights to land, markets are still missing for many of the most important interactive effects between right-holders (Pearce and Warford, 1993).

In addition to missing markets, many existing markets have been prevented from operating efficiently by agricultural policies and institutions. During the 1980s this was argued to have led to the degradation of the agroecosystems by increasing pressure on grazing, arable and forest resources, and by inhibiting responses to climatically induced changes in the sensitivity of the environment to such pressure (Berry, 1984; World Bank, 1986; Repetto, 1989). It was argued that fiscal, price and incomes policies directly increased the pressure on soils, vegetation, and water. Subsidies designed to promote cash cropping as a means of increasing export revenue, for example, were argued to have contributed to leaching, soil acidification, and nutrient loss, and to the reduction in the resilience of key ecosystems (Grainger, 1990). Administered prices were also argued to have reduced producer income and so discouraged investment in land conservation (Warford, 1987).

The reforms of the last ten years have begun to alter this pattern of distortion in agricultural prices, but agricultural subsidies nevertheless remain one of the main driving forces behind biodiversity loss. Pearce (1998) has recently estimated that subsidies to biodiversity-threatening activities worldwide are currently running at $684–808 billion, $151 billion of which occur in non-OECD countries. Some agricultural subsidies have been reduced or eliminated in Sub-Saharan African countries, frequently as part of a structural adjustment programme agreed with the International Monetary Fund and/or the World Bank. The study of deforestation in Ghana in Part II of this volume explores the implications of the changes in relative prices associated with one such set of reforms. But only a small number of countries (the Cairns Group) have come close to the elimination of distortionary price interventions in agriculture. 'Policy failures' of this sort are widely recognized to be at the heart of the biodiversity problem (Barbier et al., 1994; Perrings et al., 1994). These issues are considered later.

A third driving force behind biodiversity loss in Sub-Saharan Africa is persistent rural poverty. The Brundtland Report (WCED, 1987) and Agenda 21 (UNCED, 1993) both asserted rural poverty to be a direct cause of environmental degradation. In recent years, however, environmental economists have paid increasing attention to an empirical relation between per capita income and certain indicators of environmental quality that seems to tell the opposite story. The relation is similar to the Kuznets curve, and shows that various indicators of environmental quality first worsen and then improve as per capita incomes rise. The relation was first observed in work undertaken by Grossman and Krueger (1993) on the environmental implications of Mexico's inclusion in the North American Free Trade Area (NAFTA), but has since been found between per capita income and emissions of sulphur dioxide (Grossman and Krueger, 1993, 1995; Seldon and Song, 1994; Shafik, 1994; Panayotou, 1995, 1997), particulates and dark matter (Grossman and Krueger, 1993), nitrogen oxides and carbon monoxide (Seldon and Song, 1994), carbon dioxide and CFCs (Cole et al., 1997). Grossman and Krueger (1995) have also found a Kuznets relation involving various indicators of water quality, including faecal coliform, biological and chemical oxygen demand and arsenic.

More importantly for purposes of this study, Panayotou (1995) and Antle and Heidebrink (1995) found the same general relation between deforestation rates – one of the proximate causes of biodiversity loss – and per capita income. Figure 1.3 shows the data plot (and fitted lines) for quadratic models relating deforestation per capita GNP over a cross-section of developing countries. Panayotou (1995) found an inverted U-shaped relation between deforestation and per capita income for 41 tropical countries. If the sample is widened to include 68 developing countries reporting positive deforestation rates, the relation is much weaker. The fitted model reveals the same general relation: deforestation rates first rise and then fall as per capita income rises. But variations in per capita incomes explain only a small part of the variation in rates of deforestation.

Not only does the existence of the Environmental Kuznets Curve (EKC) appear to suggest that the post-Brundtland view on the environmental consequences of consumption are wrong about the effects of poverty and affluence, it also appears to suggest that growth in the level of consumption may be environmentally beneficial. While there may be negative environmental effects during the early stages of growth, these will be counteracted by later environmental quality improvements. To the proponents of market-led development strategies, the EKC hypothesis has been interpreted as both a rationale for growth and an argument against growth-inhibiting environmental protection measures.

It is interesting, therefore, that in the 1980s when deforestation rates were purportedly at their highest, rural poverty in Sub-Saharan Africa appeared to be deepening. In 1985, average consumption in Sub-Saharan

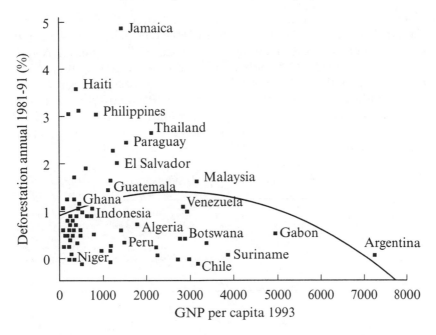

Source: The World Resources Institute (1994).

Figure 1.3   Deforestation and per capita income

Africa was not only less than it had been in 1975, it was less than it had been in 1965. In nutritional terms, mean daily calorie supply as a percentage of requirements is estimated to have fallen slightly in the whole of Sub-Saharan Africa over this period, while the variance of this measure has increased sharply. Two groups of countries experienced a significant decline in average nutrition. These are Senegal, Mauritania, Niger, Chad, Sudan, Somalia and Ethiopia in the Sudano-Sahelian region; and the Central African Republic, Zaire, Uganda, Zambia and Tanzania in East and Central Africa. Of these, the hardest hit were the Sudano-Sahelian countries. Between 1964–6 and 1984–6, daily per capita calorie supply fell by an average of nearly 20 per cent in Ethiopia, Sudan and Chad. Indeed, by the mid-1980s the populations of the Sudano-Sahelian region were reckoned to be the most deprived in the world by the UNDP's human development index (UNDP, 1990).

Nor was the burden born evenly within each country. With the exception of Zambia, the countries already mentioned are predominantly rural economies, agriculture accounting for over 70 per cent of the labour force

in all but two, and it is in the rural sector that poverty is most highly concentrated (see Table 1.4). Indeed, the same feature characterizes many of
the seemingly less disadvantaged countries of Sub-Saharan Africa,
Botswana included. Other indices of poverty tell a similar story. All of
the countries in the two groups referred to recorded zero or negative average annual per capita GNP growth between 1965 and 1988. Moreover,
although measures such as life expectancy and infant mortality did not
worsen in the period, the rate of improvement in these countries was less
than elsewhere.

Table 1.4   Profile of rural population in developing countries, 1988

	Rural population (millions)	Percentage of total population	Agricultural population: percentage of rural population	Population below the poverty line: percentage of rural population	Landless population: percentage of rural population	Refugee population: percentage of rural population
Asia	2019	74	83	31	26	5
Asia (excluding China and India)	567	70	74	46	20	5
Sub-Saharan Africa	337	73	98	60	11	6
Near East & N. Africa	106	51	73	26	23	13
Latin America & Caribbean	123	29	96	61	31	1
Least Developed Countries	368	80	89	69	18	7

Source: Jazairy et al. (1992).

Both information about future effects and the rate at which they are
discounted turn out to be sensitive to the level of market income.
Information is not costless. Although poor resource users often understand the value of resources in the uses available given the technology at
their command, their understanding of the wider value of the same
resources under different technologies tends to be limited. The poor command less information than the rich. In addition, there is a strong
relationship between income and the rate at which people discount the
future. Because what matters is consumption today, people in poverty
tend to discount the future costs of resource use at a very high rate so dis-

torting the private value they place on future effects (Perrings, 1989; Holden, Shiferaw and Wik, 1998). For similar reasons, poverty turns out to be positively correlated with high rates of population growth, or at least with high rates of fertility – with all that this implies for pressure on environmental resources (Dasgupta, 1993).

The root causes of the decline in these rural economies in this period included the declining productivity associated with the degradation of the natural resource base, the increasing level of dependence on food imports, and the sharp fall in those non-food imports – spare parts, fuels and fertilizers – on which agricultural intensification depends. Increasing pressure on grazing, arable and forest resources occurred alongside climatically induced changes in the sensitivity of the environment to such pressure. Population growth is usually thought to be the immediate source of such pressure, and it is certainly the case that high levels of population growth are associated with increasing levels of pressure on the natural resource base (Myers, 1992). But the strong positive correlation between the rate of population growth, resource degradation, and poverty does not necessarily imply a causal relationship running in one direction only. While average fertility in Sub-Saharan Africa fell over the period 1965–88, it increased in just those countries where environmental degradation and rural impoverishment had been most marked: Central African Republic, Zaire, Uganda, Zambia, and Tanzania (World Resources Institute, 1991).

One factor in this has been the fact that resources have tended to be locked into traditional activities and traditional technologies. The result is livestock densities in pastoral areas that are unsustainably high given the variance in climatic conditions in the arid and semi-arid zones, fallow periods in arable areas that are unsustainably low, and an exponential increase in the demand for construction timber and fuelwood. Overgrazing, overcultivation and deforestation have, in turn, led to reduced productivity of desirable plants, undesirable alterations in the biomass and the diversity of microfauna and flora, and accelerated soil deterioration from bush encroachment at one extreme to the increasing soil aridity at the other.

In addition, poverty is linked to the same market and policy failures that lie behind the gap between private and social value. There is considerable evidence that a major source of poverty among the users of natural resources in many of the least resilient ecosystems has been due to manipulation of the set of prices they face. In some cases, such manipulation reflects government intervention. It has, for example, been observed that a major effect of price intervention in agricultural markets in the less developed economies has been the reduction of producer incomes (cf. Warford, 1987).

An additional 'cause' of biodiversity loss is the distribution of assets, whether marketed or non-marketed. Farmers with 'uneconomic' holdings of land and other natural resources, and who have no other source of income, will tend to overexploit those holdings. It is of some concern, therefore, that there has been a marked and continuing tendency for the distribution of both assets and income to widen over time in many of the low income countries, reflecting both the erosion of traditional rights of access to the resource base and increasing human population pressure. It turns out that gender is an important factor in this trend. Female-headed households typically have access to a much smaller asset base than male-headed households, and it is not coincidental that relative poverty in the sense of relative deprivation is reckoned to bear most heavily on women (UNDP, 1992). In addition, the lower the security of tenure attaching to the use of an asset, the higher tends to be the rate at which the future costs of resource use are discounted: i.e. the lower the incentive to manage it on a sustainable basis.

1.5 THE VALUE OF BIODIVERSITY

In most cases the value of individual biological resources depends on the existence of other biological resources. The value of domesticated plant species, for example, is generally reduced by the presence of pests and diseases but enhanced by the presence of microorganisms and invertebrates which increase soil fertility (Hawksworth, 1991) or control undesirable species (Heywood, 1995). The value of the diversity of biological resources accordingly lies in the benefits offered by their combination, different combinations of species generally being of different value. In some cases, indeed in very many cases, a combination involving few species will be more valuable than a combination involving many species. Historically, environmental management has sought to enhance the value of ecosystems by eliminating undesirable species – whether pests, pathogens, predators or competitors. The problem confronted by the Convention on Biological Diversity is that whereas the private benefits from species deletion are obvious and are often reflected in market prices, the social costs are not. The valuation of biodiversity is generally concerned with the estimation of either the social cost of the deletion of species, or the social benefits of their conservation.

This section considers the evidence on the value of biodiversity in Sub-Saharan Africa. Even more than elsewhere, this evidence is patchy in both quality and quantity. The point has already been made that in much of Sub-Saharan Africa markets for ecological goods and services are either non-existent or poorly developed, and less effort has been put into their valuation than elsewhere. The available evidence derives from a number of quite different valuation studies, most of which use widely divergent valuation methods and rely on raw data of variable quality. Estimation of the value of resources in particular systems, such as wetlands or forests, is complicated by uncertainty about system boundaries, threshold levels for tolerance to pollution or depletion and so on. It is, for example, frequently impossible to specify minimum viable populations and minimum habitat sizes for the survival of species in different ecosystems. An additional source of difficulty lies in the fact that the same resources have widely divergent value to different groups of people. This is partly because of differences in preferences and technology, income and endowments. But it is also because of differences in ethical and cultural 'values'.

A 'conservationist bias' of traditional hunter–gatherer societies (McNeely and Pitt, 1985) is argued to have been the product of a long and gradual accumulation of experience of environmental responses to human pressure on the resource under a given technology (Gadgil, Berkes and Folke, 1993). Although the early settlers of Madagascar were responsible for extinction of some of the largest species of lemurs, for example, over time the remaining species came to be treated as 'sacred' and were until recently protected against hunting (Jolly, 1980). In many other traditional societies, protection of keystone species or their habitats through designation of sacred sites and supporting sanctions is a common culturally evolved response to the stresses imposed on exploited ecosystems (Gadgil and Berkes, 1991). The same species or habitats will not, however, be regarded in the same way by other societies. Although members of other societies might be willing to commit resources to their conservation, they would also be willing to trade them off against other benefits. Such differences in perception are a major source of difficulty in estimating the value of such resources.

The greatest value of biodiversity to private consumers in Sub-Saharan Africa, as elsewhere, arises from the use of domesticated plant and animal species. The main species originally domesticated in Africa were, among plants, African rice, sorghum, (pearl) millet, yam, watermelon, cowpea, coffee, cotton and sesame (the last two thought to have been independently domesticated in South Asia) and, among animals, donkey and guinea fowl (Heywood, 1995). Domesticated plant species represent a very small proportion of the total number of plant species. Domesticated food plants, for example, constitute less than 0.01 per cent of vascular plants worldwide. Given that more than 90 per cent of food supplies derives from less than 3 per cent of the domesticated species, it is clear that a small number of species – some 15–20 food crops to be precise – are more valuable to humankind than the vast majority of vascular plants. Domesticated animals are similarly concentrated. Globally, domesticated animals are dominated by just four species: cattle, sheep, pigs and chickens. In Sub-Saharan Africa goats and donkeys are more significant than sheep and pigs, but the picture is the same. A very small number of domesticated animals are more valuable than the vast majority of vertebrates.

The point has already been made that the value of domesticated plants and animals is mainly in their use. That is, the value of the genetic makeup of domesticated species derives from the consumptive and non-consumptive use to which they are put. In most cases, although the original genetic material derived from wild resources, breeding programmes and biotechnological development have improved the productivity and quality of the goods and services concerned, and so increased their value. This is not to say that the pool of domesticated genetic material is independent of the stock of wild resources. *Ex situ* conservation of domesticated genetic diversity through germ plasma technologies cannot conserve more than a sample of the range of an organism's genetic diversity. Genes transferred to domestic crop plants from their wild relatives have increased yields, improved quality, provided resistance to pests and diseases, extended growing ranges and permitted hybridization between crop species and wild relatives species (Weissinger, 1990).

Hence many non-marketed wild species derive value from the use of domesticated species. Such wild species are then said to have indirect use value. More generally, the value of biodiversity lies in the role of the composition of species in maintaining ecological services over a range of states of nature. This reflects three propositions in ecology: that the dynamics of ecological systems depend on a small set of key ecological processes (Holling et al., 1995; Holling, 1992); that animals and plants can shape their ecosystems (Schindler, 1977; McNaughton et al., 1988); and that species are more sensitive to stress than are ecosystem processes (Vitousek, 1990). The diversity of species reduces the risks of fluctuating environmental conditions. The value of biodiversity, in this sense, lies in the insurance it provides against fluctuating environmental conditions.

This last category of value may be thought of as an option value: i.e. the value of the option to use the resources if environmental conditions change. Similarly, resources that may have no use under one technology or one state of knowledge may have use under another technology or another state of knowledge. Their conservation accordingly maintains the option to use those resources under a different state of knowledge. This is conventionally defined as a quasi-option value: the value of the future information made available through the preservation of a resource (Arrow and Fisher, 1974).

Empirical Results: Species and Habitats

There are a relatively small number of studies specifically aimed at the valuation of non-marketed biological resources or biodiversity in Sub-Saharan Africa. An early and influential example was a study of the viewing value of elephants in East Africa undertaken by Brown and Henry (1993). The survey focused on foreign tourists in Kenya in 1988. It used both open ended and dichotomous choice questions to elicit tourists stated willingness to pay to maintain elephant populations at existing levels, along with a travel cost estimate of revealed preference for the same sites. The payment vehicle in the dichotomous and open ended choice questions was a special 100 dollar annual permit or equivalent increase in the safari costs. Converting the sample values to the adult safari population yielded an estimate of the annual viewing value of conservation to lie between $22 and $30 million dollars per year (in 1988 US dollars) depending on the choice of median or mean value and size of the safari population. Estimates of consumer surplus using the travel cost technique appeared to confirm these numbers, varying between $23 and $27 million dollars annually depending on the size of the safari population.

Similar market research in a number of game reserves and hunting concessions in Sub-Saharan Africa has been used to estimate the consumer surplus in both forms of recreation. Combined with research into the price elasticity of tourist demand it has been used to recalculate park fees. While such studies have helped to generate additional resources for conservation they say little about the value of the diversity of species. The viewing value of elephants is only one component of the use value of elephant conservation. For example, Barbier et al. (1990) estimated that pre-ban ivory exports from Africa were $35–45 million/year, a substantial proportion of which derived from Kenya. More recently, Moran (1994) estimated the wider value of the protection of wildlife habitats in Kenya, and concluded that the consumer surplus attached to non-consumptive use of Kenya's protected areas by foreign visitors was some $540 million (in 1994 US dollars).

Other studies of the direct use value of wild-living resources in Africa show that many activities that are marginal when evaluated in terms of direct use value at market prices have a high social rate of return when non-marketed direct use values are taken into account. Barnes and Pearce (1991) and Barnes and de Jager (1995) show that small-scale group harvesting, ostrich farming, crocodile farming, tourism, safari hunting and game ranching in wildlife areas in Botswana all offer a higher social rate of return than cattle ranching in the same areas if the non-marketed direct use values are taken into account. Barbier, Adams and Kimmage

(1991) similarly show that direct use of the Hadejia-Jama'are floodplain in Northern Nigeria for fishing, fuelwood and flood recession agriculture offers higher economic returns than commercial upstream irrigation developments that are diverting water away from the floodplain when non-market use values are included. The same issues in Northern Nigeria and Namibia have been studied in more detail in Chapters 2 and 5.

What such studies illustrate is that economic activities involving joint products, some of which are marketed and some of which are not, should be evaluated in terms of both marketed and non-marketed costs and benefits. From this point of view, the focus on foreign visitors in evaluations of tourism in Africa is potentially misleading. A World Bank study has assessed the costs and benefits across different socio-economic groups resulting from the creation of Mantadia National Park in Madagascar (Kramer et al., 1992; Kramer, 1993; Munasinghe, 1993). Mantadia and other new national parks are a response to the threat posed by deforestation and biodiversity loss in Madagascar. But they are also seen as investments that will yield a return both to the government and to the local population. To compensate for the opportunity cost to local people of park creation a number of the park projects include tourism.

The Mantadia study used both stated (contingent valuation) and revealed preference (production function and travel cost) methods to assess the potential value of tourism. Direct use benefits to local villagers from forest protection, in terms of agricultural output, fuelwood, crayfish, crab, tenreck and frogs, were valued using a production function approach. Direct use benefits to tourists were estimated using the travel cost method. Other benefits to local villagers and tourists including, for instance, the benefits of lemur conservation, were estimated using contingent valuation methods. The results (in 1992 US dollars per annum) are summarized in Table 1.5.

The opportunity cost of park creation to the local villagers includes comprised forgone benefits in the form of fuelwood, fish, animals, grasses, and land for shifting agriculture. A survey of households in the area estimated this to be $91 per household per year, implying a total of $566k. A contingent valuation survey was then undertaken to establish the villagers' willingness to accept compensation for the loss, and found this to be equivalent to 108 kg of rice for a total of $673k. In addition, both travel cost and contingent valuation studies were undertaken of visitors to the Perinet Forest Reserve, adjacent to Mantadia National Park. While the travel cost revealed quite modest benefits, the contingent valuation study estimated the annual willingness to pay for the new destination to be $6.34 million. This is probably an overestimate, but it does indicate that the park option is likely to be economically viable.

Table 1.5   Benefits from the establishment of Mantadia Park, Madagascar

Items valued	Aggregated net present value (20 years and 10% DR) (US$000)
1. Direct use benefits of forest by local villagers – agriculture, fuelwood, crayfish, crab, tenreck, frog.	566
2. Net benefit of forest for local villagers – including use and non-use costs and benefits.	673
3. Direct use benefits of tourists – tourism benefits only.	797
4. Net benefit of park creation for tourists – may include tourism and other perceived benefits and costs of park creation, e.g. lemur conservation.	2 160

Sources: Munasinghe (1993) and Kramer (1993).

The local opportunity cost of conservation may be expected to vary significantly. The scope for transferring results from one system and one location to another is therefore quite limited. A study by Campbell (1993) of the direct use value of woodland resources in Zimbabwe, again using both revealed and stated preference methods, found the annual value to the household of fruits and other wild foods, fuelwood, construction materials, crop and livestock production attributable to the woodlands to lie between $223 and $267. Contingent valuation of the same resource yielded an annual value to the household of $537. Moreover, these estimates excluded the local benefits of hunting, estimated at $2.6 per hectare per year (Murindagomo, 1988). With limited scope for benefit transfer other than within national borders and ecosystem types, it follows that valuation studies need to be undertaken afresh if they are to provide policymakers considering new projects with useful data. There are advantages to the replication of studies, but it is more important to ensure that the study includes all relevant costs.

The Mantadia exercise, for example, was directed to a restricted set of direct use benefits, and offered no estimates of indirect use, passive use or non-use benefits of the resource (Barbier, 1994). In many instances, where conservation of biological resources or ecological systems is not a viable option in the absence of indirect non-marketed use benefits, it is a viable option when those benefits are taken into account. For example, Barbier (1992) evaluated the financial return on gum arabic (*Acacia senegal*) relative to a number of existing crops in the Sudan: the existing crops including sorghum, millet, groundnuts and sesame. He showed that *Acacia senegal* was dominated by other crops in all areas of the Sudan if no account were taken of the non-marketed indirect use benefits of the crop. These include the provision of fodder for livestock, fuelwood and shade, the reduction of soil erosion and run-off, nitrogen fixation, wind-break and dune fixation. Since the tree is the preferred species in bush-fallow rotation and intercropping farming systems in the arid areas of western Sudan, it is clear that the farmers do place value on the indi-rect benefits of *Acacia senegal* cultivation. Specifically, Barbier notes that environmental benefits of gum arabic trees are significant in maintaining the yields of field crops. In addition, its role in controlling desertification supports and protects farming systems in the region and, although this is a public good, traditional farming communities in the gum belt region are aware of this benefit.

One of the key benefits of *Acacia senegal* in Sudan is its role in pro-tecting the option to undertake agricultural activity in the future. That is, it has an option value. Other examples of option and quasi-option value of wild resources in Africa include the value of wild genetic resources in plant breeding, biotechnology and pharmaceuticals. Many plants, fungi, animals and microbes, for example, have yielded pharmacologically active alkaloids and glycosides important in western medicine. The option value of a wild or weedy species lies in the fact that it provides the raw genetic material for improving existing crops. Among the better known examples of genetic transfers, a wild relative of barley from Ethiopia currently pro-tects US crops from yellow dwarf virus. On the other side, genes from a wild Mexican bean have been used to improve resistance to the Mexican bean weevil which destroys as much as 25 per cent of stored beans in Africa (WCMC, 1992).

Empirical Evidence: Ecosystem Functions

To estimate the full opportunity cost of the deletion or conservation of some species requires valuing its role in the provision of a range of ecosystem functions including nutrient cycling, watershed protection, waste assimilation, microclimatic stabilization and carbon storage. If the role of species in mediating such functions is understood, it is possible to derive the indirect use value of such species. To return to the example of elephants, in addition to a 'viewing value', elephants are known to have a role in African savannas and forests that includes ecosystem diversifica-tion, seed dispersal, expanding grasslands and reducing tsetse fly, all of which may be of value to livestock grazing (Western, 1989). Such ecologi-cal functions are important in maintaining the dynamics and health of the ecosystem, and hence its capacity to sustain the various organisms dependent on it.

A recent highly publicized attempt at valuation of the ecological services deriving from all major biomes, Costanza et al. (1997), sought to aggregate estimates obtained from various local valuation exercises to yield a single global figure that would capture the importance of ecological functions. To do this, local estimates were obtained for a range of alternative uses for 17 ecological functions. These were used to estimate values for ecosystem services per unit area in each biome, the values then being multiplied by the area of the biome, and summed across biomes. The list of ecological functions that were valued in this way is in Table 1.6.

There are serious doubts about the wisdom of estimating a single value (or even a range of values) for ecosystem services on the basis of a series of ad hoc, partial studies of particular resources and particular uses. Moreover, since the exercise is based on non-market valuation studies it ignores ecosystem functions that support arable or pastoral activity simply because their value is thought to be reflected in land prices. Given that ecosystem functions obtain value from the economic outputs they support, however, functions that support production of foods and fibres, such as nutrient cycling, erosion control, water regulation and so on, will have high derived value. Cultivation or grazing may reduce the effectiveness of key ecological functions and may reduce the resilience of those functions. A poorly functioning system that supports high value crops or livestock may nevertheless yield a greater flow of benefits than a well functioning system that supports no exploitable species. Hence Costanza et al.'s estimates of the value of ecosystem functions on croplands and grazing lands are probably misleading.

The important point of the exercise, though, is to underscore the fact that the value of ecological resources reflects the range of benefits flowing from those resources. This includes the private use, option, quasi-option, bequest and scientific values already referred to. But it also includes the indirect use value of the ecological functions supported by those resources and reflected in Table 1.6. In many cases these may be traded off against the production of economically valued goods and services. The problem for policy is to determine the appropriate trade-off given available information, market imperfections and the like.

Consider the case of tropical moist forests – thought to provide a habitat for between 60 and 80 per cent of all species. Tropical forests provide a diverse range of functions and services, including sustainable timber production, non-timber forest products, soil conservation and watershed protection, recreational services, amelioration of microclimate and carbon fixation and sequestration as well as habitat provision. Their conversion affects some ecological functions more than others. For example,

Table 1.6 Ecosystem services and functions

Ecosystem service*	Ecosystem functions	Examples
1 Gas regulation	Regulation of atmospheric chemical composition.	CO_2/O_2 balance, O_3 for UVB protection, and SO_x levels.
2 Climate regulation	Regulation of global temperature, precipitation, and other biologically mediated climatic processes at global or local levels.	Greenhouse gas regulation, DMS production affecting cloud formation.
3 Disturbance regulation	Capacitance, damping, and integrity of ecosystem response to environmental fluctuations.	Storm protection, flood control, drought recovery, and other aspects of habitat response to environmental variability mainly controlled by vegetation structure.
4 Water regulation	Regulation of hydrological flows.	Provisioning of water for agricultural (e.g. irrigation) or industrial (e.g. milling) processes or transportation.
5 Water supply	Storage and retention of water.	Provisioning of water by watersheds, reservoirs, and aquifers.
6 Erosion control and sediment retention	Retention of soil within an ecosystem.	Prevention of loss of soil by wind, run-off, or other removal processes, storage of silt in lakes and wetlands.
7 Soil formation	Soil formation processes.	Weathering of rock and the accumulation of organic material.
8 Nutrient cycling	Storage, internal cycling, processing, and acquisition of nutrients.	Nitrogen fixation, N, P, and other elemental or nutrient cycles.

9	Waste treatment	Recovery of mobile nutrients and removal or breakdown of excess or xenic nutrients and compounds.	Waste treatment, pollution control, detoxification.
10	Pollination	Movement of floral gametes.	Provisioning of pollinators for the reproduction of plant populations.
11	Biological control	Trophic-dynamic regulations of populations.	Keystone predator control of prey species, reduction of herbivory by top predators.
12	Refugia	Habitat for resident and transient populations.	Nurseries, habitat for migratory species, regional habitats for locally harvested species, or over-wintering grounds.
13	Food production	That portion of gross primary production extractable as food.	Production of fish, game, crops, nuts, fruits by hunting, gathering, subsistence farming, or fishing.
14	Raw materials	That portion of gross primary production extractable as raw materials.	The production of lumber, fuel, or fodder.
15	Genetic resources	Sources of unique biological materials and products.	Medicine, products for materials science, genes for resistance to plant pathogens and crop pests, ornamental species (pets and horticultural varieties of plants).
16	Recreation	Providing opportunities for recreational activities.	Ecotourism, sport fishing, and other outdoor recreational activities.
17	Cultural	Providing opportunities for non-commercial uses.	Aesthetic, artistic, educational, spiritual and/or scientific values of ecosystems.

Note: *Ecosystem 'goods' included with ecosystem services.

Source: Costanza et al. (1997).

managed plantations maintain rainfall regimes and cycle carbon at a rate similar to that of natural forests. However, managed plantations are genetically much poorer than natural forests. The aim of conservation should be to optimize provision of ecological and other goods and services taking these trade-offs into account. It does not necessarily imply the preservation of the existing resource in all its facets.

Historically, timber production and the potential use of forest land for agriculture have dominated forestry management, while indirect uses have tended to be ignored. This is partly because of the difficulty of valuing those uses, and partly because of perverse incentives that encourage timber extraction or conversion to agriculture. The economic value of tropical forests consists of the sum of their many distinct values. Direct use values include, non-timber forest products, medicinal plants, plant genetics, hunting and fishing, recreation and tourism, and education and human habitat. Indirect use values include soil conservation and soil productivity (through nutrient cycling), watershed protection, water supply and storage, flood control, microclimatic amelioration and carbon sequestration. They also include option and quasi-option values for future (direct or indirect) use.

In Sub-Saharan Africa there has been at least one analysis of the range of values associated with the conservation of tropical forest. The Korup Project in Cameroon is a forest conservation project that is thought to deliver (a) direct use value in the form of non-timber forest products, subsistence, tourism and genetic material and (b) indirect use value in the form of watershed protection, flood control and erosion control. Evaluation of the project compared this set of benefits with the direct operating and capital costs of the project together with forgone timber earnings and forgone agricultural and other output from the resettlement of users (Ruitenbeek, 1989). The results are summarized in Table 1.7. They show that, if correct, the Project offered substantial net economic benefits as a land-use option.

While there are a number of difficulties with this particular exercise, and while the assumptions behind the calculation of both costs and benefits may be unrealistic (Aylward and Barbier, 1992), it does indicate the potential difference that inclusion of ecological functions can make to the economic analysis of land-use options. In fact, logging would be unlikely to have as significant an effect on fishery production as Ruitenbeek assumes in this case, but the point remains that inclusion of ecological functions in the appraisal of conservation investments can substantially improve the rate of return on those investments (Anderson, 1987).

Table 1.7 Cameroon: cost–benefit analysis of Korup Project

Direct costs of conservation	**–11913**
Opportunity costs	**–3326**
Lost stumpage value	–706
Lost forest use	–2620
Direct benefits	**11995**
Sustained forest use	3291
Replaced subsistence production	977
Tourism	1360
Genetic value	481
Watershed protection of fisheries	3776
Control of flood risk	1578
Soil fertility maintenance	532
Induced benefits	**4328**
Agricultural productivity gain	905
Induced forestry	207
Induced cash crops	3216
Net benefit – project	**1084**
Adjustments	6462
External trade credit	7246
Uncaptured genetic value	433
Uncaptured watershed benefits	–351
Net benefit – Cameroon	**7546**

Notes: Base case result (NPV £ 000, 8% discount rate).

Source: Ruitenbeek (1989).

1.6 THE STRUCTURE OF THE BOOK

We take the proximate causes of biodiversity loss to be found in activities that modify habitat – such as land clearance or land conversion – and the underlying causes to be found in the divergence between the private and social cost of resource use. As illustrated in the cases of Kenya, Chapter 4, and Ghana, Chapters 6–8, if the cost of forest clearance to the user is less than the cost of forest clearance to society the result will be excessive deforestation. The social costs of biodiversity loss are frequently very indirect, and are difficult to estimate. However, it may be possible to identify the direction of bias in current conditions, and that is often enough to motivate a change of policy in the right direction.

This volume focuses on the incentives to biodiversity conservation offered by institutional, policy and market conditions in a number of different ecosystem types: lowland and montane forests, semi-arid rangelands, wetlands and freshwater lakes. Accordingly, it addresses Article 11 of the Convention on Biological Diversity which, it will be recalled, requires the Contracting Parties to create incentives that are conducive to the conservation of biodiversity. The importance of incentives for biodiversity conservation in Sub-Saharan Africa has certainly been recognized in the literature (see, for example, McNeely, 1993). But the studies reported here provide greater depth. They consider what the incentive effects of current conditions are, what the biodiversity costs of those incentives may be, and what options policymakers have to address the problem.

Following the GBA, our starting assumption is that the principal objective in the biodiversity problem is not the preservation of a particular set of species now threatened with extinction, but the conservation of enough biodiversity to maintain the resilience and the productivity of those ecosystems on which human activity depends. We take it that the main value of biodiversity (as distinct from the value of individual biological resources) lies in its role in the provision of ecological services. Hence demand for biodiversity derives from demand for such ecological services. If an individual species harvested from some ecosystem is valued for specific properties that make it useful in either production or consumption, the biodiversity of the system will be valued to the extent that it supports that species. If not all species in an ecosystem are necessary for the health or resilience of that ecosystem, then not all species will be positively valued. In Chapters 2 and 4, Acharya and Adano offer case studies of the value of biodiversity in wetlands in Northern Nigeria and montane forests in Kenya respectively. In both, the problem is to identify the benefit stream from a particular mix of species. This provides a way of estimating the opportunity cost of policies, institutions, regulations or market conditions that reduce biodiversity in those systems.

It is, however, worth repeating that though some species may be 'redundant' in terms of current technology, preferences, environmental or market conditions, they may become important if there is a change in any of these things. The best example of this is offered by Kasulo's study of fisheries in Lake Malawi, Chapter 3. The main threat to the diversity of fish species is shown to be overharvesting, due to the incentive effects of institutional and market conditions. In the Lake Malawi fisheries, as in so many others, the composition of the catch has changed over the years as fishers have removed the most easily caught or highly desirable species. Species that were at one time low-valued, have become high-valued. Species that were at one time high-valued have been driven to extinction.

These three chapters, along with the study of wildlife utilization in semi-arid rangelands in Namibia, by Matundu and Perrings, comprise Part I. They are all microstudies of particular but quite widely representative biodiversity problems in Sub-Saharan Africa. Chapter 4 focuses on the problem of forest use and encroachment at Marsabit in Kenya. It addresses a mix of issues that recur with monotonous frequency not just in Africa, but also in Latin America, South Asia and South East Asia: the effect of population growth and migration, encroachment on and policing of protected areas, deforestation and fuelwood supplies, damage to watershed functions and water supply. It is, in a sense, the classic biodiversity problem (Dixon and Sherman, 1990). But in this chapter, as in others in this section, the authors have attempted to link biodiversity and a range of production and consumption activities. They have tested the importance of biodiversity in the day-to-day activities of rural households. This is in sharp contrast to the view that biodiversity is essentially a problem of the *ex situ* and *in situ* preservation of rare species. These chapters show how and why biodiversity supports both the commercial and the subsistence activities of rural households. They discuss the effect of current incentive structures on biodiversity use, and the external costs associated with that use.

In Chapter 3, and in the chapters of Part II, the authors consider the implications of changes in the mix of species in two major activities: fisheries and agriculture. In both cases the mix of species harvested or cropped has implications for a range of ecological functions. In freshwater lakes this includes nutrient cycles and the capacity of the lake to assimilate nitrates and phosphates (Bundy and Pitcher, 1995). In agroecosystems it includes the regulation of hydrological flows, the maintenance of soil structure and nutrients and plant reproduction. It also affects ecosystem structures, food-webs and the fragmentation of habitats. We have already seen that the introduction of the Nile Perch into Lake Victoria is thought to have led to the loss of some 200 haplochromine cichlids. Deforestation through agricultural extensification has also been cited as one of the main proximate causes of biodiversity loss. However, it is seldom the simple process it appears in state-of-the-environment reports. The conversion of natural forest to sustainable yield selective logging has very different implications for the species it can support than, for example, conversion to clear-cut logging, plantation forestry, tree crop production or arable agriculture. The social costs of species deletion in the Lake Malawi fisheries or forest conversion in Ghana may not have been taken into account by the individual fishers or farmers concerned, but these chapters show that there are socially relevant trade-offs between private resource use and biodiversity conservation. There does exist a socially optimal mix of species and this may be different to the mix that exists under the current structure of incentives.

To illustrate the nature of the decision problem at a microlevel, Chapter 5 addresses a very specific issue: the mix of wildlife and livestock in the Nyae Nyae region of Namibia. It argues that biodiversity conservation may be seen in terms of a choice between alternative strategies, each of which is associated with a different level of biodiversity. In the rangelands of Sub-Saharan Africa the choice is typically between strategies involving different combinations of wildlife and livestock. In the Nyae Nyae, the options considered involve livestock farming only, or livestock farming with tourism (consumptive or non-consumptive). The decision variable is the amount of land to be allocated to tourism-based wildlife protection, and this turns out to be sensitive to the value of the non-market benefits of wildlife conservation. The case indicates the structure of incentives required for conservation in a particular environment. More importantly it provides a way of thinking about the questions raised by Article 8 of the Convention which requires Contracting Parties to establish protected areas. The Nyae Nyae case provides a way of determining the optimal area to be allocated to protection.

In Part II, three chapters by Benhin and Barbier provide an in-depth analysis of the environmental consequences of the macroeconomic policy reforms of the type that have swept Sub-Saharan Africa since the mid-1980s. While this follows the case study approach of the rest of the volume, it takes a much broader view of the policy reform process and its sectoral effects, before considering the implications this has for biodiversity. That is, it inquires into the nature of the structural adjustment programme undertaken by Ghana, and the way in which this has impacted on the agricultural sector. The biodiversity consequences of the reform process are then identified through the proximate effects on habitat of changes in the crop mix.

NOTE

1.   I am indebted to Jon Lovett for the points in this paragraph, and for Figure 1.1.

REFERENCES

Anderson, D. (1987), *The Economics of Afforestation: A Case Study in Africa*, World Bank Occasional Paper Number 1, Baltimore and London: Johns Hopkins University Press.

Antle, J.M. and G. Heidebrink (1995), 'Environment and development: theory and international evidence', *Economic Development and Cultural Change*, **43**(3), 603–25.

Arrow, K.J. and A.C. Fisher (1974), 'Environmental preservation, uncertainty, and irreversibility', *Quarterly Journal of Economics*, **88**(2) 312–19.

Aylward, B.A. and E.B. Barbier (1992), 'Valuing environmental functions in developing countries', *Biodiversity and Conservation*, 1: 34–50.

Barbier, E.B. (1992), 'Rehabilitating gum arabic systems in Sudan: economic and environmental implications', *Environmental and Resource Economics*, **2**, 335–41.

Barbier, E.B. (1994), 'Valuing environmental functions: tropical wetlands', *Land Economics*, **70**(2), 155–73.

Barbier, E.B., J.C. Burgess, T.M. Swanson, and D.W. Pearce (1990), *Elephants, Economics and Ivory*, London: Earthscan.

Barbier, E.B., W.M. Adams, and K. Kimmage (1991); Economic valuation of wetland benefits: the Hadejia-Jama'are Floodplain, Nigeria, LEEC Discussion Paper 91–102. London: IIED.

Barbier, E.B., J.C. Burgess, and C. Folke (1994), *Paradise Lost? The Ecological Economics of Biodiversity*, London: Earthscan.

Barnes, D.L. (1979), 'Cattle ranching in the semi-arid savannas of East and Southern Africa', in B.H. Walker (ed.), *Management of Semi-Arid Ecosystems*, Amsterdam, Elsevier, pp. 9–54.

Barnes, J.I. and J.L.V. de Jager (1995), 'Economic and financial incentives for wildlife use on private land in Namibia and the implications for policy', Research Discussion Paper No. 8, Windhoek: DEA.

Barnes, J. and D.W. Pearce (1991), *The Mixed Use of Habitat*, London: Centre for Social and Economic Research on the Global Environment.

Berry, L. (1984), 'Assessment of desertification in the Sudano-Sahelian Region 1978–1984', UNEP Governing Council, 12th Session, Nairobi, UNEP.

Biswas, M.R. (1994), 'Agriculture and environment: a review 1972–1992', *Ambio*, **23**, 192–97.

Brown, G.M. and W. Henry (1993), 'The economic value of elephants', in E.B. Barbier E.B. (ed.), *Economics and Ecology: New Frontiers and Sustainable Development*, London: Chapman and Hall.

Bundy, A. and A.J. Pitcher (1995), 'An analysis of species change in Lake Victoria: did the Nile perch act alone', in A.J. Pitcher and P.J.B. Hart (eds), *The Impact of Species Changes in African Lakes*, London: Chapman and Hall, pp. 111–36.

Campbell, B.M. (1993), 'The monetary valuation of tree-based resources in Zimbabwe: experience and outlook', paper prepared for the FAO.

Cole, M.A., A.J. Rayner and J.M. Bates (1997), 'The Environmental Kuznets curve: an empirical analysis', *Environment and Development Economics*, **2**(4), 401–16.

Costanza, R., R. d'Arge, R. de Groot, S. Farber, M. Grasso, B. Hannon, S. Naeem, K. Limburg, J. Paruelo, R.V. O'Neill, R. Raskin, P. Sutton and M. van den Belt (1997), 'The value of the world's ecosystem services and natural capital', *Nature*, 15 May.

Cumming, D.H.M., R.F. du Toit, and S.N. Stuart (1990), *African Elephants and Rhinos: Status Survey and Conservation Action Plan*, Geneva: IUCN.

Daily, G. (ed.) (1997), *Nature's Services: Societal Dependence on Natural Systems*, Washington DC: Island Press.

Dasgupta, P. (1993), *An Inquiry into Wellbeing and Poverty*, Oxford: Blackwell.

Dixon, J.A. and P.B. Sherman (1990), *Economics of Protected Areas: A New Look at Benefits and Costs*, Washington, DC: Island Press.

Dregne, H.E. (1983), *Desertification of Arid Lands*, New York: Harwood.

Gadgil, M. and F. Berkes (1991), 'Traditional resource management systems', *Resource Management and Optimisation*, **18**(3–4), 127-41.

Gadgil, M., F. Berkes and C. Folke (1993), 'Indigenous knowledge for biodiversity conservation', *Ambio*, **XXII** (2–3), 151–5.

Githinji, M. and C. Perrings (1993), 'Social and economic sustainability in the use of biotic resources in Sub-Saharan Africa', *Ambio*, **27**, 110–16.

Grainger, A. (1990), *The Threatening Desert – Controlling Desertification*, London: Earthscan.

Grossman, G.M. and A.B. Krueger (1993), 'Environmental impacts of a North American free trade agreement', in P. Garber (ed.), *The U.S.–Mexico free trade agreement*. Cambridge, MA: MIT Press, pp. 165–77.

Grossman, G.M. and A.B. Krueger (1995), 'Economic growth and the environment', *Quarterly Journal of Economics*, **110**(2), 353–77.

Grout, P. (1981), 'Social welfare and exhaustible resources', in J. Butlin (ed.), *Economics of the Environment and Natural Resource Policy*, Boulder CO: Westview Press.

Hawksworth, D.L. (1991), *The Biodiversity of Microorganisms and Invertebrates: Its Role in Sustainable Agriculture*, Wallingford: CAB International.

Heywood, V. (ed.) (1995), *Global Biodiversity Assessment*, Cambridge: Cambridge University Press.

Holden, S.T., B. Shiferaw, and M. Wik, (1998), 'Poverty, market imperfections and time preferences: of relevance for environmental policy?', *Environment and Development Economics*, **3**(l), 105–30.

Holling, C.S. (1992), 'Cross-scale morphology, geometry and dynamics of ecosystems', *Ecological Monographs*, **62**, 447–502.

Holling, C.S., D.W. Schindler, B.H. Walker and J. Roughgarden (1995), 'Biodiversity in the functioning of ecosystems: an ecological synthesis', in C. Perrings, C. Folke, C.S. Holling, B.O. Jansson and K.G. Mäler (eds) *Biological Diversity: Economic and Ecological Issues*, Cambridge: Cambridge University Press, 44–8.

IUCN (1994), *Report of the Global Biodiversity Forum*, Gland: IUCN.

Jazairy, I., M. Almagir and T. Panuccio (1992), *The State of World Rural Poverty*, IT Publications for IFAD.

Jolly, A. (1980), 'A World Like Our own: Man and Nature in Madagascar', New Haven and London: Yale University Press.

Jones, D.D. (1975), 'The applications of catastrophe theory to ecological systems', in G.S. Innes (ed.), *New Directions in the Analysis of Ecological Systems*, La Jolla, CA: Simulation Councils.

Karenge, L. and J. Kolding (1995), 'Inshore fish populations and species changes in Lake Kariba, Zimbabwe', In A.J. Pitcher and P.J.B. Hart (eds), *The Impact of Species Changes in African Lakes*, London: Chapman and Hall, pp. 245–76.

Knoop, W.T. and B.H. Walker (1985), 'Interactions of woody and herbaceous vegetation in a southern African savanna', *Journal of Ecology*, **73**, 235–53.

Kramer, R.A. (1993), 'Tropical forest protection in Madagascar', paper prepared for Northeast Universities Development Consortium, Williams College, 15–16 October.

Kramer, R., M. Munasinghe, N. Sharma, E. Mercer and P. Shyamsundar (1992) 'Valuing a protected tropical forest: a case study in Madagascar', IVth World Congress on National Parks and Protected Areas, Caracas, Venezuela, 14–16 February.

MacDonald, I.A.W., L.L. Loope, M.B. Usher and O. Hamman (1989), 'Wildlife conservation and the invasion of nature reserves by introduced species: a global perspective', in J.A. Drake, H.A. Mooney, F. di Castri, R.H. Groves, F.J. Kruger, M. Rejmanek and M. Williamson (eds), *Biological Invasions: A Global Perspective, SCOPE 37*, New York: John Wiley, pp. 215–55.

MacKinnon, J. and K. MacKinnon (1986), *Review of the Protected Areas System in the Afrotropical Realm*, Gland: IUCN.

Marshall, B. (1995), 'Why is *Limnothrissa miodon* such a successful introduced species and is there anywhere else we should put it?', in A.J. Pitcher and P.J.B. Hart (eds), *The Impact of Species Changes in African Lakes*, London: Chapman and Hall, pp. 527–46.

McNaughton, S.J. (1985), 'Ecology of a grazing ecosystem: the Serengeti', *Ecological Monographs*, **55**, 259–94.

McNeely, J. (1993), 'Economic incentives for conserving biodiversity – lessons for Africa', *Ambio*, **22**(2–3), 144–50.

McNeely, LA. and D. Pitt (eds) (1985), *Culture and Conservation*, Dublin: Croom Helm.

Moran, D. (1994), 'Contingent valuation and biodiversity conservation in Kenyan protected areas', *Biodiversity and Conservation*, **3**.

Munasinghe, M. (1993), 'Environmental economics and biodiversity management in developing countries', *Ambio*, **22**(2–3), 126–35.

Murindagomo, F. (1988), 'Preliminary investigation into wildlife utilisation and Land Use in Angwa, Mid-Zambezi Valley, Zimbabwe', M.Phil. thesis, Dept. of Agricultural Economics, University of Zimbabwe, Harare, Zimbabwe.

Myers, N. (1992), 'Population/environment linkages: discontinuities ahead', *Ambio*, **21**, 116–11.

Nicholson, S.E. (1994), 'Recent rainfall fluctuations in Africa and their relationship to past conditions over the continent', *The Holocene*, **4**(2), 121–31.

Ogutu-Ohwayo, R. (1995), 'Diversity and stability of fish stocks in Lakes Victoria, Kyoga and Nabugabo after establishment of introduced species', in A.J. Pitcher and P.J.B. Hart (eds), *The Impact of Species Changes in African Lakes*, London: Chapman and Hall, pp. 59-82.

Panayotou, T. (1995), 'Environmental degradation at different stages of economic development', in I. Ahmed and J.A. Doelman (eds), *Beyond Rio: The Environmental Crisis and Sustainable Livelihoods in the Third World*, Macmillan, London: pp. 13–36.

Panayotou, T. (1997), 'Demystifying the Environmental Kuznets Curve: turning a black box into a policy tool', *Environment and Development Economics*, **2**, 465–84.

Pearce, D.W. (1999), 'Economics and biodiversity conservation in the developing world', *Environment and Development Economics*, **4**(2).

Pearce, D.W. and D. Moran (1994), *The Economic Value of Biological Diversity*, London: Earthscan.

Pearce, D.W. and J.J. Warford (1993), *World Without End: Economics, Environment and Sustainable Development*, Oxford and New York: Oxford University Press for the World Bank.

Perrings, C. (1989), 'An optimal path to extinction? Poverty and resource degradation in the open agrarian economy', *Journal of Development Economics*, **30**(1), 1–24.

Perrings, C., K.-G. Mäler, C. Folke, C.S. Holling and B.-O. Jansson (eds) (1994), *Biodiversity Conservation: Problems and Policies*, Dordrecht: Kluwer Academic Press.

Perrings C., K.-G., Mäler, C. Folke, C.S. Holling and B.-O. Jansson (eds) (1995), *Biological Diversity: Economic and Ecological Issues*, Cambridge: Cambridge University Press.

Perrings, C. and B.H. Walker (1995), 'Biodiversity loss and the economics of discontinuous change in semi-arid rangelands', in C. Perrings, K.-G. Mäler, C. Folke, C.S. Holling, and B.-O. Jansson (eds), *Biological Diversity: Economic and Ecological Issues*, Cambridge: Cambridge University Press, 190–210.

Perrings, C. and B.H. Walker (1997), 'Biodiversity, resilience and the control of ecological-economic systems: the case of fire-driven rangelands', *Ecological Economics*, **22**(l), 73–83.

Ramakrishnan, P.S. and P.M. Vitousek (1989), 'Ecosystem-level processes and the consequences of biological invasions', in J.A. Drake, H.A. Mooney, F. di Castri, R.H. Groves, F.J. Kruger, M. Rejmanek and M. Williamson (eds), *Biological Invasions: A Global Perspective*, SCOPE 37, New York: John Wiley, pp. 281–96.

Repetto, R. (1989), 'Economic incentives for sustainable production', in G. Schramme and J.J. Warford (eds), *Environmental Management and Economic Development*, Baltimore: Johns Hopkins for the World Bank, pp. 69-86.

Ruitenbeek, H.J. (1989), *Social Cost-Benefit Analysis of the Korup Project, Cameroon*, London: World Wide Fund for Nature Publication 3206/A14.1.

Schindler, D.W. (1977), 'Evolution of phosphorus limitation in lakes: natural mechanisms compensate for deficiencies of nitrogen and carbon in eutrophied lakes', *Science*, **195**, 260–62.

Schindler, D.W. (1990), 'Experimental perturbations of whole lakes as tests of hypotheses concerning ecosystem structure and function', Proceedings of 1987 Crafoord Symposium, *Oikos*, **57**, 25–41.

Seldon, T.M. and D. Song (1994), 'Environmental quality and development: is there a Kuznets curve for air pollution emissions?', *Journal of Environmental Economics and Management*, **27**, 147–62.

Shafik, N. (1994), 'Economic development and environmental quality: an econometric analysis', *Oxford Economic Papers*, **46**, 757–73.

Silva, J. (1987), 'Responses of savannas to stress and disturbance: species dynamics', in B.H. Walker (ed.), *Determinants of Tropical Savannas*, Oxford: IRL Press, pp. 141–56.

Skole, D.L. and C. Tucker (1993), 'Tropical deforestation and habitat fragmentation in the Amazon: satellite data from 1978–1988', *Science*, **260**, 314-22.

Swanson, T. (1995), *The Economics and Ecology of Biodiversity Decline*, Cambridge: Cambridge University Press.

Tolba, M.K., O.A. El-Kholy, E. El-Hinnawi, M.W. Holdgate, D.F. McMichael and R.E. Munn (eds) (1992), *The World Environment 1972-1992: Two Decades of Challenge*, United Nations Environment Programme, London: Chapman and Hall.

Tucker, C.J. et al. (1991), 'Expansion and contraction of the Sahara Desert from 1980 to 1990', *Science*, **253**, 299–301.

Turner, G.F., D. Tweddle and R.D. Makwinja (1995), 'Changes in demersal communities as a result of trawling in Southern Lake Malawi', in T.J. Pitcher and P.J.B. Hart (eds), *The Impact of Species Changes in African Lakes*, London: Chapman and Hall.

United Nations Conference on Environment and Development (UNCED) (1993), *Agenda 21: The United Nations Programme of Action from Rio*, New York: UN.

United Nations Development Programme (UNDP) (1990), *Human Development Report 1990*, Oxford: Oxford University Press.

United Nations Development Programme (UNDP) (1992), *African Development Indicators: 1980–1990*, New York: UNDP and World Bank.

Vitousek, P.M. (1990), 'Biological invasions and ecosystem processes: towards an integration of population biology and ecosystem studies', *Oikos*, **57**, 7–13.

Walker, B.H. (1988), 'Autecology, synecology, climate and livestock as agents of rangelands dynamics', *Australian Range Journal*, **10**, 69–75.

Walker, B.H., D. Ludwig, C.S. Holling, and R.M. Peterman (1969), 'Stability of semi-arid savanna grazing systems', *Ecology*, **69**, 473–49.

Warford, J. (1987), Environment and Development, Washington DC: World Bank/IMF Development Committee.

Weisinger, A.K. (1990), 'Technologies for germ plasm conservation ex situ', in G.H. Orians, G.M. Brown, W.E. Kunin and J.E. Swierbzinski (eds), *The Preservation and Valuation of Biological Resources*, Seattle: University of Washington Press, pp. 3–31.

Weitzman, M.L. (1995), 'Diversity functions', in C. Perrings, K.G. Mäler, C. Folke, C.S. Holling and B.O. Jansson (eds), *Biological Diversity: Economic and Ecological Issues*, Cambridge: Cambridge University Press, pp. 21–43.

Western, D. (1989), 'The ecological value of elephants: a keystone role in African ecosystems', in the ITRG Report, *The Ivory Trade and the Future of the African Elephant*, prepared for the Second Meeting of the CITES African Elephant Working Group, Gaborone, Botswana, July.

Williamson, M. (1996), *Biological Invasions*, London: Chapman and Hall.

World Bank (1986), *Sudan Forestry Sector Review*, Washington DC: World Bank.

World Bank (1996), *World Development Report 1996*, Oxford: Oxford University Press.

World Commission on Environment and Development (WCED) (1987), *Our Common Future*, Oxford: Oxford University Press.

World Conservation Monitoring Centre (WCMC) (1992), *Global Biodiversity: Status of the Earth's Living Resources*, London: Chapman and Hall.

World Resources Institute (WRI) (1991), *World Resources 1990–1991*, Oxford: Oxford University Press.

World Resources Institute (WRI) (1992), *World Resources 1992–1993*, World Resources Institute in collaboration with the United Nations Environment Programme and the United Nations Development Programme, Oxford: Oxford University Press.

World Resources Institute (WRI) (1994), *World Resources 1994–1995: People and the Environment*, World Resources Institute in collaboration with the United Nations Environment programme and the United Nations Development Programme, Oxford: Oxford University Press.

PART I

The Microeconomics of Biodiversity
Loss: Case Studies from Nigeria,
Malawi, Kenya and Namibia

2. The value of biodiversity in the Hadejia-Nguru wetlands of Northern Nigeria

Gayatri Acharya[1]

2.1 INTRODUCTION

Under the Convention on Biological Diversity, inland water biodiversity is a matter of concern since it relies on ecosystems and habitats containing high diversity and large numbers of endemic and threatened species, which are unique or associated with key evolutionary processes. The underlying causes of biodiversity loss in inland water ecosystems generally stem from habitat alterations, introduction of invasive species, overexploitation or pollution and land conversion. The stress caused by one or more of these may have cumulative or discrete impacts on habitats. Article 14 of the Convention requires each contracting party to 'introduce appropriate procedures requiring environmental impact assessment of its proposed projects that are likely to have significant adverse impacts on biological diversity' and to identify processes and categories of activities that are or are likely to have significant adverse impacts on the conservation and sustainable use of biological diversity. Specific investment projects such as water development projects can have discrete and large (significant) impacts on ecosystems found downstream of these developments. Linkages within water systems, from catchment area to the river mouth are therefore relevant in understanding and identifying possible biodiversity loss due to development projects.

The basin of the Komadugu-Yobe River covers an area of 84 138 km^2 in North-eastern Nigeria. The rivers Hadejia and Kano, arising in Kano state, and the Jama'are river arising in Plateau and Bauchi states, drain into the Yobe, and flow into Lake Chad. The portion of the floodplain where the Hadejia and Jama'are rivers meet is known as the Hadejia-Jama'are wetlands while the area of floodplain lying between the towns of Hadejia and Gashua and South of Nguru, is widely referred to as the Hadejia-Nguru wetlands (see Figure 2.1). The semi-arid zone of West Africa is subject to strongly seasonal patterns of rainfall and river flow.

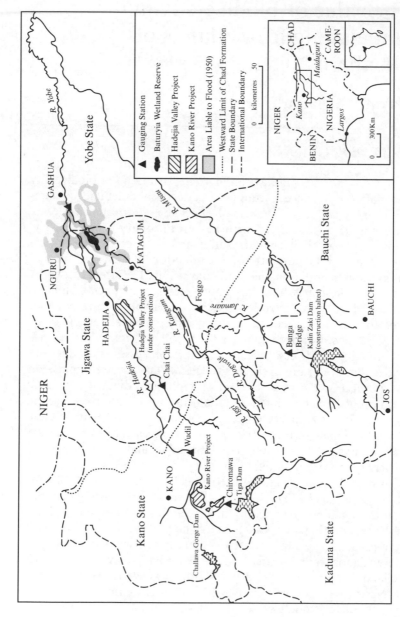

Figure 2.1   The Hadejia-Nguru wetlands

Most of the annual rainfall in Northern Nigeria occurs in just 3–4 months, between June and September. During this season, the rivers flood, providing support for a large number of varied activities, dependent on the floodplain and admirably adapted to the seasonal fluctuations within the area. The rivers that maintain this floodplain are affected by a number of dam and reservoir projects, some built and some proposed. Dam construction and the withdrawal of water for irrigation and industrial uses can cause changes in water volumes, velocities and general hydrological circulation and flow patterns. The biological diversity associated with flooding patterns can therefore be affected without any clear indication of changes occurring.

The harsh and variable natural conditions that prevail in this region can be exacerbated by inappropriate changes in water regimes induced by water resource development schemes. By minimizing water flow within floodplains, by-pass canals and dams essentially reduce flood extent in downstream areas, resulting in ecological and economic changes in these areas. Adams (1985) notes that the Bakalori Dam in northwest Nigeria reduced flood extent and depth by over 50 per cent in parts of the downstream floodplain of the Sokoto River. As a result, in areas below Bakalori Dam, cultivators have shifted from growing rice to lower value millet. The size and species diversity of fish catches has declined and many fishermen have left the floodplain to fish elsewhere.

Water diverted to upstream areas as a result of these projects does however benefit upstream areas, albeit at a cost to downstream areas. Water resource development projects are often designed to meet increasing demands for drinking water, electricity, and other urban requirements. However, any water development schemes that affect water allocation decisions for upstream and downstream uses must be based on a careful assessment of relative benefits of water used within the river basin. Failing this, changes in flooding patterns in downstream areas may result in the loss of flood-dependent resources, causing large welfare losses for a significant section of the society.

Previous studies have calculated the value of the Hadejia-Nguru wetlands in terms of agricultural production, fisheries and forestry (Barbier et al., 1993). It has also been demonstrated that the recharge of groundwater resources is maintained by regular flooding of the wetlands (Thompson and Goes, 1997) and that changes in the recharge function would result in welfare losses for wetland populations (Acharya, 1998). The dependency of wetland populations on the wild, uncultivated resources found within the wetlands, and which are an important source of materials, food and income, has also been investigated by a recent study (Eaton and Sarch, 1997). Drawing on the hydrological and economic evidence, the primary purpose of this chapter is therefore to show the impact of hydrological changes on floodplain productivity and resulting welfare changes stemming from losses in agricultural productivity and wild resource availability. The second purpose of this chapter is to present the evidence regarding the use of wild resources and to explicitly calculate welfare change for wetland populations due to the impact of flooding on the availability and diversity of these resources.

In Section 2.2 we briefly describe the upstream development projects and downstream impacts of these hydrological projects. We then discuss the nature and scale of biodiversity loss within the wetlands, resulting from changes in flood extent, as a direct result of upstream developments. In Section 2.4 we show, with the aid of an optimal control framework, the decision rules determining allocation of water resources within the Komadugu-Yobe river basin, with a view to maximizing the economic value of water used within the entire river basin. Section 2.5 presents some preliminary calculations of economic value from wild wetland resources. We conclude by summarizing these values together with values from groundwater use and other floodplain benefits to give an indication of the impact of dam construction on net productivity within the river basin.

2.2 UPSTREAM DEVELOPMENTS AND DOWNSTREAM IMPACTS

The logic of river basin planning is simply to co-ordinate the different uses of water in each river basin. The Tennessee Valley Authority (TVA) from the 1930s is cited as one of the first integrated river basin planning authorities where the development of the river basin was planned and carried out by a centralized authority. River basin planning was initiated in Nigeria in the 1960s with the establishment of the Niger Delta Development Board and the Niger Dams Authority (Adams, 1992). This includes the Lake Chad Basin Commission which provides an international forum for planning development of all the rivers draining into Lake Chad, involving Chad, Cameroon, Nigeria and Niger. The first two River Basin Development Authorities (RBDAs) were set up in Sokoto-Rima, and Lake Chad in 1973, followed by seven others in 1976. Since then, with boundary changes and the creation of numerous new states, a number of new RBDAs have been created and are now known as River Basin and Rural Development Authorities (Adams, 1992).

However, the boundaries of these authorities are not related to actual river basin boundaries and are subject to political whims and fancies. Project development within the river basin is not directed by a single coherent plan (Hollis and Thompson, 1993) and as such, the requirements of the various ecosystems associated with the river basin are not consciously included within the planning process. Table 2.3 shows the number and location of the main dam and irrigation schemes (Thompson, 1995).

Large-scale Irrigation Schemes

Most irrigation in Nigeria is classified as small-scale or indigenous (Adams, 1992) and development schemes on the Hadejia and Jama'are rivers have been directed towards increasing the area under large-scale, formal irrigation. In the early 1970s the Federal Military Government initiated a number of large-scale irrigation projects, including the South Chad Irrigation Project in Borno State, the Sokoto-Rima Project in Sokoto State, and the Kano River Irrigation Project at the upstream end of the Hadejia River system in Kano State (Wallace, 1980).

The largest of these schemes is the Kano River Irrigation Project (KRIP). Phase I of KRIP (KRIP-I), aims to irrigate an area of 27 000 hectares while Phase II (KRIP-II) is expected to irrigate an additional 40 000 hectares. Around 14 000 hectares are presently irrigated from the project. Water supplies for this project are provided by the Tiga Dam that also supplies water to Kano River for abstraction downstream by the Kano City Waterworks. The major crops supported by these irrigated projects are rice, maize, cowpeas and millet, which are grown in the wet season and tomatoes and wheat, which are grown in the dry season. Barbier et al., (1993) calculated that the present economic value of the scheme ranged from 153 and 233 Naira per hectare.[2] These figures include the project operating costs, which range from 7.5 per cent to 37 per cent of total value of crop production, but neglect the substantial sunk capital costs which in 1988 amounted to 180 million Naira.

The second major irrigation scheme within the river basin is the Hadejia Valley Project (HVP) which is still under construction. A barrage built across the Hadejia River has created a storage pond capable of holding a week's irrigation water requirements for 12 500 hectares of land and the scheme has so far demarcated 7000–8000 hectares of land (Thompson, 1996). A third dam, the Challawa Gorge Dam, on the Challawa River, one of the tributaries of the Hadejia River, was completed in 1992. At present only one dam has been completed in the Jama'are Basin. This dam, at Birnin Kudu, has a capacity of $1 \times 10^6 \, m^3$. The largest dam planned for the basin, Kafin Zaki, has an envisaged total storage of $2700 \times 10^6 \, m^3$ and aims to provide irrigation water to 84 000 hectares of land (Thompson, 1995).

In addition to large-scale irrigation schemes, a number of channelization schemes have been proposed (IWACO, 1985; Chifana, 1986). The IWACO (1985) plan consists of the construction of a new river channel that would shorten the length of the Hadejia River by 50 per cent and allow navigation, hydro-power and fish ponds through the provision of control structures. The water would be utilized for irrigation, hydro-electric power and town water supply predominantly between Gashua and Geidam although water would be supplied to Nguru lake and could irrigate 6800 hectares along the Burum Gana as well. Chifana (1986) suggested the need for a new channel (with an annual capacity of $400 \times 10^6 \, \mathrm{m}^3$) for the Hadejia River, intended to carry water from Hadejia town to Geidam. The water supply would be used for irrigation downstream of Gashua and upstream of Katagum and for rice cultivation in the *fadamas* (lowlying areas) around Hadejia. However, Hollis and Thompson (1993) note that groundwater, small-scale irrigation, wetland cultivation and pastoralism would be affected by the implementation of these channelization schemes.

The Hadejia-Jama'are Floodplain and Wetlands

The main area of concern in this chapter are the floodplain wetlands located at the downstream end of the Hadejia-Jama'are River Basin (see Figure 2.1). The wetlands are maintained by the regular flooding of the two rivers which meet to form the Komadugu Yobe river, flowing northeast into Lake Chad. This water rejuvenates the floodplain, providing new soil and moisture. Floodplain activities have adapted to suit this cycle, making use of the floodwaters and the *fadamas* in an ingenious way and taking advantage of a combination of the wetland's resources. However, as populations of cities like Kano grow and the water demands of the urban areas increase, more water will be diverted upstream, resulting in a reduction of the flow in the rivers as they pass through the floodplain. Competing uses for water from the Hadejia and Jama'are rivers divert water away from the floodplain to feed the upstream projects described in the previous section.

Historically, the floodplain of the Hadejia and Jama'are rivers may have spanned an area of over $2000 \, \mathrm{km}^2$ at peak flood (Thompson and Goes, 1997). Inundation begins in July and peak flood extents are attained in August/September (Thompson, 1995). The climate of the region is dominated by the annual migration of the Inter Tropical Convergence Zone (ITCZ) which produces the distinct wet and dry seasons, characteristic of Sub-Saharan Africa. The rivers have periods of no flow in the dry season (October–April) with almost 80 per cent of the total annual run-off occurring in August and September. The flood waters of the Hadejia and Jama'are rivers accumulate in lowlying areas known as *fadamas* in Hausa, which then provide valuable opportunities for grazing, agriculture and other economic uses. *Fadamas* are waterlogged or flooded during the wet season and gradually dry out until they are flooded again during the next wet season.

Studies of the hydrological and economic environment of the Hadejia-Nguru wetlands have noted that these wetlands support a wide range of economic activities, including wet and dry season agriculture, fishing, fuelwood collection, livestock rearing and forestry (Hollis et al., 1993; Thomas et al., 1993). The wetlands are, in addition, a valuable site for wildlife conservation and, in particular, for waterfowl. The wetlands support over 60 water bird species from 15 families (Hollis et al., 1993) and are considered to be of international importance as habitats for waterfowl populations. Table 2.1 summarizes the available key floodplain resources and the main methods of utilization within the wetlands. Changes in hydrological conditions are therefore expected to affect the range of resources outlined in Table 2.1, resulting from changes in habitat, water availability and flooding patterns within the wetlands.

Table 2.1   Resource utilization

Resource	Utilization
Water	Domestic use, irrigation, livestock watering, navigation
Vegetation	Food, thatching material, ropes, fuel
Land (*fadamas* and upland), soil	Flooded agriculture, irrigated agriculture, dryland farming, building material
Fish	Fishing, important source of protein
Birds, reptiles, amphibians	Food, hunting, tourism, minor trade

Source: Acharya (1998).

Cultivated floodplain species The flood cycle is very important in the order and intensity of activities undertaken. In agriculture, the seasonal rise and fall of floodwaters results in the establishment of four cropping systems, namely, rain-fed upland cropping, *fadama* or flood cultivation, recession farming and irrigated cropping (Table 2.2). Rain-fed upland farm lands are called *tudu* in Hausa. This type of farming entails mainly bullrush millet and sorghum or guinea corn. These two crops make up a large proportion of the agricultural production of the area and are dominant in the diet of the villagers. Planting occurs with the beginning of the rains in early June and the growing season lasts for 100 to 120 days (Adams, 1993; Kimmage and Adams, 1992).

Table 2.2   Agricultural technologies

A. Flood cropping
   • rising flood cropping (planted before flood rises)
   • decrue cropping (residual soil moisture cropping)
   • flood defence cropping (with bunds)

B. Stream diversion
   • permanent stream diversion or canal supply
   • storm spate diversion (rainwater harvesting)

C. Lift irrigation
   • from openwater
   • from groundwater
   • well
     – bucket
     – *shadoof*
     – animal powered
     – motorized
   • tubewell (generally < 9–10 metres depth)
   • borehole (up to 30 metres depth)

Source: Adapted from Adams (1992).

Flood cultivation is an important aspect of farming in the floodplain and *fadama* lands are highly prized possessions. Rice cultivation and some sorghum is grown. Recession farming follows the *fadama* cultivation. As the floods recede the exposed *fadama* land is planted with recession crops such as beans, cotton or cassava. These crops utilize the residual moisture in the soil. Dry season irrigated farming has been traditionally practised in the area with irrigation technologies such as *shadoofs* (Adams, 1993). These irrigated or *lambu* lands are now increasingly (since the 1980s) being irrigated with the use of small petrol-powered pumps, which can lift water relatively short distances from river channels or from shallow groundwater within the wetlands. Although agriculture is often cited as a factor in bio-diversity loss, it is recognized that small-scale or traditional systems may in fact enhance or maintain biodiversity.

Fisheries Mathes (1990) and Thomas et al. (1993) note that the wetlands have long been recognized as an important centre of fish production in the region. Fishing is undertaken mainly during the flooded season although some villages and individuals fish throughout the year. The main fishing period begins at the start of the dry season when fish return to areas of permanent water and are more concentrated (Thomas et al. 1993). The intensity of fishing activity varies between different parts of the wetland, with some villages specializing in fishing. Thomas et al. (1993) estimated that the annual fish production from the wetlands may vary between 1620 and 8100 metric tonnes, and may well be an underestimate. Barbier et al. (1993) estimate a market value of Naira 480 million based on an estimated annual catch of over 6000 metric tonnes of fish.

Natural vegetation: fuel, food and fibre resources Trees, grasses and other naturally occurring vegetation within the wetlands provide a multitude of resources for wetland populations. Pastoralists use the wetlands seasonally, moving into the wetlands as the surrounding rangelands dry out. Grazing within the wetlands is crucial for the cattle and livestock owned by the nomadic Fulani populations and by some sedentary farmers. It is estimated that the Fulani herds may number around 250 000 animals (Rodenburg, 1987). During the dry season the Fulani from both the north and the south of the wetlands move their camps and their herds on to the seasonally exposed grasslands. The wetlands are a part of the seasonal cycle of migration undertaken by the nomadic Fulani and traditionally, the Fulani and farmers have had a tense but cordial relationship. Certain traditions such as allowing the Fulani herds to graze on the last of the harvest crops in return for some compensation are still practised, although these are becoming increasingly rare and wrought with conflict. Eaton and Sarch (1997) estimate that over 250 000 head of cattle may be reared in the wetlands, supporting a cattle trade with an annual turnover of over Naira 400 million (1995 prices, N80 = 1US$).

Based on a case study of two villages within the wetlands, Eaton and Sarch (1997) find that other than fish and fuelwood, there are a number of other resources used by wetland populations to provide food, building materials and income. Doum palm, potash, fuelwood and foods from wild fruits and leaves were studied in greater detail. They find that many of these wild food sources are critically important for a number of disadvantaged groups, in terms of both income generation and as food supplements.

2.3 BIODIVERSITY LOSS AND FLOOD EXTENT WITHIN THE WETLANDS

Hydrological predictions based on studies of the Komadugu-Yobe river basin indicate that the flooding within the wetlands would be dramatically reduced with the construction of the proposed upstream dams. Tables 2.3 and 2.4 outline the simulated results of a hydrological model of the wetlands and show a fall in both flood extent and groundwater tables under different scenarios of upstream project completion.

*Table 2.3   Scenarios for upstream projects in the Hadejia-Jama'are River
             basin*

Scenario (time period)	Dams	Regulated releases ($10^6 m^3$)	Irrigation schemes
1 (1974– 1985)	Tiga	Naturalized Wudil flow (1974–1985)	No KRIP-I
1a (1974– 1990)	Tiga	Naturalized Wudil flow (1974–1990)	No KRIP-I
2 (1964– 1985)	Tiga	None	KRIP-I at 27 000 ha
3 (1964– 1985)	Tiga	400 in August for sustaining floodplain	KRIP-I at 14 000 ha
4 (1964– 1985)	Tiga Challawa Gorge Small dams on Hadejia tributaries	None 348 yr^{-1} * for downstream users	KRIP-I at 27 000 ha
5 (1964– 1985)	Tiga Challawa Gorge Small dams on Hadejia tributaries	None 348 yr^{-1} * for HVP	KRIP-I at 27 000 ha
	Kafin Zaki HVP	None None	84 000 ha 12 500 ha
6 (1964– 1985)	Tiga Challawa Gorge Small dams on Hadejia tributaries	350 in August 248 yr^{-1} * and 100 in July	KRIP-I at 14 000 ha
	Kafin Zaki HVP	100 per month: Oct–Mar and 550 in August Barrage open in August	None 8 000 ha

Notes
*Distributed based on Haskoning (1977).
KRIP-I = Kano River Irrigation Project Phase I.
HVP = Hadejia Valley Project.

Source: Barbier and Thompson (1997).

Table 2.4   Changes in flood extent and water table change associated with dam scenarios

Scenario	Change in flood extent (hectares)		Change in water table elevations (m)	
	Scenario 1	Scenario 1a	Scenario 1	Scenario 1a
Scenario 2	97775	91697	−1.13	−1.27
Scenario 3	103592	107234	−0.82	−0.95
Scenario 4	86315	80257	−1.21	−1.34
Scenario 5	25768	19710	−4.28	−4.41
Scenario 6	55350	49292	−1.21	−1.34

Source: Adapted from Thompson and Goes (1997) and Thompson, pers. communication (1988).

The impact of diversions to upstream areas will be felt within the wetlands primarily through a reduction in flooding and subsequently through changes in groundwater tables. This will, in turn result in (a) loss of habitat and water resources for uncultivated species; (b) loss of water and available soil moisture for cultivated species and (c) increased pressure on fewer food and water resources. Table 2.3 gives the level of flood reduction and corresponding change in water tables within the wetlands.

Scenarios 1 and 1a represent the production of naturalized discharge data for the Hadejia River at the Wudil gauging station downstream of Tiga Dam, under two alternative discharge assumptions. The remaining five scenarios represent the impacts of a range of operating regimes for various combinations of the proposed water resource schemes. The simulation periods for these scenarios are limited to either 1964–1985 or 1964–87. The impacts of the different scenarios are evaluated by assuming that the dams and irrigation schemes were operational at the start of the simulation period and continued to function in the same manner throughout this period.

In terms of biodiversity loss therefore, the impacts of these hydrological changes on the wetland environment and dependent economy are expected to occur in the following ways:

a. Loss of agricultural productivity from floodplain agriculture;
b. Loss of agricultural productivity from groundwater-dependent agriculture;
c. Loss of natural distribution and abundance of uncultivated wetland species.

Loss of agricultural productivity will not only result in reduced output of cultivated species but may result in the ousting of low-intensity farming based on a wide variety of crops to intensive wheat cultivation. Furthermore, it has been suggested that wheat cultivation is unsustainable and would result in significant economic upheaval within the wetlands.

There is already evidence that the natural distribution and abundance of uncultivated species is changing as a result of altered flooding. Vast areas within the wetlands are now covered by *Typha* sp., known locally as *kachalla* grass. It is believed that the spread of the species, which is difficult to eradicate and has resulted in blocked waterways and reduced areas suitable for rice cultivation, has been due largely to changes in the flow regime of the rivers (Akinsola, 1998). Villagers report reduced availability of a number of uncultivated plant and tree species, not only due to increased demand but due to lower regeneration and survival of seedlings as a direct consequence of changing flood patterns (Eaton and Sarch, 1996). Other resources such as potash are also dependent on the flood. Potash appears on the soil surface after the floodwaters recede and is an important plant nutrient.

In the next section we model the impact of water allocation within the river basin to better understand the trade-offs associated with changes in downstream flooding patterns.

2.4 A MODEL OF WATER ALLOCATION WITH DIRECT AND INDIRECT FLOOD BENEFITS

Previous studies of the Komadugu-Yobe river basin have noted that the upstream dam projects are likely to cause a number of externalities to downstream inhabitants. The Hadejia-Nguru wetlands are expected to undergo changes in hydrology and, associated with this, in the mix of both cultivated and harvested wild species. These costs are expected to have significant implications for the welfare of human populations in the area. In order to fully appreciate the manner in which downstream benefits may enter into a social planner's objective function for optimal allocation of water resources within the river basin, we develop an optimal control model which captures both direct and indirect benefits of water in upstream and downstream portions of the Komadugu-Yobe river basin. This section is derived from Acharya (1998).

We account for the direct and indirect benefits of water used in upstream areas and within the wetlands in the welfare maximization problem presented below. We assume that the main productive use of water diverted by these schemes is in upstream agriculture. We expect that the total irrigated area in upstream areas could increase through dam construction and thus the total accumulated diversion contributes to agricultural production in upstream areas. Furthermore, since newly irrigated areas are expected to respond favourably to water inputs, the more water diverted in the current period, the higher will be the aggregate output. Agricultural production in upstream areas is therefore assumed to depend upon the current rate of diversion, $D(t)$, and the cumulative amount of diverted water at time t, $\int_0^t D(t)dt$, as well as on a number of other variable inputs. In addition, farmers are assumed to be price takers, i.e., we expect that the price effects resulting from changes in crop acreage would be small. The change in the extent of downstream flooding will be determined by the cumulative amount of water diverted upstream, i.e. $F(t)-F(0) = -\int_0^t D(t)dt$.

The production technology describing upstream production can be defined as:

$$Y_1 = f_1 (x_i, \dots x_j, D, F(0) - F(t)) \tag{2.1}$$

where:

$$F(t) = F(0) - \int_0^t D(t)dt \quad F(0) = F_0 \quad D(0) = 0$$

with Y_1: an agricultural good
    x_i: variable inputs (for $i = 1, \dots j$)
    $D(t)$: diverted river flow used as water input
    $F(t)$: flood stock
    $dY_1/dD > 0$
    $dY_1/d\,[F(0)-F(t)] > 0$
    $Y_1(.)'' < 0$

Note that the subscript t has been dropped for notational convenience. We assume that the production function for the agricultural good Y_1 is increasing, concave and twice differentiable. The partial derivative, $dY_1/d [F(0)-F(t)]$ is positive, suggesting that aggregate agricultural production increases with an increase in the total amount of water diverted up to time t. This implies that as water is diverted, the total amount of water available for irrigation in upstream areas increases, thus, effectively, increasing total irrigated area used in upstream agricultural production. However, since newly irrigated areas generally receive a greater boost to yields in initial periods (Carruthers and Clark, 1981), the more water diverted in the current period, the higher the aggregate output and $dY_1/dD > 0$.

If we consider that the price of the agricultural output, P_a, varies according to the inverse demand curve for the good, i.e.

$$P_a = P(Y_1) \tag{2.2}$$

where $P'(Y_1) < 0$, and we assume that $P(Y_1)$ is a reasonable approximation to the income-compensated demand curve, then the net benefits from $Y(t)$ are measured as the area under the demand curve integrated from 0 to $Y(t)$, less the costs of inputs. Hence, the welfare measure, S_i, which is the sum of consumer and producer surplus associated with the production of Y, can be expressed by the net benefit function $B^1(D, F(0)-F(t))$, where:

$$B^1(D, F(0)-F(t)) = \int_0^{Y_1} P_a(Y_1) \, dY - c_x x_J - c_1 D \tag{2.3}$$

for all i and where $c_x x_J$ is the vector of costs associated with the use of variable inputs in the production process.[3] In actual production decisions, farmers in upstream areas face no water charges.[4] However, we note that there is a social opportunity cost associated with diverting this water and therefore $c_1 D > 0$.

The Hadejia-Nguru wetlands are highly productive in terms of agricultural production and other uncultivated resources. The level of diversion determines changing hydrological conditions within the wetlands and in addition, floodplain water may be lost due to evaporation and infiltration to groundwater. The remaining water, net of evaporation and infiltration losses, is then available for floodplain activities such as floodplain and recession agriculture, fishing and forestry and also supports the diverse flora and fauna of the floodplain. Hence, F represents the maximum amount of water stored on the floodplain at time t, net of evaporation losses and available for use by floodplain activities.

For the purpose of our analysis, we assume that there are two types of resources supported by the floodplain: (1) cultivated species used in floodplain agriculture and groundwater irrigated agriculture, and (2) uncultivated resources such as doum palm, potash, trees and fruits gathered from naturally occurring species. We will define the production technologies and benefit functions for each of these resources below.

Cultivated floodplain species As described earlier, farmers use floodwater and soil moisture to grow a number of crops within the wetlands. The water available on the floodplain (F) is used with other inputs ($x_i \ldots x_j$) to produce an agricultural good (Y_2).[5] Farmers are assumed to be price takers and produce agricultural goods similar to those produced by upstream farmers, vegetables such as tomatoes, onions and grains such as wheat, rice, millet. We therefore use the same notation to describe costs associated with the use of variable inputs in the production process for floodplain agriculture.

We assume that the production function for the agricultural good Y_2 is increasing, concave and twice differentiable with respect to its inputs and can be expressed as:

$$Y_2 = f_2(x_i, \ldots x_j, F) \qquad (2.4)$$

Since Y_1 (upstream agricultural production) and Y_2 are similar agricultural products and are both produced for the same local and regional markets, we assume that both upstream and floodplain producers face the same inverse demand schedule for agricultural production, i.e.:

$$P_a(Y_1) = P_a(Y_2) = P_a(Y)$$

The net benefit or welfare function for floodplain agriculture, $B^2(F_1)$ is defined as:

$$B^2(F_1) = \int_0^{Y_2} P_a(Y_2)\, dY_2 c_x x_J \qquad (2.5)$$

where the benefits derived from the floodplain agriculture are the value of the production less the costs of variable inputs, assuming constant prices. Since floodwater is not diverted and is used *in situ*, there are no costs of diversion associated with this sector.

Cultivated species using groundwater resources As asserted by previous research in the wetlands, the floodplain provides various environmental benefits such as groundwater recharge and habitat for migratory waterfowl (Hollis et al., 1993). These environmental benefits are *indirect* benefits deriving from the regular inundation of the floodplain. Groundwater recharge is regarded as possibly the most important environmental function supported by the wetlands.

Groundwater is used within the wetlands for two main uses, namely, dry season agricultural production and domestic water consumption. Irrigation is carried out mainly with the use of small pumps and shallow tubewells and draws water from the shallow aquifer within the wetlands. Domestic water use also relies on the shallow aquifer, and water is abstracted from village wells.[6]

We include the use of groundwater resources for groundwater-irrigated agriculture as $B(w)$. The recharge rate, r, is a function of the area of flood extent, F, as well as a function of groundwater stock, A, that is, $r = r(A,F)$. As in the case of floodplain agriculture, water abstracted for irrigation (w) is combined with other resources (x_i) and is used to produce an agricultural good (Y_3).[7]

$$Y_3 = f_3(x_i, \dots x_J, w) \tag{2.6}$$

However, in this case, because of the use of shallow tubewells, there is a cost associated with water abstraction for irrigation. This pumping cost is represented by $c_w(r)$ and is assumed to vary inversely with the height of the water table. We assume that costs are dependent on the recharge rate since lower water levels in the aquifer would result in higher pumping costs, assuming no technological change.

We assume that an inverse demand curve for this sector exists and is also equal to $P_a(Y)$. The benefit function associated with agricultural production using groundwater, $B^3(w)$, can then be expressed as:

$$B^3(w) = \int_0^{Y_3} (P_a(Y_3)dY_3 - \mathbf{c_x x_J} - c_w(r)w) \tag{2.7}$$

where P_a is the per unit price for the agricultural good Y_3, $\mathbf{c_x x_J}$ is the vector of costs associated with inputs.

Harvested wild floodplain resources The second major production from the wetlands derives from the harvest of uncultivated species. Many of these species are sold in the market, some are processed before being sold. The net benefit function for uncultivated species, where q is the harvested quantity of these resources, and the only other input is labour, X, is described by:

$$B^2(F_2) = \int_0^q (P_q(q)dq \ c_X X \tag{2.8}$$

where C_X is the unit cost of labour used to harvest q_i and P_q is the market or shadow price of the resource.[8]

We are interested in understanding the impact of reduced flooding on cultivated species and uncultivated, harvested species within the wetlands, as opposed to the benefits of diverting water to upstream areas. Above we have identified four outputs, Y_1, Y_2, Y_3, and q, each of which is a composite product comprising a mix of either cultivated or harvested species. We can further define these outputs as functions of species diversity (S_i),[9] as:

$$Y_1(S_1), \ Y_2(S_2), \ Y_3(S_3), \ q(S_4), \ \text{where} \ S_1 \leq S_3 \leq S_2 \ \text{and} \ S_4 \geq 0$$

and Y_i refers to the cultivated agricultural outputs and q refers to the harvested quantity of uncultivated species. Since upstream and downstream agriculture support similar species, we assume that the diversity of surface-irrigated agriculture upstream or groundwater-irrigated downstream agriculture is strictly less than the combined species diversity of floodplain agriculture and harvested wild species, $S_1 \leq S_3 < (S_2 + S_4)$. This implies that the species diversity supported by the floodplain, in terms of cultivated and uncultivated species, is higher than the species diversity supported by upstream or downstream agriculture.

Furthermore, since floodplain species, cultivated and uncultivated, are dependent on flooding and soil moisture and do not include any irrigation costs, we define $B^2(F) = B^2(F_1) + B^2(F_2)$, where $B^2(F)$ is defined as the sum of net benefits from floodplain use, including cultivated and harvested species from the floodplain. This, together with groundwater benefits (B_3), comprise the combined net benefits of downstream flooding.

Having defined benefit functions for each of the above noted sectors, we assume the existence of a social planner and a social objective to maximize net benefits from water used within the river basin. We recognize that the benefits of water used within the river basin come from upstream and downstream uses as noted above. The objective function can therefore be expressed as:

$$\text{Max}_{D(t), \ w(t)} = \int_0^\infty e^{\delta t} \left[B^1(D, F(0) - F(t)) + B^2(F) + B^3(w) \right] dt \qquad (2.9)$$

subject to:

$$\dot{A} = r(A, F) \, w(t)$$
$$\dot{F} = D(t)$$
$$\lim_{t \to \infty} e^{-\delta t} \mu_1(t) = 0$$

The corresponding Hamiltonian can be expressed as:

$$H = B^1(D, F(0) - F(t)) + B^2(F) + B^3(w) - \mu_1(D) + \mu_2(r(A, F)w) \qquad (2.10)$$

The control variables for this problem are $D(t)$ and $w(t)$, the rate of diversion and the rate of groundwater abstraction, and the stock variables are the flood (F) and the aquifer (A). The co-state variable (μ_2) captures the value of a marginal change in the resource stock, it is the shadow price of the groundwater resource. Applying the maximum principle, we derive the following first-order conditions:

$$\frac{\partial H}{\partial D} = B_D^1 - \mu_1 \Rightarrow P_a(Y_1) \frac{\partial Y_1}{\partial D} - c_1 = \mu_1 \qquad (2.11)$$

$$\frac{\partial H}{\partial w} = B_w^3 = \mu_2 \Rightarrow P_a(Y_3) \frac{\partial Y_3}{\partial w} - c_w(r(A, F)) = \mu_2 \qquad (2.12)$$

$$\dot{\mu}_1 - \delta\mu_1 = \frac{-\partial H}{\partial F} = -B_F^2 - B_F^1 + \left(\frac{\partial c_w}{\partial r} w - \mu_2\right) r_F$$

$$\dot{\mu}_1 - \delta\mu_1 = -P_a(Y_2) \frac{\partial Y_2}{\partial F} + P_a(Y_1) \frac{\partial Y_1}{\partial[F(0) - F(t)]} + \left(\frac{\partial c_w}{\partial r} w - \mu_2\right) r_F \qquad (2.13)$$

where $B_F^1 = -\dfrac{\partial B^1}{\partial[F(0) - F(t)]} < 0, \ B_F^1 > 0, \ \dfrac{\partial c_w}{\partial r} < 0$

$$\dot{\mu}_2 - \delta\mu_2 = -\frac{\partial H}{\partial A} = -\mu_2 r_A + \frac{\partial c_w}{\partial r} r_A \qquad (2.14)$$

$$\frac{\partial H}{\partial \mu_1} = -D = \dot{F} \qquad (2.15)$$

$$\frac{\partial H}{\partial \mu_2} = r(F, A) - w = \dot{A} \qquad (2.16)$$

From (2.12) we note that the shadow price of groundwater is equal to the marginal net benefits derived from groundwater use, w, that is, $\mu_2 = B_w$. We define $\mu_2 r_F$ as the value of a marginal change in recharge, in terms of additional returns to downstream productive activities dependent on groundwater abstraction. Equation (2.13) therefore implies that the flood should be diverted up to the point where the marginal benefits of downstream flooding are equal to the opportunity cost of allowing the flooding to occur and accumulate.

The marginal floodplain benefits include capital gains and the marginal benefits of current floodplain production, B_F^2, as well as the value of a marginal change in recharge to downstream uses of groundwater ($\mu_2 r_F$), less the marginal changes in costs of abstracting w, due to changes in r. The sum of the terms $(\mu_2 - (\partial c_w/\partial_r)w)r_F$ can be defined as the indirect benefits from an increase in the recharge function of the floodplain wetlands. Marginal floodplain benefits, B_F^2, include benefits from the production of cultivated and uncultivated species from the floodplain. The opportunity costs of maintaining F in (2.13) are comprised of the sum of the interest payment term, $\delta\mu$, and the opportunity cost of reduced accumulated diversion, $(-B_F^1)$.

Hydrological data from the Komadugu-Yobe river basin suggest that the relationship between flooding and groundwater recharge is linear and dependent solely on flood extent within the wetlands (Thompson and Goes, 1997). We therefore define $r(A) = 0$ and this relationship implies that $r_A = 0$ and equation (2.14) then simplifies to:

$$\mu_2 / \mu_2 = \delta \qquad (2.17)$$

implying that the shadow price of the groundwater stock is constant over time and that its rate of change is equal to the discount rate, δ. We derive the following expression for the optimal rate of diversion of water from downstream to upstream areas, from (2.11), (2.12) and (2.13) and from noting that $B_D = \mu_1$. Thus,

$$\mu_1 = \delta\, B_D^1 - B_F^2 - B_F^1 + \left(\frac{\partial c_w}{\partial r} - \mu_2 \right) r_F = D\, B_{DD}^1 \qquad (2.18)$$

The rate of change in water diversion along the optimal path is thus determined by the following condition:

$$\dot{D} = \frac{\delta\left(P_a(Y_1) \frac{\partial Y_1}{\partial D} \right) - \left(P_a(Y_2) \frac{\partial Y_2}{\partial F} \right) + \left(P_a(Y_1) \frac{\partial Y_1}{\partial [F(0) - F(t)]} \right) - \left(\frac{\partial c_w}{\partial r} - P_a(Y_3) \frac{\partial Y_3}{\partial w_1} + c_w \right) r_F}{P_a{}'(Y_1)\left(\frac{\partial Y_1}{\partial D} \right)^2 + P_a(Y_1) \frac{\partial^2 Y_1}{\partial D_2}} \qquad (2.19)$$

which further implies that:

$$D = 0 \text{ if } \frac{B_F^2}{\delta} + \frac{\left(\mu_2 - \frac{\partial c_w}{\partial r} \right) r_F}{\delta} = B_D^1 - \frac{B_F^1}{\delta} \qquad (2.20)$$

Equation (2.18) tells us that if the present value net benefits from diverted water are higher than net direct and indirect benefits from the floodplain wetlands, then the rate of diversion falls over time. The rate of diversion will *increase* over time if the present value net benefits from diversion are less than the benefits from flooding. However, given that flood extent, F, is finite, it is feasible for $\dot{D} > 0$ only for the initial periods, and the rate of diversion must eventually fall.

The optimal path for $D(t)$ is therefore affected by two types of present value benefits derived from the floodplain, namely, discounted floodplain production benefits, B_F^2/δ and discounted floodplain recharge benefits,

$$\frac{\left(\mu_2 - \dfrac{\partial c_w}{\partial r}\right) r_F}{\delta}$$

The relative costs and benefits of diverting water from downstream to upstream areas of the river basin therefore determine the initial level of diversion and influence the level of diversion over the time path. Clearly therefore, the present value benefits derived from the floodplain and from the upstream areas must be known before the social planner can determine the initial level of diversion and, subsequently, the optimal path of the rate of diversion. Determining the relative levels of these net benefits is therefore the subject of the next section.

2.5 BIODIVERSITY AND FLOODING WITHIN THE WETLANDS

The above model has shown that direct and indirect benefits of the wetlands, if positive, will have an impact on the optimal level of diversion to upstream areas. In terms of floodplain agriculture, Barbier et al. (1993) and Barbier and Thompson (1997) have shown that reduced flooding within the wetlands would result in welfare losses due to reduced productivity of the wetlands. Acharya (1998) has further shown that the indirect effects of changes in flood extent would cause groundwater levels to fall within the wetlands, resulting in welfare losses from reduced agricultural productivity during the dry season and from increased prices or higher opportunity costs of time for water used in domestic consumption.

As noted earlier, the floodplain is a producer of large quantities of doum palm, reeds and sedges. Polet and Shaibu (in prep.) estimate that the annual market value of doum palm produced from the area may be around 35 million Naira.[10] These values have been included in the above model as $B(F_1)$. However, we do not know the welfare impacts of changes in flood extent, resulting from changes in the distribution and availability of harvested species such as doum palm. The objective of this section is therefore to (1) present the existing data on upstream gains and floodplain benefits, and (2) to partially measure the biodiversity value of the wetlands, in terms of harvested wild species. We use available data to illustrate how this may be carried out for the various species and resources collected from the wetlands and which are dependent on continued flooding to meet the demands of wetland populations.

Assessing the Value of Upstream and Partial Floodplain Benefits

Barbier et al. (1993) find that both on an area and water use basis the total production from *fadamas* of the Hadejia-Nguru wetlands exceeds that derived from the Kano River Irrigation Project (Table 2.5). Barbier and Thompson (1997) expand on this analysis and suggest that the construction of the proposed dams would have a large impact on floodplain production. The high productivity of the floodplain is evident in that the losses in economic benefits due to changes in flood extent for all scenarios are large, ranging from US$2.6–4.2 million to US$23.4–24.0 million. Scenario 3, which yields the lowest upstream irrigation gains, also has the least impact in terms of floodplain losses, whereas Scenario 5 has both the highest irrigation gains and floodplain losses.

Table 2.5   Present value net economic benefits from KRIP and wetlands

Present value net economic benefits from overall land-use system	
Kano River Irrigation Project	233 Naira/ha
Hadejia-Nguru wetlands	1276 Naira/ha
Present value net economic benefits per 1000 m³ of water used	
Kano River Irrigation Project	0.3 Naira
Hadejia-Nguru wetlands	565 Naira

Source: Barbier et al. (1993).

The hydrological simulations are combined with the economic estimates of floodplain agricultural, fishing and fuelwood benefits and the returns to the Kano River Irrigation Project – Phase 1 (KRIP-I) (Barbier et al., 1993). These are used to determine for each scenario the likely overall gains in terms of economic benefits of additional upstream irrigation production versus the subsequent losses in floodplain benefits from reduced flooding. Barbier and Thompson (1997) conclude that in all the scenarios the additional value of production from large-scale irrigation schemes does not replace the lost production attributable to the downstream wetlands, since gains in irrigation values account for at most around 17 per cent of the losses in floodplain benefits.

Assessing the Value of Groundwater-irrigated Cultivation

The regular inundation of the wetlands ensures the annual recharge of the shallow aquifer within the wetlands, which is used extensively for domestic water consumption and increasingly for irrigated agriculture during the dry season. Using agricultural production data from the wetlands, Acharya (1998) shows that the floodplain recharge benefits are in fact positive and significant. Using a production function approach, the change in welfare associated with a decrease in recharge to the aquifer is estimated as 2863 Naira (US$32.5) for each vegetable farmer and as 29 110 Naira (US$331) for farmers growing wheat and vegetables. The total loss associated with the 1 metre change in naturally recharged groundwater levels (resulting in a decline of groundwater levels to approximately 7 metres) is estimated as 36 308 Naira (US$413) per hectare. Since wheat is a newly introduced crop within the wetlands it displays a high yield response to water inputs. However, continued production of wheat within the wetlands could therefore be subject to declining yields over time and is therefore generally considered to be unsustainable within the wetlands over the long run. Therefore, we disregard wheat production and estimate a lower bound welfare loss of US$82 832 for the wetlands, due to a decrease in groundwater levels to approximately 7 metres in depth.[11] Although there is some difference in the level of welfare loss with and without consideration of wheat production, the value of groundwater recharge in terms of irrigated agriculture is positive and significant.

Valuing Uncultivated Floodplain Benefits

Although there is some evidence available for direct floodplain benefits as given by the above studies, the value of wild resources (with the exception of fuelwood and fisheries) is missing from the analysis. As noted earlier, there is evidence to show that these resources are used widely within the wetlands and have economic value. Eaton and Sarch (1997) find that wild resources are an integral part of the wetland economy with linkages to other income-generating activities such as mat making and fishing, as sources of income for disadvantaged groups and as a source of goods and materials for the wider regional economy. They conclude that the wealth of wild resources in the wetlands depends directly on the maintenance of annual flooding.

Biodiversity of wild resources, in terms of species abundance and species distribution, is likely to be determined by flood extent and groundwater levels. Changes in either flood extent, flooding patterns and/or groundwater levels may impact species distribution and abundance. We therefore try to capture this effect on some species which are not cultivated and are dependent on the flooding pattern within the wetlands. The example below is developed for the benefits derived from the collection of doum palm fronds.

We assume a log–linear relationship where flood extent appears as an input in the production function for uncultivated, wild resources. We base this assumption on the log–linear relationships shown to be appropriate for agricultural production within the wetlands (Acharya, 1998). To collect these resources, however, requires labour and labour is therefore a second input in the production function for these garnered resources.

We begin by assuming that the production of q_i, an uncultivated resource, requires a water input W_i (flood area). The aggregate production function for resource i can be expressed as:

$$q_i = q_i(W, X) \text{ for all } i \qquad (2.21)$$

and the associated costs of producing q_i are:

$$C_i = C_x X \text{ for all } i \qquad (2.22)$$

where C_i is the minimum costs associated with producing q_i during a single growing season and C_x is a cost of harvesting q_i. We assume that there exists an inverse demand curve for the aggregate output, q_i, such that:

$$P_i = P_i(q_i) \text{ for all } i \qquad (2.23)$$

where P_i is the market price for q_i, and all other marketed input prices are assumed to be constant.

We further assume that the production function (2.21) can be expressed as a log–linear, in this case, Cobb–Douglas, form. We make this assumption based on the evidence that irrigated agricultural production in the wetlands is described by a log–linear functional form for the production function (see Acharya, 1998 and Acharya and Barbier, 1997). Substituting the Cobb–Douglas functional form for (2.20), we can write the production function as:

$$q_i = AW^a X^b \text{ for all } i \qquad (2.24)$$

where A, a and b are parameters, q is the output.

Denoting S_i as the social welfare arising from producing q_i, S_i is measured as the area under the demand curve (2.23), less the cost of the inputs used in production:[12]

$$S_i = S_i(W,X) = \int_0^{qi} P_i(q)dq - C_X X \text{ for all } i \qquad (2.25)$$

To maximize (2.25) we find the optimal values of input X_i and water input W_i through setting the following first-order conditions to zero:

$$\frac{\partial S_i}{\partial X_i} = P_i(q_i) \frac{\partial q_i}{\partial X_i} - C_X = 0 \text{ for all } i \qquad (2.26)$$

$$\frac{\partial S_i}{\partial W} = P_i(q_i) \frac{\partial q_i}{\partial W} = 0 \text{ for all } i \qquad (2.27)$$

Equations (2.26) and (2.27) are the standard optimality conditions indicating that the socially efficient level of input use occurs where the value of the marginal product of each variable input equals its price. If each resource user is a price-taker, then this welfare optimum is also the competitive equilibrium. For a constant labour input, the net welfare change from a change in wetland area is therefore the effect of a change in flood extent on the value of the marginal product of water in production.

Following Ellis and Fisher (1987), the optimization problem faced by a price-taking individual can also be characterized as a cost minimization problem where:

$$\min L = rX + \lambda(q - AX^a W^b) \qquad (2.28)$$

where r is the opportunity cost of labour used in collecting the resource q. Differentiating the Lagrangian to derive first-order conditions, we get:

$$\frac{\partial L}{\partial X} = r - \lambda AW^b aX^{a-1} = 0 \qquad (2.29)$$

$$\frac{\partial L}{\partial X} = q - AX^a W^b = 0 \qquad (2.30)$$

Since the production function is characterized only by the labour decision variable, X, we solve for the cost function $C(x)$ as

$$X = \left[\frac{q}{AW^b} \right]^{1/a} \qquad (2.31)$$

$$C(r,W,q) = r\, A^{-1/a}\, W^{-b/a}\, q^{1/a} \qquad (2.32)$$

and differentiating the cost function (2.30) with respect to output generates the following expression for marginal cost:

$$\frac{\partial C}{\partial q} = \frac{r}{a}\, A^{-1/a}\, W^{-b/a}\, q^{(1-a)/a} \qquad (2.33)$$

We assume that the collectors of wild resources are price-takers and face a horizontal demand function. Assuming further that the collectors equate price to marginal cost, we find that the equilibrium level of harvesting q is given by:

$$q = \frac{r}{a}\, AW^b \qquad (2.34)$$

We use input and output data from Eaton and Sarch (1997) who estimate a market value of 10 million Naira from annual doum palm collection in the village of Adiani. We also incorporate the econometric findings from Acharya and Barbier (1997) to calibrate the parameters for the above model.

The expression (2.32) is used to calculate equilibrium output for different levels of flood extent, based on the scenarios presented in Tables 2.4 and 2.5. The level of labour input, X is held constant at 3486 days of labour, for an initial (maximum) flood extent of 112817 hectares. For a non-marginal change in W, from W^0 to W^1, the aggregate welfare change can be found by integrating under (2.25), holding all other inputs constant. The welfare changes associated with changes in flood extent under the various dam scenarios are presented in Table 2.6. Flood extent refers to the estimated flood extent under the scenarios presented in Tables 2.3 and 2.4.

2.6 CONCLUSIONS

Development of waterways to provide irrigation and drinking water supplies does not necessarily have to be an antithesis of biodiversity conservation in the ecosystems dependent on these water systems. The analysis here shows that development should stop at the point where marginal benefits equal marginal costs (in terms of biodiversity loss and

Table 2.6   Welfare change associated with change in flood extent and reduced harvest of doum palm fronds

Flood extent (ha)	Quantity harvested (tons)	Welfare change (Naira)	Flood extent (ha)	Quantity harvested (tons)	Welfare change (Naira)
97 755	66 064	779 400	91 697	64 395	1 113 200
103 592	67 614	469 400	107 234	68 555	281 200
86 315	62 855	1 421 200	80 257	61 052	1 781 800
25 768	38 756	6 241 000	19 710	34 816	7 029 000
55 350	52 620	2 312 053	49 292	50 236	3 945 000

Note: Initial flood extent = 112 817 hectares; q = 69 961; X = 3485.6.

other floodplain related productivity) to allow the remaining resources to support the downstream floodplain. Under the Biodiversity Convention, the environmental consequences of a country's programmes and policies should be fully taken into account. However, without adequate recognition of the marginal value of biodiversity conservation (or the opportunity costs of development) it is unlikely that such disturbances and conversions will stop at an optimal level, thereby resulting in excessive loss of biodiversity, and hence social and economic welfare, in downstream communities.

This chapter has explored how the biodiversity impacts of water development activities may be assessed. The analysis presented here shows the importance of valuing floodplain productivity in making water allocation decisions in semi-arid river basins such as the Komadugu-Yobe river basin in Northern Nigeria. Using an optimal control framework, it shows that the basin-wide economic value of water can be maximized when net benefits from water used in both upstream and downstream areas are considered. Drawing on the results reported in Sections 2.3 and 2.4, the impact of dam construction on the net basin-wide economic benefits of water can also be shown. The results of all the valuation studies presented in this chapter, for cultivated and harvested species, are summarized in Table 2.7. It is clear from these results that floodplain productivity would be severely affected by changes in hydrological conditions within the wetlands.

This analysis shows the potential impact of upstream dam construction on species diversity supported by the regular inundation of the wetlands. The relationship between the productivity and distribution of these species and flooding is, however, complex and requires further study of changes in productivity due to changes in flooding patterns.

Table 2.7 Losses in floodplain and groundwater use benefits versus gains in irrigated upstream production

		Scenario 1				Scenario 1a			
	Irrigation value[a] [1]	Floodplain loss (1)[b] [2]	Floodplain loss (2)[c] [3]	Groundwater welfare[d] loss [4]	Net loss [2+3+4] – [1]	Floodplain loss[b] [5]	Floodplain loss (2) [6]	Groundwater welfare loss [7]	Net loss [5+6+7] – [1]
Scenario 2	682 983	−4 045 024	−349	−34 265	−3 396 655	−5 671 973	−498	−38 510	−5 027 998
Scenario 3	354 139	−2 558 051	−210	−24 865	−2 228 987	−4 184 999	−126	−28 807	−3 859 793
Scenario 4	682 963	−7 117 291	−636	−36 691	−6 471 655	−8 744 240	−797	−40 633	−8 102 707
Scenario 5	3 124 015	−23 377 302	−2 793	−129 783	−20 385 863	−24 004 251	−3 146	−133 725	−21 017 107
Scenario 6	556 505	−15 432 952	−10 433	−36 691	−14 923 571	−17 059 901	−1 766	−40 633	−16 545 795

Notes
[a] Based on the mean of the net present values of per hectare production benefits for the Kano River Irrigation Project Phase I applied to the gains in total irrigated area (Source: Barbier and Thompson, 1997).
[b] Based on the mean of the net present values of total benefits for the Hadejia-Jama'are floodplain averaged over the actual peak flood extent for the wetlands of 112 817 ha in 1989/1990 and applied to the differences in mean peak flood extent (Source: Barbier and Thompson, 1997).
[c] Based on the mean of the net present values of welfare loss (from Table 2.6) from reduced doum palm collection due to a reduction in flood extent (in hectares), using discount rates of 5 per cent and 8 per cent with time horizons of 30 and 50 years for each discount rate and converted to US$ using the 1997 rate of US$1 = 88 Naira.
[d] Based on the mean of the net present values of welfare loss from a 1 metre reduction in well levels in the Hadejia-Nguru wetlands (using discount rates of 5 per cent and 8 per cent with time horizons of 30 and 50 years for each discount rate), averaged over an area of 19 000 ha of land within the wetlands which could support groundwater irrigated agriculture. A welfare loss of 3566 Naira per ha is used for all the scenarios. Values are converted to US$ using the 1997 rate of US$1 = 88 Naira.

Nonetheless, it has been possible to compare effects of proposed upstream developments. Scenarios which allow for regulated flooding (scenarios 3 and 6) to some extent succeed in mitigating the adverse downstream impacts of dam construction. In particular, by identifying the level of species diversity in the outputs of activities dominated by different hydrological regimes, this analysis has shown that upstream agricultural production not only fails to make up for lost floodplain productivity in terms of monetary value, but also supports a lower level of species diversity. Furthermore, the values identified in Table 2.7 as Floodplain loss (2) are indicative only of a single harvested species and it is likely that were we to account for the market value of other harvested species (or the shadow value of non-marketed species) losses in floodplain benefits as a consequence of upstream developments would be even higher. The full assessment of environmental and social impacts of water development projects therefore requires a more complete appreciation of the opportunity cost of development in terms of water requirements by households, farmers and naturally occurring species within the wetlands.

NOTES

1. I am grateful to Charles Perrings for helpful suggestions and comments.
2. 1989/90 prices: US$1 = 7 Naira.
3. For convenience of notation this is written as $c_x x_j$ for all the agricultural production functions described later in this chapter. However, each production function will have its own, unique vector of associated input costs.
4. If there are no water use charges for farmers *and* no externalities, then we could assume zero costs of diversion, $c_1 D = 0$, by further noting that investments in pipes and dams have already been made.
5. The other main uses of floodwater are fishing and forestry (see Barbier, Adams and Kimmage, 1993). Net benefits from these activities can be similarly described by appropriate production functions. However, to keep the analysis simple and to maintain symmetry between the sectors we include only agricultural production in the model.
6. The use of groundwater in domestic water consumption is a major use within the wetlands. In the present chapter this use is omitted from the model to simplify analysis. However, see Acharya (1988) for an alternative formulation of this model, including net benefits derived from groundwater used for domestic consumption.
7. Note that we assume that the diverted water, the flood and the groundwater serve distinct areas. The area irrigated by flooding is not irrigated by groundwater abstraction and vice versa.
8. Here, we consider only the use values of these species and not their non-use or existence values, although these are likely to be significant for some species.
9. There is little consensus in ecological literature on the best diversity measure to use. A species diversity index such as Simpson's diversity index reflects both the number of species (species richness) and their relative abundance. Since we make the assumption that the output Y_i is a function of species richness and the present distribution of these species, this index is appropriate for our purpose. We also assume that $dY/dS > 0$ and $d^2Y/dS^2 < 0$, since the present farming system, especially in the floodplain, is dependent on a relatively diverse composition of cultivated species. For uncultivated species,

$dq/dS > 0$ and $d^2q/dS^2 < 0$, since the wetland populations rely on the use of a wide variety of uncultivated, harvested species.
10. 88 Naira = US$1.
11. This is based on the assumption that 19000 hectares within the wetlands could be irrigation through the use of small tubewells (DIYAM, 1987).
12. We assume here that the demand function in (2.23) is compensated, so that consumer welfare can be measured by the appropriate areas. Welfare change is the sum of the consumer and producer surplus measures. However, if the production units are small relative to the market for the final output, and they are essentially price-takers, it can be assumed that product and variable input prices will remain fixed after a change in the environmental resource, W. In this case the benefits of a change in W will accrue to the producers (Freeman, 1993).

REFERENCES

Acharya, G. (1998), 'Hydrological-economic linkages in water resource management', unpublished PhD thesis, University of York.

Acharya, G. and E.B. Barbier, (1997), 'Using the production function approach to value environmental functions: groundwater recharge in the Hadejia-Nguru wetlands', Environment Department, discussion paper in Environmental Economics and Environmental Management, University of York.

Adams, W.M. (1985), 'The downstream impacts of dam construction: a case study from Nigeria', *Transactions of the Institute of British Geographers*, **10**, 292–302.

Adams, W.M. (1992), *Wasting the Rain: Rivers, People and Planning in Africa*, London: Earthscan Publications.

Adams, W.M. (1993), 'Economy of the floodplain', in Hollis et al. (eds), *The Hadejia-Nguru Wetlands*, Gland: IUCN.

Akinsola, O.A. (1988), 'The invasion of Hadejia-Nguru', *World Conservation*, 4/97–1/98, 16.

Barbier, E.B. and J.R. Thompson (1997), 'The value of water: floodplain versus large-scale irrigation benefits in Northern Nigeria', forthcoming in *Ambio*.

Barbier, E.B., W. Adams and K. Kimmage (1993), 'Economic valuation of wetland benefits', in Hollis et al. (eds), *The Hadejia-Nguru Wetlands*, Gland: IUCN.

Carruthers, I. and C. Clark (1981), *The Economics of Irrigation*, Liverpool: Liverpool University Press.

Chifana (1986), *Improvements of River Channels along River Hadejia between Geidam and Hadejia: Final Report*. Lagos: Federal Ministry of Water Resources.

DIYAM (1987), *Shallow Aquifer Study*, 3 Volumes, Kano: Kano State Agricultural and Rural Development Authority.

Eaton, D. and T.-M. Sarch (1997), 'The economic importance of wild resources in the Hadejia-Nguru wetlands', Collaborative Research in the Economics of Environment and Development (CREED) Working Paper no. 13, London: International Institute for Environment and Development (IIED).

Ellis, G. and A. Fisher (1987), 'Valuing the environment as an input', *Journal of Environmental Management*, **25**, 149–56.

Freeman, A. M. (1993), *The Measurement of Environmental and Resource Values: Theory and Methods*, Washington DC: Resources for the Future.

Hadejia-Nguru Wetlands, mimeo, Nguru: Hadejia-Nguru Wetlands Conservation Project.

Haskoning (1977), *Hadejia Irrigation Project: Masterplan and Preliminary Design*, 6 vols, Lagos: Haskoning Engineering Consultants (Nigeria).

Hollis, G.E. and J.R. Thompson (1993), 'Water resource developments and their hydrological impacts', in Hollis et al. (eds), *The Hadejia-Nguru Wetlands*, Gland, IUCN.

Hollis, G.E., W.M. Adams and M. Aminu-Kano (eds) (1993), *The Hadejia-Nguru Wetlands : Environment, Economy and Sustainable Development of a Sahelian Floodplain Wetland*, Gland, Switzerland: IUCN.

IWACO, B.V. (1985), *Study of the Water Resources in the Komadugu-Yobe Basin, General Report,* Rotterdam: Report for the Nigeria-Niger Joint Commission for Cooperation.

Kimmage, K. and W.M. Adams (1992), 'Wetland agricultural production and river basin development in the Hadejia-Jama'are valley, Nigeria', *Geographical Journal*, **158**, 1–12.

Matthes, H. (1990), *Report on the Fishery Related Aspects of the Hadejia-Nguru Wetlands Conservation Project*, Gland: Mission Report to IUCN.

NEAZDP (1994), *Groundwater Report*, Gashua, Nigeria: North East Arid Zone Development Programme.

Rodenburg, W.F. (1987), *Report of a Mission to Nigeria and Burkina Faso: Part 1 Nigeria*, Leiden: Centre for Environmental Studies.

Thomas, D.H.L., M.A. Jomoh and H. Mathes (1993), 'Fishing', in Hollis et al. (eds), *The Hadejia-Nguru Wetlands*, Gland: IUCN.

Thompson, J.R. and G. Hollis (1995), 'Hydrological modelling and the sustainable development of the Hadejia-Nguru wetlands, Nigeria', *Hydrological Science Journal*, **40**, 97–116.

Thompson, J.R. (1995), 'Hydrology, water management and wetlands of the Hadejia-Jama'are Basin, Northern Nigeria', unpublished PhD thesis, University of London.

Thompson, J.R. and B.J.M. Goes (1997), 'Inundation and groundwater recharge in the Hadejia-Nguru wetlands, Northeast Nigeria: hydrological analysis', Wetland Research Unit, Department of Geography, University College London.

Wallace, T. (1980), 'Agricultural projects and land in northern Nigeria', *Review of African Political Economy*, **17**, 59–70.

3. The loss of biodiversity in aquatic ecosystems: the case of demersal and gillnet fisheries in Malawi

Victor Kasulo

3.1 INTRODUCTION

Biodiversity is fundamental to the functioning and resilience of freshwater ecosystems, many of which supply goods and services that are important for human welfare. However, economic utilization of such systems may lead to biodiversity loss either directly through overexploitation or indirectly through habitat destruction. The fundamental problem of biodiversity conservation is to maintain that level of biodiversity which will guarantee the functioning of ecosystems on which human consumption and production depend (Barbier et al., 1995; Perrings et al., 1995).

Terrestrial and freshwater ecosystems are linked by powerful feedbacks. Soil erosion in watersheds affects both siltation and nutrient inputs into water bodies. Freshwater bodies are a magnet for human settlement and use. Both the harvesting of resources and waste emissions to water can qualitatively and quantitatively affect freshwater habitats. Freshwater bodies are insular habitats in which biotic interactions can have major consequences. Species introduction and fish manipulations have significantly changed productivity, nutrient cycling and physical characteristics of fresh waters. The net consequences of land-use changes and species introductions has been to increase the similarity among freshwater ecosystems through eutrophication and community change (Heywood and Watson, 1995).

The main driving forces behind biodiversity loss stem from human activities. It is possible to distinguish proximate and underlying causes. Proximate causes include the direct overexploitation of species, for example through hunting, fishing and collection or gathering and their indirect impact on ecosystem degradation that leads to species loss. Habitat destruction and conversion can be given as examples. Underlying causes comprise the economic, social-political and cultural factors that lie

behind the activities that lead to direct depletion of species and degradation of their habitat. These underlying causes include growth of
population, culture and ethics, economic incentives, policies and institutions (Barbier et al., 1995; Heywood and Watson, 1995).

As an example, agriculture and construction activities promote erosion
and nutrient loading which cause eutrophication of fresh waters. Input of
sewage or household wastes can also result in eutrophication.
Eutrophication reduces water quality and affects microbial activity. It
may also have atmospheric effects. The introduction of exotic species and
overharvesting have complex effects on sediments and nutrients. They can
alter sediment accumulation rates, while changes in the fish community
affect recycling rates of limiting nutrients and can shift the limiting nutrient between nitrogen and phosphorus. Because of the insularity of fresh
waters, species introductions, overharvesting and management actions
targeted on particular species can have effects that ramify throughout
freshwater systems, affecting production, decomposition and nutrient
recycling as well as other species. These changes may also affect wildlife
and waterfowl that use freshwater systems for drinking, habitat and food.
It may be pointed out that despite these facts, there is still considerable
scientific uncertainty about the responses of freshwater ecosystems to
changes in biodiversity (Heywood and Watson, 1995).

In the analysis of loss of biodiversity in aquatic ecosystems, fish are
usually used as indicators of trends in aquatic biodiversity. The main
reason for using fish to monitor biodiversity is that they are better known
than most aquatic organisms, and are relatively easy to collect and identify. They are also enormously diverse, with different species reflecting
different environmental conditions. Some fish species can also be considered as keystone species in that they have major effects on the distribution
and abundance of other organisms in the waters they inhabit. In lakes, for
example, zooplankton-feeding fish can cause major changes in the abundance and species of zooplankton, which in turn causes cascading
changes in the food web (Moyle, 1992). It has been argued that populations of grazing sea urchins are strongly affected by the abundance of fish
predators, particularly trigger-fish and puffer-fish. Such observations
have been made in places as widespread as the Red Sea, Kenya and the
Caribbean (Roberts, 1995). Studies in the Atlantic, Pacific, and Antarctic
Oceans of the effects of fisheries on marine ecosystems all show that the
removal of predators may have various effects, including a replacement of
exploited species by alternative species in the same trophic position, an
increase in production at lower trophic levels, or long-term effects involving ecosystem change (Boehlert, 1996; Parsons, 1992).

Common patterns of development have been observed in diverse fisheries. As fisheries develop, they are said to go through a fishing-up process. The geographic range of the fishery expands as the local population of the preferred species decline. With time the fishery moves to less desirable species. In a multispecies fishery, for instance, where many species are caught using the same gear, the very easily caught species can be completely fished out before catches start to decline. This is because other less easily caught species continue to support the fishery. Once the easily caught species disappear, catches are propped up by increasing effort, adding a few more traps or fishing for longer periods (Boehlert, 1996; Heywood and Watson, 1995 and Roberts and Polunin, 1993).

Empirical evidence shows that most of the recorded extinctions of fish species and subspecies in the present century are from freshwater habitats. Fishing is involved in only a few cases, and as a relatively minor factor. The main causes have been loss of, or degradation of habitat, interruption of migration routes and the introduction of exotic species. This does not mean, however, that fishing is unimportant for the persistence and well-being of the exploited populations. On the contrary, fisheries have frequently depleted fish populations thereby heavily influencing the diversity and dynamics of aquatic ecosystems. Overfishing causes a reduction in the size and age of fish in the catch, and alters the genetic structure of the stock. This is because fishing adds to the natural mortality of species and so decreases the average life span. Most of the fish species caught grow continuously throughout their lives. Shorter lifespans, therefore, mean a reduction in mean size. Apart from a shift of fish catches towards the smaller end of the size spectrum of the fish community, clear-cut evidence of the effects of fishing on the substantive structure and function of the aquatic ecosystem is scarce (Roberts and Polunin, 1993).

Twenty per cent of Malawi's terrestrial area is covered by water. This freshwater ecosystem provides fresh water for drinking, fishing, industry, irrigation, recreation (tourism) and transportation. These uses are impaired by landscape changes that fill, eutrophicate or pollute lakes and rivers, by exotic species introductions and by overharvesting of existing species. Turner et al. (1995) noted that declining populations of molluscivores and large arthropod feeders in Lake Malawi may lead to the diversion of production from fish to benthic invertebrates. Deepburrowing invertebrates, such as bivalves and some ephemeroptera can probably be exploited by large long-snouted haplochromines such as *Taeniolethrinops praeorbitalis* while specialized mollusc-crushers such as *Mylochromis anaphyrmus* and *Lethrinops mylodon* can take large tough-shelled snails. As these species are likely to be inaccessible to small unspecialized fish species, populations of larger benthic invertebrates may rise in heavily fished areas. This could result into an increase in snail populations which may lead to an increase in the incidence of human and animal schistosomiasis (bilharzia) in the lake region. An outbreak of schistosomiasis can have negative effects not only on the health of the people around the lake but also on the tourism industry.

The FAO (1982) suggested that the existence of large populations of chaoborid larvae in the pelagic zone of Lake Malawi would lead to a loss of energy and nutrients from the aquatic foodweb as the adult insects are often consumed by terrestrial or aerial predators. They recommended that consideration be given to introducing the Lake Tanganyika chipeid, *Limnothrissa miodon*, to exploit this resource. However, it is now believed that this is unlikely to be beneficial since there are numerous indigenous pelagic cichlids which eat chaoborid larvae (Turner et al., 1995).

Malawi's freshwater resources support diversified fish resources. This fish biodiversity is reflected in the degree of speciation among fish (there are estimated to be over 500 species in Lake Malawi), the genetic variability within species and the range and number of ecosystems. This biodiversity is currently under threat. The Malawi National Environment Action Plan (NEAP) identified fish depletion and biodiversity loss as major environmental issues that have to be addressed. Although there is no overall assessment of the current status of exploitation or level of depletion of fish resources in Malawi, new trends in traditional fisheries show a large and widespread increase in fishing effort together with declining catch rates. Severe depletion of fish species is known to have occurred both in rivers and lakes, though lakes have been the more severely affected. The most dramatic case is the Nchila (*Labeo mesops*). In the 1950s this species was the major commercial fish in Malawi, but is now threatened with extinction (DREA, 1994; Tweddle et al., 1994).

Overfishing is the proximate cause of loss of fish biodiversity. There are several indirect causes including reduction in water flows and increased sedimentation because of agricultural and deforestation activities. Increasing agricultural pressure from the growing population within the catchment areas and subsequent land degradation have led to increasing nutrient and sediment loads in the lakes and rivers, resulting in habitat alteration. Water pollution, the introduction of non-indigenous fish and the spread of water hyacinth are also believed to have contributed towards loss of fish biodiversity. Water pollution is due to human waste, agricultural waste and run-off and industrial waste. Exotic pond fish are carried away to the rivers and lakes through flooding. The culture of carp in fish ponds in preference to indigenous species, for instance, was stopped, to avoid its transfer to the lakes and rivers (DREA, 1994).

The water hyacinth, introduced to Africa in the late 19th century as an ornamental plant has proliferated explosively in the last forty years. In lakes and rivers the hyacinth has displaced native aquatic plants. The blanket of the weed cuts out light causing native plants to die and rot, and depleting the oxygen in the water. It has also affected fish species together with algae and some invertebrates. The plant is a breeding ground for snakes and disease-carrying mosquitoes and snails which spread malaria and schistosomiasis, respectively. The weed can be so thick that fishing boats cannot leave the shores and ferries may be stranded for hours at a time.

This chapter focuses on one cause of biodiversity change: fisheries. The study offers an assessment of the current status of fish depletion in Malawi and its impact on the fish community and aquatic biodiversity. In particular, it considers how the institutional structure of the fisheries has influenced the level of fishing effort and, through this, the mix of exploited species. It also aims to identify policy options for the conservation of aquatic biodiversity, through reforms to the fishing industry. More especially it has the following goals:

a.   to estimate the optimal, free-entry and maximum sustainable yield (MSY) solutions for the demersal and gillnet fisheries;
b.   to analyse the impact of fishing on fish biodiversity;
c.   to examine the economic factors that influence fish production; and
d.   to identify economically and socially sound measures relating to the sustainable utilization of fisheries for the conservation of aquatic biodiversity.

The empirical data derive from the commercial demersal fishery and the traditional gillnet fishery in the southwest arm of Lake Malawi. This area is approximately 50 km long by 30 km across and reaches a depth of 100 m in the centre. Most of the shoreline, and particularly the south coast, is heavily reeded with extensive marshes and small lagoons. For the demersal fishery, the study period is from 1976 to 1995 and for the gillnet fishery it is from 1976 to 1993. The difference is due to data availability.

3.2   FISHERIES IN THE MALAWI ECONOMY

Fisheries play a significant role in the economy of Malawi. The industry experienced rapid growth between the 1960s and the 1980s. Estimated landings in 1964 were 15 000 tons. Production peaked in 1987 at 88 000 tons. It now averages around 70 000 tons. The industry's contribution to

Gross Domestic Product (GDP) is around 4 per cent. It is, however, an important and rapidly growing source of primary and secondary employment, particularly in rural areas. According to the 1994 annual census on employment, primary employment in the sector totalled 43 227 people in 1993, consisting of 10 602 gear owners and 32 625 assistants. It was estimated that about 200 000 people work ashore in secondary employment. Secondary employment involves boat building and repair, gear manufacturing, fish processing and trading (Malawi Government, 1994).

The capture fisheries sector in Malawi is also an important source of nutrition and food security. Fish provides between 60 and 70 per cent of the nation's animal protein supply and 40 per cent of the total protein supply. It is accessible to the vast majority of the people. Fish production has almost exclusively been geared towards supplying the local market. However, Malawi has been a net exporter of fish since 1969, and between the early 1970s and the early 1980s exports grew steadily. There is a flourishing export trade in aquarium fish. Most aquarium fish are exported to North America, Germany, France, Belgium, and other European countries. Table 3.1 shows the fish export trend since 1976. Food fish exports to neighbouring countries declined in the 1980s, probably due to foreign exchange restrictions in the importing countries, to liberalization of fish markets, and to the increase in domestic demand.

The fisheries of Malawi can be categorized into two major groups, namely commercial fisheries and traditional (artisanal) fisheries. The fish resources of Malawi's lakes and rivers have been exploited by traditional methods for many centuries. Commercial fishing started in 1835 when purse seining was introduced on Lake Malawi, but it was not until 1968 when trawling was introduced that commercial exploitation became a significant industry (Tweddle and Magasa, 1989). There is an overlap in the stocks exploited by the two fisheries. Traditional fisheries produce over 90 per cent of the country's fish output.

Lake Malawi is the largest and most significant water body in terms of fish production. It is 600 km long and 22 to 50 km wide, and covers a total area of about 72 000 km^2. The lake is bordered by Tanzania in the north east and Mozambican waters in the south east. The northern part of the lake is very deep (700 m) and the shelf area suitable for fishing is very narrow. The southern part of the lake, especially in the southeast arm, is shallower with a depth of 50–60 m and a wider shelf area. This creates suitable conditions for fishing. Fish landed from Lake Malawi consistently represents between 40 and 50 per cent of the total national production. Lake Chilwa is the second in importance. Catches from this

Table 3.1   Fish landings and exports, 1976–93

| Year | Landings | | Exports | |
	(m. tons)	Value (MK'000)	(m. tons)	Value (MK'1000)
1976	74 900	7 490	1 945	451
1977	68 200	6 800	1 030	754
1978	67 800	8 798	800	512
1979	59 800	8 372	1 415	671
1980	65 800	10 521	2 000	1 508
1981	51 300	8 220	3 690	2 782
1982	58 400	9 346	2 358	1 778
1983	64 900	12 981	584	682
1984	65 400	17 649	82	260
1985	62 100	20 513	120	330
1986	72 800	27 646	203	500
1987	88 500	37 128	101	548
1988	78 800	40 580	62	82
1989	70 810	71 706	5	6
1990	74 100	77 345	4	7
1991	63 700	65 000	3	7
1992	69 500	82 418	–	–
1993	68 201	113 600	–	–

Note: MK denotes Malawi Kwacha.

Source: Malawi Fisheries Department/Malawi Government: *Economic Report* (various issues).

source fluctuate from year to year and this affects the national catch. The other lakes, Chiuta and Malombe and the Shire River are also important and contribute varying amounts to the total production.

Table 3.2 shows the contribution of traditional and commercial fisheries to total fish production and the distribution of total catch by productive area from 1976 (when the current statistical system was introduced) to 1993. The southeast arm of Lake Malawi is considered to be the most important fishery. Resources are considered to be exploited at or near capacity, with occasional overfishing of certain species. The southwest arm is the second area in importance. Catch records show potential for expansion but careful research is needed to determine the limit of expansion. The fisheries of the northern region of Lake Malawi are con-

Table 3.2   Fish production by source, 1976–93 (metric tons)

Year	Lake Malawi Trad.	Comm.	Total	Lake Malombe	Lake Chilwa	Chiuta	Lower & Mid Shire	Total
1976	29 000	7 500	36 500	6 100	21 200	1 800	9 300	74 900
1977	27 200	6 700	33 900	6 400	20 800	1 500	5 600	68 200
1978	26 400	7 200	33 600	6 100	17 800	1 700	6 600	65 800
1979	15 300	7 100	22 400	3 600	25 800	1 600	6 400	59 800
1980	28 000	7 200	35 200	6 500	19 400	800	3 900	65 800
1981	21 700	7 600	29 300	8 500	8 600	900	4 000	51 300
1982	17 800	6 400	24 200	12 100	15 500	1 400	5 200	58 400
1983	23 400	7 800	31 200	9 700	16 800	1 100	6 100	64 900
1984	25 000	7 600	32 600	11 300	14 600	2 000	4 900	65 400
1985	21 000	8 000	29 000	8 600	15 200	1 700	7 600	62 100
1986	29 200	7 200	36 400	12 700	13 800	700	9 200	72 800
1987	41 800	8 200	50 000	13 000	14 000	4 000	7 500	88 500
1988	40 400	6 700	47 100	10 900	10 800	1 800	8 200	78 800
1989	33 800	4 900	38 700	7 100	11 900	910	12 200	70 810
1990	31 600	6 200	37 800	12 200	14 200	2 400	7 500	74 100
1991	30 000	5 700	35 700	9 900	7 400	1 700	9 000	63 700
1992	35 500	4 900	40 400	8 000	14 500	3 600	3 000	69 500
1993	38 155	5 931	44 086	6 709	11 079	3 433	2 892	68 199

Source: Malawi Fisheries Department.

ducted largely at subsistence level and the low level of landings suggest that there is not much scope for expansion. The same applies to the northern shelf, which adjoins Tanzania. It is suggested that Tanzania and Mozambique together may land between 20 000 and 30 000 tons of fish annually and that this consists principally of *Haplochromine spp*, *Engraulicypris sardella* and certain off-shore species (Watson, 1987).

Commercial Fisheries

Commercial fishing operations fall into the following categories: demer-sal trawling; ringnetting for Chambo (or Tilapia–*Oreochromis spp*); ringnetting for Utaka (a group of semi-pelagic, shoaling zooplanktivo-rous, haplochromine cichlids); and midwater trawling for Chambo and Utaka (Tweddle and Magasa, 1989).

Demersal trawl fishery The demersal trawl fishery is the major commercial fishery in Malawi. Commercial trawling was introduced on the southeast arm of Lake Malawi in 1968, following trawling research in 1965. Since then, the fishery has undergone steady expansion. Initial reports on the fishery (Tarbit, 1972) were followed by a detailed investigation into the changes taking place as the fishery developed (FAO, 1976; Turner, 1977; and Tweddle and Turner, 1977). Results from these studies showed large changes in species composition of catches as the trawl fishery intensified with larger cichlid species disappearing from the catches while small species increased in abundance.

The FAO (1976) carried out experimental trawling from 1971 to 1975. They divided the southern portion of the lake into seven fishing areas and estimated total fish biomass and tentative MSY for each fishing area. These estimates were used to specify total allowable catches and to determine the number of trawling licences to be issued by the Fisheries Department. The minimum legal trawl cod-end mesh size was also increased from 25 to 38 mm. This was intended to reverse the decline in populations of the larger cichlid species.

No attempt was made to see if the hoped-for recovery of the large cichlid species had occurred, until 1989 when experimental trawls were used to estimate total fish biomass and the species composition of the catch. The experimental trawls used up to 1992 showed that species such as *Lethrinops mylodon* and *Lethrinops macracanthus*, which had declined substantially in the 1970s, had become locally extinct. Other large species had also declined. This showed that the recommended total allowable catch and mesh size had not been successful in reversing the decline in large species. Further changes in the fish community were noted. In the areas where most trawling had taken place, large and medium-sized benthic zooplanktivores, large sediment feeders and large piscivores had all declined. The standing stock of small sediment feeders and pelagic species had remained largely unchanged (Tweddle et al., 1995).

Chambo ringnet Chambo ringnets were used in the southeast arm of Lake Malawi from the 1940s following the depletion of inshore stocks of Chambo exploited by intensive beach seine. The first assessment of the fishery was made by Lowe (1952), with subsequent reports made by Williamson (1966), FAO (1976), Mkoko (1981), Lewis (1986) and Tweddle and Magasa (1989). Williamson's (1966) report outlined changes in the fishery since its inception. These included an increase in the minimum mesh size of the nets from 51 mm (2 inches) to 102 mm (4 inches), creation of a one-month close season (December) in 1951, and the extension of the close season to two months (November and December) in 1960. Mkoko (1981) showed that in the period following the FAO (1976) report, catches in the ringnet fishery had declined considerably in this area. This coincided with the introduction of midwater trawling for Chambo. Later studies by Lewis (1986) and Tweddle and Magasa (1989) found that the change in mesh size had no influence on the long-term catch and catch per unit effort of the ringnet fishery (Tweddle and Magasa, 1989).

Traditional (Artisanal) Fisheries

Traditional fisheries use several types of fishing gear. These include: gill-net, *chilimila*, *kambuzi* (beach seine), *chambo* seine, mosquito nets, handlines, long lines, scoop nets and fish traps. The most commonly used gear is the gillnet, which accounts for over 47 per cent of total traditional catches. This type of gear appears to have reached maximum development. Species caught are Tilapia (*Oreochromis spp.*, *Oreochromis shiranus*, and *Tilapia rendalli*), Kampango (*Bagrus meridionalis*) Mlamba (*clariid catfishes*) and Nchila (*Labeo mesops*). Walker (1976) carried out a statistical study of traditional fisheries of Malawi, showing that catch per unit effort in the southwest arm of Lake Malawi using gillnets had declined from about 20 kg per set in the mid-1950s to 5 kg per set in the early 1970s. The decline was largely accounted for by the disappearance of Nchila (*Labeo mesops*) which comprised about half of the catch in the 1950s.

Chilimila net is the second most important gear accounting for around 18 per cent of total traditional catch. This is a sort of modified purse seine. The net is operated by two dugout canoes or planked boats. The species caught are Utaka (*Copadichromis spp*) and Usipa (*Engraulicypris sardella*). *Kambuzi* or beach seine is now used for inshore cichlid (*haplochromine*) species, and represent 9 per cent of total traditional catches while *chambo* seine and mosquito nets represents 5 per cent. Handlines, long lines, scoop nets and fish traps are also used. Their contribution to total catch is low but the fish caught are of high quality.

The growth of the traditional fishery has occurred in a remarkably short period of time and it is therefore not without problems. However, unlike the commercial fishery, few studies have been undertaken in this fishery. It is, therefore, important to appraise the present situation of the fishery and to make necessary recommendations for future management to avoid damage to the fish stocks, which are relatively vulnerable to overexploitation.

3.3 POLICIES AND THE REGULATORY FRAMEWORK OF FISHERIES IN MALAWI

The current policies of the Government of Malawi are laid down in the Statement of Development Policies (DEVPOL, 1987–1996). The policy focus has recently shifted towards food security and alleviation of poverty. Sectoral ministries have developed new policy statements which aim to revise the detail of DEVPOL in light of changes in the country from the political, environmental social and economic perspectives. DEVPOL (1987–1996) states that the aim of the government's policy on fisheries is to maximize the safe sustainable yield from these fish stocks that can economically be exploited from the national waters; improve the efficiency of exploitation, processing and marketing; promote investment in viable rural fish farming units; and exploit all opportunities to expand existing and develop new aquatic resources. Several specific strategies were identified to achieve these objectives. These objectives and strategies were established some time ago and reflect the orientation of the sector at that time. That orientation was very much focused on the status of the fish resources. The Fisheries Department was seen as a guardian of those resources. In recent years, the emphasis of government has moved more towards a concern for the needs of the fishing community and consumers, and fish resources are now seen more as a source of sustainable benefits to the fishing community itself and to the wider national community.

The major statute for the regulation and control of fisheries is the Fisheries Act 1974. The administration of the Act is the responsibility of the Department of Fisheries. The principal function of the Act is to prevent depletion of fish resources and make harvesting of fish sustainable. In this regard, three strategies are employed, namely licensing, gear restrictions and closed seasons. First, the Act requires that certain types of fishing should only be conducted with a licence issued in terms of the Act.

The type of fishing licences which may be issued under the Act include commercial fishing licences, fishing vehicle licences, trout fishing licences, and trade fishing licences. The licences contain terms and conditions prescribed for a particular licence. Recreational fishing by rod or handline and private fishing by hand net do not require licences. There is also a provision in the Act to limit the number of fishing licences for any class of fishing in Malawi, in general, or in a specified area. The intention behind this provision is to ensure that where fish resources are threatened by too many fishermen, the Department of Fisheries should be able to avoid depletion of fish stocks by limiting the number of licences. The second way in which the Act seeks to ensure that fish resources are not depleted is through prohibition of certain methods of fishing. These include use of certain nets (including mesh size), explosives and poison. Thirdly, the Act also prohibits fishing during certain specified periods. This may apply in general or with respect to a particular area of Malawi. This ensures that fish can breed during that period and that fishermen do not catch young fish.

Policing of these regulations is constrained by lack of trained staff and patrol equipment due to inadequate funds, and also by the low level of penalties for non-compliance. Again, although the Act covers most of the important aspects of fisheries, it lacks coordination with other relevant Acts like the Forestry Act, the Land Act, and the Water Resources Act. For example it is silent on cross-sectoral issues such as pollution of waters and its effect on the fish. An Environmental Management Act was established in 1996 in order to deal with such cross-sectoral issues. There is also no mention in the Fisheries Act of the involvement of local communities in the management of fish resources. It is now realized that local knowledge and skills can enhance conservation and management of fisheries and reduce pressure on enforcement. To this end efforts are underway to come up with a new 'Fisheries Conservation and Management' act which would include the involvement of local communities in the management of fish resources. In addition, the Fisheries Act does not take into account the effect of the transboundary nature of Malawi's major fishing waters. Lakes Malawi and Chilwa and Shire River are shared with neighbouring countries. Fishing in shared waters may deplete fish in Malawi. There is, therefore, need for a mechanism to ensure that transboundary issues are properly taken care of.

In summary, it can be stated that overfishing is the main proximate cause of loss of fish biodiversity in Malawi. The factors that cause overfishing include property rights and weak institutional structures. All natural water bodies in Malawi are owned by the state. The Fisheries Department as a government institution has the mandate to issue fishing licences for the purpose of controlling fishing effort. This goal has not been achieved, especially in the traditional fisheries. The traditional fishermen are widely spread all over the lake-shore and this makes it impossible for full coverage of the whole area by licensing teams, who also happen to be part of the enforcement team. This has resulted in the present near open-access situation in the fisheries.

The recent change in policy to focus more on the fishermen may have encouraged increasing levels of effort which has driven profits down to almost zero, thereby reducing the income of existing fishing communities. This situation has been worsened by lack of alternative income-generating activities. Fishermen are locked into a short-run survival strategy whereby they are unable to curtail effort in order to conserve stocks or increase economic efficiency, for this would mean going without food. The lack of income-generating alternatives is also a contributory factor. Poor enforcement of fisheries' regulations reflects lack of effective institutional structures to carry out this task. The enforcement section of the Fisheries Department has insufficient manpower and equipment. It also receives little support from other related institutions like the police and judiciary (Bland and Donda, 1994).

3.4   A FISHERIES MODEL

Most empirical work on fisheries is based on the theoretical relationships between species stock levels, growth functions, harvest rates, effort and fish catch. One classical study which outlined this relationship was by Gordon (1954). This developed the theory of optimum utilization of the fishery resources and the reasons for suboptimal utilization. The optimal degree of utilization on any fishery was defined in terms of total cost and total production functions of the fishery. Total cost and total production were each expressed as a function of fishing effort (degree of fishing intensity). The study also established the very important property of open-access fisheries: that is where a fishery is not privately owned the rent it yields may not be appropriated by anyone. Competition among fishermen will then lead to dissipation of the rent and to higher levels of effort than in a regulated access fishery (Gordon, 1954).

Two characteristics of fisheries are important here. The first characteristic is that as the level of effort rises, it initially results in increasing output. But later, an increase in effort will lead to a fall in the level of output. In such a case there is a maximum sustainable catch which the harvested population can provide. The second characteristic is that the level of effort depends on the nature of property rights in the fishery. When access to fisheries is open (there is no effective regulation), the bioeconomic system will be overexploited beyond the maximum sustainable level (Beddington et al., 1990). These characteristics can be illustrated using mathematical models. The first component of any such model involves a relationship between the population growth of a resource and its abundance. There are a variety of different population models in use for fisheries.

Background

The model that has been used to describe the Malawian fishery is the logistic population growth model. It is given as:

$$dX/dt = rX(1 - X/K) \tag{3.1}$$

where dX/dt is the change in fish stock, X is the fish stock biomass, r is the maximum intrinsic rate of increase in stock, and K is the unexploited level of the stock or environmental carrying capacity.

The second component of the model entails the production function for the catching process. This is the return in catches which can be expected from fishing operations. The catch is related to the inputs (E – fishing effort) and the stock size. In its simplest form, the relationship can be given by:

$$Y = qEX \tag{3.2}$$

where Y is the fish catch, q is a catchability coefficient and E represents the effort. The two components can be combined to describe the rate of change in harvested fish stock. One such model is the Schaefer model:

$$dX/dt = rX(1 - [X/K]) - qEX \tag{3.3}$$

The change in the size of the stock is simply the difference between natural growth and harvest.

A common objective in fisheries management, and a stated objective of Malawian fishery policy, is to maintain the stock (X) which affords MSY. For the logistic growth function, when there is no change in stock, $rX(1 - X/K) - qEX = 0$. This implies that,

$$Y = rX(1 - X/K) = qEX \tag{3.4}$$

Solving for X gives: $X = K(1 - qE/r)$, hence

$$Y = qEX = qKE(1 - qE/r) \tag{3.5}$$

Equation (3.5) is the sustainable-yield function for the Gordon–Schaefer model. It is parabolic and, therefore, for sufficiently high effort, the yield will be zero. The effort level at MSY is derived from the sustainable-yield function as below:

$$\partial Y/\partial E = qK(1 - 2q\,E/r) = 0$$

$$1 = 2q\,E/r$$

$$E_{msy} = r/2q \tag{3.6}$$

The associated levels of stock and catch are calculated as follows. Differentiating the logistic growth function (equation (3.1)) with respect to X gives;

$$r - 2Xr/K = 0 \quad \text{implying that } r = 2Xr/k$$
$$\text{and}$$
$$X_{msy} = K/2 \tag{3.7}$$

Substituting the value of X_{msy} above in the sustainable yield function gives:

$$Y_{msy} = rK/4 \tag{3.8}$$

The MSY is denoted by equation (3.8) above and occurs at $X_{msy} = K/2$ and $E_{msy} = r/2q$ (Beddington et al., 1990; Conrad, 1996; Conrad and Adu-Asamoah, 1986; Conrad and Clark, 1994).

Although MSY has been a stated goal of Malawian fisheries policy, this is not consistent with the nature of property rights in the fishery. To see this, suppose that some price, p, can be put on the level of catch and that some cost, c, is associated with the level of effort. The economic rent, π, is then given by:

$$\pi = pqEY - cY \tag{3.9}$$

Gordon (1954), showed that in an open access fishery the fishing effort adjusts to a level where this economic rent is driven to almost zero. This is because if access is open and a positive rent is being made new entrants will be attracted into the industry, while if rent is negative some participants will leave.

Henderson and Tugwell (1979) analysed the optimal and free market utilization of the lobster fishery in two fishing areas in Canada – Port Maitland and Miminegash. They assumed the growth function of the lobster fishery to be of quadratic form, and the production function to be of Cobb–Douglas form. Using data for the period between 1954 and 1969 for Port Maitland and between 1957 and 1971 for Miminegash, they estimated both the growth function and the production function. Using these estimates the authors calculated the stationary values of both the free-entry and the profit-maximizing solutions. It was noted from the results that the free-entry solutions for both catches and stocks and the actual situations in the two areas were similar. The model, therefore, predicted very well. It was also noted that although the free-entry solution had higher catches, the associated effort was much greater because the equilibrium stocks were smaller. Free entry did not lead this fishery to ruin but it did reduce the net benefits of fishing to all those in the industry (Henderson and Tugwell, 1979).

Another study by Lynne et al. (1981) considered an approach for quantifying and evaluating the contribution of marsh estuarine areas to the production of marketable marine life. A bioeconomic model of the blue crab fishery on the Gulf Coast of Florida was developed. The study covered the period between 1952 and 1974. Fish production was expressed as a function of acreage of marsh (wetland), effort, and catch rate in the previous period.

The ordinary least square method (OLS) was used to estimate the model parameters. The results of the study showed that annual catch was significantly related to the product of effort and the natural logarithm of marsh acreage. The logged catch variable was also significant. Using the estimated coefficients, a marginal product for an acre of marsh was calculated and the value of the marginal product for an acre was computed using dockside price. From their results, it was concluded that both effort and marsh acreage had a significant effect on fish production. However, the authors noted the need for a better dynamic model for improved knowledge on the policy formulation process as regards to marsh preservation (Lynne et al., 1981).

Ellis and Fisher (1987) subsequently sought to value the environmental resource service flows from wetlands using data from Lynne et al.'s (1981) study of the commercial blue crab fishery. They assumed that production of blue crabs could be represented as a Cobb–Douglas process. Blue crab production was expressed as a function of effort and wetland acreage. They calculated the equilibrium output associated with various levels of wetland acreage, and the equilibrium price corresponding to the output. Welfare gains associated with an increase in wetland habitat were calculated as the change in consumer and producer surplus. Successive increments in acreage added less to estimated benefits due to diminishing returns to the wetland input. The results of a sensitivity analysis in which different elasticities were used to calibrate the model indicated that the estimates of welfare gains were reasonably robust (Ellis and Fisher, 1987).

This study was, however, subsequently criticized for neglecting the impact on output, price and resource values of alternative management regimes for the fishery (Freeman, 1991). The fact that many fisheries are under open access with little or no control of effort and catch was ignored (the area under study was confirmed to be under free entry). Freeman argued that open access implies rent dissipation, total cost equal to total revenue, and price equal to average cost. Freeman (1991) modified Ellis et al.'s (1987) model to reflect the open access nature of the Gulf Coast blue crab fishery during the period of study. He calculated the unit cost of effort consistent with zero profit where the average cost curve intersected with the demand curve. He also calculated welfare gains associated with increase in wetland acreage under optimal regulation and open access. The results of the study were contrary to the expected result that the value of the resource would be lower under optimum management, and showed that resource values are influenced not only by biological and economic factors, but also by institutions and management policies (Freeman, 1991).

Another instructive study by Gallastegui (1983) considered the management of the sardine fishery of the Gulf of Valencia (Spain). Using data that described the fishery exploitation, optimum levels of catch, effort, and stock were calculated. In addition, the welfare gains that could be achieved by a movement from the open access equilibrium to the socially optimum solution were demonstrated. The results of the study showed that sardine catches were above the MSY over the period of study (Gallastegui, 1983).

The Model

This study adapts Conrad and Adu-Asamoah's (1986) model of the bioeconomics of commercial tuna fisheries in the Eastern Tropical Atlantic. It is thought to be appropriate to the freshwater fisheries of Malawi, since it uses data on landings (catch), and effort, to estimate the bioeconomic parameters of the Gordon–Schaefer model. Based on these parameters, open access and bioeconomic equilibria may be identified for a combination of price, cost and discount rate. Management policies may be explored using these results. Conrad and Adu-Asamoah (1986) adopted the logistic growth function, as given in equation (3.1) and the simple production function as in equation (3.2). The instantaneous rate of the change in biomass was, therefore, given by $dX/dt = rX(1 - X/K) - Y$ as in equation (3.3). By assuming that the cost of harvest depends on stock abundance, net revenues would depend on fish catch and fish stock. The general form of the net revenue function is $\pi = \pi(Y, X)$ where π is the net revenue. For the Gordon–Schaefer model, the specific form of this function may be given by:

$$\pi = (p - c/qX)Y \qquad (3.10)$$

where p is the per unit price of fish and c is the per unit cost of effort. The cost function ($Y(c/qX)$) is a negative stock-dependent average cost function (a larger stock lowers average cost). We assume a profit maximizing objective function (the management strategy of maximizing sustainable yield has been discussed earlier). This entails maximization of the present value of net revenues subject to the change in biomass and to an initial condition on fish stock. This can be put as:

$$\text{Max } \pi = \int_0^\infty ((p - c/qX)Y) \, e^{-\delta t} \, dt \tag{3.11}$$

Subject to:

$$dX/dt = rX(1 - X/K) - Y$$
$$X_{(0)} = X_0$$

Fish catch (Y) is the control variable while fish stock (X) is the state variable. The current value Hamiltonian for this problem is:

$$H(.) = ((p - c/qX)Y) + \mu(rX(1 - X/K) - Y) \tag{3.12}$$

Where μ is the current value shadow price associated with an incremental change in the fish stock (marginal value of the fish stock which is equivalent to user cost). The first-order necessary conditions for a maximum are:

$$dH/dY = \partial\pi/\partial Y - \mu = (p - c/qX) - \mu = 0 \tag{3.13}$$

$$dH/dX = -cY/qX^2 + \mu(d - r(1 - 2X/K)) \tag{3.14}$$

$$dX/dt = rX(1 - X/K) - Y \tag{3.15}$$

In the steady state, $\dot{\mu} = \dot{X} = 0$, which together with equations (3.13), (3.14) and (3.15) implies:

$$\mu = (p - c/qX) \tag{3.16}$$

$$cY/qX^2 = \mu(d - r(1 - 2X/K)) \tag{3.17}$$

$$Y = rX(1 - X/K) \tag{3.18}$$

Substituting the expression for μ from equation (3.16) into equation (3.17) and isolating δ on the right-hand side yields:

$$r(1 - 2X/K) + \frac{cY/qX^2}{p - c/qX} = \delta \tag{3.19}$$

Equation (3.19) is the fundamental equation of renewable resources. On the left-hand side, the first term ($r - 2X/K$) is the marginal net growth rate (the rate of change in net growth associated with an increment to fish stock). The second term is the marginal stock effect. It measures the marginal value of fish stock relative to the marginal value of fish catch. The terms together represent a fishery's internal rate of return. The equation implies that the optimal steady state value of fish catch and stock will cause the fishery's internal rate of return to equal to the discount rate.

Substituting the expression $Y = rX(1 - X/K)$ (equation (3.18)) into the fundamental equation and solving for the fish stock (X) gives:

$$X^* = \frac{K}{4}\left[\left(\frac{c}{pqK} + 1 - \frac{\delta}{r}\right) + \sqrt{\left(\frac{c}{pqK} + 1 - \frac{\delta}{r}\right)^2 + \frac{8c\delta}{pqKr}}\right] \qquad (3.20)$$

Equation (3.20) may be used to calculate the optimum stock of fish where profit maximization is the objective. Alternately, the steady state can be expressed in terms of the two-equation system:

$$Y^* = [\delta - r(1 - 2X^*/K)][X^*(pqX^*/c - 1)] \qquad (3.21)$$

and

$$Y^* = rX^*(1 - X^*/K) \qquad (3.22)$$

Equation (3.21) is derived from equation (3.17) by solving for Y, while equation (3.22) is the sustainable yield function, equating fish catch to its logistic growth. This equation is used to calculate the optimum level of fish catch. The optimum level of effort is calculated by using:

$$E^* = Y^*/qX^* \qquad (3.23)$$

derived from the production function of the fishery (equation (3.2)).

In Malawi, we are interested in the three outcomes: the MSY management objective, the profit maximizing outcome and the open access outcome. As before, the MSY is $Y_{msy} = rK/4$. The associated levels of stock and effort are $X_{msy} = K/2$ and $E_{msy} = r/2q$, respectively.

The open access equilibrium occurs when the fishery rent is zero (fishery rents are dissipated). For positive stock and harvest (no extinction) this occurs at:

$$X_\infty = c/pq \qquad (3.24)$$

Equation (3.24) is derived from the revenue function (equation (3.10) by making revenue equal to zero ($p = 0$), and solving for fish stock (X). The associated levels of catch and effort are: $Y_\infty = rX_\infty (1 - X_\infty/K)$ and $E_\infty = Y_\infty/qX_\infty$, (or $E_\infty = r/q(1 - c/pqK)$), respectively.

The Gordon–Schaefer model involves the use of known values of catches (Y) and effort (E), and the unknown parameters q and r. Data on catch and effort have been used to obtain estimates of the parameters r and q as follows. The sustainable yield (yield-effort) function for the Schaefer model (equation (3.5)) can be written in the form:

$$Y/E = qK - q^2 KE/r = a - bE$$

where $a = qK$, and $b = q^2K/r$. The coefficients a and b can be estimated by means of a linear regression of Y/E against E (Conrad and Clark, 1994). Setting $U = Y/E$, we have

$$dU/dt = qU(a/b - E^* - U/b)$$

The integral of the above equation after rearranging terms is:

$$\frac{dU}{U(a/b - E^* - U/b)} = qdt$$

or

$$q_t^* = ln\left[|(ZU_t^{-1} - 1/b)/(ZU_{t+1}^{-1} - 1/b)|\right]/Z \tag{3.25}$$

Where $Z = a/b - E^*$ and $E^* = (E_t + E_{t+1})/2$, the effective effort exerted between years t and $t+1$. Equation (3.25) is used to estimate the sequential values of q^* which are supposed to be positive. The absolute value operator guarantees that this is the case. With time series for q^*, an integral assessment can be obtained by taking the arithmetic or geometric mean (Fox, 1975; Conrad and Adu-Asamoah, 1986). It may be noted that given the values of a, b, and q^*, estimates can be made for K and r, where:

$$K^* = a/q \tag{3.26}$$

and

$$r^* = q^2K/b \tag{3.27}$$

The estimates of q, r, and K may then be used to estimate the optimal stock, X^*, using equation (3.20), by selecting appropriate values for cost of effort, c, average price of fish, p, and discount rate, δ.

Measures of the Loss of Fish Biodiversity

The model discussed in Section 3.4 identifies the optimal catch as a function of (a) either a management objective such as maximizing sustainable yield or an economic objective such as maximizing profit, and (b) the property rights/regulatory regime. The optimal catch is measured in metric tons, and does not depend on the mix of species involved. Given the proposition that the main proximate cause of biodiversity loss in Malawi fisheries is overharvesting, we need to understand the relation between the level of catch and the species composition of the catch. Implicitly it has been assumed that the species composition of the catch and the relative abundance of individual species in the catch depend upon the total harvest. What lies behind this is the observation that catchability differs between species: that species which are 'easiest' to catch tend to be fished out first. This section considers the link between the level of total harvest and species composition for harvest (and hence the species composition of the fish stock).

The idea of species diversity has two distinct concepts: species richness and evenness. Species richness is the number of species in a community, while evenness explains the abundance of each species in the community. The term that combines the two concepts of richness and evenness is heterogeneity. It is synonymous with diversity and popular because it is relatively easy to measure. One such measure is the Simpson's index of diversity.

The Simpson's index is based on the fact that diversity is inversely related to the probability that two individuals picked at random belong to the same species. For a population of infinite size, this is given by:

$$D = \sum P_i^2 \tag{3.28}$$

where D is the Simpson index, and P_i is the proportion of species i in the community.

For a measure of diversity, the complement of Simpson's index is used. It is given as:

$$1 - D = 1 - \sum (P_i)^2 \tag{3.29}$$

where $1 - D$ is the Simpson index of diversity.

For a population of finite size, the appropriate estimator is:

$$1 - D = 1 - \sum_{i=1}^{s} [ni(ni - 1)/N(N - 1)] \tag{3.30}$$

where ni is the number of individuals of species i in the sample, N is the total number of individuals in the sample and s is the number of species in the sample. The Simpson's index of diversity ranges from zero for low diversity to almost 1.

It should be noted that the Simpson's index of diversity is sensitive to changes in the more abundant species. One index of diversity which is more sensitive to changes in the rare species is the Shannon–Weiner index. This index is based on information theory and deals with predicting correctly the species of the next individual collected in a sample. It is given by:

$$H^* = \sum_{i=1}^{s} (p_i)(\log p_i) \qquad (3.31)$$

where H^* is the index of species diversity, s is the number of species and p_i is the proportion of total sample belonging to the ith species. The larger the value of H^*, the greater the diversity. Units of H^* are decits per individual if base 10 logs are used (Krebs, 1989).

In order to apply these indexes to the case of Malawi fisheries, the unit of measurement is changed from number of individuals in a sample population to biomass in the total catch (Goda and Matsuoka, 1986). That is, the estimation for a total catch of finite size in a particular period, t, is:

$$D_t = 1 - \sum_{i=1}^{s_t} [Y_{it}(Y_{it} - 1)/Y_t(Y_t - 1)] \qquad (3.32)$$

for the Simpson's index (D_t), and

$$H_t = 1 - \sum_{i=1}^{s_t} (Y_{it}/Y_{it})(\log(Y_{it}(Y_t)) \qquad (3.33)$$

for the Shannon–Weiner index (H_t).

In both of these, Y_{it} is the catch of the ith species harvested in period t (in metric tons), Y_t is the total catch in period t (in metric tons) and s_t is the number of species harvested in period t. The use of these estimates enables us to identify an empirical relation between the diversity indexes and total catch. The time paths for the two diversity indexes and the two fisheries considered, are shown in Figures 3.1 and 3.2.

Regression of the indexes against total catch then provides us with a specific form for the general functions:

$$D_t = f(Y_t) \text{ and } H_t = g(Y_t) \qquad (3.34)$$

With these it is possible to identify the MSY, open access and profit maximizing (optimal) levels of biodiversity in the fishery. It is also possible to identify the biodiversity implications of changes in economic parameters and institutional conditions in the fishery.

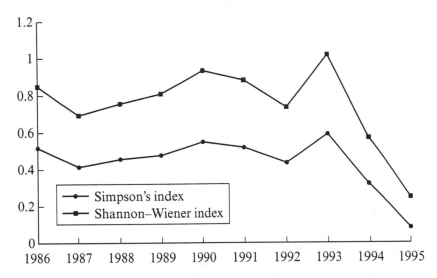

Figure 3.1 Biodiversity index of demersal fishery

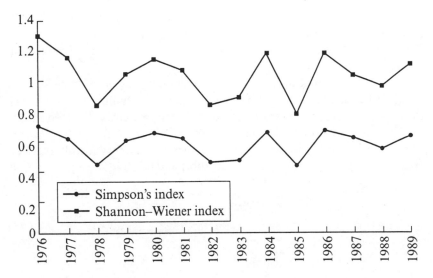

Figure 3.2 Biodiversity index of gillnet fishery

Data Sources and Definitions

All fisheries data used in this study were obtained from the Malawi
Fisheries Department. Fish catch, effort and other data are recorded at
selected landing places in all the main fish producing areas. The raw data
are collected monthly by fisheries' staff at district and regional level
where a preliminary analysis is done. It is then submitted to the Fisheries
Department Headquarters in Lilongwe and the Fisheries Research Unit
in Monkey Bay, Mangochil, where it is finally processed in a form which
provide guidance for fisheries management.

Annual frame surveys are also carried out to establish fleet size,
number of fishermen and nets. The data are analysed by species.
The major species groups are the following:

Chambo (tilapia)	=	*Oreochromis spp* excluding *O. shiranus*
Other tilapia	=	*O. shiranus* and *Tilapia rendalli*
Kambuzi	=	inshore cichlid (haplochromine) species
Utaka	=	*Copadichromis spp.*
Kampango	=	*Bagrus meriodionalis* Günther
Mlamba	=	clariid catfishes
Nchila	=	*Labeo mesops*
Usipa	=	*Engraulicypris sardella* Günther
Chisawasawa	=	offshore, demersal haplochromines

Catch is expressed in metric tons (unless otherwise stated). Effort for gillnet fishery is expressed as number of sets of 91 m (stretched length) net.
Effort for demersal trawl fishery is expressed in fishing days. One fishing
day equals eight hours.

There are no good data on the cost of effort. For both demersal and
gillnet fisheries the cost of effort is calculated by assuming that the situation is one of complete rent dissipation due to free entry. Defined in this
way, the cost of effort includes the opportunity income, or the income
that could be earned in alternative employment (the forgone alternative).
It is obtained by substituting data on effort and catch in the equation:

$$c = \frac{\sum_{i=1}^{n} (Y_i)/n}{\sum_{i=1}^{n} (E_i)/n} \quad \text{for} \quad i = 1,2,3,...,n \qquad (3.35)$$

where $n = 20$ for the demersal trawl fishery, and $n = 18$ for the gillnet fishery.

The price of fish is calculated based on the information on fish catch and value as given in Table 3.1. Total fish value is divided by the total catch to give the price per metric ton. This is expressed as an index with 1993 as the base year.

3.5 EMPIRICAL RESULTS

By using the methodology outlined above, estimates are made for the values of the intrinsic growth rate, r, the catchability coefficient, q, and the environmental carrying capacity, K, of the whole fishery. Table 3.3 shows the estimated values of a, b, q, r and K for the demersal and gillnet fisheries.

Notice that these are averaged across all species caught in each of the fisheries over the period 1976 to 1995 for the demersal fishery and 1976 to 1993 for the gillnet fishery.

The fish price is set at MIC 100.00 per ton. The unit cost of effort assuming complete rent dissipation due to free entry is MK 129.78 for the demersal fishery and MK 0.60 for the gillnet fishery. Estimates of optimal, MSY and open access solutions assuming zero discount rate (future catches are valued in the same way as present ones), are presented in Tables 3.4a and 3.4b for the demersal and gillnet fisheries, respectively.

Table 3.3   Estimates of a, b, q, r *and* K *for the demersal and gillnet fisheries*

Fishery	a	b	q	r	K (m. tons)
Demersal	1.709	−0.00034	0.000323	1.608	5290.75
Gillnet	0.0072	−2.84E-9	1.2E-7	1.443	12664.46

Table 3.4a   Optimal, MSY and open access solutions for the demersal fishery

Optimal	MSY	Open access	Actual average
$Y^* = 900.41$	$Y_{msy} = 2126.25$	$Y^. = 1554.42$	$Y = 1496.61$
$E^* = 599$	$E_{msy} = 2488$	$E^. = 1197$	$E = 1198$
$X^* = 4654.00$	$X_{msy} = 2645.36$	$X^. = 4017.24$	

Note: $p = 100$, $c = 129.78$ and $\delta = 0$.

The microeconomics of biodiversity loss

Table 3.4b   Optimal, MSY and open access solutions for the gillnet fishery

Optimal	MSY	Open access	Actual average
$Y^* = 1352.23$	$Y_{msy} = 4567.34$	$Y \cdot = 2467.75$	$Y = 2404.27$
$E^* = 204284$	$E_{msy} = 1268881$	$E \cdot = 408568$	$E = 408614$
$X^* = 11645$	$X_{msy} = 6332.23$	$X \cdot = 10625.54$	

Note: $p = 100$, $c = 0.60$ and $\delta = 0$.

For the demersal fishery, the results show that average catches were below the MSY level. Fish catches were above the MSY level in the years 1987, 1988 and 1993. It may be noted that the actual average is very close to the open access level and not to the optimal solution, probably due to free entry.

For the gillnet fishery, average catches were also below the MSY level. Fish catches were above the MSY only in 1979 when they were recorded at 5906.93 tons. Like the demersal fishery, the actual average is very close to the open access level and not to the optimal solution. In both cases, open access levels of catch and effort are less than MSY levels, implying a situation of high cost of one unit of effort (Schaefer, 1957).

The financial implications of these results can be demonstrated by considering the profits associated with each situation. Profit is calculated by subtracting the product of effort and cost from the product of catch and price. For the demersal fishery, the optimal solution leads to a profit of MK12 303.78 while the MSY solution leads to a loss of MK110 267.64. For the gillnet fishery, the optimal solution leads to a profit of MK12 655.00 while the MSY solution leads to a loss of MK304 594.60. By assumption, the open access solution leads to zero profit for both the demersal and gillnet fisheries.

Loss of fish biodiversity is linked to the levels of fish catch and stock. Regressions of the Simpson's and Shannon–Weiner indexes against total fish catch shows a negative relationship between the two variables. Results for such regressions are presented below from the gillnet fishery: the figures in parentheses are standard errors.

$$D = 0.619307 - 0.000015\,Y$$
$$(0.0929)\ (0.000022)$$

$$H = 1.05 - 0.0000074\,Y$$
$$(0.161)\ \ (0.000039)$$

The results show that an increase in fish catch would lead to loss of fish biodiversity. The biodiversity indexes for the optimal, MSY and open access levels of catch for the demersal and gillnet fisheries can be inferred from the index functions. The results are shown in Table 3.5.

Table 3.5   Biodiversity index for actual average, optimal, MSY and open access catches

		Demersal				Gillnet		
Index	Actual average	Optimal	MSY	Open access	Actual average	Optimal	MSY	Open access
D	0.5969	0.6058	0.5874	0.5959	0.5832	0.5990	0.5508	0.5823
H	1.0389	1.0433	1.0343	1.0385	1.0322	1.0399	1.0162	1.0317

For both indexes, the optimal level of biodiversity is greater than the actual average. The actual average is greater than the open access level, which is greater than the MSY index. This holds for both the demersal and gillnet fisheries. There is a small difference in the biodiversity indexes between the actual average and open access levels, reflecting the assumption of free entry. It can be concluded that the optimal solution, which is a profit maximizing solution is also associated with high levels of biodiversity (since the larger the value of the indexes the greater the diversity). It can, therefore, be used to reduce loss of biodiversity. The MSY may not be the best solution for the conservation and sustainable utilization of biodiversity.

3.6   SUMMARY AND POLICY IMPLICATIONS

The preceding section established the fact that increases in fish catch leads to a reduction in total stock and loss of fish biodiversity. There is a negative relationship between the biodiversity indexes and total fish catch. In a multispecies fishery, an increase in fish harvesting may be expected, therefore, to lead to loss of biodiversity. It has also been shown that fish catches are lowest under the optimal (profit maximizing) condition. The open access solution has higher levels of catch and effort but lower levels of fish stock than the optimum solution. MSY catches may not necessarily be equal to the optimal level and at times, as this study has shown, they can be greater than the open access levels.

Since the optimal solution has the lowest catches and highest stocks, it is associated with higher levels of biodiversity than the open access solution. The MSY level may not necessarily be the best for biodiversity conservation. It therefore follows that profit maximization may be 'good' for the conservation and sustainable utilization of biodiversity. It would therefore be necessary to identify strategies that could make the fisheries operate at the optimal level to reduce loss of biodiversity.

There are a wide variety of regulatory tools that are used for the conservation and sustainable use of biological resources. However, these traditional management tools, which mainly rely on command and control, have not been sufficient for the conservation of biological diversity. They fail to adquately address the underlying national economic forces which drive biodiversity loss at the local level. In recent years, applying economic instruments to biodiversity problems has gained wider acceptance. The Convention on Biological Diversity also reflects this trend. The Convention urges Contracting Parties to develop strategies and policies for the conservation and sustainable use of biological resources, in order to avoid or minimize adverse impacts on biodiversity. In particular, it calls for the adoption of economically and socially sound measures that act as incentives for the conservation and sustainable use of components of biological diversity (Glowka et al., 1994; UNEP, 1994: Articles 6, 10 and 11).

Malawi implements three traditional fisheries management policies: gear restrictions, closed seasons and licensing. These policies are designed to protect against the decline in stocks below the MSY level. They are driven by a management goal – maximizing sustainable yield not an economic one. Choice of the goal has implications for both biodiversity conservation and the efficiency of the fishery. Economic incentives can be used to complement traditional policies in the conservation and sustainable utilization of fish biodiversity. Such incentives would involve changes in price of fish, discount rate and cost of effort. Sensitivity analysis of the optimal and open access solutions to changes in the discount rate, cost of effort, and price can be used to demonstrate their effectiveness. Tables 3.6a and 3.6b show the results of the sensitivity analysis for the demersal and gillnet fisheries, respectively. Each variable is changed while holding the other two constant.

It is clear from these that, for the two fisheries under consideration, higher discount rates imply lower optimum values for the stock variable and higher optimum values for both catch and effort. Open access levels remain constant because dissipation of economic rent in the open access is equivalent to setting an infinite rate of discount, which gives zero value on future profits. These results agree with theoretical conclusions which state that the optimum population level, X^*, lies between the open access level, X_∞, and the level where the discount is equal to zero, X_0, and that X^* decreases monotonically from X_0 to X_∞ as the discount rate, δ, increases from zero to infinity (Clark, 1990). It can be concluded that under optimum conditions, increase in discount rate will lead to loss of fish

Table 3.6a   Sensitivity analysis of the optimal and open access solutions to changes in δ, c and p for the demersal fishery

Variable	Optimal			Open access		
	X^*	Y^*	E^*	$X\cdot$	$Y\cdot$	$E\cdot$
δ						
0.00	4654.00	900.41	599	4017.24	1554.42	1198
0.05	4642.91	913.90	609	4017.24	1554.42	1198
0.10	4632.15	926.92	619	4017.24	1554.42	1198
0.15	4621.71	939.50	629	4017.24	1554.42	1198
c						
70	3728.79	1769.61	1469	2166.82	2056.66	2938
80	3883.56	1660.44	1323	2476.37	2117.57	2647
100	4193.11	1398.42	1032	3095.46	2064.69	2065
129.78	4654.00	900.41	599	4017.24	1554.42	1198
p						
100	4654.00	900.41	599	4017.24	1554.42	1198
130	4190.47	1400.90	1035	3090.19	2066.13	2070
160	3900.76	1647.40	1647	2510.78	2120.74	2615
190	3702.54	1786.68	1494	2114.34	2040.56	2987

biodiversity through an increase in catch and effort and a decline in stock.

A rise in the cost of effort increases the optimal level of fish stock and decreases the optimal level of fish catch and effort. This is in agreement with the theory. It implies that rising costs lead to high levels of biodiversity since they reduce harvest levels and raise optimal stocks.

Conversely, a rise in fish prices leads to a reduction in optimal stock levels and an increase in fish catch and effort in both demersal and gillnet fisheries. This is not in agreement with capital theory, which holds that when asset prices are increasing, it is desirable to exploit the stock less heavily now – that the stocks are worth holding on to (Clark, 1990). For an open access fishery, a price increase (other factors remaining constant) would induce more fishermen to enter and exploit the fishery until the rents associated with the price increase are dissipated. This may be expected to result in the loss of biodiversity due to the reduction in fish stock.

It should be noted that the equilibrium level of catch is determined by both biological and economic parameters. Given the biological parameters (r, q and K), catch becomes a function of the cost–price ratio. If fishing costs are sufficiently high relative to the price of fish, the fishery

Table 3.6b   Sensitivity analysis of the optimal and open access solutions to changes in δ, c and p for the gillnet fishery

Variable	Optimal			Open access		
	X^*	Y^*	E^*	$X\cdot$	$Y\cdot$	$E\cdot$
δ						
0.00	11 645	1 352.26	204 284	10 625.54	2 467.75	408 568
0.05	11 626.11	1 375.08	208 069	10 625.54	2 467.75	408 568
0.10	11 607.86	1 397.06	211 728	10 625.54	2 467.75	408 568
0.15	11 590.20	1 418.24	215 265	10 625.54	2 467.75	408 568
c						
0.30	8 971.03	3 774.18	740 107	5 277.59	4 440.66	1 480 215
0.40	9 850.62	3 157.28	563 850	7 036.78	4 510.80	1 127 699
0.50	10 730.22	2 364.12	387 592	8 795.98	3 875.92	775 184
0.60	1 1645	1 352.26	204 284	10 625.54	2 467.75	408 568
p						
100	11 645	1 352.26	204 284	10 625.54	2 467.75	408 568
140	10 127.07	2 926.99	508 454	7 589.67	4 387.24	1 016 909
180	9 283.77	3 575.03	677 438	5 903.08	4 546.36	1 354 876
220	8 747.13	3 903.07	784 973	4 829.79	4 310.22	1 569 946

will not be exploited. But at some lower cost level (higher price level), the fishery would become profitable, and an open access level can be established at the point where economic rent is dissipated. Market-based incentives can be used to vary the economic parameters and reduce loss of biodiversity. For instance, a tax can be imposed on fish catch to reduce the price and improve the level of biodiversity.

Conrad and Clark (1994) show that a competitive resource exploiter always exerts excessive levels of effort relative to the cooperative (social) optimum. Competitive resource exploiters attempt to maximize their own net revenues over the short term ignoring the long-term effects that their harvest will have on the resource stock. In the case of fisheries, the primary externality can be identified as a stock externality, since individual fishermen ignore the effect that their catch may have upon future productivity of the fishery. The competitive fisherman behaves as if the user cost of the fishery (the shadow price μ in equation (3.12) of the model) is zero. Tax can be used to counteract this externality. A fisheries management agency can force fishermen to recognize this user cost by imposing it as a tax on catch. The price received by the fisherman will be reduced by the amount of the tax, and the fisherman will be forced to exert the optimal level of effort. It can therefore, be concluded that a tax on catches that is equal to the shadow price or user cost will force fishermen to reduce their effort to the optimum levels and improve the level of biodiversity.

Changes in the discount rate have also been found to have effects on fish catch and loss of biodiversity. The higher the discount rate or rate of interest on a project the smaller the present value of a given payment in the future. It is important to consider the factors that lead to changes in the discount rate. These include the following: an excess demand for money; expansionary fiscal policies including income tax cuts and/or increases in government spending. Conversely, a decrease in government spending would lead to a reduction in interest rate and discount rate. In summary, policies that lead to a reduction in interest and discount rates will also lead to a loss of biodiversity. Such policies may include changes in government expenditure, income tax, money supply and improvements in financial markets.

With open access it has been assumed that fishermen will enter a fishery until no economic rent is made. The income earned can be considered as 'opportunity-cost income', because the cost of effort includes the opportunity cost. The cost of effort can be changed by changing this opportunity cost. Specifically, the opportunity cost can be increased by creating better rewarding alternative employment opportunities, increasing the minimum wage, and improving the availability of credit for small-scale business and agriculture. These incentives can help to move fishermen out of the fishing industry and reduce the fishing effort. In addition, it can be argued that the low opportunity cost in the fishing industry contributes to poverty, which leads to overexploitation of the fisheries. Any policy that aims at reducing poverty will also assist in reducing fishing effort and loss of fish biodiversity.

The focus of this study has been on the impact of fisheries on fish biodiversity. However, fish biodiversity is also affected by other factors such as water pollution and the introduction of exotic species. In addition, the single species fish model used in this study is inadequate since it does not consider the interactions of the exploited species with predators, prey and competitors within the ecosystem. Inclusion of these interactions would have called for the use of a multispecies model whose parameters are not easy to estimate. Finally, the biodiversity indexes used in this study fail to reflect the socioeconomic values of the species. For instance, the indexes may not reflect a gradual transition in fish catch from high-valued species on top of the foodweb to low-valued planktivorous fish. This would require biodiversity indexes that are sensitive to changes in trophic levels and economic values of the species. All these factors are important in the review of fisheries, and, though not included in this study, remain a major focus for future research.

APPENDIX 3.1 SOUTH WEST ARM OF LAKE MALAWI: DEMERSAL TRAWL FISHERY, CATCH AND EFFORT

Year	Catch (m. tons)	Effort (days)	CPUE
1976	1557.76	864	1.802963
1977	1472.87	1621	0.9086181
1978	1440.41	1473	0.9778751
1979	1229.22	1037	1.1853616
1980	884.33	684	1.2928801
1981	1593.37	1080	1.4753426
1982	533.91	550	0.9707455
1983	721.05	535	1.347757
1984	1406.72	978	1.438364
1985	1511.88	1819	0.83116
1986	1595.51	1150	1.3874
1987	2140.75	1288	1.662073
1988	2168.38	1172	1.8501536
1989	1633.4	960	1.7014583
1990	1543.87	1422	1.0857032
1991	1612.01	1598	1.0087672
1992	1603.38	1328	1.2073645
1993	2190.2	2237	0.9790791
1994	1778.43	1201	1.480791
1995	1304.64	958	1.3618372

Note: CPUE = catch per unit effort.

APPENDIX 3.2 SOUTH WEST ARM OF LAKE MALAWI: DEMERSAL TRAWL FISHERY, CATCH BY SPECIES*

Year	Chambo	Chisawasawa	Utaka	Mlamba
1986	35.93	1120.16	737.71	50.92
1987	17.21	395.37	1117.31	25.1
1988	20.75	687.09	1623.65	65.65
1989	23.16	915.7	439.02	37.09
1990	46.9	822.56	679.4	58.08
1991	23.87	515.58	307.01	24.95
1992	18.82	930.39	338.8	29.28
1993	21.21	508.4	334.38	98.79
1994	1.43	1090.99	249.44	23.83
1995	4.47	755.3	21.43	13.64

Note: *Metric tons.

APPENDIX 3.3   SOUTH WEST ARM OF LAKE MALAWI: GILLNET FISHERY, CATCH AND EFFORT

Year	Catch (m. tons)	Effort (days)	CPUE
1976	2562.85	463 578	0.0055284
1977	5906.93	703 139	0.0084008
1978	4186.94	541 195	0.0077365
1979	1761.66	345 778	0.0050948
1980	1619.46	341 246	0.0047457
1981	2311.19	460 318	0.0050209
1982	2645.57	255 069	0.010372
1983	2534.4	217 332	0.0116614
1984	1425.05	499 957	0.0028503
1985	1868.35	327 770	0.0057002
1986	2112.43	456 651	0.0046259
1987	1728.78	252 800	0.0068385
1988	1906.84	357 581	0.0053326
1989	1735.91	319 866	0.005427
1990	1352.6	291 183	0.0046452
1991	4518.7	826 032	0.0054704
1992	1559.91	271 609	0.0057432
1993	1539.22	443 947	0.0034671

Note: CPUE = catch per unit effort.

APPENDIX 3.4   SOUTH WEST ARM OF LAKE MALAWI: GILLNET FISHERY, CATCH BY SPECIES*

Year	Chambo	Kampango	Mlamba	Nchila
1976	659.82	759.01	433.72	225.73
1977	2851.13	1416.64	764	402.69
1978	2656.72	566.65	424.82	64.38
1979	782.65	374.08	287.51	13.24
1980	579.08	462.15	313.86	30.21
1981	1002.31	543.52	471.98	11.92
1982	1655.15	457.8	243.36	21.31
1983	1523.99	459.41	222.41	36.03
1984	534	386.77	256.99	48.66
1985	1207.62	310.18	157.79	2.38
1986	719.66	600.19	360.75	61.87
1987	581.78	547.99	196.51	2.32
1988	901.51	370.31	198.18	12.12
1989	613.83	488.54	250.37	19.26

Note: *Metric tons.

APPENDIX 3.5 MANAGEMENT AREAS IN SOUTHERN LAKE MALAWI

Note: The lake is divided into several management areas: areas A, B and C make the south east arm of the lake; areas D, E, F, G and H make the south west arm of the lake, which is the study area.

Source: Tweddle et al. (1995).

REFERENCES

Bland, S.J.R and S.J. Donda (1994), 'Management initiatives for the fisheries of Malawi', *Fisheries Bulletin*, No. 9.

Clark, C.W. (1990), *Mathematical Biocononomics: The Optimal Management of Renewable Resources*, New York: Wiley.

Conrad, J.M. (1996), 'Bioeconomic models of the fishery, in: D.W. Bromley (ed.) *The Handbook of Environmental Economics*, Oxford: Blackwell.

Conrad, J.M. and Adu-Asamoah (1986), 'Single and multispecies systems: the case of tuna in the Eastern Tropical Atlantic', *Journal of Environmental Economics and Management*, **13**, 50–68.

Conrad, J.M., and C.W. Clark (1994), *Natural Resource Economics: Notes and Problems*, Cambridge: Cambridge University Press.

Department of Research and Environmental Affairs (DREA), (1994), *Malawi: National Environmental Action Plan*, Lilongwe.

FAO (1976), 'An analysis of the various fisheries of Lake Malawi', based on the work of J. Turner FI: DP/MLW/71/516 Tech. Rep., 1, 1–73.

Fox, W.W. (1975), 'Fitting the generalized stock production model by least squares and equilibrium approximation', *Fishery Bulletin*, **73**, 23–7.

Gallastegui, C. (1983), 'An economic analysis of the sardine fishing in the Gulf of Valencia (Spain)', *Journal of Environmental Economics and Management*, **10**, 138–50.

Glowka, L., F. Burhenne-Gulmin and H. Synge (1994) *A Guide to the Convention on Biological Diversity*, Gland and Cambridge: IUCN.

Goda, T. and T. Matsuoka (1986), 'Synthesis and analysis of a comprehensive lake model – with evaluation of ecosystem', *Ecological Modelling*, **31**, 11–32.

Henderson, J.V. and M. Tugwell, (1979), 'Exploitation of the lobster fishery: some empirical results', *Journal of Environmental Economics and Management*, **6**, 287–96.

Heywood, V. and R. Watson (1995), *Global Biodiversity Assessment*, Cambridge: Cambridge University Press.

Krebs, C.J. (1989), *Ecological Methodology*, New York: Harper.

Lewis, D.S.C. (1986), 'A review of the research conducted: Chambo and the Chambo fisheries of Lake Malawi and Malombe 1951–1985', Malawi Fisheries Department Report.

Lowe, R. H. (1952), 'Report on the tilapia and other fish and fisheries of Lake Nyasa 1945–47', *Colonial Office Fisheries Publication*, **1**, 1–26.

Mkoko, B.J. (1981), The Chambo fishery of S. E. arm of Lake Malawi', Malawi Fisheries Department Report.

Moyle, C. (1992), 'Loss of biodiversity in aquatic ecosystems', in C.F. Peggy, K.J. Subodh (eds), *Conservation Biology*, New York: Chapman and Hall.

Perrings, C., K. Mäler, C. Folke, C. Holling and B. Jansson (eds) (1995), *Biodiversity Loss: Economic and Ecological Issues*, Cambridge: Cambridge University Press.

Roberts, C.M. (1995), 'Effects of fishing on the ecosystem structure of coral reefs', *Conservation Biology*, **9**(5), 988–95.

Roberts, C.M. and N.V.C. Polunin (1993), 'Marine reserves: simple solutions to managing complex fisheries', *Ambio*, **22** (6), 363–8.

Schaefer, M.B. (1957), 'Some considerations of population dynamics and economics in relation to the management of commercial marine fisheries', *Journal of the Fisheries Research Board of Canada*, **14**(5), 669–81.

Tarbit, J. (1972), 'Lake Malawi trawling survey: Interim Report 1969–1971', *Malawi Fish Bulletin*, **2**, 1–16.

Turner, J. L. (1977), 'Changes in the size structure of cichlid populations of Lake Malawi resulting from bottom trawling', *Journal of the Fisheries Research Board of Canada*, **34**, 232–8.

Tweddle, D. and J.L. Turner (1977), 'Age, growth and natural mortality rates of some cichlids fishes of Lake Malawi', *Journal of Fisheries Biology*, **10**, 385–98.

Tweddle, D., and J.H. Magasa (1989), 'Assessment of multispecies cichlid fisheries of the south east arm of Lake Malawi, Africa', *Journal du Conseil*, **45**, 223–30.

Tweddle, D., S.B. Alimonso and G. Sodzapanja (1994), 'Analysis of catch and effort data for the fisheries of south west arm of Lake Malawi', *Fisheries Bulletin*, No. 14.

Tweddle, D., R.D. Makwinja and J.H. Magasa (1995), 'Demersal fisheries re-assessment project: final report', *Fisheries Bulletin*, No. 29.

UNEP (1994), 'Convention on Biological Diversity: text and annexes', Switzerland: Geneva Executive Center.

Walker, R.S., (1976), *Statistical Studies of the Traditional Fisheries of Malawi: A Final Report Prepared for the Malawi Government*, Rome: FAO.

Watson C.E.P. (1987), *Malawi Fisheries Development Study*, GOPA – Consultants.

Williamson, R.B. (1966), 'Analysis of ringnet catch data from the south east arm of Lake Malawi 1946–1966', Malawi Fisheries Department, mimeo.

4. Costs and benefits of protected areas: Marsabit Forest Reserve, Northern Kenya

Adano Wario Roba[1]

4.1 INTRODUCTION

Forests account for 3.6 billion ha (28 per cent) of the world's land area.[2] They are the world's most extensive terrestrial ecosystems (World Bank, 1991). However their distribution is uneven. Some twenty countries account for 85 per cent of tropical moist forests. In Latin America, for example, Brazil alone accounts for more than half of all forests. In Africa, forests occupy around 24 per cent of the total land area but are again concentrated in a relatively small number of countries (World Bank, 1991, p. 68). The annual loss of forest cover is currently about 1 per cent, and this exceeds its regeneration rate (World Bank, 1991, p. 5). In developing countries, annual forest loss is between 17 million and 20 million ha.

The 1992 United Nations Conference on Environment and Development (UNCED) meeting in Rio de Janeiro made forest protection and management a major focus. In 1994, the International Tropical Timber Agreement continued a commitment to link conservation and development issues and established 'Objective 2000' which was a challenge to source all trade in tropical timber from sustainably[3] managed forests by the turn of the century. This, although a non-binding commitment in the legal sense, marked a milestone in sharing of goals and objectives to achieve sustainable management of national forests by the end of the century. In 1995, the UN Commission on Sustainable Development reviewed trends since the Rio meeting. The Commission was unable to demonstrate progress in addressing global forest concerns. Thus the Intergovernmental Panel on Forests was instituted, and mandated to formulate plans to combat deforestation and forest degradation. In 1997 the panel made a series of recommendations for promoting forest management, conservation, and sustainable development (MacArthur, 1997).

Forest systems are important for a variety of reasons. The vast majority of terrestrial species with significant environmental and economic values are found in forests. Indeed, they provide nearly 500 million people with their livelihood (World Bank, 1991; Barbier et al., 1994). Forest conversion is a critical factor in the loss of biodiversity and remains the main challenge to its conservation. It has been estimated that between 50 and 90 per cent of the world's species are held by closed tropical forests (Reid and Miller, 1989), and that 85 per cent of tropical moist forests are seriously threatened by encroachment and destruction. But forests need to be conserved for other reasons as well. They provide a range of essential services, few of which are priced in the market (Heywood, 1995).

The proximate causes of forest conversion include the spread of small-scale farming, commercial logging, fuelwood gathering and intensive grazing from domestic animals (Mahar, 1989) in that order of severity. These factors are often exacerbated by poverty, skewed land distribution and declining agricultural output. To be added to this list are government policies which inadvertently or otherwise influence the manner in which environmental resources are used. Inadequately defined property rights also encourage resource users to ignore the effects of their actions on third parties (Heywood 1995; Hanna et al., 1995).

Among goods provided by forests, fuelwood accounts for the largest share (80 per cent in Africa) (World Bank, 1991). This is particularly true for Kenya. In fact, at the global level, the need for woodfuel has been argued to be the most widespread cause of the degradation (as opposed to the destruction) of habitat (Dasgupta, 1982). This study explores the effects of human activities on Marsabit Forest Reserve, not just in terms of habitat disturbance, but also in terms of the provision of a range of forest services. It focuses on the community of settled villages around the forest reserve who are mainly small-scale rural farmers.

Marsabit Mountain is suitable for rain-fed agriculture and, when weather conditions are favourable, contributes over 90 per cent of the District agricultural output (Agricultural Production Officer personal communication, 1997). The area also contains a rich mix of biological resources – both wild (in Marsabit National Reserve and Forest Reserve) and domesticated. Farming on Marsabit Mountain began in the 1920s when colonial administrators, in need of maize and fresh vegetables for the civil servants, called down some Burji peasants from southern Ethiopia to take up farming near the little town of Marsabit (Tablino, 1997). This move inadvertently initiated the destruction of the forest on the mountain. Subsequently, other ethnic groups[4] with different cultural backgrounds migrated to the region either to settle or to provide labour for farm activities. This gave rise to fast population growth on the mountain and increasing pressure on environmental resources. Demand for firewood grew rapidly and supplies were obtained by exploiting the available natural forest.

The process is a continuing one. The population density of some areas on the mountain increased from 9 persons/km^2 in 1979 to 15 persons/km^2 in 1989, and the trend has continued since then. As a measure of the process, land prices have risen from Ksh.3000 per ha in 1986 to Ksh.45 000 in 1997 – implying a very significant real increase. This is largely driven by immigration.[5] The process has given rise to competition for environmental resources for livestock grazing and domestic needs.

The reserve is privately managed and conserved by an autonomous state agency. The demand for natural resources by the local population is reflected in illegal access to the reserve resources. The outcome is a growing conflict between the local populations and the state agency. The local population is notionally excluded from forest resources, but levels of enforcement are such that access can be described as, at best, 'weakly regulated'. To the local communities, the reserve resources are in the nature of a public good: one household's harvest does not exclude another's. Since each household's use of the resource imposes costs on others, however, present resource use inflicts costs on the entire reserve system and society at large.

Not all use of the forest is illegal. A system of licences gives some households legal access to the reserve. However, the forest licence fee was determined in the 1960s and has not been adjusted with changing demand. The low fee influences the way local resources are used. Due to the near-open access nature of the resource use, private individuals are encouraged to excessively harvest reserve resources. Ecological and wider values of biodiversity are not reflected in prevailing forest products' prices. Overuse of the ecosystem resources by local people in turn alters the carrying capacity of the reserve for wildlife. For example, baboons require a greater range than is now available, and their predation on local crops is an indication of this. Their conflict with inhabitants on the forest borders is one concern of this chapter.

In 1988–89 an area of 540 km^2 was excised from the Forest Reserve for human settlement and for the expansion of Marsabit town (Government of Kenya, 1989a). This further increased demand for forest resources. The local communities around the reserve source most of their requirements for wood products (fuelwood and poles) and water from the forest. This has effects on the ecosystem's resources and disturbs habitat.

In this chapter we assess the factors influencing resource use by local populations bordering a forest reserve. Individual behaviour is determined by existing institutions and local settings. However, the value of environmental goods to private individuals (households) and society as a whole are often at variance. We consider various forest products that local people obtain from the reserve and the rules of their access. We explore the causes and probable consequences of the prevailing resource use regime on the functional diversity of the reserve in the region. On the basis of this we make recommendations and evaluate policy options relevant for conservation and sustained management of the resources.

4.2 MARSABIT[6]

Marsabit Forest Reserve is among the least studied in the country (Litoroh et al., 1994). Marsabit District is situated in northern Kenya between 36° 02' to 39° 23' East and 4° 45' to 1° North (Government of Kenya, 1994) (see Appendix 4.1). The District has four (4) different agroecological zones. One of these zones is commonly referred to as a 'high potential' area. Marsabit Mountain and Mt Kulal are included in this category. These areas are endowed with fertile volcanic soils suitable for arable farming given adequate rains and proper planting.

The 'high potential' areas receive a bi-modal rainfall pattern occurring (when they do) in the months of March to May and October to December. Farming activities are enabled solely by the modified climate of the mountain. Marsabit mountain has the highest annual mean rainfall among the three 'high potential' areas (see Table 4.1). It is surrounded by low plains which are at best suited for nomadic pastoralism. The

Table 4.1   Total annual rainfall, Marsabit Mountain, 1967–97 (mm)

Year	Rainfall	Year	Rainfall	Year	Rainfall
1967	1227.3	1977	839.4	1987	687
1968	1113.8	1978	1037	1988	1022.2
1969	1021.6	1979	842	1989	757.6
1970	960.7	1980	358	1990	777.2
1971	602.6	1981	1138	1991	409.6
1972	720.8	1982	1367	1992	556.8
1973	258.0	1983	1028	1993	832.8
1974	436.4	1984	544	1994	710.2
1975	500.4	1985	1151	1995	851.4
1976	324.8	1986	509	1996	320.5
				1997	1490.0

Source: Marsabit Meteorological Station and Development Plans.

Note: Figures for 1978–87 are rounded off to whole numbers.

nomadic groups in the area are the Rendille and Samburu in the south and south-east, and the Gabbra in the north-west, north and north-eastern part. All fall back on the reserve and its embodied resources for dry season grazing (Oba, 1994; Lusigi, 1984). We selected our study sites from a number of villages on the periphery of the Forest Reserve and within the borders of the Marsabit National Park (see Appendix 4.1).

In 1962 Marsabit District had a total population of 47 252 people with a density of 1 per km². Between 1962 and 1979, the population almost doubled. By 1979 about 23 per cent of the total population was based in towns. In 1989 the District population had reached 129 262 people. Since then Moyale District has split from Marsabit to form an independent District in 1995. This increase in human settlement around towns was attributed to migration of people attracted by social amenities.

During this time most immigration was from southern Ethiopia. Marsabit Mountain (an area of 2090 km²) had a population of 17 268 (about 18 per cent of the total District population) in 1979. Between 1979 and 1989 numerous administrative divisions were created which involved splitting and criss-crossing of the former boundaries. This makes consistent comparison over time of population change of specific areas impossible. A brief look at a few divisions on the mountain, at the end of the 1980s is shown in Table 4.2.

The area around Marsabit Mountain is the most densely populated area in the District. The main cause of population growth is, as has

Table 4.2 Population, households, area and density: Marsabit, 1989

Area	Total population	No. of households	Area (km²)	Density
Marsabit District	**129 262**	**29 110**	**72 290**	**2**
Marsabit Central	30 685	6 945	2 055	15
Mountain	15 175	3 408	478	32
Marsabit township	11 355	2 673	397	29
Dakabaricha	3 820	735	81	47
Sagante	5 333	1 141	390	14
Dirib Gombo	4 855	1 085	213	23
Karare	1 824	445	538	3
Songa	2 173	514	242	9
Hula Ula	1 325	352	194	7

Source: Kenya Population Census, 1989, pp. 1–66 and 1–67.

already been remarked, rural–urban migration.[7] This is characterized by an influx of pastoral people from the surrounding lowlands whose economy has been depressed by recent droughts.

The process of human settlement and consequent encroachment on the protected area is well established (Marekia, 1991). Every year a portion of the reserve is allocated to influential individuals from the area. The allocation decision is often justified by the assertion that the land belongs to the county council and not the forest department or Kenya Wildlife Service (KWS). This has been a source of conflict between the parties concerned. On 6 October 1996 the Marsabit District Development Committee nullified all land allocations by the County Council within the protected areas. However, this decision was later revoked and plots allotted to private developers.

Agricultural Production

Marsabit District had a total area of about 78 079 km^2 before the creation of Moyale District in 1995. Of this, about 75 per cent is range land. Only about 2.5 per cent of the District gets enough rainfall to sustain crops. The rest (13 807 km^2) has been set aside for conservation. It comprises Marsabit Forest Reserve (about 2000 km^2), game reserves and parks and public amenities, the Losai Game Reserve (1807 km^2) and Sibiloi National Park (1570 km^2) in the north-eastern part of the District on the eastern shores of L. Turkana. In this report we confine ourselves to the interface between Marsabit Forest Reserve and/or Marsabit National Reserve, the activities of agro-pastoral groups in the area, and the ways in which they make use of forest resources.

Marsabit Mountain lies between 1345 m and 1700 m above sea level. Soils are generally fertile. The possibility of arable cultivation on the mountain has increased pressure both on the land and other environmental resources. There was a general increase in acreage after 1983. This was attributed to government initiation of an adjudication exercise over the same period. In practice this meant opening up new lands to farmers for cultivation and also erection of electric fences and construction of a moat around the reserve which reduced crop predation by wildlife. The main crops grown in the region are maize, teff, wheat and beans. Other crops include sorghum, cow peas, pigeon peas, green vegetables (kale, pumpkins), horticultural crops (tomato, onion) and fruits (oranges, bananas and mangoes among others). Crops are sold to the Marsabit National Cereals and Produce Board. Farm sizes are relatively small, but productivity is rising. Average yields increased by 50 per cent in the 1980s due to on-farm use of waste manure to boost production.

Livestock held include cattle, sheep and goats, with the cattle being of highest value about 35 per cent. The main products are meat, milk, hides and skins (Government of Kenya, 1994). Since the late 1970s the District has had more small stock (goats and sheep) than camels and cattle. From the mid-1980s to the present, the livestock population has been on the decline. In per capita terms it fell from 16 to 12 between 1979 and 1989. Using population projections,[8] this reduces to only 6 livestock per capita in 1996. The decline in livestock population is partly explained by a series of severe droughts the District has experienced over the years. Our sampled households held a total livestock population of 3944 implying average livestock per capita of about 3. By extrapolation, the total livestock population (projection based on 1989 population using annual growth rate of 5 per cent) on the mountain in 1996 was about 3.23 million. This is about 32 per cent of the livestock population in the whole district.

The Forest Reserve

The potential for tourism in the District was realized in 1902 when the Northern Game Reserve was established encompassing the whole area east of L. Turkana to Isiolo and Mathew Ranges. This area remained under the National Park ordinance until December 1960 when the reserve was reduced to its present size of some 2000 km² around Marsabit Mountain. Our focus is primarily on Marsabit National Forest Reserve. Within the reserve, Marsabit Mountain was designated a Forest Reserve in 1931. Today the Forest Reserve covers 141 km² of Marsabit Mountain. The reserve is, in turn, part of Marsabit National Park.

The most important services provided by the reserve are various watershed functions. The vegetation cover of the reserve protects what is a very important watershed and retards soil erosion. It has already been noted that the forest is a source of water for wild game, livestock and the human population. There are a series of hand-dug wells in the forest and livestock watering is allowed. Watering of livestock in the forest has a number of impacts. The routes into water sources are active areas of erosion and run-off during the rainy season. The wells are often located along valleys and the water rights are owned by individuals/groups. They set access rules and determine watering rotas, thus giving water from particular wells the property of a club good. Access to individual wells is often based on ethnic considerations. Due to excessive use during dry seasons, many well sites have become areas of weakness in the forest and the source of landslides. Well sites are also starting points in the destruction of habitat.

Although livestock grazing in the forest is illegal even in stress periods, in practice livestock do graze on the way to wells and the forest is used for dry season grazing. The penalty for illegal grazing is a fine of Ksh.100 and Ksh.50 per head for cattle and goats, respectively. These penalties were last fixed in the late 1960s and offer little disincentive to cattle owners. Illegal grazing seriously hampers plant regeneration.

The most important collected resource is fuelwood. Fuelwood collection is legal through possession of a permit costing Ksh.35 per month. In fact fuelwood provides about 96 per cent of rural households in the District with cooking fuel. It is also the source of the main type of lighting for about 63 per cent of the rural households in the District (Government of Kenya, 1989b). Firewood collection is mostly carried out by women. The forest is also a source of construction timber. Accessing of construction timber is legally restricted, but collection does take place anyway. Poles are sold in black markets, providing an important source of cash income for some. A number of tree species are, however, legally exploited. Marketable tree species include *Croton megalocarpus*; *Olea africana*; *Strombosia scheffleri*; *Cassipourea molosana*; *Diospyros abyssinica*; *Ekerbergia rueppaliana*; *Premna maxima*; *Ocotea usambareusis*, *Olea hochstetter*, *Olea capensis*, *Cordia abyssinica*, *Casearia spp.* and *Apodytes dimidiata*. This provides a source of revenue for the Forest Department (on average Ksh.40 000/annum).

Up to now the biological resources of the reserve have attracted fewer tourists than might be expected. Marsabit National Reserve, Losai Game Reserve and Sibiloi National Park areas are accessible to tourists, but are off the 'tourist circuit'. They are, however, rich in wildlife resources. Among the larger mammals (the main attraction to tourists) are eland, elephant, buffalo, lion, monkeys, baboon, hyena, aardwolf, leopard, black rhino, lesser and greater kudu and topi. There are 13 species of bats and more than 350 bird species including 52 birds of prey. The greater kudu and elephant are the two keystone species in the reserve. The lowlands surrounding the reserve are acacia plains. In this belt of acacia are found other native game species such as gerenuk, reticulated giraffe, cheetah, caracal, klipspringer, Grant gazelle, oryx and bushbuck. No comprehensive wildlife population censuses have been conducted in the region, except for elephant which were last counted in 1984. Warnings already exist that many of these species are threatened by poaching, encroachment of farming and habitat destruction through human activities (Government of Kenya, Development Plan, 1984).

Land Tenure

The mountain (which also covers the forest reserve) is subject to two conflicting jurisdictions. On the one hand, it is part of Marsabit Forest Reserve administered by the Forest Department of the Ministry of Environment and Natural Resources. The forest reserve land is a trust land under the jurisdiction of Marsabit County Council. On the other hand, it is managed by the Kenya Wildlife Service, a parastatal created by act of parliament in 1989. The national reserve land is the property of the Kenya Government. This jurisdictional overlap is a persistent source of difficulty for the regulation of forest access.

Many parts of the district suitable for cultivation fall within the jurisdiction of 'protected areas'. Local farmers in these areas cannot hold title deeds to the farm plots they occupy. Their right to use the land is based on an institutionally defined and legally authenticated ownership, but this form of property right lowers the incentives to manage land resources on a sustainable basis. This has had consequences for the way in which local farm and environmental resources are used. In the absence of secure property rights in form of title deeds, local farmers have had difficulty in securing agricultural loans and lack the motivation to invest in their land. Table 4.3 summarizes the early settlement schemes around Marsabit Forest.

All these villages are within the borders of the reserve and individual farmers have use rights only. These reserve villages are now recognized as 'officially' settled by the authorities concerned. They are the most densely populated (15 000–17 000) parts of the District due to the favourable climate as compared to the rest of the District. Their proximity to the reserve encourages wildlife–human conflicts. Every crop season people are stationed on farm-fringes guarding crops from wild animals. Baboons, elephants and monkeys are particularly notorious. Village inhabitants complain of heavy crop losses attributed to these animals.

The survey reported in this chapter finds that the rural farm sizes are small, and that land distribution is skewed. A large proportion of the land is in the hands of a few individuals who own as much as 100 acres. Some individuals own different patches of land at different sites on the mountain. They often leave parcels fallow for several seasons, which otherwise would have been sown to improve food security in the region. Recent migrants to the mountain are landless, and unoccupied land is not available. Most migrants provide farm labour during periods of high agricultural activity.

Table 4.3   Settlement schemes around Marsabit Forest

Scheme	Families	Crops grown	Farm size	Remarks
Soncla	20	maize, kales, sorghum, c/peas, pawpaw, fruits	1–2 ha	Under NCCK and about 20 plots were under irrigation (piped water). The scheme is subsistence except chillies are sold in Nairobi (Ksh.12000, 1978).
Nasikakwe	73	beans, chillies, c/peas, maize, s/flower, sorghum	1–1.5 ha	Run by NCCK. Population decreased from 480 to 378.
Kituruni	68	maize and beans	1–1.5 ha	Seasonal cultivation due to lack of water.
Manyatta Jillo	20	maize and beans	1–2 ha	Started by CARE(K), spent about Ksh.72 000 on the project; includes housing, 8 goats to each family, Catholic mission spent Ksh.20 000 which included 8 oxen for ploughing.
Badassa	24	maize, beans, and fruits	1.5 ha	Ksh.125 418.40 Spent to resettle refugees from Ethiopia. Money spent for housing, land cultivation and social amenities (hall).
Gabbra scheme	55	maize and beans	2 ha	Started 1977, 22 families, corrugated iron sheet houses, CARE(K) Ksh.89 744.50, Catholic mission Ksh.5000. Plan to provide the scheme with 10 oxen for ploughing for the whole scheme and 10 goats/family by the Catholic Relief Services

Source: Marsabit District Development Plan, 1979.

4.3 THE SURVEY

Methods and Selection of the Study Sites

The study uses both primary and secondary data. The primary data has been collected through a household survey. In the preparation stage, a number of villages around the forest were visited and population concentration sites identified. Thereafter, a draft questionnaire was designed and tested through a pilot survey. On the basis of answers to the pilot survey, a final questionnaire was developed. An appropriate number of households (203 HH) were selected for the survey. On the basis of the population clusters, 34 households (Karare) in the southern margin of the forest, 33 households (Manyatta Jillo) in the north and 136 households (Sagante I and II) in the east and north-eastern margin of the forest were selected and interviewed. The latter section mainly covered Gabbra Scheme, Dirib Gombo and Badassa areas. The survey questions were addressed to the head of households.

Information on household composition, size of farm plot, years of farm plot occupancy; crops grown and their outputs; livestock owned, their sales and income; farm outputs, forest products collected, distance to the forest, frequency of forest visits, and prices and quantities of forest products gathered was collected. Also livestock and crop losses incurred by households, replacement and protection costs and sources of household income were obtained. These data are presented below. A separate questionnaire was used to obtain information on charcoal burning, fuelwood collection, period of use of one back-load of firewood per household and type of cooking stove used apart from the three-stone fireplace.

The aims of the survey were:

1. To identify main forest products and services provided by Marsabit Forest Reserve to local communities;
2. To identify the market prices of forest products used by the local communities bordering the reserve;
3. To determine the access regime to forest resources;
4. To evaluate the role of public policies in influencing/determining the pattern of forest resource use; and
5. To assess the impact of the existing resource use pattern in the area on biodiversity.

Our results show that local people draw heavily on forest resources. Such information is necessary for the development of incentives to influence use of resources by local populations bordering such areas.

Munasinghe (1993) employed a similar approach to estimate the costs and benefits of a National Park. In the current study, we assess the causes of resource use, the role of government policy in influencing household decisions in resource use patterns and the implications of different resource uses for the conservation of biological species. We finally describe how such causes contribute to the problem of biodiversity in the region.

Household Characteristics

The household heads were interviewed because their decisions are assumed to determine how local natural resources are used.

Real assets are traditionally vested in males, and women would therefore be expected to have less assets than men. Yet except for Manyatta Jillo, the majority of respondents were female heads (Table 4.4). Overall, 53 percent of the respondents were female. The position of a respondent in the household is important in terms of the role played in the community. For example, the collection of the firewood is traditionally a female task. This position has an influence on household decisions regarding the use of available resources. The predominance of women may be due to absentee male household heads (men often move animals to other parts of the district for better forage). It may also indicate partial sedentarization of respondents. Manyatta Jillo has a lower population of livestock than the other sites. The local population rear livestock which are often moved to other areas for grazing and water. This normally coincides with the seasons when there are minimal on-farm activities. Household sizes (Table 4.5) are largest in Karare and Manyatta Jillo, and average household sizes for the sites are higher than that of the district (4 persons per household). We assume that household size influences its demand for forest resources.

Table 4.4   Gender of respondents by site

Survey site	Gender Male	Female	Total
Karare	14 (41.1 %)	20 (58.8 %)	34
Manyatta Jillo	22 (66.7 %)	11 (33.3 %)	33
Sagante I	33 (47.1 %)	37 (52.9 %)	70
Sagante II	26 (39.4 %)	40 (60.6 %)	66

Note: The figure in parentheses is the proportion of households expressed as a percentage of the site's total households sampled.

Source: Own survey. 1997.

Table 4.5   Household composition by site

Sites	Male pop.	Female pop.	Total pop	H/Hold size	At home	Wage employee	In school
Karare	118	205	323	9	63	5	113
M. Jillo	125	119	244	7	116	4	90
Sagante I	231	227	458	6	100	**	126
Sagante II	255	182	437	6	190	1	158
Total	729	733	1462	7	469	10	487

Source: Own survey, 1997

The majority of the respondents are in the age group 33 to 57 years. Ages of respondents are normally distributed (Table 4.6). The years of occupancy of the farm-plot (Table 4.7) refers to the number of years that a given family has lived on the stated piece of land. About 65 per cent of the sample's land area is in the possession of people who have lived on the farm-plots for more than a decade. Those farmers who settled earlier have relatively bigger farm-plots than the latecomers. Later we consider how the year of occupancy, the quantity of forest used and farm output of a household are related.

Average farm sizes (Table 4.8) lie between 3 and 11 hectares. Except for Karare, a majority of the households have farm-sizes only marginally larger (2 ha) than the lower bound of farm-plots. Despite the size of farm plots, most households did not consider that they were short of land. Respondents were asked whether they perceive land shortage to be a

Table 4.6   Age of respondents by site

Average	Karare	Manyatta Jillo	Sagante I	Sagante II	Total
25	4	4	3	2	13
33	8	9	7	19	43
41	5	4	21	13	43
49	9	4	16	12	41
57	2	4	13	9	28
65	1	2	8	10	21
68+	3	5	2	1	11

Source: Own survey, 1997

Table 4.7   Respondents' years of occupancy of the farm-plot

Average	Karare	Manyatta Jillo	Sagante I	Sagante II	Total
<5	2	1	6	5	14
6–8	3	3	13	4	23
9–11	7	4	3	11	25
12–14	4	0	5	13	22
15–17	8	4	13	15	40
18–20	7	10	15	14	46
21–23	0	1	3	1	5
24+	3	11	8	1	23

Source: Own survey, 1997.

Table 4.8   Land area available to households

Land area (ha)	Karare	Manyatta Jillo	Sagante I	Sagante II
<2	1	2	14	7
3–5	3	16	27	35
6–8	10	10	15	16
9–11	14	4	11	4
12–14	3	1	3	3
15 +	3	0	0	1
Average area	9	9	5	5

Source: Own survey, 1997.

problem. It was only at Sagante I (34 per cent) and Manyatta Jillo (39 per cent) that the respondents affirmed the problem of land shortage. This may be related to the fact that many have exogenous sources of income which may include livestock subsistence production and environmental resources. We shall pay attention to these issues later in the chapter.

Respondents were also asked if they held title deeds to the land they occupied. Except in Sagante II, where 27 per cent of the respondents have title deeds, the majority of the rest had no secure title deeds to the land they occupy. Lack of land security is a disincentive to invest in land. However, it is important to understand farmers' perceptions of the implications of owning or not owning a title deed. This was posed as an open-ended question in the questionnaire. The results are reported in Table 4.9.

At Sagante II, 18 households already held a title deed for their plots, and this may explain the perception in both Sagante I and Sagante II of the potential importance of deeds in settling disputes. In all the sites respondents cited the acquisition of a commercial loan for farm development from relevant institutions as a motive for obtaining a title deed, but the proportion of respondents who saw this as an advantage is surprisingly small. It is clear that respondents are aware that lack of title has consequences, but it is not clear that they necessarily see title deeds as the precursor to the development of an active land market, or as a necessary condition for the development of rural credit markets.

Table 4.9   Perceptions of the importance of secure title (%)

	Karare	Manyatta Jillo	Sagante I	Sagante II
Acquisition of commercial loan	20.6	9.1	12.9	9.1
Gives proper land ownership	55.9	78.1	1.4	31.8
Creates a sense of belonging	20.7		5.7	10.6
Creates confidence in ownership		3.0		3.0
Can be used to settle land disputes			54.3	36.4
Confirms land ownership		9.3	25.7	
Can be used to pay tax to government				4.5
Enables owner to lease land to others				1.5

Source: Own survey, 1997.

Agriculture

On-farm activities are dictated by the erratic occurrence of the rainfall (except for Songa area where some irrigation is done). We did not sample from Songa during our survey exercise. Agricultural production in the area is heavily dependent on the highly variable rainfall. Table 4.10 shows agricultural crops grown (in hectares) and their output (in 90 kg. bags) from the sample or survey site.

These figures do not give an indication of trend in on-farm production. In the respondents view, crop yields and land productivity in general has declined compared to 10 years ago. Various reasons have been offered to explain this phenomenon. These range from the introduction of 'foreign' and unsuitable seeds on the mountain, frequent rain failure and

Table 4.10   Agricultural crops

Crop		Karare	Survey sites Manyatta Jillo	Sagante I	Sagante II
Maize:	Area	118	95.5	218.5	232.5
	Output	760	359.0	1058.0	1017.0
Beans:	Area	111.8	35.0	63.8	63.0
	Output	922.0	93.3	66.3	50.0
Kale:*	Area	13.5	0.4	Nil	Nil
Wheat:	Area	—	7.0	3.0	4.5
	Output	—	11.0	103.0	7.0
Others:	Area	1.5	3.0	1.0	12.5
	Output	11.0	8.0	54.0	11.0
Fallow		54.8	45.0	98.8	39.0

Notes
Output of 'other crops' is in 'bundles'; output of maize, beans and wheat in 90kg bags, area in ha.
The figure for bundles under others for Sagante II refers to bundles of khat sold.
*Kale production is mostly for home consumption. Its production is spread over a long period such that over a short period its production is trivial.

Source: Own survey, 1996–1997.

growing interference from wildlife to loss of soil fertility. It is not yet clear though what proportion of the agricultural crop loss is attributable to wild game. Their perception is supported by the decline in average agricultural production figures, which are lower in the 1990s than in the 1980s (when maize and beans productions were quoted well above 7 bags per hectare). A reduction in agricultural production may mean increasing demand on Marsabit reserve.

Minimal land area is left fallow by farmers on the mountain. Over 80 per cent of the sample area's land is devoted to the production of maize and beans. The remaining areas are used to grow crops such as bananas, cassava, vegetables, horticultural crops and khat. The latter is grown to complement household earnings throughout the year. Khat (*Mirraa*) is a mild leafy stimulant used by local people for leisure. The plant has been introduced by farmers from Meru (Kenya).

Farm sizes dictate, to some extent, the type of technology used by households. This in turn determines the level of on-farm production. Farmers generally use a low level technology. They rely on the use of oxen and hoe for ploughing, and *panga* for clearing bushes and bringing more land under cultivation. The size of the farms and farm income do not allow the use of modern farm equipment. Farming activities are often carried out through pooling labour. This is done in rotation and on a reciprocal basis; one time for one farmer and the next round for another. Such labour arrangements serve as a payment for labour efforts in kind. In the recent past labour payments in cash have become more frequent. This is thought to be weakening the social cohesion.

Most respondents are of pastoral origin, and combine crop cultivation with livestock rearing. Less than 5 per cent of the people do not own live-stock. Table 4.11 describes the livestock holdings of the balance of households. In many cases animals are sold to meet specific needs. The reasons mentioned for the sale of animals included payment of school fees, ceremonies, and general household needs. Household needs tend to be highest during the dry season. During that season the number of the animals sold is high relative to demand, and prices tend to fall. During the dry season, too, more women invest time in hawking bags of charcoal in the urban centres. Once again, since there are many charcoal burners and sellers, prices for the product fall.

Table 4.11   Livestock holdings

Livestock	Karare	Manyatta Jillo	Sagante I	Sagante II
Cattle	445 (34)	222 (33)	556 (67)	601 (65)
Camel	34 (6)	10 (10)	–	8 (2)
Donkey	26 (10)	21 (16)	80 (67)	46 (25)
Sheep	274 (24)	91 (14)	318 (44)	293 (24)
Goat	302 (25)	105 (14)	334 (54)	351 (40)
Chicken	149 (22)	105 (16)	73 (20)	194 (36)

Note: The figures in parentheses are the total number of households with the preceding total number of livestock.

Source: Own survey, 1996–1997.

Household Income and Asset Holdings

Sources of household income are reported in Table 4.12, which indicates a degree of specialization between the study sites, with arable production dominant in the Sagantes, livestock production dominant in Karare, and 'other' income dominant in Manyatta Jillo. There is no charcoal income

Table 4.12   Sources of annual household income (Ksh.)

Source of income	Karare	Manyatta Jillo	Sagante I	Sagante II
Crop sales	288	1164	1151	761
Livestock sales	3609	1121	131	92
Milk sales	765	0	512	573
Charcoal sales	0	527	524	233
Other sources	0	1595	169	305
Total	4662	4408	2487	1964

Source: Own survey, 1997.

in Karare. Traditionally, charcoal burning has been seen as a dirty activity and has been undertaken by individuals in the lowest social strata. This activity is, however, now common as a way of earning cash income along with other alternative sources.

This implies a change in local people's perceptions. In addition, milk sales, which has traditionally been perceived as a cultural offence, now constitutes a sizeable source of income for some households. Other sources of income for households include petty trade, casual wage earnings, sale of forest products (other than charcoal) and donations from charitable organizations during emergencies.

The characteristic feature of the area is the existence of a range of income sources. To get a sense of the balance between elements in the income 'portfolio', Table 4.13 ranks household income, starting with the most important source as rank I. These rankings reflect the importance of different sources of income to households in each village. For Sagante II and Karare areas, livestock and agricultural earnings are the dominant sources of income. Manyatta Jillo has wage earnings and forest products as important sources of income. In Sagante I, agricultural proceeds are the commonest source of income. Earnings from alternative sources are uniformly distributed across households. In Karare there is less diversification of income earning activities. In general, labour is employed for on-farm activities to meet seasonal demand which reaches a peak during the wet season when numerous farm tasks are carried out over a short period. By far the greatest number of wage employees[9] is found in Sagante I, but only 7.1 per cent of households in Sagante I report wage income as their most important source.

Table 4.13   Sources of income ranking (%)

	Rank I	Rank II	Rank III
Karare			
Sales from agricultural proceeds	14.7 (5)	52.7 (18)	8.8 (3)
Sale of forest products	–	–	2.9 (1)
Earnings from livestock sales	67.6 (23)	23.5 (8)	–
Labour wage earnings	14.7 (5)	–	–
Sale of livestock products	–	8.8 (3)	–
Charitable offer	2.9 (1)	–	–
Manyatta Jillo			
Sales from agricultural proceeds	15.2 (5)	45.5 (15)	24.2 (8)
Earnings from livestock sales	21.2 (7)	–	–
Sale of forest products	15.2 (5)	60.6 (20)	3.0 (1)
Labour wage earnings	45.5 (15)	12.1 (4)	–
Gains from petty trade	3.0 (1)	9.1 (3)	6.1 (2)
Other sources	–	–	12.1 (4)
Sagante I			
Sales from agricultural proceeds	42.9 (30)	50.0 (35)	7.1 (5)
Earnings from sale of livestock	10.0 (7)	12.9 (9)	14.3 (10)
Sale of forest products	25.7 (18)	12.9 (9)	12.9 (9)
Earnings from livestock products	12.9 (9)	24.3 (17)	38.6 (27)
Labour wage earnings	7.1 (5)	4.3 (3)	–
Other sources	1.4 (1)	–	1.4 (1)
Sagante II			
Sales from agricultural proceeds	42.4 (28)	28.8 (19)	16.7 (11)
Earnings from sale of livestock	4.5 (3)	3.9 (2)	1.5 (1)
Sale of forest products	9.1 (6)	40.9 (27)	16.7 (11)
Earnings from livestock products	24.2 (16)	40.9 (27)	19.7 (13)
Labour wage earnings	9.1 (6)	–	1.5 (1)
Other sources	9.1 (6)	10.6 (7)	19.7 (13)

Note: Entries in parentheses are the number of households which gave stated source of income under the respective ranks.

Source: Own survey, 1997.

4.4   ACCESS TO FOREST RESOURCES

So far we have been looking at various household characteristics, composition and asset holdings and the situation regarding on farm labour allocation. Now, with this background, we consider how people make use of local forest resources. In highlighting the general access rule of forest resources, we confine our views to the area of legally gazetted forest (15 280 ha) which is protected by the Forest Act (cap. 385) of Kenya. The forest resources are owned by the central government. The Forest Reserve and the National Park (of which the forest is a part) resources are protected by the Laws of Kenya under the Wildlife Management and Conservation Act (cap. 376), the Forest Act (cap. 385), the Agriculture Act and also by the Water Act (cap. 372) (Ogolla, 1992). The local communities treat these resources as a common property resource. Their use by an individual household does not in any way exclude their use by other households. The demand for forest products is purely influenced by household factors, fees and the level of penalty in the case of illegal access. The latter, to a great extent, depends on the efficiency of forest rangers and collaborating agencies such as KWS patrol staff. The number of technical staff in the forest department and KWS were stated to be below the optimal human resource requirement for the efficient monitoring and conservation of the ecosystem (personal communication, 1997).

In addition to forest products directly obtained by local communities, the forest has a crucial watershed function. For Marsabit town, water is harnessed, piped and supplied to part of the urban population by the Water Department. In 1989 this provided about 80 per cent of the urban water demand (Government of Kenya, 1989a). Local communities also have access and use rights to water sources within the forest. They are allowed to use the wells in the forest, provided they do not cause unnecessary disturbance (although inevitable) to, and exploit, forest resources. The growing water demand resulting from the swelling population deprives flora and fauna (including microorganisms) of water.

Access to forest resources is allowed by possession of a licence issued by the Forest Department. Licence holders are allowed to obtain products from the reserve only during weekdays and extraction is mainly for fuelwood. In both Sagante I and Sagante II all households reported harvesting forest products. In Manyatta Jillo, 91 per cent of households harvested forest products, while in Karare 74 per cent of households did so. Not all respondents who collect forest products possess permits. Indeed, official records reveal that there are only 180 households with forest licence permits, with about 40 regular collectors. There are more households who admit to collecting forest products in our own sample than there are licence holders.

Permits currently cost Ksh.35 per month. Permit holders (households or individuals) are allowed to collect one back-load of firewood every weekday. If sold in the market, this yields between Ksh.150 and 200 per trip depending on the quantity harvested per trip and the season of the year.[10] This implies potential gross revenue of between Ksh.3300 and 4400 per month, using 22 as the number of working days in a month: between 94 and 125 times the permit value. Such low permit prices of forest products encourages exploitation of the forest by the local communities.

Local Use of Forest Products

The reserve's resources are used by local communities for an array of purposes. They include herbs, fuelwood, poles, charcoal, dry season grazing and water for livestock. Table 4.14 shows the number (and percentage) of households in each study site collecting forest products.

Table 4.14 Forest products collected

Product	Survey site			
	Karare	Manyatta Jillo	Sagante I	Sagante II
Fuelwood	34 (100 %)	33 (100%)	70 (100%)	66 (100%)
Poles	8 (23.5%)	6 (18.2%)	31 (44.3%)	43 (65%)
Charcoal	–	2 (6.1 %)	36 (51.4%)	34 (51.5%)
Grass	–	3 (9.1 %)	51 (72.9 %)	13 (19.7%)
Herbs	–	1 (3.0%)	2 (2.9%)	–

Note: Number and percentage (in parentheses) of households in each study site collecting forest products.

Source: Own survey, 1997.

Frequently collected products include poles (used for the construction of semi-permanent houses, erection of maize granaries and ploughing equipment), charcoal and firewood – the dominant source of fuel for rural households in the region. Fuelwood is the most commonly extracted product (see the previous section on firewood collection). Grass harvesting is seasonal and occasional. It occurs during dry seasons when rangeland forage has diminished and young, disabled or sick animals need complementary feedstuff. Herb collection from the reserve is also very irregular. The knowledge to identify and obtain specific plant parts or roots with medicinal value is restricted to experts. This knowledge is passed from old people to their first sons and remains within the family and is always passed to first-born sons.

Most environmental goods are not priced as their harvesting is illegal (see previous section on access rules). The market prices of these products (if they exist) are low relative to processed or manufactured goods in the market. Often user charges are centrally determined by the relevant department. These charges do not reflect the value of the wider environmental costs or costs imposed by the individual user on others through their use of the products. Given the range of complex and interdependent ecosystem functions, the use of forest resources carries both social and environmental costs. When environmental costs of forest products are included, the value of forest resources typically exceeds their market price by a wide margin.

We also attempted to obtain estimates of the quantity of forest products extracted and repeat visits made for harvesting by a household per month. The results are shown in Table 4.15.

Table 4.15   Extraction of forest products

| | Survey site | | | |
Product	Karare	Manyatta Jillo	Sagante I	Sagante II
Fuelwood	1026 (9)	988 (6)	2800 (7)	2727 (5)
Poles	110 (6)	7105 (1)	610 (3)	763 (6)
Charcoal	–	–	1585 (5)	1460 (6)
Grass	–	25 (3)	1715 (2)	360 (7)

Note: The first figure is the number of trips for collecting the stated forest product per month and that in parentheses is the site's household average number of trips for a particular product.

Source: Own survey, 1997.

Fuelwood Most trips to the forest were made for the collection of fuelwood. Every household uses wood as a source of energy. Collection of fuelwood from the forest is permitted, and a majority of the respondents choose to collect as opposed to buying fuelwood. An average back-load of firewood weighed 40 kg. Earlier surveys revealed higher weights of 55 kg (MDP/GTZ, 1997) and 65 kg (Inter-Aid, 1993). Using the mean of these estimates gives the rate of firewood extraction at 385.1 kJ (Karare 51.3 kJ, Manyatta Jillo 49.4 kJ, Sagante I 140 kJ and Sagante II 136.4 kJ) per month.

It is often assumed that provided the fuelwood is collected from fallen dry/dead wood, then firewood collection has no impact on forest ecosystems. If dead wood (used for firewood) is left to decompose within the forest, with the help of microorganisms, it adds to the stock of existing humus, strengthens soil structure, enriches soil composition and retards soil loss and erosion. The decomposers are only part of the ecosystem's components, which are interconnected through a complex web. This complements the role of other species in supporting specific and ecological functions and services. As long as firewood extraction impacts on the reserve ecosystem, there is a need to treat this issue with caution. Added to this are the consequences of illegal access and harvesting of forest resources, as revealed by our survey. The collectors of firewood (main forest product) ignore the ecological role of the resource in climate modification and watershed protection.

Charcoal Related to fuelwood, charcoal is the second most frequently extracted product. The source of charcoal is not only restricted to the forest reserve. Those villages far away (about 15 km) from the reserve burn charcoal from outlying woodlands (referred to by the local population as '*Woroma*' – thick woodland). Where woody material used for making charcoal comes from the forest, conversion is done around the homesteads: the charcoal materials are collected from the forest and converted to charcoal at house sites. The price (September 1997) for 8 kg of charcoal was Ksh.40 (equivalent to Ksh.200 per 40 kg bag during the wet season).

Poles The other timber product is poles, whose harvesting is generally illegal. Indeed, it is more of a threat to the existence of reserve species than any other product. Poles are often collected by labourers hired to load tractors with fuelwood. The poles are used in fencing and construction (houses and toilets). Poles weigh between 8 and 12 kg per piece and, in 1997 sold at a price of about Ksh.100 per piece: i.e. between Ksh.330 and Ksh.500 per 40 kg.

Turning to availability, there appears to be an increasing distance between villages and woodfuel sites. As a result permit holders tend to lop trees for firewood to add to available dead stock. We also observed people lopping tree branches which were then left to dry awaiting collection at a deferred date. A similar problem was reported by MDP/GTZ (1997) which found that 28 per cent of all the firewood collected by women contained wet wood. Illegal practices of this nature speeds up the deterioration of ecosystem functions. This pattern of resource use is encouraged by the open access conditions. This undermines the resilience of the forest ecosystem to withstand external shocks without collapsing to another and different state. Overuse of habitat results in deterioration of the state of the natural environment which may be difficult to reverse. Damage of this nature is either absolutely irreversible or very costly to reverse.

An example of this is the role of the reserve in regulating run-off. The high altitude of the mountain directly feeds the surrounding low-lying plains and acquifer with water through groundwater recharge and surface run-off. Deforestation leads to both higher levels of run-off and lower rates of groundwater recharge. It also alters the wild mix of species. The process of habitat alteration through uncontrolled human activities for private financial gains, have reciprocal effects also on the pastoral population in the arid low lands.

Other products harvested are *grass* and *herbs* for medicinal purposes. Their collection has minimal effects on the reserve. The quantity of herbs collected is small and with minimal effect on the forest. The frequency of forest visits to collect necessary herbs is based on the frequency of the patient's visit to a herbalist. The use of the forest in this manner has no deleterious consequences for the forest. Herbalists in society are aware of the usefulness of natural resources and appreciate conservation efforts. They may be used as partners in conservation efforts as forest guards. Involving such members of the local population in the sustainable management and production of forest resources would reduce the costs of effective forest protection and conservation.

Given the dominance of fuelwood/charcoal and poles, the survey paid particular attention to timber products. The collection and transportation of firewood for households and some firms (hotels) is done by women. Urban based households and firms use motorized transport to obtain firewood, primarily from the reserve. In this report we focus on rural households. In the recent past, women have travelled for more than 6 hours per trip (to and from the collection site) to obtain firewood. This implies a distance of between 10 and 20 km per day.[11] Legal possession of a permit does not give users the right to harvest unlimited forest resources. But users typically find ways to avoid the legal restrictions on collection. Women frequently use each others' permits. The growing demand for poles for construction purposes has also given rise to illegal extraction of forest resources. In 1988, the District Forest Product Licensing Committee proscribed pole extraction from the forest and banned animal-assisted transport. However, the use of poles for construction purposes by the local population has not stopped.

Specific types of trees are preferred by local people. For example, hardwood (*Olea* spp.) is preferred over others because of its higher market value, less smoky indoor cooking, more hot coal when used for charcoal making and resistance to rodents when used for construction and fencing. In the previous section we considered wood energy availability. One indicator of growing scarcity and accessibility is a shift in the preference of tree species used as fuelwood over time. Some records exist to support this scenario (Adano, 1995; MDP/GTZ, 1997). Table 4.16 summarizes the species used in the area as reported by the two surveys.

Table 4.16   Tree species used for fuelwood, 1995 and 1997

Tree species	Preference frequency (%)	
	1995	1997
Olea africana	62.3	39.5
Teclea nobilis	–	43.4
Diospyros scabra	56.3	13.2
Grivettea robusta	41.3	–
Croton megalocarpus	31.3	–
Others	15	3.95

Source: Adano (1995, p. 103) and MDP/GTZ (1997, p. 24).

Following the diminished availability of certain tree species in Marsabit Forest Reserve, there has been a change in gatherers' preference for tree types collected for firewood. For instance, *Olea* spp. which was the predominant source of firewood among households in 1995, ranked second in importance in 1997. Other tree species which previously were not preferred emerged as important sources of firewood over the same period. Two points are pertinent here. First, the increasing distance to be travelled by fuelwood collectors has forced women to shift their choice of firewood trees. Second, the scarcity of certain tree species reflects the fact that their rate of regeneration is less than their rate of harvest. This influences the diversity and composition of the forest through depletions of preferred tree species. This diminishes diversity. The shift in tree species preferred by the local population ignores the role of these trees in the functioning of the ecosystem.

In our survey, the dwindling availability of fuel wood and forest products over the years was attributed to more settlements around the forest and to frequent droughts. The respondents are, however, aware of the effects of human interference on the forest resources. It has also been observed that the periphery of the forest is devoid of plant under-growth due to constant human activities (Forest Officer, personal communication, 1997).

Dry wood/logs are used for firewood, converted to charcoal for cash earnings, sold in urban centres for cash or used as poles for construction purposes. Demand for these products is driven by the growing settlements around the forest. Maize cob (Table 4.17) is also mentioned as a source of firewood but its use is restricted to the short period immediately after harvests. This happens to be when the opportunity cost of labour for col-

Table 4.17   Type of fuel and cooking fire used by respondents by site

Fuel used	Karare	Manyatta Jillo	Sagante I	Sagante II
Firewood	34	33	68	64
Maize cob	–	32	65	62
Others	2 (5.9 %)	1 (3.0 %)	–	–
3-stone fireplaces	3	32	1	3

Note: The figures corresponding to the stated fuel type, are the number of households using that particular source.

Source: Own survey, 1997.

lecting firewood or any other forest products is high because of the many competing activities on the farm. This is exacerbated by the persistence of inefficient cooking technologies. The majority of the respondents use a three-stone fireplace for cooking. This cooking device is very inefficient from a resource use perspective and a source of health (eye and breathing) problems among rural women.

4.5   INTERPRETING THE SURVEY DATA

To interpret the survey data we first consider the nature of the household decision problem. Households are assumed to maximize the net benefits of three main activities: arable agriculture, livestock rearing and the collection of forest products — principally fuelwood and construction timber. The objectives of the ith household may be described by the following:

$$\text{Max}_{VF,Vc,LQ}\Pi^i = [p_Q Q^i(A^i, L_Q^i, H^i(V)) - wL_Q^i] + [p_F F - wT_F^i(V_F) \\ - P_V]V_F^{\frac{1}{2}} + [p_c G^i(C^i, R^i(C), K^i(V), W^i)\, wT_C^i(V_C)]V_C^i$$

where

P_0 = price of agricultural output
P_C = price of livestock products
P_V = price of reserve entry permit
W = wage rate
V = total number of visits to the reserve
V_F^i = number of wood collection visits by the ith household

V_F = total number of wood collection visits
V_C^i = number of watering and water collection visits by the ith household
V_C = total number of watering and water collection visits
L_Q^i = labour time committed to arable production
T_F^i = labour time committed to wood collection per visit
T_C^i = labour time committed to watering and water collection per visit
Q^i = arable output by the ith household
G^i = livestock output by the ith household
A^i = arable area committed by the ith household
R^i = rangeland available to the ith household
W^i = water available to the ith household
F = wood load per visit
C^i = livestock held by the ith household
C = total number of livestock
$H^i(V)$ = damage to crops of the ith household from the reserve
$K^i(V)$ = damage to livestock of the ith household from the reserve.

That is, the ith household is assumed to maximize the net benefits of the three activities by choice of the labour time it commits to each. The time each household must commit to either water or fuelwood visits depends on the total level of usage. This is approximated here by the total number of visits for either wood or water collection. It is assumed that $dT_F^i/dV_F > 0$ and $dT_C^i/dV_C > 0$: i.e. the time committed to both wood and water collection increases with the total number of visits for each purpose. The effectiveness of land use depends on the nature and extent of crop damage or livestock predation by wild animals from the forest reserve. This again depends on the level of usage of the forest, and is approximated by the total number of visits. It is assumed that $dQ/dV < 0$: i.e. the greater the overall level of pressure on the reserve, the greater the level of crop loss. Similarly, $dG/dV < 0$: i.e. the greater the overall level of pressure on the reserve, the greater the level of livestock loss. In both cases this reflects (a) the fact that arable and rangelands become more accessible to the species in the reserve the more land is converted to farming use, and (b) that greater incursions into the reserve reduce the resources of the reserve that are available to species in the reserve.

It is worth pointing out that there is also an open access problem, reflected in the relation $G^i(R^i(C))$. The range effectively available to the ith houseold depends on the total number of livestock, and since $dG^i/dC < 0$ the larger the size of the total herd, the smaller the level of output from livestock in the ith household. Since this is not the problem at hand, however, we do not discuss it here.

The problem with the use made of the reserve can be seen very simply by taking the first-order conditions for the optimization of the household's problem, and by comparing those with the first-order conditions for the optimization of the social problem—where we consider all of the households that use the resource. The first order necessary conditions (f.o.n.c.) for the three choice variables in the household problem are:

$$L_Q^i: \ p_Q(dQ^i/dL_Q) - w = 0$$

$$V_F^i: \ p_F F - wT_F - p_V + w(dT_F^i/dV_F^i)V_F^i - p_Q(dQ^i/dV_F^i) - p_C(dG^i/dV_F^i)V_C^i = 0$$

$$V_C^i: \ P_C G^i(.) - wT_C^i + [p_C(dG^i/dV_C^i) - w(dT_C^i/dV_C^i)]V_C^i - p_Q(dQ^i/dV_C^i) = 0$$

In the case of arable farming the f.o.n.c. require only that the marginal revenue product and marginal cost of labour be equal. The f.o.n.c. for livestock and forest products are more complicated, requiring that the household takes into account not only the marginal direct costs and benefits of forest visits for water and wood collection, but also the marginal indirect effects of the household's own forest visits on arable production, livestock products and the time taken by each visit. Compare these with the f.o.n.c for the *i*th household when the problem is evaluated from the perspective of the whole community, assuming that there are *n* households ($i = 1,...,n$) in the community:

$$L_Q^i: \ p_Q(dQ^i/dL_Q^i) - w = 0$$

$$V_F^i: p_F F - wT_F^i - p_V + \sum_j [w(dT_F^j/dV_F^i)V_F^i - p_Q(dQ^j/dV_F^i) - p_C(dG^j/dV_F^i)V_C^i = 0$$

$$V_C^i: \ P_C G^i(.) - wT_C^i + \sum_j [[p_C(dG^j/dV_C^i) - w(dT_C^j/dV_C^i)]V_C^i - p_Q(dQ^j/dV_C^i)] = 0$$

The costs imposed by each household on the rest of the community, $\sum_j[w(dT_F^j/dV_F^i)V_F^i - p_Q(dQ^j/dV_F^i) - p_C(dG^j/dV_F^i)V_C^i]$ and $\sum_j[[p_C(dG^j/dV_C^i) - w(dT_C^j/dV_C^i)]V_C^i - p_Q(dQ^j/dV_C^i)]$, $j \neq i$, are ignored in the private optimization problem. We now consider what the survey data reveals about the nature of these costs.

Demand for Forest Products

The main forest ecosystem resources use by the local population are poles, water and firewood. Our interest in this section is to find the factors determining the existing forest resource usage by households on the Marsabit Mountain and Forest Reserve. Formally, watering of livestock in the forest is done free of charge while access to other reserve resources is controlled. Fuelwood collection is subject to the monthly licence fee of Ksh.35, and livestock grazing and collection of construction timber is proscribed. However, the majority of users of forest resources neither observe the restriction on grazing or construction timber, nor pay the monthly fuelwood collection fee (although there may be a market developing in the use of licences). Consequently it is reasonable to take the labour time committed to collection of these products as a proxy for their price.

Poles are harvested to support development of houses to shelter the growing human population. The harvesting of poles is done illegally as this survey reveals. The probability of detection of illegal access to the reserve depends on the staff members of KWS and the Forest Department (which are charged with conservation and management of the reserve). Together the agencies employed 61 people in 1997 (36 KWS and 25 Forest Dept.) for the daily surveillance of the reserve resources (personal communication, 1997). This is less than they need for efficient conservation (KWS, 1990). Only 5 per cent of the households interviewed had permits to harvest firewood legally. It is common practice among rural households to use the wood from maize granaries for firewood in the event of scarcity and later to obtain replacement timber from the forest.

To estimate the demand for forest products we relate monthly collection visits to this proxy for the price of such products, household income, livestock holdings, and land holdings. That is, we consider the relation:

$$Q_i = F(W_i, Y_i, X_j, Z_i)$$

in which W_i = labour time invested in collection by the ith household, itself proxied by distance walked to the forest; Y_i = the ith household's monthly income; $X_i = C_i$, S_i, G_i = livestock (cattle, sheep and goat) holdings of the ith household; $Z_i = T_i$, O_i = farm area and years of occupancy of the ith household. Collections, as might be expected fall with our proxy for the price of collection—collection labour time or distance to the reserve—but increase with livestock and land holdings, both of which are positively correlated with household income. The overall fit of the model is, however, modest, with an adjusted r-square of 0.63. While there are insufficient data to test the relation between demand for forest products and the external costs of private activity, the survey does yield some insights into the nature of these costs. However, there remains a good deal of uncertainty.

In particular, certain indigenous tree species have already been depleted from the reserve because of their high market value, yet their role and contribution to the forest ecosystem functioning may be important. The effects of the depletion of certain indigenous tree species (*Olea* and *Teclea*), for example, are not known. The forest provides vegetation cover on the mountain and retards soil erosion. It also supports the downstream population both in reducing soil and water run-off and sedimentation deposition. The rains on the mountains recharge water sources in the low-lying plains used by the pastoral populations. These are notably the Sura water source in the east, Logologo borehole in the south and Medate and Maikona water sources in the north-west. Change in the species composition of the forest, and change in the pattern of run-off as a result of the heavy use of wells may affect its capacity to recharge these sources.

Benefits of the Forest Reserve

The Marsabit Reserve has both direct and indirect value to a range of stakeholders. In addition to the local communities these include the Kenya Wildlife Service (KWS), Forest Department and Ministry of Water Development. The Ministry of Water Development harnesses water sources in the watershed. KWS has the mandate to conserve and manage the national reserve's habitats. KWS also maintains the roads within the reserve and thus provides support services to the tourist industry. The Forest Department oversees the daily management of the forest reserve. The costs and benefits of protected areas that are 'counted' by local decisionmakers are usually the only direct use benefits measurable in money terms.

Aside from timber revenues, one such direct use benefit is tourism. Marsabit National/Forest Reserve is a source of attraction for tourists. Between 1975 and 1979 the area received some fifteen thousand visitors (both residents and non-residents). The number fell back sharply in the first half of the 1980s, but by the early 1990s was again running at the level of the late 1970s. The revenue earned by tourism is at risk from both forest encroachment and the associated loss of biodiversity. Table 4.18 summarizes the number of visitors and the revenue earned by the reserves.

Urban Water Supply

The forest provides over 80 per cent of the water used within Marsabit township (Government of Kenya, 1989a). The water comes from two springs: Bakuli I and Bakuli II in the forest, the output of which varies between seasons. During the rainy season, they are capable of producing 470 m^3/day, although only 235 m^3/day can be pumped out. During dry seasons the water table falls tremendously reducing the springs' yield to 150 m^3/day. The forest is also the main source of water for livestock and

Table 4.18   Visitors' entry to Marsabit National Reserve, 1981–92

Year	1	2	3	Total visitors	Revenue
1981	982	1487	107	2576	–
1982	609	1051	61	1721	–
1983	421	606	39	1066	–
1984	690	906	69	1501	–
1985	1120	779	101	2000	–
1986	1948	1110	130	3188	–
1987	1344	809	150	2313	101641
1988	775	872	84	1731	123918
1989	964	753	99	1825	115011
1990	1435	800	47	3167	262033
1991	1533	816	85	3440	425791
1992	1598	530	96	2745	615945

Notes
1 = Adult residents, 2 Adult n/residents; 3 Children.
Total visitors not equal to sum of 1, 2 and 3.

Source: Kenya Wildlife Service (1990 and 1993).

for the surrounding villages. A number of water sources exist in the forest. Present demand for urban water is 600 m³ /day. There are no estimates for demand by the village communities. A survey of water discharge rates carried out by the Department of Water Development recorded the information reported in Table 4.19.

Table 4.19   Water sources in the reserve and their discharge rates, 1995–96

Survey	Name of site	Year surveyed	Average discharge rate (l/s)
S1	Marsabit Lodge	1995/96	1.4
S8	Badassa spring	1995/96	1.60
S9	Songa spring	1995/96	2.3
S10	Bakuli I	1995/96	5.20
S11	Bakuli II	1995	5.3
S12	Ichuta	1995/96	6.84

Source: Water Resource Assessment and Planning, 1997.

Water is supplied to the urban population through meters. Most of the water meters on individual connections are old and defective, and although metered, most of the consumers are on average assessment connections. For instance in 1996, out of Ksh.632 655 of gross revenue earned only Ksh.470 685.00 (about 75 per cent of the total) was collected. This indicates substantial loss of water revenue earned by the department to defaulters or through average assessment. This presents a huge revenue loss to the department and underestimates ecological functions of the Reserve to the local population even in terms of direct use values.

'Vermin', Crop Destruction and Compensation Claims

The proximity of human settlements to the protected area and its wild inhabitants is a source of additional cost: the cost of predation. Respondents were asked about livestock and crop losses due to forest wildlife. All the respondents in Sagante II and the vast majority of respondents in two other sites (97.1 per cent in Karare and 80.6 per cent in Sagante I) claimed to suffer crop or livestock losses to wildlife. However less than 10 per cent of respondents in Manyatta Jillo claimed to have suffered losses. Crop and livestock losses are clearly a 'normal' phenomenon in the area. Respondents were asked to specify the causes of such losses. While they cite management failures, such as late planting or planting of 'foreign' and unsuitable seeds for the mountain conditions, they also cite destruction from both wildlife and domestic animals. Table 4.20 presents details of these. Damage blamed on wild animals is one measure of the external cost (a) of the conservation of wild species, and (b) of human disturbance of the protected area. The survey did not reveal wildlife interference as the dominant cause of damage. Nevertheless, wildlife does cause some crop and livestock losses on the mountain. Moreover, farmers do incur costs of protection. Estimates of the annual costs of protection against wildlife reported in the survey are shown in Table 4.21.

Most defensive expenditures against wildlife take the form of hiring labour on the farm to chase wildlife away from crops or livestock. Although Sagante I had the highest number of people employed in this way, the cost of this to farmers was reported to be comparatively low. The estimates may, however, reflect an upward bias — exaggeration of costs by respondents in the expectation of compensation. Nor is it clear as to whether the cost of wildlife predation is rising or falling. Wildlife crop destruction and livestock killing was, for example, reported to have adverse affects on agricultural and livestock produc-

Table 4.20   Causes of agricultural losses (%)

	Survey site			
		Manyatta		
Causes of losses incurred	Karare	Jillo	Sagante I	Sagante II
Most frequently cited cause				
Attack from diseases	17.6	63.6	30.0	53.0
Political insecurity	47.1	3.0	4.3	25.8
Destruction from wildlife	23.5	–	32.8	19.6
Loss of soil fertility	2.9	12.1	32.9	–
Lack of veterinary service	2.9	–	–	–
Second most frequently cited cause				
Attack from diseases	23.5	27.3	–	21.2
Political insecurity	26.5	–	–	18.2
Destruction from wildlife	17.6	–	80.0	48.4
Destruction from domestic animals	–	3.0	5.7	–
Loss of soil fertility	–	15.2	11.4	–
Third most frequently cited cause				
Attack from diseases	5.9	–	10.0	4.5
Political insecurity	–	3.0	–	–
Destruction from wildlife	5.9	–	53.8	34.8
Loss of soil fertility	–	–	10.0	–

Source: Own survey, 1997.

Table 4.21   Costs of protecting crops and livestock against wildlife

		Manyatta		
	Karare	Jillo	Sagante I	Sagante II
Proportion incurring costs	26%	87.9%	97.1%	71.2%
No. of people involved	23 (8)	18 (7)	98 (66)	56 (47)
Labour cost (Ksh.)	7050	28500	9815	6730
Year of loss	1990–96	1995–96	1993–96	1995–96

Note: The numbers in parentheses are the number of households with preceding total number of people engaged in crops and livestock protection against wildlife. These show that property protection takes up household labour-time. However, it is not clear either how many people are engaged in a specific protection activity or how many people divide their time between different activities.

Source: Own survey, 1997.

tion in the district during the 1980s (Government of Kenya, 1989). Indeed, during the mid-1980s, annual compensation paid for crop losses due to wildlife was of the order of Ksh.360 000, while compensation for livestock lost was around half that amount (Government of Kenya, Development Plan, 1984).

To obtain a sense of people's perception of the indirect costs of damage to forest habitat, respondents were asked their views on the consequences of forest conversion. The responses are summarised in Table 4.22, and are grouped into three levels of (decreasing) severity. The

Table 4.22   Perceived consequences of forest conversion

Consequences of conversion	Karare	Manyatta Jillo	Segante I	Segante II
Agree that there will be consequences	34	33	70	63
Level I				
Desertification	47%	9.1%	–	25.5%
Reduction in supply of forest resources	38%	51.5%	21.4%	4.5%
Destruction of habitat	–	18.2%	5.7%	9.1%
Shortage of fuelwood	12%	27.3%	30.0%	9.2%
Reduced rain (and shade)	3%	3.0%	27.1%	1.5%
Life of forest dependants threatened	–	–	–	12.1%
Level II				
Desertification	–	6.0%	–	9.1%
Reduced forest resources	75%	18.2%	31.2%	1.5%
Destruction of the habitat	–	3.0%	2.9%	1.5%
Lack of firewood	25%	23.5%	45.8%	28.8%
Reduced rain and shade	–	–	29.1%	6.0%
Survival of dependants reduced	–	–	6.2%	19.7%
Level III				
Reduced forest resources	–	–	14.7%	4.5%
Lack of firewood	–	–	11.7%	3.0%
Reduced rain (and shade)	–	–	20.5%	3.0%
Destruction of habitat	–	–	17.6%	–
Survival of dependants reduced	–	–	38.3%	13.6%

Source: Own survey, 1997.

respondents agreed that the forest ecosystem might be cleared for alternative land uses such as agriculture, and that this would have consequences for their well-being. However, they differed as to their perceptions of the main impact of forest clearance. In Karare, nearly half of the respondents perceived that forest clearance might have negative effects on surrounding areas—leading to their desertification. This effect was, however, not even mentioned in Sagante I. In other villages, respondents tended to consider the important outcomes of forest conversion to be the direct loss of forest products: water, fuelwood, construction timber and grazing. There is little doubt that the low weight given to the watershed functions of the forest is a major factor in the increasing pressure being placed on forest resources.

4.6 IMPLICATIONS OF THE IMPLEMENTATION OF THE CONVENTION ON BIOLOGICAL DIVERSITY

The problem in Marsabit Forest, as in many other protected areas, is that local communities obtain a range of goods from the forest either at low prices or they access them illegally. The economic incentives encourage overuse of these resources. In the long run, growing scarcity may lead to price increases which will reduce demand. But the market for wood is hampered by inadequate property rights and relaxed access rules. The private cost of wood comprises only the time costs of harvest. These values ignore the social value of wood to the community. To address this, concerned parties (government and non-governmental agencies) need to influence the structure of incentives to encourage conservation as required by Article 11 of the Convention on Biological Diversity. Substantial public capital inflow (free seedlings and say Food-for-Work) may be needed to supplement these incentives by establishing farm agroforestry. The Food-for-Work programme has the advantage of already being in the region. To kick off such programmes a government subsidy may be important. In addition, a certain level of political support would be necessary.

Access to forest resources is governed by Forest Policy, drafted in 1968. It is still in operation. The levy for use of forest products (firewood) was established at that time, and remained unchanged until 1995 when it increased from Ksh.4 to Ksh.35. In principle, permit holders are allowed to collect firewood only on weekdays. At present, the monthly forest licence fee is about as costly as one litre of kerosene (Ksh.30 per litre). It is economically rational for households to prefer firewood to kerosene for domestic use. The private benefits of obtaining forest products (even with a permit) is less than the marginal economic value of the forest resources. The pricing policy and other relevant institutions need to address this problem. The prices of environmental resources should be adjusted upward in response to the prices of non-forest goods which are complementary to or substitute for forest resources. The current system of centrally determined pricing of forest products at the head-quarters needs to be decentralized. By so doing, local access prices may be better attuned to local resource scarcities. Local people would also get the chance to make decisions and their socio-economic conditions could be taken into account.

Poles are also obtained from the reserve although their harvesting is illegal. Empirical data are not available but the process of human settle-ment on the mountain has been increasing – poles are mostly used for construction purposes. Royalties or stumpage fees should be set at appropriate levels to discourage people from overexploiting the resource. At present, penalties for illegal access are biased in favour of violators, and take little account of the environmental and social costs of overuse of the reserve. These charges should also be adjusted upward to reduce illegal access. This should be supported by effective monitoring of the reserve. Such penalty prices should be predetermined rather than left to market forces.

A number of springs originate in the reserve. These have been tapped and supply water through meters to the urban population of Marsabit Town. This system makes it possible to charge users an appropriate rate. In addition, however, several hand dug wells exist in or on the periphery of the reserve for livestock and rural household water supply. Livestock frequently visit the wells for water and access is 'free'. There is scope for introducing an appropriate system of abstraction charges to well owners. Alternatively, local communities should be charged for watering their ani-mals in the forest and for their harvest of forest products. The water use charges might then support a miscellaneous fund for conserving biologi-cal resources in the area.

Our survey reveals that while most households rely on collection of forest resources, only about 5 per cent of the sampled households have forest access permits. Harvesting of forest products provides households both some level of earnings and direct consumption benefits. Local people depend heavily on the forest for wood energy and there has been a significant reduction in certain indigenous tree species used for firewood (Adano, 1995; MDP/GTZ, 1997). To address this there is a need to pro-mote people-oriented agro-forestry (consisting of both exotic and native tree species) projects, education on environmental issues to raise aware-ness of the role of trees in retarding soil erosion, retaining soil fertility and, by extension, conserving biodiversity. On-farm forestry will also help reduce demand for forest products that require the cutting of trees.

Over the last three decades, Marsabit Mountain has been a net recipient of immigrants, particularly from southern Ethiopia, from the surrounding plains and from other parts of the country. There is a growing gap between the supply and demand for firewood. On both environmental and equity grounds, government intervention through policies that encourage the establishment of farm woodlots and fodder at a commercial level is necessary. To support this there is a need to change people's attitudes from seeing forest products merely as free resources to be 'mined', to commodities to be raised by farmers on their farms. Special attention should be paid to women's groups as women bear the burden of providing the larger proportion of rural households with fuelwood. Women might thus be more responsive to on-farm forestry and woodlot development. Therefore they should be at the centre of tree planting and woodlot management.

Forestry and agricultural extension in Kenya falls under separate ministries; the Ministry of Environment and Natural Resources and the Ministry of Agriculture, Livestock Production and Marketing. Separation does not always mean incompatibility. The forest and reserve resources come under the Forest Department and Kenya Wildlife Service (KWS), respectively. KWS is an autonomous private entity mandated to conserve and manage rich ecological areas in Kenya. To the best of my knowledge there exists a memorandum of understanding between KWS and the Forest Department. But conservation efforts might be improved through the development of a close working relationship between forest guards and KWS staff.

To achieve farm forestry with some degree of success, the forestry extension should be built into the mandate of existing agricultural extensions, with foresters serving as trainers in management and planting technologies. It is significant that the incentive to farmers to undertake farm forestry is limited by policies that restrict their rights to use on-farm trees—in an effort to control tree cutting. In order to achieve success in farm forestry, farmers need a high level of autonomy in making decisions on the use of farm trees and improvements in the rights to land. Practical experience has shown that such approaches work well among small-scale farmers in other developing countries (World Bank, 1991). But in the short-run, public support to reduce additional environmental damage through cultivation of tree crops would provide farmers private earnings and allows for regeneration of the reserve.

The growing distance travelled by collectors has had some impact on demand, particularly after the ban on the use of animals to assist in transport. But this does impact most severely on the poor and on women, who undertake most of the collection. It might be more equitable to lift the ban on draught animal transport alongside a reduction in the number of forest entrance gates, and the number of forest permits issued each month.

Local people believe that the reserve makes no contribution towards their wellbeing. Their argument is that revenue raised from the reserve benefits private agencies. The problem here is that while the benefits yielded by ecological goods and services from forests are significant, they are not captured in market prices. Prices fail to reflect the social value of the reserve. Since the values of the externalities are not incorporated into households' decisions regarding resource use, these goods and services are inevitably overused. The decision to use reserve resources is made by individual households. Individual households fail to recognize and account for the costs they impose on other households ('hidden' users and beneficiaries). This is further exacerbated by pseudo-ownership of farm plots. To enhance use and conservation of resources, local people need to be educated, involved and integrated into the conservation exercise. There is a need for sufficient human resources for surveillance by KWS and the forest department, and collaboration with other relevant agencies to increase the probability of detection of illegal harvesters.

Marsabit Mountain is presently inhabited by groups with different cultural backgrounds and approaches to environmental resource management. What exists now is a 'vague culture'. What to some groups used to be a cultural offence and deviant behaviour is now just a way of making a living. The amalgamation of these groups has changed their views concerning norms of resource use. This has negative implications for the conservation of biological resources.

Specific Recommendations

The following specific recommendations are thought relevant for the mountain region:

1. *Electric power connections* The existing Marsabit Power plant has sufficient capacity to supply a greater number of households with electricity. The plant is currently operating at suboptimal level. The high initial installation cost (especially of the transformer) is prohibitive for the majority of the poor communities. This could be waived through introduction of a subsidized rural electrification programme by the government.

2. *Close control of livestock per capita on the mountain* Farm based livestock on the mountain depend on the forest for both grazing and water. In collaboration with and through the relevant line ministries, incentives should be put in place to reduce animal populations to a level more consistent with the carrying capacity both of individual land holdings and the forest ecosystem as a whole.

3. *Channelling of the existing water supply for livestock use to the periphery of the reserve* Frequent visits of human and livestock to the water sources inevitably interfere with wildlife and reserve's resources. Water should be piped out of the reserve. This must be done with caution, however, as doing so will detach the local people from the protected areas and increase the rate of illegal extraction of reserve resources.

4. *Growing demand and diminishing supply* The increasing demand for forest products, diminishing supplies of wood and destruction of forest resources should encourage a move towards integration of the ecological and economic management of the forest ecosystem. To achieve this, small-scale farmers should be offered economic incentives to encourage on-farm investment as opposed to forest harvesting. The development of agroforestry systems and the involvement of farmers in conservation programmes are called for.

5. *Research and training* Empirical data are crucial inputs for development planning and making informed decisions about the use of resources. Marsabit National and Forest Reserves are among the least studied not only in Kenya but in East Africa. There is a need to generate data through research programmes aimed at enabling the reserve to continue to provide valuable watershed and biodiversity functions in the region. Such initiatives could be fostered through joint ventures involving the relevant authorities; KWS, Water Development, Ministry of Agriculture and Forest Department.

6. *Pricing* At present, households make independent decisions on resource use without due considerations of their effects on others and the ecosystem. Under the current pricing system, the effects of resource users on third parties are not taken into account. The problem is that the individual resource users lack incentives to take the social costs of their actions into consideration. A policy that aims at reducing anomalies between private individual profits and the social benefits of wild resource use is necessary so as to internalize the external costs of the use of biological resources. Prices of environmental resources and violator penalties should both be adjusted accordingly.

4.7 CONCLUDING REMARKS

The main value of biodiversity derives from the functions the mix of biological species plays in supporting specific ecological services
(MacArthur, 1997b). With increasing human settlement on the mountain,
and with heavy dependence on forest products, the future of many
species, whether harvested or targeted as competitors or predators, is
insecure. Farm forestry can satisfy the individual household needs for
some forest products, and should complement the management and conservation of natural forests. This chapter has explored the different
economic uses that local people make of a forest resource. It shows that
local communities use the reserve for firewood for domestic use, poles for
the construction of semi-permanent housing, production of charcoal for
sale in urban centres and livestock grazing. It also shows that access to
the forest products is at best weakly regulated, and at worst open. A combination of forces – population pressure resulting from rural–urban
migrations, resource pricing policy, ill-defined properly rights, a bottle-
neck in forest resource management and access rules, and low licence fees
– are among many factors which influence resource use. These encourage
habitat destruction and loss of biodiversity in the reserve. This in turn has
serious implications for the flow of benefits from the forest system.

   Licence fees for forest products, where they exist, are low. They are
based on administrative pricing without regards to conversion, harvest
and extraction costs. They fail to reflect ecological values. The pricing
system thus encourages people to use forest products. Government policy
currently tends to be responsive neither to the scarcity of forest resources
nor to the socio-economic characteristics of the local population. Policies
ought to be amended to conform with realities on the ground while the
environmental resource pricing system ought to incorporate the social
value of environmental goods. Natural resource managers should be
aware of and sensitive to the local farming systems, household energy
usage, and socio-economic conditions. Finally, most environmental problems result from interaction between different ecological processes,
economic forces and household decisions. Therefore there is a need for
collaborative research comprising of scholars with backgrounds in different disciplines. The adoption of such research and management strategies
will help not only to reconcile resource conservation problems arising
from human use but also to promote conservation of biodiversity.

APPENDIX 4.1   MAP OF MARSABIT DISTRICT

5 0 5 10 15

Kilometres

Key

- ● Urban centres
- ▲ Rural centres
- —·— District boundary
- —··— Division boundary
- —— Location boundary

NOTES

1. This chapter presents findings of a research programme on the problem of biodiversity loss in Sub-Saharan Africa under the auspices of the Environment Department at the University of York, UK. My efforts to undertake this study have benefited from the support of Charles Perrings, University of York. Special thanks to Dr Mohamud Jama of the Environmental Economics Network of Eastern and Southern Africa (EENESA-Nairobi), through whom participation in both the training component (UK) and subsequent research programme of the project has been made possible. Many thanks to my research assistants; Samson Teko, Waqo Gololcha, Mamo Gutu and Roba Shamma for tireless efforts in the collection of data. I feel indebted to all our respondents for disclosing to us the necessary information for the study. Thanks to Marsabit District Forest Officer Mr J.M. Mburu and Mr J. Kariuki of Kenya Wildlife Service (KWS Marsabit) who willingly shared their experience and relevant materials with me. My utmost thanks goes to Dr Karen Witsenburg for sacrificing hours to ensure accurate data entry. Thanks too for the social support and tolerance at the height of field challenges. My sincere thanks to Godanna and Nasibo for taking good care of our daughter, Naomi Talasso over the period.
2. Out of the total global forest cover, about 2.9 billion ha are closed forests, 700 million ha are open forests and 1.7 billion ha other wooded land; giving the total area of wooded vegetation as 5.3 billion ha of the world's land area.
3. In this report we confine ourselves to 'Sustainable Forestry' to mean — 'to meet the needs of the present without compromising the ability of future generations to meet their own needs by practising a land stewardship ethic which integrates the reforestation, management, growing, nurturing, and harvesting of trees for useful products with the conservation of soil, air and water quality, wildlife and fish habitat, and aesthetics' (MacArthur Foundation, 1997a, p. 15)
4. These included Boran, Turkana, Rendille, Gabbra and Samburu among others. For the role of culture and ethics in natural resources use decisions and loss of biodiversity, see Barbier et al. (1994: pp. 83–7).
5. Migration figures for the mountain do not exist from the available reports, except for intra-district migrations.
6. Much of the information in this section derives from District Development Plans, Population Census reports and annual reports of government ministries.
7. There are no hard data on this form of migration (within the District).
8. Population projections based on 1989 Population Census. I believe this figure is higher than the actual population.
9. The survey reveals 24 hired labourers in Karare, 16 in Manyatta Jillo, 421 in Sagante I and 67 in Sagante II. This means that rural employments are based on social arrangements rather than on monetary income.
10. During the rainy season the market value of firewood sales increases due to difficulties of access and transport, and also firewood collection has an opportunity cost as it competes with farm activities.
11. MDP/GTZ (1997) estimate that users of motorized transport (tractors and Landrovers) currently drive about 25 km into the interior of the forest to access fuelwood.

REFERENCES

Adano, W. (1995), 'Economic analysis of the environmental impacts of water projects: a contingent valuation survey of Maikona and Sagante areas, Northern Kenya', Unpublished M. Phil. manuscript. Moi University, Eldoret, Kenya.

Barbier, E., J. Burgess and C. Folke (1994), *Paradise Lost? The Ecological Economies of Biodiversity*, London: Earthscan.

Dasgupta, P. (1982), *The Control of Resources*, Cambridge, MA: Harvard University Press.

Government of Kenya (1979), *Marsabit District Development Plan, 1979–1983*, Nairobi: Government Printer.

Government of Kenya (1984), *Marsabit District Development Plan, 1984–1988*, Nairobi: Government Printer.

Government of Kenya (1989a), *Marsabit District Development Plan, 1989–1993*, Nairobi: Government Printer.

Government of Kenya (1989b), *Kenya Population Census, 1989*. Housing, Analytical Report, Vol. X. Nairobi: Government Printer.

Government of Kenya (1994), *Marsabit District Development Plan, 1994–1996*, Nairobi: Government Printer.

Hanna, S., C. Folke and K.G. Mäler (1995), 'Property rights and environmental resources', in: S. Hanna and M. Munasinghe (eds), *Property Rights and the Environment, Social and Ecological Issues*, The Beijer International Institute of Ecological Economics and The World Bank, Chapter 2.

Heywood, V. (1995), 'The economic value of biodiversity', in V. Heywood (ed.), *Global Biodiversity Assessment*, Cambridge: Cambridge University Press.

Inter-Aid (1993), 'Institutional firewood consumption: a cross-sectional survey in Central, Sololo and Moyale Divisions, Marsabit District', unpublished survey report.

Kenya Wildlife Service (1990), 'Policy framework and development programme, 1991–1996: community conservation and wildlife management outside parks and reserves. Annex 6', unpublished manuscript.

Kenya Wildlife Service (1993), 'Statistical abstract, 1981–1992: visitors entry to parks and reserves', Wildlife Policy Planning Department, unpublished.

Litoroh, M., N. Aaron and P. Masinde (1994), 'A survey of the Marsabit National Reserve: elephant and large mammal population', Kenya Wildlife Service Elephant Programme, unpublished manuscript.

Lusigi, J.W. (1984), 'Integrated resource assessment and use, development and management. Guideline for Western Marsabit District', Northern Kenya. IPAL-UNESCO-FRG-MAB report.

MacArthur Foundation (1997a), *Sustaining Profits and Forests. The Business of Sustainable Forestry*, Chicago: MacArthur Foundation.

MacArthur Foundation (1997b), *Balancing Economic Growth and Conservation. World Environment and Resources*. No. 161997, Chicago: MacArthur Foundation.

Mahar, D. J. (1989), *Government Policies and Deforestation in Brazil's Amazon Region*, World Bank.

Marekia, E.N. (1991), 'Managing wildlife in Kenya', in A. Kiririo and C. Juma (eds), *Gaining Ground: Institutional Innovations in Kenya*, Nairobi: African Centre for Technology Studies, pp. 155–76.

Marsabit Development Programme/GTZ–Marsabit (1997), 'Environmental impact of wood energy consumption in arid and semi-arid lands ASAL: a case study of Marsabit Central Division, Kenya', unpublished preliminary report.

Munasinghe, M. (1993), 'Environmental economics and biodiversity management in developing countries', *Ambio*, **22**, 126–35.

Oba, G. (1994), 'The role of indigenous range management knowledge for deser-
    tification control in Northern Kenya', EPOS-Research Report, No. 4, Uppsala
    and Linkoping Universities.
Ogolla, D. B. (1992), 'Environmental management policy and law in Kenya',
    Journal of Environmental Policy and Law, **22**(3), 163–75.
Reid, W.V. and K.R. Miller (1989), *Keeping Options Alive: The Scientific Basis of
    Conserving Biodiversity*, Washington, DC: World Resource Institute.
Tablino, P. (1999), *The Gabra: Camel Nomads of Northern Kenya*, Nairobi:
    Paulines Publishers (Africa).
World Bank (1991), 'The Forest Sector', a World Bank policy paper, Washington,
    DC: World Bank.

5. Biodiversity conservation and land-use options in semi-arid lands: the case of Nyae Nyae in Namibia

Omu Kakujaha-Matundu and Charles Perrings

5.1 INTRODUCTION

The primary use of semi-arid rangelands in Sub-Saharan Africa is for livestock production (Walker, 1995). Management systems vary from nomadic pastoralism, through mixed subsistence farming relying mainly on livestock, to commercial ranching. In most areas land policies have virtually wiped out nomadic pastoralism. Livestock production has assumed a more sedentary mixed subsistence farming character. One effect of this has been to increase the level of grazing pressure by domestic livestock. This has radically changed the composition of vegetation and wildlife. In both sedentary mixed subsistence farming areas and marginal lands a combination of factors (including overstocking, drought, inappropriate management systems, and so on) has led to a fundamental change in the biodiversity of semi-arid rangelands.

Aside from livestock farming, the rich flora and fauna on semi-arid rangelands is the basis for a rapidly expanding tourist industry. But while tourism is an important contributor to GDP in the semi-arid savannas of east, central and southern Africa, its development has divorced local communities from any control over or rights to wildlife. Coupled with law enforcement efforts by the central and local authorities to protect wildlife, this has meant that local farming communities have had little incentive to explore the potential benefits from tourism or to protect the wildlife resource (Swanson and Barbier, 1992).

The net result has been deepening rural poverty, accelerated environmental degradation and biodiversity loss in livestock areas, and a growing conflict between different land uses. One example of this is the conflict between livestock herders and hunter-gatherers in the Kalahari. In the Nyae Nyae area, which is one of the few areas still available to huntergatherers, there is currently a very low density of livestock. But the area has been targeted for development of the livestock sector. This raises the question as to whether it is possible simultaneously to meet the needs and interests of the hunter-gatherer communities and to develop the livestock sector. Because the various options imply a different mix of species, this is a biodiversity issue. The problem is to determine the optimal mix of species.

Failure to appreciate the economic value of biodiversity can result in a distortion of economic incentives (Barbier et al., 1994). Where biodiversity values are not fully recognized and integrated into decision-making processes there may be an excessive loss of biodiversity. The Biodiversity Convention accordingly includes provisions not just to establish protected areas, but also to correct economic incentives that lead to biodiversity loss away from protected areas. In many cases in Sub-Saharan Africa the disincentive to conservation by livestock farmers lies in the loss of property rights in wild living resources. This chapter considers the scope for development of the Nyae Nyae in a way that conserves the diversity of the region whilst meeting the competing claims of the hunter-gatherer and livestock farming communities.

The chapter also considers the nature of the appraisal problem. Because the changes induced by committing resources to one land-use option or another may be permanent or at least very long-lived, a cost–benefit analysis (CBA) of the social advantages and disadvantages of alternative courses of action should factor irreversibility into the analysis (Abelson, 1979). Indeed, this should be the characteristic feature of the cost–benefit analysis of land-uses that change the probability of species extinction. This chapter estimates the economic return to different land use options in the Nyae Nyae. These include tourism-based wildlife conservation and livestock production. Neither is thought to change the probability of the global extinction of species, and only livestock production affects the probability of local extinction.

The Nyae Nyae

The Nyae Nyae area borders Botswana in the east, former Hereroland in the south, Kaudum game reserve in the north and former Western Bushmanland in the west. The current area is about 6400 km^2, with a population of approximately 4500. This includes all inhabitants in Tsumkwe township and the surrounding villages.

The original Nyae Nyae area was occupied by the Ju'hoan people. This included Tsumkwe and the Kaudum game reserve. To the south it stretched beyond Gam into the Omaheke region and to the east into Botswana. The area has subsequently contracted. The division of

Namibia into ethnic homelands by South Africa in the 1960s and the proclamation of the game reserve contributed to the shrinking of the territory of the Ju'hoansi. In the 1970s, the authorities concentrated the inhabitants at Tsumkwe, the administrative capital of the former Bushmanland. The result was a near collapse of their social system as the population was left without access to their traditional means of support. Since the early 1980s the Nyae Nyae Development Foundation of Namibia, a local NGO, has assisted the Ju'hoansi to move away from Tsumkwe to their former living areas. The Foundation is also assisting them in making a transition into a mixed economy of hunting and gathering and subsistence livestock and dryland cropping.

The area consists of a system of seasonal pans and wetlands. The pans and wetlands attract a large number of water and wading birds in the summer months, including flamingos and pelicans. Endangered wattle cranes, snipe and many migrants from Europe are found here when the pans are full. Although wildlife is not abundant, a number of animal species that are rare or endangered in the region are found in this area. Elephant, wild dog, leopard and roan antelope are among species recognized to be in need of protection. A small number of lion and cheetah are also found. Other species include giraffe, blue wildebeest, red hartebeest, eland and buffalo. Alongside such charismatic megafauna the area is also characterized by equally charismatic megaflora: it is dotted with spectacular giant baobab trees.

This combination of resources makes the Nyae Nyae a potential destination for tourists seeking a wilderness experience in a remote area (Jones, 1994). Although the area has potential as a tourist destination, few tourists currently pass through the area. This is due to a lack of tourist facilities. The community does get some revenue from providing tour guides, craft sales, cultural dancing and singing, photographs taken and camping fees from Makuri Campsite, but this is currently very limited. The situation may change if the government approves conservancy status for the Nyae Nyae. Indeed, the land-use alternatives considered in this chapter may be considered the alternatives with and without conservancy status.

Historically, the colonial administration believed that animal husbandry, primarily cattle, was the way for the inhabitants (traditionally hunter-gatherers) to increase their productivity most rapidly by their own efforts. In 1973 the administration introduced cattle into the area. The repatriation of Ovaherero pastoralists from Botswana after the Namibian independence increased the population of livestock in the general area, and there have since been several attempts by the Herero to move their livestock into the Nyae Nyae. Nevertheless, the livestock population remains very low. A livestock census conducted in May 1996 gave the numbers as: 625 cattle, 22 goats, 15 donkeys and 14 horses. Cattle are sometimes sold to middlemen, who buy the animals at very low prices compared with the meat-buying parastatal, MEATCO.

The area is accordingly the focus of interest for a number of different, conflicting groups. Aside from the people who currently live in the Nyae Nyae and the Herero pastoralists, these include industry (CDM and Texaco Petroleum), together with a number of government and non-governmental agencies. The Department of Agriculture and Rural Development (DARD) is the principal government institution involved with the agricultural sector. The DARD works in close liaison with other agencies such as the Ministry of Lands, Resettlement and Rehabilitation, the Directorates of Forestry and Environmental Affairs, the agricultural unions, the Namibia Development Corporation and various NGOs involved in agriculture related interventions. DARD suffers from a shortage of trained personnel. At the same time, the farming community is poorly educated and this complicates the work of the extension staff in eliciting the problems being experienced by the fanning community and in passing on the possible solutions to them.

Other organizations involved in the agricultural sector include the Namibia National Farmers Union which was established in 1992 to promote and advance the interest of farmers and promote the development of a viable agricultural industry in the communal land tenure areas. The Namibia Agricultural Union represents the interests of the private-tenure farmers. The Meat Marketing Board is responsible for regulating the export of meat and livestock exports and for organizing the smooth flow of cattle to the export abattoirs for slaughter. The government has a limited representation on the board and monitors its operations. Livestock processing and beef marketing is organized by MEATCO. Its main activities are livestock slaughter, the processing of meat and meat products and the marketing of these products both in Namibia and abroad.

The Ministry of Environment and Tourism (MET) has responsibility for wildlife and conservation. Tourism and wildlife are interdependent, wildlife being the basic attraction of the Namibian tourism. There are a total of 19 parks and reserves in the country, but there are also substantial wildlife populations outside the parks and reserves. Many of these are found on commercial farms where sustainable use for recreational hunting and tourism is encouraged by the legal and policy framework. There are some wildlife populations in communal areas. Although user rights were denied to the residents in the past, opportunities for income generation from fauna and flora are becoming viable. MET is currently reviewing its policy on wildlife utilization on commercial farmland as well as on communal land. New legislation is expected to improve communal area wildlife utilization (GRN, 1996). This legislation will allow people in the communal areas to exploit wildlife resources in the way that the CAMP-FIRE programme in Zimbabwe, among others, is beginning to do.

Agriculture and Tourism: Contributions to GDP, Employment and Exports

Agriculture is important mainly for its role in employment. It is the largest source of employment in Namibia supporting 70 per cent of the population directly or indirectly. It is the second most important sector in terms of its contribution to exports with a 12 per cent share. Extensive stock farming is the dominant agricultural activity, accounting for 65 per cent of the sector's gross value of output. Beef is the major product. Aside from cattle other livestock and livestock products include sheep, goats, pigs, karakul pelts, poultry, dairy and wildlife. About half or 444 000 km^2 of the country's land area is suitable for farmland. Low rainfall and high evaporation limit dryland arable farming in the north. Table 5.1 summarizes the agricultural sector's contribution to GDP. It contributed on average 7.6 per cent to GDP between 1990 and 1996. The commercial sector's contribution was about 5.1 per cent, while the subsistence sector contributed the remaining 2.5 per cent.

Table 5.1   Agricultural activity as percentage of GDP

	1990	1991	1992	1993	1994	1995	1996
Agriculture	9.0	8.8	6.6	6.8	7.6	6.9	7.8
Commercial	6.0	5.7	5.0	4.9	4.8	4.1	5.5
Subsistence	3.0	3.1	1.6	1.9	2.8	2.8	2.4

Source: Directorate of Planning and Marketing.

While tourism accounts for a much smaller proportion of total employment, its contribution to GDP is only just below that of agriculture. A visitor survey undertaken in 1992 yielded an estimated total turnover in the tourism sector of N$509 million, with net export earnings of N$315 million. The income generated by the tourism sector makes up about 6 per cent of GDP, which is similar to the share of commercial agriculture. Earnings from tourism are equivalent to around 11 per cent of all export of goods and services , which means that tourism is the third biggest foreign exchange earner after mining and agriculture. By contrast with agriculture, direct employment in tourism accounted for only 10 000 people, while total employment was estimated to be approximately twice this number (GRN, 1996).

Objectives of the Study

The main objective of the study is to evaluate the resource use options in the Nyae Nyae in the light of both Namibia's commitments under the Biodiversity Convention and the proposals to develop the area through commercial livestock farming in the area. Specifically, the chapter aims to evaluate the social profitability of the main livestock and wildlife use options, and to make policy recommendations.

Two ecological interactions are particularly important in the semi-arid savannas in Sub-Saharan Africa (SSA). One is the interaction between herbivore grazing pressure and vegetation. The productivity of rangelands depends on the balance between palatable and unpalatable grasses available to herbivores, and between woody plants and grasses. The relation between these is influenced by the patch structure of rangelands (Pickup, 1991; Tongway and Ludwig, 1989). Patchiness can be associated with a change in the composition of species in favour of woody plants, which reduces the economic productivity of the range (Walker, 1995). Both the patch structure of rangelands and the mix of palatable grasses and woody plants depends on the level of grazing pressure. The higher the stocking density, and hence the level of grazing pressure, the greater the probability that the system will converge to a state dominated by thorny thicket which is not only less productive in terms of livestock, but is also less productive in terms of wild herbivores (Perrings and Walker, 1997).

The other ecological interaction is that between wild and domestic herbivores. In rangelands, wild herbivores directly compete with livestock for graze and browse. As a result, wildlife populations have been substantially reduced in areas where there are cattle usually through direct depletion (hunting) but also through habitat conversion (Jansen, 1990; Kiss, 1990; Jones, 1994; Mishra, 1994). This has led to a conflict of interest between pastoralists and wildlife conservationists, for example, ministries of wildlife and tourism/environment, recreational hunters, tourism and hunting concessions operators and other interested parties. The planned proclamation of the area as wildlife reserve led to clashes between the Ju'hoansi (assisted by the Foundation) and the wildlife authorities. Although the reserve would not have excluded the Ju'hoansi, they would have lost control over the land. The Foundation launched a successful campaign to halt proclamation of the reserve. But new threats began to surface. Predators and the resettlement of the Ovaherero people from Botswana, to the south, at Gam, presented a new threat.

Any increase in the number of people and livestock places further pressure on the region's wildlife. In order to prevent herders moving further north from Gam and invading the area of the Ju'hoansi, a new fence has been built to separate the two areas. As with the veterinary cordon fences elsewhere in the region, this fence poses a threat to migratory species. On the positive side, however, both the Ministry of Environment and the Foundation have undergone a major evolution in terms of staff and philosophy and are working together to strike a balance between development and conservation.

One outcome of this is the proposal to establish a nature conservancy.[1] The proposal is modelled on the conservancies developed elsewhere in the region, and is an attempt to allow local communities to utilize wildlife and other natural resources on a sustainable basis, while permitting development of the tourist potential of the region. This chapter tests the hypothesis that the allocation of resources associated with the conservancy – a combination of wildlife and livestock use will yield greater net social benefits than the alternative. The alternative in this case is assumed to be commercial livestock farming on land freed up for the purpose by government.

5.2 EVALUATING BIODIVERSITY PROJECTS

Evaluating land-use options with different biodiversity risks is a complex task, involving both the valuation of non-marketed environmental resources and political/ethical considerations that are beyond the scope of normal cost–benefit analysis. As in the evaluation of all projects, the decision-maker implicitly or explicitly transforms all values to a single dimension to compare them. Once all benefits and costs have been expressed in monetary units, the social profitability of the considered project can be assessed. This requires the full valuation of costs and benefits of the options being considered (Johansson, 1993; Munasinghe and McNeely, 1994). We consider the valuation of non-marketed environmental resources later.

A particular problem posed by land-use options with different biodiversity risks is that some alternatives may involve changes that are to all intents and purposes irreversible. That is, the options forgone may never again be part of the set of choices open to the decision-maker. This is obvious in the case of species extinction. But a land use that drives the vegetation of semi-arid rangelands into a state dominated by thorny thicket, for example, may change the habitat for such a long period that it is all but irreversible. In both cases conservation of a particular mix of species or habitat has an option value.

Many economists distinguish between direct and indirect use values and a remainder, termed non-use value. People may not wish to make immediate use of some environmental resource but may wish to retain the option to use the resource in the future, or to make the resource available to others to use it in the future. The resource in this case is said to have an option value. There are three main categories of option value: option value proper (the value of the option to make use of the resource in the future; bequest value (the value of keeping a resource intact for one's heirs); or 'quasi-option' value (the value of the future information protected by preserving a resource) (Heywood, 1995; Pearce and Moran, 1994). All of these values are real and potentially very significant. All are also uncertain.

The irreversibility of the costs associated with biodiversity or habitat loss means that it is not sufficient to estimate the value of the environmental damage or forgone benefits of biodiversity loss over the time horizon of the project. Any environmental damages (or benefits) that extend beyond the life of the project should be added to the terminal costs (or benefits) of the project. So if there are forgone options that are irreversible, the present value of these options from the end of the project should be added to the terminal cost of the project.

Suppose that conversion of semi-arid rangelands to livestock production in this period, $t = 0$, yields a flow of net-benefits with a present value denoted by B_0. Denote the per period future costs of conversion by C_1. This describes the net bequest, option or quasi-option value of the species lost to the system for $t = 1, 2,...,\infty$. The present value of the net benefits of a decision to convert the rangelands today is then

$$PVB = B_0 - \rho C_1(1 + \rho + \rho^2 + ...) = B_0 - \rho C_1(1 + \delta)/\delta = B_0 - C_1/\delta$$

in which ρ is the discount factor $1/(1 + \delta)$ and δ is the discount rate. The second term is the discounted value over infinite time of the irreversible costs of species or habitat loss.

To see the value of conservation and the effect of uncertainty, take a slightly more complicated case. Suppose that the range can exist in one of two states. State one is a thorny thicket that supports only subsistence pastoralism and involves a narrow range of species. The net benefits associated with that state at time t are denoted B_t. State two is an open savanna that supports a mixed livestock/wildlife regime and involves a wide range of species. The net benefits associated with that state at time t are denoted V_t. Denote the (stationary) probability that the system is in state 1 by P. P reflects the probability that the system will be driven by exogenous shocks, perhaps by drought, to flip from the more desirable state into the less desirable state. The present value of conservation (maintenance of the system in state 2) in period $t = 0$ takes the following form:

$$PVV = V_0 + \rho(PB_1 + (1 - P)V_2) - P\rho^2C_1(1 + \rho + \rho^2 + \ldots)$$
$$+ (1 - P)\rho^2(PB_1 + (1 - P)V_2) - (1 - P)P\rho^3C_1(1 + \rho + \rho^2 + \ldots)$$
$$+ (1 - P)^2\rho^3(PB_1 + (1 - P)V_2) + \ldots$$

in which V_0 is the economic value of biodiversity conservation in period $t = 0$. $\rho_1(PB_1 + (1 - P)V_2)$ is the discounted expected value of conservation in period $t = 1$ given conservation in period $t = 0$. $P\rho^2C_1(1 + \rho + \rho^2 + \ldots) + (1 - P)\rho^2(PB_1 + (1 - P)V_2)$ is the discounted expected value of conservation in $t = 2$ given conservation in period 1. $(1 - P)P\rho^3C_1(1 + \rho + \rho^2 + \ldots) + (1 - P)^2\rho^3(PB_1 + (1 - P)V_2)$ is the discounted expected value of conservation in period $t = 3$ given conservation in period 2 and so on. Since $(1 + \rho + \rho^2 + \ldots)$ converges to $(1 + \delta)/\delta$ and since $\rho(1 + (1 - P)\rho + ((1 - P)\rho)^2 + ((1 - P)\rho)^3 \ldots))$ converges to $\rho((1 + \delta)/(\delta + P))$ we have

$$PVV = V_0 + (PB_1 + (1 - P)V_2)/(\delta + P) - PC_1/(\delta(\delta + P))$$

If the probability that the range is in state 1 is zero (the open savannah is resilient with respect to all shocks), then the present value of biodiversty conservation is

$$PVV = V_0 + V_2/\delta$$

If the probability that the range is in state 1 is one (the open savannah has lost all resilience), then the present value of biodiversity conservation is

$$PVV = V_0 + \rho(B_1 - C_1/\delta)$$

C, in this case, has been assumed to be an option value of the conservation of wild living resources. It is also possible to evaluate a problem in which conversion of the range from state 2 to state 1 generates a flow of net benefits—the returns to subsistence pastoral production in the degraded state. In this case the present value of conservation may take the form:

$$PVV = V_0 + \rho(B_1 - W_1/\delta)$$

where W_1 denotes the net benefits from exploitation of the resource in the degraded state.

The problem considered in this chapter has both elements. It is proposed to convert part of the Nyae Nyae to pastoral use, retaining the balance for wildlife. Conversion will involve an opportunity cost in the form of an social option value. Conservation will yield benefits over and above those accruing to investors and employees in wildlife-based activities. The chapter evaluates the options in the light of these non-marketed costs and benefits.

The Valuation of Non-marketed Environmental Resources

To estimate the flow of net benefits of environmental projects in which resources do not have market prices requires non-market valuation. Two methods used to estimate non-market benefits in Namibia have been the Travel Cost Method (a revealed preference approach), and the Contingent Valuation Method (a stated preference approach). The Travel Cost Method has been widely used to value benefits of improvements in recreational facilities in parks, or the value of cultural sites that are visited by people from many different places or countries. It is an extension of the theory of consumer demand and is based on the assumption that individuals from different countries bear different costs for the same quality of safaris. It is also assumed that individuals purchase different amounts of safaris. Price and the quantity of safaris demanded are then used to construct demand functions. An example is:

$$V_i/N = f(C_i, C_1, \dots C_{i-1}, C_{i+1} \dots C_m, Y)$$

where V_i/N = visits to the ith site per capita per annum; C_i = a vector of travel costs to the ith site, assumed to be a function of both distance and time spent travelling; C_j ($j \neq i$) = a vector of travel costs sites other than the ith site; and Y = a vector of incomes and other socio-economic characteristics of the population. The total consumer surplus obtained from the demand curve approximates the value of the flow of services provided by the recreational site.

The Contingent Valuation Method (CVM) is used when relevant market behaviour is not observable. It involves asking respondents hypothetical questions about their monetary valuation. of alternatives. Typically, individuals are asked how much they would be willing to pay for an environmental resource, or how much they would be willing to accept if they were deprived of the same resource, using one of the number of methods (open ended and dichotomous choice questions being the most common). The willingness-to-pay (WTP) for the conservation of biodiversity inside protected areas is generally hypothesised to depend on a set of natural attributes summarised by the vector R, i.e.:

$$WTP_{ij} = f(Y_i, P, R_j, R_1,.... R_{j-1}, R_{j+1}, ... R_K)$$

where: WTP_{ij} = willingness to pay of the ith visitor for the jth ecological characteristic; Y_i = a vector of income and other attributes of the ith visitor; P = a vector of relative prices; and R = a vector of ecological characteristics.

Where resource or other constraints make it impossible to elicit statement of preference or to infer preference from market behaviour, economists are increasingly relying on the techniques of 'benefit transfer' (Brookshire and Neill, 1992). This involves applying estimates of value derived by either revealed or stated preference methods for one decision problem in one site (the study site) to another problem at another site (the policy site). In this chapter estimates of the costs and benefits of different options involving non-marketed environmental resources have been made on this basis.

Three empirical studies undertaken in the region are pertinent to the problem in the Nyae Nyae area. The first is a financial assessment of the returns from wildlife and cattle on private ranches in Zimbabwe undertaken in the mid-1980s. This study showed revenue from cattle to be much higher than from wildlife (Z\$13.57/ha vs Z\$3.36/ha), but also that the higher costs of running cattle compared with wildlife moderated the difference in profitability between the two activities (Z\$4.52/ha vs Z\$2.93/ha).[2] Nevertheless, from a financial perspective, cattle were shown to dominate wildlife as a land use option (Jansen, 1990). The study explains why attempts to encourage local communities to make use of wildlife in the 1980s were not very successful in Zimbabwe. A combination of the lack of effective management regimes in the communal lands and the structure of market incentives meant that many local inhabitants saw little or no benefits from wildlife utilization.

Later studies of wildlife use options in Namibia (Barnes and Pearce, 1991; Barnes and de Jager, 1995) demonstrate that full consideration of the commercial and non-commercial use values of different wildlife management operations in Botswana, such as small-scale group harvesting, ostrich farming, crocodile farming, tourism, safari hunting and game ranching would make these various wildlife management options more attractive than cattle ranching. Barnes and de Jager (1995) analysed the economic and financial efficiency of land use involving wildlife on private land. They showed that financial profitability is generally low for both livestock-game production for consumptive use and wildlife production for nonconsumptive use. However, both activities were shown to be viable, and the difference between them was shown to be much narrower than in the Zimbabwe study.

Finally, a study by Barnes et al. (1997) considered the consumer surplus in the wildlife-based activities. This study involved a contingent valuation of wildlife viewing in Namibia based on surveys of tourists at government resorts both inside and outside national parks. The study estimated that foreign tourists enjoyed consumer surpluses from wildlife viewing in the order of N\$627 per tourist or N\$121.0 million per annum in aggregate. The Namibian studies, because of their proximity in time and space to the Nyae Nyae, are thought to provide a reasonable basis on which to estimate the non-marketed costs and benefits of the tourism-based land use options in the area.

5.3   WILDLIFE AND LIVESTOCK OPTIONS IN THE NYAE NYAE

The options considered here are livestock production and tourism-based wildlife conservation. Tourism-based wildlife conservation may involve either non-consumptive uses (photographic safaris) or consumptive uses (hunting safaris). Evidence from elsewhere suggests that hunting safaris may be more profitable in the Nyae Nyae, but we have used data from nonconsumptive tourism in this study. We make the following key assumptions:

a.   That biodiversity is an increasing function of the size of the area devoted to wildlife conservation;
b.   That the main benefits of wildlife conservation accrue as tourist revenue, and are an increasing function of biodiversity;
c.   That livestock should be free from predation – fences separate wildlife from livestock; and
d.   That existing livestock owners should retain rights of access to land.

Our aim, given these assumptions, is to evaluate these two options. To estimate the net benefits of the livestock proposals the study uses the Department of Environmental Affairs' livestock enterprise model together with data on former Eastern Hereroland (i.e. Hereroland East, Rietfontein and Aminius) agro-ecological region classified as 8A (Adams et al., 1990), savannah forest region. Specifically, it covers the Kaukau forest area where extensive stock farming is taking place. In benefit transfer terms, this is the 'study site'. The area is more or less similar to the Nyae Nyae: the 'policy site'. The total area is approximately 94 000 km^2 with a carrying capacity estimated at LSU/10 ha. It carried 217 971 LSU during 1996 (Livestock

Census 96), implying that it is overstocked according to DARD guidelines by 123 641 units of livestock – more than 50 per cent. This level of stocking is consistent with the open access solution, and is thought to have led to serious degradation of the range (Sardep Report). It is assumed that under the mixed wildlife/livestock option it would be possible to restrict stocking density to 1 LSU/10 ha for the policy area, instead of the stocking density observed in Eastern Hereroland.

There are currently 22 holdings in the Nyae Nyae. Each holding is provided with a borehole (Powell, 1993). The wildlife/livestock option presumes that these holdings will be enlarged and fenced off with a game-proof fence as prescribed in the revised version of the Regulation governing game-proof fencing laid down in the Government Gazette No. 55477.[3] The costs of such fencing are N$6559.86 per kilometre. To estimate fencing costs we assume that the length of fencing required for each holding is minimized. The materials cost for fencing a holding of 96 km^2 has thus been calculated at

$$\text{Cost} = \text{N\$}6559.86 \times 2\pi \sqrt{\frac{96}{\pi}}$$

Assuming a zero shadow wage rate for unskilled labour in an area of excess labour supply, we take this as our approximation of fencing costs.

Our estimates of the rate of herd growth and the costs of livestock production are drawn from the Department of Environmental Affairs' livestock enterprise model. According to the DEA model a 96 km^2 holding should be stocked at 1 LSU: 10 ha, which implies a herd size of 960 LSU per holding. The DEA assumptions about the composition of such an idealized herd are reported in Table 5.2. The costs of a herd of this size and composition are summarized in Table 5.3.

It is assumed, as already indicated, that every holding is equipped with a fully depreciated borehole and accessories. The Ministry of Water Affairs estimates the sinking of borehole and installation of engine and pipes at N$180 000 (Mr Christallus – personal communication) but this cost is not included in the estimates. It does, however, include the following operating costs: diesel fuel and lubricants at N$18 432 p.a.; maintenance to the engine and pipes at N$2400 p.a. (including a pump operators wage of N$1200 p.a. – as pump operators are skilled employees in excess demand, their wage costs are included in the cost of pump operation); and the costs of disease control at N$1195.12 p.a. This last involves vaccination for botulism (N$34.34 per 50 head of cattle), blackwater (N$25.63 per 50 calves), anthrax (N$40.87 per 100 head of cattle) and brucellosis (N$15.98 per 20 second-year heifers). Once again, the shadow wage rate for labour in herd and fence maintenance has been taken to be zero.

Table 5.2   Cattle per holding of 96 km² according to the DEA model

Herd structure	% share	Number (960)	Survival rates	Number of surviving animals	Offtake	Number of animals sold	N$ at an average of N$1500 per head
Cows	0.4	384	0.936	359.4	0.12	43.1	64 650
Calves	0.22	211.2	0.884	186.7	0	–	
1st yr heifers	0.0375	36	0.936	33.7	0	–	
2nd yr heifers	0.0375	36	0.936	33.7	0	–	
1st yr oxen	0.0375	36	0.936	33.7	0	–	
2nd year oxen	0.0375	36	0.936	33.7	0.12	4.3	6450
Bulls	0.04	38.4	0.936	35.9	0.1	3. 8	5700
Oxen	0.19	182.4	0.936	170.7	0.12	21.8	32 700
Total		960	–	887.5	–	68.7	103 050

Source: Department of Environmental Affairs' livestock enterprise models.

Table 5.3   Investment and operating costs in the DEA livestock model

	Per holding (96 km²) or 960 LSU (N$)
Initial investment	662 198.60
Boreholes	0.00
game-proof fences	65 598.60
breeding stock	59 6600.00
Annual operating costs	22 027.12
diesel fuel & lubricants	18 432.00
maintenance of water installations	1200.00
pump operator's wage	1200.00
disease control	1195.12

5.4 AN OPTIMAL MIX OF LIVESTOCK PRODUCTION AND WILDLIFE CONSERVATION

To evaluate the livestock and wildlife options in the Nyae Nyae using these data we first identify the privately optimal livestock management regime. This regime assumes that the farmer's objective is to maximize the present value of the net benefits of commercial meat production. This may not be a reasonable approximation of current farmer objectives, but we choose to make the assumption for two reasons. First, the government's development strategies for the region assume that the introduction of well defined property rights in rangeland and market opportunities will induce farmers to behave as if they were profit maximizers. Second, the financial internal rate of return on livestock production under the assumption of profit maximization defines the upper bound on the private opportunity cost of wildlife conservation. If wildlife conservation is efficient relative to livestock production under the assumption of profit-maximizing farmer objectives, then it will *a fortiori* be efficient relative to livestock production under most other farmer objectives.

In the absence of irreversible effects, alternative land uses are evaluated over a 21-year time horizon using a dynamic programming approach. To ensure that this does not result in the sale of the stock at the close of the period, the terminal value of the stock is constrained to be no less than the steady state value. That is, the farmer's problem is taken to be the following:

$$Max_u \sum_{t=0}^{20} \rho^t (pu_t - cx_t)$$

subject to

$$x_{t+1} = x_t + \alpha x_t (1 - x_t / x_{max}) - u_t$$

x_0 given

$$x_T = \frac{\left(\sum_t x_t\right)}{T}$$

Given the following values for both ecological and economic parameters

$\alpha = 0.22$ = the growth rate of livestock
$\kappa = 1920$ = the maximum carrying capacity of the range
$p = 1500$ = the sale price of livestock
$c = 22.95$ = the maintenance cost of livestock
$\rho = 1/(1+0.05)$ = the discount factor.

the privately optimal offtake policy yields, for each holding, net benefits with a present value of N$919 113.60, and a financial internal rate of return of 12.44 per cent. The time path for livestock and offtake under such a privately optimal strategy is indicated in Table 5.4.

Table 5.4　Privately optimal herd size and offtake

t	X_t	U_t	PV net benefits
0	749	0	−850 221.31
1	849	0	−27 842.13
2	954	418	538 827.33
3	641	94	102 896.71
4	641	139	153 206.55
5	596	0	−16 067.00
6	686	141	140 203.07
7	642	94	84 595.72
8	642	94	80 641.46
9	642	94	76 947.20
10	641	94	73 292.37
11	641	94	69 595.48
12	641	94	65 962.95
13	641	93	62 444.15
14	641	93	59 462.96
15	642	93	56 818.32
16	642	94	54 516.76
17	642	94	51 683.10
18	643	98	52 121.85
19	638	178	97 206.82
20	553	0	−7 178.75

Source:　Own estimates.

It is worth noting that offtake rates are higher than those recommended in the Department of Environmental Affairs' livestock enterprise model, while stocking densities are lower. It is also worth noting that the strategy is assumed to be based on the financial costs and benefits of livestock operations only. It ignores all benefits derived from the stock of cattle – draft power, milk products and so on – other than revenues derived from cattle sales (offtake). It also ignores any environmental costs or benefits of livestock production.

Our estimate of the social value of biodiversity conservation forgone through conversion, N$146/km², is significantly less than existing estimates of the value of biodiversity for other protected areas. Examples include $800/ km² for Sarawak, Malaysia (Caldecott, 1987); $106/ km² for Korup National Park (Ruitenbeek, 1989); $300/km² for Mudumalai Sanctuary, South India (Sukamar, 1989); $50–$318/km² for Ituri Forest, Zaire (Wilkie and Curran, 1991). It is, however, consistent with (a) Barnes et al.'s (1997) estimate of tourist consumer surplus from wildlife in Namibia, and (b) estimates of the value of subsistence hunting in analogous systems, for example, Murindagomo (1988). We take this to be a reasonable lower bound on the social value of wildlife conservation in the Nyae Nyae. If we include the social cost of biodiversity loss in the calculation of the return on livestock farming in the region, the internal rate of return on investment in livestock falls from 12.44 per cent to 10.06 per cent.

To calculate the NPV of options which combine wildlife conservation and livestock production taking the benefits of biodiversity conservation into account, we estimate a relation between the returns to investment in wildlife-based tourist resorts and the area committed to conservation. It is hypothesized that the net benefits of wildlife-based tourism depend on the richness of species and ecosystem diversity, and that this is an increasing function of the area committed to conservation. That is, the net revenues from tourism are hypothesized to increase with the area under conservation. Indicative support for this notion is offered by a recent survey of tourists and their preferences. A high proportion of tourists identified both variety of landscape and wildlife as the principal attractions of the area (see Table 5.5).

Table 5.5   Tourist preferences

Attraction named	Number of responses	Percentage
Unique, unspoiled nature/landscape	252	25.7
Wildlife/animals	161	16.5
Etosha National Park	88	9.0
Dunes/Namib desert	77	7.9
Game parks/natural resorts	31	3.2
Other (40 other attractions: each with < 30 responses)	368	36.6
Totals	977	100.0

Source: Barnes et al. (1997)

Net revenues from a sample of Namibian resorts have been used to estimate a net revenue–conservation area relation. This exercise is limited by the small size of the sample, but it provides at least a first approximation of the relation needed to identify what proportion of the Nyae Nyae should be committed to wildlife conservation. Table 5.6 reports the data.

Table 5.6   Net revenue and area of selected Namibian tourist resorts, 1997

Resort	Net revenues (N$)	Area (ha)
Daan Viljoen	84 021	40
Halali	2 760 059	7 000
Kaudum	31 597	3 841
Namutoni	5 726 754	7 000
Okaukuejo	4 804 113	7 000
Von Bach	23 951	42
Waterberg	318 739	405

Source: Ministry of Environment and Tourism, 1997.

The estimated model,

$$\text{Net revenue} = 39778.20 + 627.28 \text{ area}$$

is then used to generate net private and social benefits of tourism-based wildlife conservation as a function of the size of the area committed to conservation. Implicitly, the study assumes both a species-area relationship for biodiversity and a relationship between tourist revenue and area. This is supported by the findings on tourist preferences reported above. But it is also supported by existing findings on the rates of return to wildlife-based activities at the farm and conservancy level. In Namibia it has been found that financial rates of return to game viewing at the farm level (4.2 per cent) are less than half those at conservancy level (10.0 per cent) (Pearce, 1998).

Although the area is currently thought to be a low potential tourist area, we assume that it could be developed to yield a flow of benefits comparable to resorts based in conservation areas of equivalent size. The Nyae Nyae is large enough that if all land were committed to wildlife it would yield a significantly higher return than if it were committed to livestock farming. Indeed, we estimate that the economic internal rate of return on investment in tourist based conservation over the whole of the Nyae Nyae would be 23.50 per cent. However, this is not the relevant question. Given the commitment to maintain livestock production in the area, the question we pose is different. What proportion of the Nyae Nyae committed to wildlife conservation would yield a rate of return on joint use at least as great as the rate of return on investment in livestock only? That is, the problem is to identify the proportion of the area that would have to be committed to wildlife conservation in order to leave landowners no worse off than if the land was committed only to live-stock. Since we suppose that wildlife conservation will yield additional benefits in terms of the Biodiversity Convention, this division of land would be welfare-improving.

Formally, the problem we pose is the following. We wish to maximize the net present value of development of the Nyae Nyae for both livestock and wildlife by choice of the proportion of land to be committed to wildlife conservation:

$$Max_z \sum_{t=0}^{21} \rho^t(\pi_L (1 - z) + \pi_W (z))$$

where π_L and π_W denote net benefits in the livestock and wildlife sectors, respectively, and where z denotes the proportion of the Nyae Nyae com-mitted to wildlife conservation. This is subject to the constraint that the IRR of the stream of net benefits associated with wildlife conservation be equated to the IRR of the stream of net benefits associated with livestock production.

The problem is formulated as a dynamic programming problem evalu-ated over a 21 year horizon. Its solution (Table 5.7) maximizes the present value of net social benefits while satisfying the constraint on rates of return. It yields a net present value of investment in both livestock production and wildlife conservation of N$41 474 496 with an economic internal rate of return of 12.44 per cent matching the private or financial internal rate of return on livestock. The economic internal rate of return is 14.52 per cent

Table 5.7   Social net benefits of wildlife conservation in the Nyae Nyae

t	PV livestock	PV wildlife	PV joint use
NPV	14 919 609	26 554 886	41 474 496
EIRR	10.06	14.52	12.44

Source: Own estimates.

on wildlife and 10.06 per cent on livestock. At the optimum (where the present value of the net benefits of joint production is at a maximum), 69.4 per cent of the Nyae Nyae is committed to wildlife conservation. We note that any greater commitment of land to wildlife conservation would further increase the economic internal rate of return on investment.

5.5   CONCLUSIONS AND RECOMMENDATIONS

These estimates of the economic internal rate of return on the main options for developing the wildlife resources of the Nyae Nyae are consistent with other findings in the literature. In northern Namibia, for example, existing estimates of the economic internal rate of return on conservancies are 12.9 per cent for mixed livestock and wildlife, and 19.5 per cent for wildlife only (Pearce, 1998). In Zimbabwe, there is now a substantial literature on the economics of wildlife utilization (Bond, 1992, 1995; du Toit, 1992, 1994; Cumming, 1993, 1995; du Toit and Cumming 1997). A survey of 89 ranches in that country revealed economic internal rates of return of 13.1 per cent on livestock only and 21.5 per cent on wildlife only (Jansen et al., 1992; Pearce, 1999). This compares closely with our estimates for the Nyae Nyae of 12.44 per cent for mixed livestock and game and 23.5 per cent for wildlife only.

These estimates are significantly lower than those on safari hunting in the region (which are upwards of 45 per cent), but what is important is that the study has shown that if account is taken of the social benefits of biodiversity conservation the option of combining livestock intensification with tourism-based wildlife conservation will yield a higher rate of return than eliminating all wildlife and concentrating on livestock alone. These findings are sensitive to assumptions made about the size of the social opportunity cost of livestock production or wildlife conservation. For this reason the chapter has reported conservative estimates of the value of wildlife and optimistic estimates of the yield on livestock. If the argument holds for these estimates, it should hold even more strongly for less conservative estimates.

Establishment of protected areas is a requirement under Article 8 of the Convention on Biological Diversity. The Government of Namibia is already committed to the establishment of protected areas to safeguard its national biodiversity. Indeed, these comprise a higher proportion of the total land area of the country – 12.6 per cent – than in most other countries in the region. The approach described in this chapter provides a way determining the optimal proportion of the land area to commit to protection.

Article 11 of the Convention on Biological Diversity requires Contracting Parties to put in place a structure of incentives that favours biodiversity conservation. This chapter has considered the question of the optimal level of conservation in an area in which current incentives favour livestock options. Although tourism-based wildlife utilization may yield a higher economic rate of return, existing incentives encourage agro-pastoral activity. Using estimates of the economic value of livestock and wildlife obtained from the experience in the livestock and wildlife sectors in analogous areas we reach the following conclusions.

First, biodiversity conservation in the form of mixed livestock/ wildlife options is warranted on economic grounds. Corrected for the non-marketed social net benefit of wildlife, tourism based wildlife conservation in Namibia yields a higher rate of return than livestock farming. Indeed, even if all wildlife were to be removed from the region and livestock farmers were able to operate without the cost of fencing, the financial internal rate of return to livestock farmers would still be less than the economic internal rate of return on wildlife.

Second, the question of how much land to commit to conservation can fruitfully be analysed as an economic problem. In this study the point of reference has been the financial internal rate of return on investment in livestock production. We have identified the area that needs to be committed to conservation in order to yield an economic internal rate of return to wildlife that is no less than the financial internal rate of return to livestock. This is a necessary though not sufficient condition for the landowners to be indifferent between wildlife conservation and livestock production. Up to now the criteria for selection of areas to protect under the Convention have been made largely on ecological grounds. This conclusion suggests that economic criteria may be used to indicate the area that is appropriate to protect.

Third, in order to be able to create the private incentives to conserve biodiversity required under Article 11 of the Convention, it is necessary that the social benefits of conservation be capturable – a point that is frequently made in the literature on biodiversity conservation (Pearce, 1998). There are many examples of mechanisms to capture the social benefits of conservation. Hunting or photographic safari fees or royalties are two of the most common. The Communal Areas Management Programme for Indigenous Resources (CAMPFIRE) scheme established in Zimbabwe is among the best known, although it is unlikely that it would pass the test we have applied in the case of the Nyae Nyae. The precise mechanism is, however, less important than the principle.

Two key recommendations follow. The first is that a conservancy that allocates a high enough proportion of the Nyae Nyae to wildlife protection will yield a higher economic internal rate of return than the development of the area for livestock production alone, and will not require the existing population to forgo either the livestock option or access to wildlife. It may be considered to be the preferred option. The second is that the bulk of the benefits to conservation may be expected to accrue as tourism revenues (whether hunting or photographic safaris), mechanisms should be in place that enable landowners to capture a significant portion of the indirect benefits of conservation. These are necessary to provide the appropriate incentives for conservation. More particularly, the incentives should be such that the financial rate of return on wildlife conservation should be at least as great as the financial rate of return on livestock production.

NOTES

1. The conservancy idea has been borrowed from commercial farmers who have more recently began to pool their resources with their neighbours and work together to manage wildlife on their farms jointly (Jones, 1994; Barnes and de Jager, 1995).
2. Z$ denotes the Zimbabwe dollar (1984, when Z$1 = U$0.72).
3. The following is recommended game-proofing for a variety of game including rhino, kudu and others:
   - a fence of approximately 2.3 m high @ N$31.24 per pole;
   - wooden (treated) or iron reinforcing poles which are 500 m apart @ N$31.24;
   - wooden (treated) or iron middle poles which are 20 m apart N$31.24;
   - galvanized steel wire, of which the space between the first and the second is 50 mm apart and that between the second and the tenth is 100 mm apart @ N$263 per 1500 m;
   - troppers or battens which are at least 50 mm thick and at the most 2 m apart @ N$2.32 per tropper.

REFERENCES

Abelson, P. (1979), *Cost Benefit Analysis and Environmental Problems*, Sydney: Teakfield.
Adams, F. et al. (1990), *The Land Issue in Namibia: An Inquiry*, Windhoek: UNAM.
Barbier, E.B., J.C. Burgess, and C. Folke (1994), *Paradise Lost? The Ecological Economics of Biodiversity*, London: Earthscan.
Barnes, J. and D.W. Pearce (1991), 'The mixed use of habitat', mimeo, CSERGE, London.
Barnes, J. et al. (1997), 'Tourist's willingness to pay for wildlife viewing and wildlife', Research Discussion Paper No. 15, DEA, Windhoek.
Barnes, J. I. and J. L. V. de Jager (1995), 'Economic and financial incentives for wildlife use on private land in Namibia and the implications for policy', Research Discussion Paper No. 8, DEA, Windhoek.
Bond, I. (1992), 'The financial and economic returns of cattle and wildlife production systems in commercial and communal farming systems in Zimbabwe', report prepared for the Zimbabwe Wildlife Management and Environmental Conservation Programme, World Bank/Price Waterhouse.

Bond, I. (1995), 'Wildlife and livestock options for land use in Zimbabwe', in J.A. Bissonette and P.A. Krausman (eds), *Integrating People and Wildlife for a Sustainable Future. Proceedings 1st International Wildlife Management Congress*, Bethesda, MD: The Wildlife Society, pp. 203–6.

Brookshire, D.S. and H. Neill (1992), 'Benefit transfers: conceptual and empirical issues', *Water Resources Research*, **28**, 651–5.

Caldecott, J. (1987), *Hunting and Wildlife Management in Sarawak, Malaysia*, Washington, DC: World Wide Fund for Nature.

Cumming, D.H.M. (1993), 'Multispecies systems: progress, prospects and challenges in sustaining range animal production and biodiversity in East and Southern Africa', in *Proceedings VII World Conference on Animal Production*, Vol 1 (invited papers), Edmonton, Canada.

Cumming, D.H.M. (1995), 'Are multispecies systems a viable land use option for southern African savannas, in R.R. Hoffman and H. Schwartz (eds), *International Symposium on Wild and Domestic Ruminants in Extensive Land Use Systems*, Okologische Hefte der Landwirtschaftlich-Gartnerischen Fakultat Berlin, Part 2: Humbolt University, pp. 203–34.

du Toit, R. (1992), 'Large-scale wildlife management in Zimbabwe: opportunities for commercial conservation of endangered species', in W. van Hoven, H. Ebedes and A. Conroy (eds), *Wildlife Ranching : A Celebration of Diversity*, Pretoria: Promedia, pp. 295–300.

du Toit, R. (1994), *The Lowveld Conservancies: New Opportunities for Productive and Sustainable Land-Use*, Harare: Price Waterhouse, pp. 17–59.

du Toit, J. and D.H.M. Cumming (1997), 'Biodiversity in African savannas: functional significance and implications for animal production', *Proceedings of the XVIII International Grassland Congress*, Saskatoon, Canada, pp. 149–59.

GRN, Directorate of Veterinary Services (1996), *Namibia Stock Census 1996*, Windhoek: CSO.

Heywood, V. (ed.) (1995), *The Global Biodiversity Assessment*, Cambridge: Cambridge University Press.

Jansen, D.J. (1990), 'Sustainable wildlife utilisation in the Zambezi Valley of Zimbabwe: economic, ecological and political tradeoffs', Project Paper No. 10, WWF Multispecies Project, Harare.

Jansen, D.J., I. Bond and B. Child (1992) 'Cattle, wildlife, both or neither: results of a financial and economic survey of commercial ranches in Southern Zimbabwe', WWF Multispecies Animal Systems Project Paper 27, Harare: WWF.

Johansson, P. (1993), *Cost-Benefit Analysis of Environmental Change*, Cambridge: Cambridge University Press.

Jones, B. (1994), 'Community-based natural resource management', in *DRFN, Proceedings of Namibia's National Workshop to Combat Desertification*, Windhoek: DRFN.

Kiss, A. (1990), *Living with Wildlife: Wildlife Resource Management with Local Participation in Africa*, Washington DC: World Bank.

Mishra, H.R. (1994), 'A delicate balance: tigers, rhinoceros, tourists and park management in Royal Chitwan National Park, Nepal', in LA. McNeely and K.R. Miller (eds), *National Parks, Conservation and Development: The Role of Protected Areas in Sustaining Society*, Washington DC: Smithsonian Institution Press.

Munasinghe, M. and J. McNeely (1994), *Protected Areas and Policy: Linking Conservation and Sustainable Development*, Washington DC: IUCN and World Bank.

Murindagomo, F. (1989), 'Preliminary investigation into wildlife utilisation and land use in Angwa, Mid-Zambezi Valley, Zimbabwe', M. Phil. thesis, Dept. of Agricultural Economics, University of Zimbabwe, Harare.

Pearce, D.W. (1998), 'Economics and biodiversity conservation in the developing world', *Environment and Development Economics*, **4**(2).

Pearce, D.W. and D. Moran (1994), *The Economic Value of Biodiversity*, London: Earthscan.

Perrings, C. and B.H. Walker (1997), 'Biodiversity, resilience and the control of ecological economic systems: the case of fire-driven rangelands', *Ecological Economics*, **22**(1), 73–83.

Pickup, G. (1991), 'Event frequency and landscape stability on the floodplain systems of arid central Australia', *Quaternary Science Reviews*, **10**, 463–73.

Powell, N.S. (1993), 'Methods development incorporating the needs and aspirations of indigeneous people in natural resource management: a case from Eastern Bushmanland, Namibia'.

Ruitenbeek, H.J. (1989), 'Social cost-benefit analysis of the Korup Project, Cameroon', World Wide Fund for Nature Publication 3206/A 14. 1, London.

Sukamar, R. (1989), *The Asian Elephant: Ecology and Management*, Cambridge: Cambridge University Press.

Swanson, T.M. and E.B. Barbier (1992), *Economics for the Wilds: Wildlife, Wildlands, Diversity and Development*, London: Earthscan.

Tongway, D.J. and J.A. Ludwig (1989), 'Vegetation and soil patterning in semi-arid mulga lands of Eastern Australia', *Australian Journal of Ecology*, **15**, 23–34.

Walker, B.H. (1995), 'Rangeland ecology: managing change in biodiversity', in C. Perrings et al. (eds), *Biodiversity Conservation: Problems and Policies*, Dordrecht: Kluwer Academic.

Wilkie, D.S. and B. Curran (1991), 'Why do Mbuti hunters use nets?' Ungulate hunting efficiency of archers and net hunters in the Ituri rain forest', *American Anthropology*, **93**.

PART II

Macroeconomics and Biodiversity Loss:
Structural Adjustment, Deforestation and
Biodiversity Loss in Ghana

6. Forestry, deforestation and biodiversity in Ghana

James K. Benhin and Edward B. Barbier

6.1 BACKGROUND AND STATEMENT OF THE PROBLEM

A number of recent studies have analysed the relative importance of timber extraction and agricultural growth in causing tropical deforestation (see Barbier et al., 1991; Brown and Pearce, 1994; Kaimowitz and Angelsen, 1997 for a review). Some have incorporated either timber extraction or agriculture expansion in their analyses while others have attempted to include both factors in their studies. A number have looked at the way in which policy changes have impacted these two activities through their effect on prices, and how this may have aggravated the problem of deforestation in the tropics. This chapter, following the latter studies, offers a theoretical and empirical investigation of the effects of the Structural Adjustment Programme (SAP) on deforestation in Ghana during the period 1965–95. The chapter goes even further to investigate the impact of the SAP on biological diversity in the same period.

Cocoa, a cash crop, and timber are very important commodities in the economy of Ghana. The SAP introduced in Ghana in April 1983, with its realignment of relative prices, among others, aimed to increase returns from these two commodities. Maize, a food crop, is also an important commodity in Ghana. It is a staple for a majority of the population. Given the high rate (2.6 per cent – 3 per cent) of population growth and the need to reduce imports in order to correct the persistence Balance of Payments (BOP) deficits as part of the SAP, it implied that maize production had to increase to meet the increased demand from the increasing population. With the backdrop of low agricultural productivity in Ghana, any increase in cocoa and maize production involves the conversion of more land either from cocoa to maize (or vice versa) or from the tropical high forest of Ghana where these crops are mainly grown. Increased timber exploitation also involves the use of the tropical high forest, which contains most of the economic timber species. Both groups of activities may lead to forest loss in one way or another and therefore the loss of biological diversity (hereafter called biodiversity).[1] Recent evidence suggests that there is a positive correlation between species diversity and the resilience of an ecosystem[2] (Pennist, 1994). Employing the typical species–area relationship as used by ecologists (UNEP, 1995), it also implies that there is a positive correlation between forest area and the resilience of the ecosystem. This means that losses in forest area may lead to biodiversity loss, which will lead to an unstable and less resilient ecosystem.

The forest is characterized by a high level of diversity in tree and animal species and other microorganisms, which depend on each other for their existence. The interactions between plant and animal species, insects and microorganisms support certain important ecosystem functions. These include watershed protection, nutrient cycling, pollution control, soil formation and photosynthesis. These ecosystem functions are, in turn, critically important to a number of human activities. The reduction of the forest means the loss of biodiversity and a reduction in these ecosystem functions.

There is prima facie evidence that human activity such as agriculture and timber exploitation are eroding the biological resources of the forest. However, estimating the precise rates of this loss, or the current status of species, is challenging because no systematic monitoring system is in place and much baseline information is lacking (Glowka et al., 1994). Few data are also available on which genes or species are particularly important in the functioning of the ecosystem so it is difficult to specify the present and future costs of loss of the forest biodiversity. Therefore the wisest course of action is to take a 'precautionary approach' and avoid actions that needlessly reduce biodiversity, since the ecological roles played by many species or populations are still partly known. The assumption is that, given the present state of knowledge, more forest area is better than less. This is why the Convention on Biological Diversity has called for the sustainable use[3] and conservation[4] of the forest natural resources. For if properly managed, biological resources which are renewable, can support human needs indefinitely.

Sustainable use of the tropical high forest of Ghana is dependent on the economic uses of the forest. The most commonly perceived (though not the most valuable) uses of the forest are timber and agriculture production. But also of great importance are non-timber and nonagricultural products such as rattan, resin, honey, fruits and nuts. There are also the displacement uses of the forest, that is, its uses for other purposes, such as the construction of hydro dams, the building of roads, and so on. Finally, there are the uses of the forest in conservation. This includes, as already stated, key ecological functions, recreation and tourism; the option value of the future use of the forest resource; together with a number of non-use or passive use values (Barbier et al., 1991).

An economically efficient strategy for the forest should maximize the net benefits from all uses. As the Convention on Biological Diversity rightly put it, the goal should be to identify the maximum benefits derived from the many direct and indirect uses of the components of bio-logical diversity. This in turn will give policymakers the additional information they need to identify the true costs and benefits of particular policy choices. Most of the uses of the forest mentioned have market values (their benefits therefore can be estimated) with the exception of the 'conservation' uses. These non-market values of the conservation uses, as noted, are of great importance. Unfortunately, non-market values of the conservation uses of the forest are difficult to measure and not easily expressed in monetary terms, and therefore are often ignored in the cost structure of the use of the forest resources.[5] The environmental values are reduced by the use of the forest either for selective cutting or clear felling of timber and/or conversion to agriculture. But the resulting loss of bene-fits (for example, ecosystem functions due to biodiversity loss) are seldom accounted for. The increase in the production of timber and agriculture from converted forest land are influenced by economic policies, which in many cases leads to the overexploitation of the forest and subsequent biodiversity loss. This is because the same policies ignore the conservation values of forests, thus compounding the problem since the direct costs of agricultural production and harvesting are often subsidized. Moreover, many macroeconomic policies (such as prescribed by the SAP) that are designed for other purposes, such as monetary, fiscal or trade policies, can have unintended side-effects on the forest resources through posi-tively influencing the incentives to exploit timber and expand agricultural activities. The problem is that the policies may be designed to 'improve' the overall macroeconomic performance in the economy, but because of the presence of market failures, the result may be incentive effects that may worsen forest loss and subsequent biodiversity loss. Economists gen-erally refer to this as the problem of the 'second best'. Policies designed with the intention of correcting or improving fiscal, monetary or trade imbalances inadvertently exacerbate another allocative failure, such as the presence of market failures with regard to biodiversity values (Barbier et al., 1995).

An economically efficient strategy can be achieved by making those who seek to exploit the forest resource for one use or another, take into account the forgone benefits from other potential uses (Barbier et al., 1991). Article 11 of the Convention on Biological Diversity proposes adopting economically and socially sound measures that act as incentives for the conservation and sustainable use of the forest. These measures may support 'command and control measures' like timber export bans. According to the Convention, the primary shortcoming has been the failure to adequately address the underlying national and international economic forces (incentives) which drive biodiversity loss at the local level. It is recognized that in most cases the underlying causes are the private net benefits from the use and/or conversion of the forest for timber and agriculture. This is the subject of this study: to investigate the incentives to excessively use the forest resources and to consider policies that can help mitigate their negative impact on the forest area and biodiversity.

The study seeks to examine the causes and consequences of forest loss and therefore biodiversity loss in Ghana. It examines the driving forces behind and evaluates policy options for addressing the problem of biodiversity loss. It also makes recommendations for an optimal strategy for the sustainable use of the forest and therefore the conservation of biodiversity. Specific questions addressed include:

1. Determining the relative importance of cocoa, maize and timber production as causes of forest loss and biodiversity loss in Ghana;
2. Examining the underlying economic forces and other factors that have aggravated or mitigated the problem;
3. Establishing whether there is a case for trade interventions in order to mitigate the environmental effects of the trade in forest-based products; and
4. Identifying complementarities of forest conservation.

To achieve these objectives, an optimal control problem approach to renewable resources is used to derive four demand equations for forest loss, cocoa land, maize land and timber production in Ghana. In each of the three latter demand functions, estimates are derived for the underlying factors (that determine the net benefits), basically prices, and other factors that influence the demand for these three latter commodities. These estimates are then used to examine how policy changes, like the SAP and other policies, impact on the demand for cocoa land, maize land and timber production and therefore impact on forest and biodiversity loss in Ghana between the period 1965–1995. The rest of the study is as follows; the second part of this chapter examines land use, forestry and agriculture and their implications for biodiversity in Ghana; an overview of the Structural Adjustment Programme, with specific reference to agricultural and forest policies are presented in Chapter 7. The model development and estimations, and a summary of the main results and some policy implications are found in Chapter 8.

6.2 FORESTRY AND BIODIVERSITY IN GHANA

The competition between agriculture and forestry in Ghana has significant implications for forest loss. This is in view of the high dependence of agricultural production on the traditional methods of shifting cultivation and slash–burn. This stems from the inaccessibility of improved technology to most farmers in Ghana, which leads to the high dependence on nutrients from the burnt forest for increased agricultural production. Timber extraction also entails use of the forest resource. This, in normal cases, is expected to lead to minimal forest loss if done in an efficient way and on a sustainable basis. But studies have shown that this is not the case. There is overexploitation of the forest resource for timber. Unsustainable timber extraction in most cases complements agricultural production by making it easier for farmers to move into the forest area and then complete the destruction of the forest. These uses which lead to forest loss have implications for biodiversity as defined for this study. This section describes the structure/production of the three main industries that utilize the forest (forestry – timber; cash crops – cocoa; and food crops – maize) and their implications for Ghana's forest and biodiversity. The section includes a description of land use and the forest in Ghana over the past three decades; a discussion of biodiversity in Ghana's forest; a description of the trend in deforestation, forest degradation and biodiversity loss in Ghana's forest; a discussion of the causes of deforestation; a review of the forestry sector; a review of the structure/production trends of cocoa and maize and finally, some conclusions.

Ghana has a surface area of approximately 23.9 million ha. It lies in the tropics between latitude 4° and 45' North and 11° 10' North and longitude 1° 13' East and 3° 14' West. It is bounded on the North by Burkina Faso, on the South by the Gulf of Guinea, on the East by Togo and on the West by Côte d'Ivoire (Asenso-Okyere et al., 1993; ITTO, 1993).

The country can conveniently be divided into two broad ecological zones; the closed forest zone (the tropical high forest) covering approximately one-third of the country (8.3 million ha), where most of the country's economic activities (timber, cocoa, oil palm, rubber, mineral production and some food crops) are concentrated. The remaining two-thirds is covered by the savanna zone (15.6 million ha). The main economic activities in this zone are annual crops and livestock production. The tropical high forest (THF) is part of the Guineo-Congolean phytogeographical region.[6] The flora and fauna have strong affinities with the forest of Côte d'Ivoire, Liberia and Sierra Leone and a lesser affinity with Nigerian forest from which they are separated by the arid 'Dahomey gap' (ITTO, 1993).

The THF can generally be separated into two types, the rainforest and moist semi-deciduous forest whose occurrence is largely conditioned by rainfall. It can also be said to comprise of four forest types, namely (a) wet evergreen forest – 0.7 million ha, (b) moist evergreen forest – 1.9 million ha, (c) moist semi-deciduous forest – 2.2 million ha, and (d) dry semi-deciduous forest – 2.2 million ha. These four types can further be divided into seven vegetation types (see Figure 1.1 of ITTO, 1993) each with distinct associations of plant species and corresponding rainfall and soil condition (Hall and Swaine, 1981).

Land use in Ghana can be grouped under seven categories (Table 6.1). Patterns of land use have changed over the years, but data are not available to follow the trend of this change. Given that the main interest of this work is the tropical high forest, attention is turned to the land use pattern in this category (Table 6.2) and how the trend has changed over the period 1962–1990 (data for periods 1991 and beyond are not available). The years selected in Table 6.2 correspond to different phases in the political/social/economic history of Ghana. The year 1962 represents the period immediately after independence; 1966–69 represents the first change in government by a military coup and the beginning of the economic crisis; 1977–78 represents the height of the economic crisis; and 1984, is the period immediately after the bushfires in 1982/83, the deportation of more than one million Ghanaians from Nigeria and the introduction of the Structural Adjustment Programme. Discussions on the trend in each land use in the tropical forest areas follows.

Table 6.1   General land use in Ghana

	Area	
	(million ha)	%
Forest reserves	2.6	11
Wildlife reserves	1.2	5
Unreserved high forest	0.5	2
Savannah woodlands	7.1	30
Tree crops	1.7	7
Annual crops	1.2	5
Unimproved pasture	3.6	15
Bush fallow and other uses	6.0	25
Total	23.9	100

Source: Forestry Department (undated), 'Ghana – progress towards the year 2000: sustainable management of tropical forests', unpublished, Accra.

Table 6.2   Land use in the tropical high forest of Ghana, 1962–90

Type of land use	1962 (km²)	(%)	1966–69 (km²)	(%)	1977–78 (km²)	(%)	1984 (km²)	(%)	1990 (km²)	(%)
Reserve forests	15185	18.5	15571	18.9	16788	20.41	16788	20.41	16788	20.41
Unreserved forests (potential farmland and private/commercial forests)	9283	11.3	6147	7.5	1674	2.03	606	0.74	308	0.37
Total forests	24468	29.8	21717	26.4	18462	22.44	17394	21.15	17096	20.78
Other lands (cocoa and food/farms/ bush/fallow)	57791	70.2	60542	73.6	63797	77.56	64865	78.85	65163	79.22
Total	82259	100	82259	100	82259	100	82259	100	82259	100

Source: Forestry Department (1962, 63,..., 1990), Annual Report of the Forestry Department, Accra.

Reserve Forests

The need for action to combat deforestation was the primary rationale for the establishment of the Forestry Department in Ghana in 1909, and with it the creation of forest reserves beginning in the 1920s and 1930s. There are now approximately 280 forest reserves in Ghana, of which 214 are in the high forest zone (see Figure 1.2 of ITTO, 1993). The remainder are in the Savannah zone. From Table 6.2, the reserves constitute about 20 per cent of the area of the high forest. They are duly constituted under the Forest Ordinance Caption 157. Most reserves were established in hilly and swampy areas and in watersheds. The reserves were created to serve two main functions – protective (comprising 47.73 per cent) and production (52.25 per cent) functions (Foggie, 1957, 1962; Foggie and Piaseck, 1962). Three main protective functions were envisaged:

a. Barrier reserves to prevent the savannah from spreading into forest country;
b. Headwater reserves, needed to protect the soil, prevent serious erosion and maintain water supplies. These were usually established in hilly regions where rivers have their source and where erosion of hillsides is a danger; and

c. Shelter belt reserves, needed to create a minimum or maintain climate
    condition favourable to agricultural crops, for example, cocoa pro-
    duction. In addition, they are to shelter neighbouring countries from
    winds (especially the dry harmattan) and thus maintain atmospheric
    humidity.

In terms of productive functions, the reserves were to circumscribe and
protect stocks of timber trees for careful management, and to protect
stocks of non-timber forest produce for the villages surrounding the
forests. Today, the reserves hold all that is left of Ghana's forest.

Hawthorne and Abu Juam (1993) have assessed the botanical diversity
of the forest reserves. Species were scored for their genetic rarity and
degree of threat from exploitation (Appendix 6.1). A 'genetic heat index'
(GHI) and 'economic index' (EI) were calculated from the weighted averages of the species scores from forest samples (see Figures 1.3 and 1.4 of
ITTO (1993) for a description of the variation of GHI and EI across the
high forest of Ghana). A high GHI signifies that the area is relatively rich
in species which are internationally rare in that area while a high EI area
signifies that the area is relatively rich in species threatened in Ghana by
over exploitation. This is in spite of the fact that the area under reserves,
as shown in Table 6.2, seems to be relatively constant. Increases after
1969 are due to new demarcation of forest reserves, pressure to exploit
reserves has grown and now virtually all have been logged at some time.
Table 6.3 shows the condition of the forest reserves as assessed by
Hawthorne and Abu Juam (1993). About half of the reserved forest,
some 9000 km^2, is in reasonable condition (condition 1 to 3) and the
remainder is 'mostly degraded' or worse. There is a general increase in
forest disturbance from the wetter to the drier forest areas. This is a consequence both of greater fire and logging damage (it should be noted
however that a significant portion of the reserves in the northern 'transition zone' was not forested at the time of the reservation in the 1920s and
1930s). It is clear however that, while reserve boundaries have been
largely protected and respected, the condition of the reserves within is
very variable, and in many cases deteriorating.

From the 1950s increasing areas of the reserve forests were exploited
under the 'selection system' (Baidoo, 1970, 1976; Asabere, 1987).
'Protection Working Circles' areas (PWCs) were set aside within the production forest reserves, usually because they were not loggable or too
poor in economic species. Other parts of the forest reserves were designed
for conversion or research (or, most often, both) but these were usually
vaguely and temporary defined management amounts. Some PWCs were
to be protected 'in perpetuity' but, even in these, District Officers had dis-

Table 6.3   The status of the forest reserves: areas of forest by reserve condition and zone

Forest zone	Condition (area) in km^2 and percentage of zone total						
	(1) Excellent (km^2) (%)	(2) Good (km^2) (%)	(3) Partly degraded (km^2) (%)	(4) Mostly degraded (km^2) (%)	(5) Very bad (km^2) (%)	(6) No forest (km^2) (%)	Total area (km^2)
WE (–ME)	346 15.7	1239 56.3	617 26.0	0 0	0 0	0 0	2202
ME (–MS)	0 0	1134 20.6	2531 46.1	633 11.5	192 3.5	1002 8.2	5492
UE (–MS)	0 0	0 0	661 99.4	0 0	4 0.6	0 0	665
MS-SE	0 0	34 1.9	1144 63.5	358 19.9	218 2.1	48 2.7	1802
MS-NW (–DS)	0 0	75 1.8	1224 30.1	1584 39.0	878 21.6	305 7.5	4066
DS	0 0	0 0	5 0.2	986 29.9	1316 39.9	991 30.1	3298
SM	0 0	3 1.9	0 0	3 1.9	18 11.4	134 8.5	158
SO	0 0	0 0	8 12.9	54 87.1	0 0	0 0	62
Total	346 1.9	2485 14.0	6190 34.9	3618 20.4	2626 14.8	2480 14.0	17745

Notes

Forest zones (after Hall and Swaine, 1981)

WE = Wet evergreen forest zone

ME = Moist evergreen forest zone

UE = Upland evergreen

MS-NW = Moist semi-deciduous (north-west subtype) forest zone

MS-SE = Moist semi-deciduous (south-east subtype) forest zone

DS = Dry semi-deciduous forest zone

SM = Southern marginal forest zone

SO = Southern outlier forest zone

Reserve conditions. Each reserve was given a single score.

(1) = EXCELLENT with few signs (<2%) of human disturbance (logging/farming or fire damage) with good canopy and virgin or late secondary forest thoughout.

(2) = GOOD with <10% heavily disturbed. Logging damage restricted or light and well dispersed. Fire damage none or peripheral.

(3) = SLIGHTLY DEGRADED. Obviously disturbed or degraded and usually patchy, but with good forest dominant. Max. 25% with serious scars and poor regeneration; max. 50% slightly disturbed, with broken upper canopy.

(4) = MOSTLY DEGRADED. Obviously disturbed and patchy, but with bad forest predominant; 25–50% serious scars but max. 75% of heavily disrupted canopy. Or forest lightly burnt through out.

(5) = VERY POOR. Forest with coherent canopy <25% (more than 3/4 disturbed), or more than half the forest with serious scars and poor or no forest regeneration; or almost all heavily burnt with conspicuous *Eupatorium* and other pioneers throughout.

(6) = NO SIGNIFICANT FOREST LEFT. Almost all deforested with savanna, plantation or farm etc; <2% good forest; 2–5% very disturbed forest left; or 5–10% left in extremely poor condition, for example, as scattered trees or riverine fragments. Remnants with little chance of surviving 10 years.

Source: ITTO (1993).

cretionary powers to permit logging or other activities. With no rational framework for the protection in the first place, this led to the increasing disturbance of the PWCs, particularly during the mid-1960s and early 1980s. On paper, the PWCs cover about one-third of the forest reserves but less than half of this supports undisturbed forests today.

The period of decline in the mid–late 1960s and to the early 1980s applied to the whole economy, not only to the management of natural resources. Although the economic collapse towards the end of this period probably helped protect some forest from logging, overexploitation had previously been rife, and legal and illegal farms proliferated inside some reserves (Martin, 1991). Large areas of forest reserves – sometimes of healthy forests – were lost to farms through the encouragement of *taungya*[7] (the *taungya* system was discontinued in 1987).

With generally limited support and control this amounted to little more than legalized deforestation because of the conflict of interest between trees and crops. For example, some reserves in the western region of the country have suffered seriously from 'illegal' farming and now virtually support no forest. Mass 'disobedience' leading to complete deforestation has also occurred in the Volta region reserves due to high demand for farmlands, associated partly with the movement of dispossessed people prior to the damming of the Volta Lake in the early 1960s, which is estimated to have submerged portions (about 149 km[2]) of the six neighbouring forest reserves (Forestry Dept, 1964).

In conclusion, it can be observed that even though the area for forest reserves shows a relatively constant figure for the periods reviewed, much has been degraded through illegal logging, bad logging practices and legal and illegal farming activities.

Unreserved Forest

Information is ambiguous with respect to areas of intact closed forest outside reserves. Estimates vary from 3700 km[2] (Nsenkyire, 1992) to 2700 km[2] (World Bank, 1987a) to 1000 km[2] (IUCN, 1992), while others (Hawthorne, 1990; and Norton, 1991) estimate that closed canopy forest outside reserves may comprise as little as a fifth of this latter amount, much of it as small scattered patches in swamps and sacred groves.

Unreserved forests, however, have generally been planned for conversion to agriculture. Virtually all of the unreserved forests have been converted to farmlands and fallow areas, in most cases after the timber has been extracted. Table 6.2 shows the rapid decline of unreserved forest from about 11.3 per cent of total closed forest area in 1962 to 0.4 per cent in 1990. It is estimated by the Forestry Department that about

389 km^2 in 1962, 1658 km^2 in 1966–69, 1554 km^2 in 1977–78, 120 km^2 in 1984 and 25 km^2 in 1990 of unreserved forest in the closed forest area was lost to farming (Forestry Dept., 1962–1990). It must be noted that these figures have decreased over the period not because the demand for the unreserved forest for agriculture has been falling but because the amount of unreserved forest has dwindled rapidly as shown in Table 6.2. This reflects the concern for the reserve forest. Because of the loss of unreserved forest, farmers are and have been increasingly diverting their attention to the reserved forests leading to illegal farming and degradation of reserved forests.

Forest Plantations

Forest plantations in Ghana date back to the first decade of this century when some were established in the Guinea savanna woodland (IUCN, 1992). In 1960, the FAO proposed a national forest plantation estate of 59 000 km^2 commencing with the planting of 50 km^2 in 1968 (FAO/UNEP, 1981). In the late 1960's a national Land Use Planning Committee revised the objectives downwards and targeted an estate of 1100 km^2 to be established over a 10 year period from 1970/71 (Nsenkyire, 1992). Many of the plantations were planned through the *taungya* system in forest reserves. It has been estimated that approximately 500 km^2 of plantation has been established by the state in the high forest zone to date of which 165 km^2 (33 per cent) is considered successful (Apumasuh, 1992). In addition to the above estimates, Ghana has about 112 km^2 of rubber plantation (General, 1993). It is, however, realized that plantations successfully established to date cover a very insignificant area. It therefore cannot be relied upon to provide for the ever increasing demand on forest resources. The implication is that the natural forest will still be under increasing threat from increased demand for timber and timber products, with ramifications for the forest and biodiversity.

Very few species have been planted in forest plantations and for one of many reasons only few have thrived. The most commonly planted species are emire (*Terminalia ivorensis*), wawa (*Triplochiton scleroxylon*), Central American cedar (*Cedrela odorata*) and teak (*Tectona grandis*). These were chosen because they establish readily under plantation conditions and grow rapidly. Afromosia (*Pericopsis elata*) has also been subjected to trials because of its very high value. However, no plantations exist; the trials did not prove to be productive and the species grows very slowly. Similarly, other valuable species, most notably mahogany (*Khaya ivorensis*) and iroko (or odum) (*Chlorophora/Milicia excelsa*) have been omitted due to difficulty in gaining establishment because of insect pests

(Friends of the Earth, 1992; Jones, 1970). Referring to Appendix 6.1 and 6.2, emire is one of the species classified as under serious threat from heavy exploitation and will be extinct in about 30 years' time. Plantations are therefore a step in the right direction to avoid this problem. However, given the rate of establishment of forest plantations this objective may not be achieved.

Other Lands

These are mainly areas under cash and food crops and fallow lands. Table 6.2 shows that this area has increased rapidly over the period 1962–1990. Unfortunately, what is not estimated is the level of infiltration into the reserved forest, which may be very substantial. It is true that farm and fallow lands may still hold some forest resources due to the nature of dominant farming systems in the high forest zone.[8] However, the fact that most of the trees have been removed (not all of the studies have been able to estimate how many trees remain on the farms they studied or whether they are reasonably substantial) and burnt to make room for cocoa and other crops has, in itself, degraded the biodiversity of the natural forest. Moreover, the combination of factors such as the neglect of most of these cocoa farms and the conversion of most of these farms to food crops during the period of economic crisis, the bush fires in 1982/83, and the movement of people, mostly to the high forest zones, have rendered and continue to render most of these farms and fallow lands and the forest itself bare of trees.

6.3   BIODIVERSITY LOSS AND DEFORESTATION

The tropical high forest of Ghana, as with other Guinea-Congolean tropical forest, is extremely heterogenous. The wet evergreen forest is the most floristically rich while the drier southern marginal forest is species-poor. The moist evergreen and moist semi-deciduous forest zones are the most important for commercial purposes. Different surveys have shown different results of tree species in the high forests but all confirm the high diversity of Ghana's plant species. Some 2100 plant species have been recorded, 23 of them endemic (Hall and Swaine, 1981). Another study also recorded 730 tree species, of which 680 attain a diameter of 5 cm or more at breast height (Hawthorne, 1989). Results from a recent national forest inventory (1989) also recorded 680 tree species of which 420 species grow to timber size, with about 126 of them in sufficient quantities for exploitation. These are grouped into four classes:

Class I   consist of species of major economic value;
Class II   consists of species of minor economic value;
Class III consists of species of possible economic value; and
Class IV   comprises of the remaining species, which have no
           economic value.

The first three classes form only about 9 per cent of the total species recorded. This implies that diversification of trees extracted will help conserve the forest diversity because it will reduce the overextraction of these few species.

The fauna of the forest zone also include more than 200 species of mammals, many of which are rare or endangered, including bongo (*Tragelaphus eurycerus*), Ogilby's duiker (*Cephalophus ogilbyis*), golden cat (*Felis ourat*), chimpanzee (*Pantroglodytes*), forest elephant (*Loxodonta africana cyclotis*), and the pygmy hippopotamus (*Choeropsis liberiensis*) (Mensah-Ntiamoa, 1989). The rainforest zone also supports 74 species of bats, 37 species of small rodents, a variety of reptiles and over 200 species of birds (IUCN, 1992). In addition the forest performs key ecological functions (Barbier et al., 1991).

As already stated, in the savannah woodland zone, very few species of current commercial interest occur in contrast to the closed forest zone. These productive forests have an important function in the production of building poles, fence posts, fuelwood, charcoal, fodder and medical plants.

Deforestation, Forest Degradation and Biodiversity Loss

Forest loss or deforestation in Ghana has been so extensive and rapid that it is becoming increasingly difficult to obtain precise figures for the country's present forest cover and rates of deforestation (Friends of the Earth, 1992). The forest reserves now contain most of the country's remaining tropical moist forest, most of which exist in isolated fragments (Figure 6.1). Comparing the two diagrams in Figure 6.1, one can see the extent to which the forest reserves and forests in general in Ghana have been depleted. Repetto (1988) put the annual rate of deforestation during the period 1981–1985 at 1.3 per cent. The same figure is estimated by the FAO (1995) for the period 1986–1990, but current estimates are as high as 2 per cent a year (Keeling, 1991).

The current state of the deforestation process, which began accelerating about a century ago, reached a peak in the 1950s through to the 1970s. About one-third of Ghana's forest is estimated to have disappeared in the 17 years between 1955 and 1972 (Hall, 1987). It is estimated that the average annual rate of deforestation since the turn of the century is $750\,km^2$

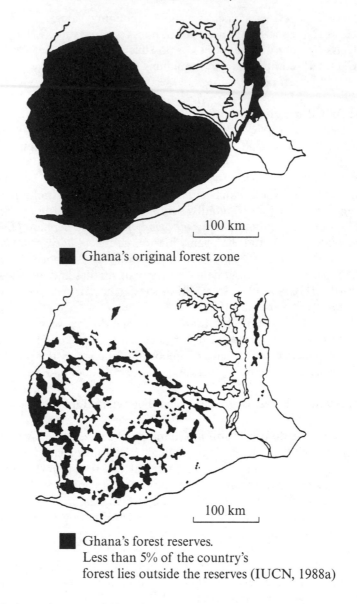

100 km

■ Ghana's original forest zone

100 km

■ Ghana's forest reserves.
Less than 5% of the country's
forest lies outside the reserves (IUCN, 1988a)

Note: Only the southern part of Ghana is shown.

Source: Friends of the Earth (1992).

Figure 6.1   Ghana's forest reserves and the extent of original forest cover

(World Bank, 1976). It is also estimated that this figure slowed down in the 1980s to about 220 km² (FAO, 1988; IUCN, 1992) and is now likely to remain low since all but a tiny fraction of the closed canopy forest outside the reserves has been converted, primarily to farmlands. This last estimate does not seem to support the trend. The evidence shows increasing extraction of timber in the second half of the 1980s and early 1990s, which should be associated with greater use of the forest and therefore increasing forest loss. It, is however, possible that in the said period more timber was extracted from previously logged areas. In addition, with the implementation of the Structural Adjustment Programme, there has been increased inflow of capital to the forest sector which may have led to improved efficiency in timber extraction such that more logs are being extracted per hectare of forest area. If this reasoning behind the fall in the estimated rate of forest loss is not true, then the rate of deforestation is being underestimated, with detrimental consequences for the forest.

More than 90 per cent of Ghana's forests have been logged since the 1940s (IUCN, 1988a). Primary forests in the country all but disappeared more than a decade ago (Plumtre et al., 1991). In 1992, the IUCN estimated that there was about 15 000 km² of 'intact closed forest' remaining in Ghana (IUCN, 1992). Another study by Hawthorne and Abu Juam (1993) showed that only 9000 km² of the reserve forest is in reasonable condition and the remainder is 'mostly degraded' or worse. A study by the International Institute for Environment and Development (IIED, 1988), conducted on behalf of ITTO, found that in 1988 timber concessions covered 50 000 km² of the country. Of those in the reserves, only about 4000 km² of unlogged productive high forest is left. The remaining concessions falling outside forest reserves have been logged and probably converted to agriculture. (This may explain why in spite of the increased timber extraction (see Figure 1.5 of ITTO, 1993) estimates of forest loss show a falling trend). Many (Chachu, 1989; Plumtre et al., 1991; Frimpong-Mensah, 1989) have observed that forestry in Ghana is presently unsustainable and the World Bank Forestry Department observed that Ghana's forests were being cut at twice the annual allowable (sustained yield) rate of 1.1 million cubic metres (World Bank, 1988).

In 1989, an inventory of more than 5000 km² of Ghana's tropical moist forest, sponsored by the UK Overseas Development Agency (ODA), was completed (Wong, 1989). The inventory undertook a comprehensive survey of 14 species, covering most of the main grades of exported hardwoods. The survey found that the extraction rate of the traditional export timbers was far greater than their annual growth, giving them a limited 'resource life' (Table 6.4). Afromosia (*Pericopsis elata*) was found to have been completely exhausted. Iroko-odum (*Chlorophora/Milicia excelsa*), a species which has never been common in the country, would also become exhausted within 10 years at current rates of exploitation but it was and continued to be exported in large volumes. Of about 350 tree species that grow to marketable size in the high forest (World Bank, 1988) only 60 were traded between 1972 and 1989 and a mere 12 species accounted for 90 per cent of exports (Oldfield, 1991).

Table 6.4   Resource life of Ghana's traditional export species

Type of species	Years
Iroko (odum)	10
Edina	18
Sapele	25
Utile	20
Mahogany	20
Afromosia	0
Wawa	114

Source: Alder (1989), in Wong (ed.) (1989).

Afromosia and iroko (odum) are listed in the report of the 5th session of the United Nations Food and Agriculture Organization (FAO) panel of experts on forest gene resources as 'endangered' species in West Africa (Oldfield,1988). The IUCN Threatened Plants Unit also lists afromosia as 'vulnerable', while the US National Academy of Sciences (1979) considered the species to be facing biological extinction in the region (Oldfield, 1991). Furthermore, the IUCN's Threatened Plants Unit database lists ten timber species in Ghana that are of conservation concern (including afromosia, and *Talbotiella genti* – the only truly endemic species in the country which is being endangered by plantation programmes). The increasing concern over the future conservation of afromosia has prompted both Governments of the UK and Denmark (with the support of the Government of Ghana), to propose that the species is listed under the Convention on International Trade in Endangered species of Wild Fauna and Flora (CITES) (Oldfield, 1991).

Other studies of tree species using reserve–harvest profiles, predict dramatic falls in the future availability of groups of tree species termed *Scarlet Red Star*[9] and *Normal Red Star*[10] species. According to an estimation by an ITTO (1993) study, if the present levels of timber harvesting are maintained over a period of 30 years, the annual harvest of *Scarlet Red* and *Normal Red Star* species will fall by 26%. And in the longer run, only very few species in these two groups will avoid commercial extinction. Moreover, total annual harvest of reserves is predicted to fall from about 405 000 m³ over a period of 50 years and later stabilize at about 268 000 m³. This represents a clear pathway towards a degraded forest estate from which the industry can extract essentially only the lower value species (wawa, *Pink-Red Star*[11] and 'other species'). This implies high biodiversity loss and negative ecological effects.

Off-reserve harvest profiles, constructed from a more meagre set of available information compared to on-reserve (as inventory data and growth estimates were not available), also indicated that all the current most valuable species will be logged out in 20 years' time. This will be caused by a total collapse in the harvest of *Scarlet Red* and *Normal Red Star* species, which may be compensated, to a limited degree, by a moderate rise in the harvest of some *Pink-Red Star* and other species. Furthermore, over 20 years, the harvest of wawa is also expected to fall drastically. After 20 years and beyond, the total annual harvest will continue to fall slightly and stabilize at around 557 000 m³, however, by then most of the important species (*Scarlet Red* and *Normal Red Star*) will be extinct (Appendix 6.2).

The increasing loss of Ghana's forest and tree species have implications for the variety of fauna in the forest. The first reaction of many animals during and after logging operations and farming activities is, in the short term, to move away (Burgess, 1971). This disrupts the complex interrelationships between plants and animals which in turn, greatly influences the mechanisms (and rates) of regeneration, reproduction and speciation in tropical forests. A variety of faunae are increasingly becoming rare in Ghana as a result of declining forests. Some of these faunae, already mentioned elsewhere, include Ogilby's duiker, forest elephant, bongo, giant forest hogs, several small antelopes, diverse primates (including chimpanzee and three species of colobus monkey) plus some species of bats and small rodents. Ghana also possesses several of West Africa's rarest birds, including a dozen species dependent on undisturbed forest (Burgess, 1971). According to Martin (1991), one species of primate, red colobus (*Colobus badius*) must be severely endangered because of the widespread timber exploitation in West Africa which reduces its habitat. The IUCN (1988) also lists the species as endangered. One study of the red colobus confirmed that 43 per cent of the primate's diet comes from commercial timber species (Martin, 1990), while another study observed that 25 per cent of the diet of the Ghanaian red colobus comes from five important species of timber trees – mahogany, iroko (odum), sapele, utile and makore (all *Scarlet Red* species) (Olsen and Curtin, 1984). The red colobus is a leaf-eating specialist (Struhsaker and Oates, 1975) and relies very heavily on the canopy for movement and shelter and thus disappears from logged forests.

The diana monkey (*Cercopithecus diana*), which Martin (1991) also considers to be endangered, feeds largely on tree species of which 20 per cent are commercially valuable, iroko and antiaris are particularly important (Olsen and Curtin, 1984). While the species does exist in secondary (disturbed) forests, it soon disappears once hunting pressure increases, a common problem in overlogged areas (Martin, 1991).

The very small and declining population of forest elephants (*Loxondonta africana cyclotis*) in Ghana (Martin estimates that, in 1987, there were only 1100 elephants left in Ghana, and of these, at least half are likely to be savanna elephants) is considered to have very severe repercussions for the natural (and sparse) regeneration of a very important timber species, makore (*Tieghemella heckelii*) and others of potential commercial interest (Hall and Swaine, 1981). These are all trees with large seeds which are known to be dispersed only by sizeable mammals. The elephant is known to favour fruits from the makore, and the seed passes through the animal's intestine unharmed and germinates very successfully in its dung (Martin, 1991).

The overall consequence of elephant loss on the composition, richness and diversity of plant species in Ghana's forest may be substantial. In neighbouring Côte d'Ivoire, 30 per cent of the seeds of tree species and 41 per cent of the seeds of tree individuals are dispersed by elephants (Alexandre, 1978). Furthermore, the decline of natural elephants browsing tracks and pathways in primary forest is one reason cited for the now very small population of white-breasted guineafowls (*Agelastes meleagrides*) which exist only in open floors beneath closed, canopy forest (Kingdom, 1990). Another reason cited for the reduction in the numbers of this bird, is logging (Kingdom, 1990; ICBP/IUCN, 1985). The IUCN considers the White-breasted Guineafowl to be endangered throughout West Africa (IUCN, 1988b).

Other species which disperse fruits and seeds, and which are vulnerable to logging throughout West Africa, include, the pygmy hippo (*Choeropsis lieriensis*) and the giant forest hog (*Hyclochoerus meinertzhagen*) (Martin, 1991). The absence of such feeding specialists will greatly influence the natural regeneration particularly for those species where seed, seedling or sapling mortality is high close to the parent tree (usually because of insect predation but also natural autotoxicity). In such instances, seed dispersal is vital. For example, saplings of idigo/framire (*Tenninalia ivorensis*) are unable to mature anywhere near a full-grown parent tree of the same species (Kingdom, 1990).

The International Council for Bird Preservation (ICBP) and the IUCN observe that the rate of forest destruction in Africa, west of the Dahomey gap, is so severe that any bird species endemic to primary forest in this region must now be considered gravely at risk (ICBP/IUCN, 1985). As well as the white-breasted guineafowl, the organizations list other Ghanaian bird species that fall into this category: rufous fishing owl (*Scotopelia ussher*), western wattled cuckoo-shrike (*Campephaga lobata*), yellow-throated olive greenbul (*Criniger Olivaceus*) and white-necked picathartes (*Picarthartes gymnocepallus*).

In a recent survey in the Cameroon forest, it was found that there are still some species of faunae which are unknown. Such species could be driven to extinction by the destruction of the forest without any knowledge of their existence and extinction. These faunae may perform some very important ecological and other functions. The same may apply to the forests in Ghana, but this is conjecture.

In addition, forest disturbance, by excess timber exploitation and/or farming activities, can radically change the microclimate of the area. The rapid transformation to a more open, dry and sunlit environment has disruptive effects on wildlife and the natural regeneration (succession) of trees. Logging has been shown to cause rapid but aberrant, rank secondary growth overtopping the usual colonizers of more natural gaps in the forest canopy (Jacobs M, 1988) Large-scale mechanized logging operations, currently practised throughout the tropics, can retard natural succession of primary tree species by as much as 20 years.

Soils become compacted and new seed banks and seedlings are destroyed under heavy logging equipment (Gartland, 1990; Ewel and Conde, 1978). Nutrient loss is significantly higher on exposed soils than under a heavy canopy (Garcia, 1981). Such events will further slow regeneration and influence species composition during succession. Moreover, according to the World Bank (1989), soil erosion in Ghana under shifting cultivation (a phenomenon that so often follows logging) exceeds that for natural forest by a factor of twelve (depending on the slope and the types of soil, forest losses are approximately six tons or less per hectare a year compared to seventy tons or more in areas under this sort of cultivation). Water courses can be greatly affected through siltation.

In addition to the above, deforestation and biodiversity loss also impact on the livelihood of local people. Non-timber forest products play an important part in everyday lives of many Ghanaians, particularly in rural areas (Friends of the Earth, 1992; World Bank, 1988). Roughly 75 per cent of the population regularly eats bushmeat, as well as a wide range of forest fruits. Plants are often used in construction or in the production of other goods (such as mats, baskets, furniture, dyes, resins and gums). The rural population (almost without exception) relies on the use of traditional medicine, which is based on forest plants, as their main (and often only) source of health care (World Bank, 1988). Approximately 2000 plants are used locally for various ailments. A number of forest plants are also presently being exported from Ghana to be manufactured into medicine in Europe (Abbiw, 1990). These benefits will be lost through excessive timber extraction and farming activities.

Causes of Deforestation and Forest Degradation

Forest loss in Ghana has been caused by the interaction of different complex factors: social, cultural, political and economic. The main proximate (direct) causes of forest loss in Ghana are fire, mining and quarrying, plantation strategy, and, more importantly, logging and farming (ITTO, 1993).

According to Hawthorne and Abu Juam (1993), fire has degraded or destroyed about 30 per cent of the moist semi-deciduous zone, much of it in the early 1980s. It is also estimated that about 4 million m^3 of high quality timber (redwoods and odum) were destroyed in the fires of 1982/83 (Hawthorne, 1991). It is also said that the state of the cocoa estates in the late 1970s and early 1980s promoted the passage of fire. The government's strategy in the 1970s of extracting maximum revenue from cocoa production and the resulting perennial low producer price led to a lack of replanting and improvement of cocoa stock. The effect was much neglected, weed inundated and combustible cocoa plantations throughout the high forest zone.

Small-scale mining for gold and diamonds and large-scale mining for bauxite, manganese and gold is a localized source of deforestation. Gold surface mining in particular continues to pose a considerable threat to forests, especially in the wet evergreen zone. Surface mining is detrimental to all aspects of the forest in that not only the forest biomass, but also the soil is removed. The main causes of forest loss have, however, been agriculture and timber production.

Plantations have replaced the biologically richest natural forest (Hawthorne and Abu Juam, 1993). This has led to biodiversity loss because of the homogeneous nature of the species planted. But even where natural forest is selectively logged, the effects have been severe.

Logging in recent decades has been more intense in the semi-deciduous than in the evergreen zones due mainly to the greater densities of desirable timber trees in the former. The forest reserves in these drier zones are today in very poor conditions partly because logging practices have encouraged the spread and intensification of the effects of fire (Hawthorne, 1989). 'Salvage felling' which allowed unlimited felling of the largest, or 'over-mature', trees on a 15-year felling cycle in the 1970s and the 'creaming' of high value species before the 1979 log export ban, took a devastating toll on total forest cover and quality in that period. Overcutting has been exacerbated by high levels of waste in timber extraction.

A recent survey by the Oxford Forestry Institute (OFI), in association with the Timber Research and Development Association (TRADA), laid much of the blame for the depletion of the forest on loggers and the export market. The report stated that 'extensive logging, legal and illegal, mainly for export did much damage when relatively uncontrolled ... Every timber processing company's prime concern is to get enough of the species it requires. This is an essential prerequisite for operating effectively and short-term pressures are often so intense that affirmation of belief in sustainability needs treating with caution' (Plumtre et al., 1991). Other observers, most notably Hawthorne (1989), have concluded that while harvesting operations showed few signs of severely damaging the forest, logging would, in all probability, make the area more susceptible to fire. This subject has been little studied in Africa but other research, most notably in the Amazon (Uhl and Katiffinan, 1990), in Sabah, east Malaysia (Woods, 1989) and in Kalimantan, Indonesia (Malingreau et al., 1985) has found a strong positive and causal relationship between logging and fire frequency. (Recent fires in the forest of Indonesia in 1997 confirm these observations.) Logging also makes the forest more accessible to farmers, which exacerbates the problem. Martin (1991) confirms that in West Africa countries, logging roads are the real reason why 90 per cent of the slash–burn activities by immigrant farmers is concentrated in exploited areas.

According to a 1988 IIED report, in addition to normal logging activities, commercially exploited areas have been repeatedly re-logged instead of being allowed to recover. Concession areas have also been too small to allow for effective and efficient management (in one case, as small as two square kilometres) and felling cycles too short (often 15 years, instead of 40). The lack of resources has made it impossible for the Forestry Department to control and manage the forest effectively (IIED, 1988).

Overcutting has been exacerbated by the very high levels of waste in timber processing and the inefficient extraction methods used in logging due to antiquated plant and machinery. Wastes associated with harvesting operations may be as high as 50 per cent while the lumber volume is invariably only 25–40 per cent of the log volume extracted (see Appendix 3 of Friends of the Earth, 1992; Chachu, 1989). The Forestry Department also observes that for every utilizable volume of wood removed from Ghana's forest, an equal volume is left waste (Chachu, 1989). Furthermore, according to the forest manager of African Timber and Plywood Company (AT&P), one of the country's largest state-owned forestry enterprises, 30–50 per cent of the forest canopy is lost when only 25 cubic metres of log (approximately two to three trees) are extracted per hectare (Nash, 1990). From an HED survey of 13 saw millers (representing 34 per cent of the processed volume), an average overall recovery factor of 37 per cent was calculated, although there is considerable variation around this mean. This may be compared with an international 'standard' of some 58 percent. For example, in 1992 some $1\,014\,000\,\text{m}^3$ were processed into an estimated $405\,600\,\text{m}^3$ lumber, plywood, veneer and other products. With a 58 per cent recovery factor some $700\,000\,\text{m}^3$ would have produced the same quantity of processed products. Thus an estimated extra $314\,000\,\text{m}^3$ was used due to the lower recovery rate (see Appendix 12, p. 3 of ITTO, 1993).

Outside reserves, logging has never been restricted beyond vague enforcement of minimum girth. Most logging off-reserves has been seen as extraction of value which would otherwise be destroyed in conversion of the land to agriculture. For example, some areas in the western region were designed to be fully extracted before being allocated to farming. Conversion of the natural forest to farmland has been legal, intentional and necessary for the development of the country. This century has seen the conversion of all but fragments of forest outside forest reserves into farm and fallow land. The pattern of forest resources remaining or grown on farmlands depends on the land availability, length of fallow period and the farming system. Opening up the new land was profitable since the major clearing and road access costs were often met by loggers and the costs were very low for those with automatic title to *stool* (royal) land. Burning the remaining forest and bush costs little and provides fertile ash which is then exploited. Where the right to land is less secure, cocoa planting and general cultivation after fallow both provide the land user with legitimate tenure under customary law. The unreserved forest has thus been used as a stock of land for cultivation and until recently land has not been scarce in the high forest zone as a whole. The high rate of increases in the rural labour force has ensured that labour is not scarce either, except at critical times in the farming year. Pressure to convert the remaining forest has thus been incessant. But given that natural forests in off-reserves are virtually non-existent pressure on the reserves continues to mount.

Farming on forest reserves has also been a major cause of forest quality decline in forest reserves. Before reservation, some forests already contained farms and these were recognized and 'admitted' on reservation. In some reserves these 'admitted' farms have since been joined by many illegal farms representing sources of fires and creeping deforestation. Recent attempts at forest reservation have been particularly hard hit by farming – about ten large reserves in the west of the high forest zone created since the mid-1960s have been almost entirely deforested by cocoa farmers (ITTO, 1993).

The Contribution of Forestry to Growth

The forestry industry consists of all the sectors of the economy that directly or indirectly utilizes forest resources for production. In this work, however, the definition is narrowed to sectors that deal with the extraction and processing of logs. Indeed the main forestry product is timber (ISSER, 1992). The forestry and logging sector, has since the early 1970s, accounted for about 5 per cent to 6 per cent of total Gross Domestic Product (GDP) and ranked third next to cocoa and minerals in foreign exchange earnings (Table 6.5). It also contributes to revenues in the form of taxes, fees and royalties (Richards, 1995). The sector employs an estimated 250 000 people and provides a livelihood for another estimated 2 million out of a population of about 17 million. It also supplies all of the country's timber needs and a major part of its energy in the form of fuelwood.

The unreserved forest and the productive forest reserves are the resource base for the sector (but as of today the focus is more on the productive forest reserve given that almost all of the unreserved forest has been at least once logged). Most of the forest is normally given out as

Table 6.5   *Foreign exchange earnings from the major export sectors of Ghana, 1986–96 (US$million)*

	1986	1987	1988	1989	1990	1991	1992	1993	1994	1995
Gross exports of which	749.3	826.6	881.0	807.9	902.4	999.3	986.3	1063.6	1270.4	1490.9
Cocoa: total	503.3	495.4	460.8	407.8	360.6	348.7	302.5	285.9	320.2	389.5
percentage	67.2	59.9	52.4	50.5	40.0	34.9	30.7	26.9	25.2	26.1
Metals: total	124.4	159.4	187.7	186.0	242.4	351.9	388.6	473.5	588.2	678.8
percentage	16.6	19.3	21.3	23.0	26.8	35.2	39.4	44.0	46.3	45.5
Timber total	44.1	89.8	106.6	80.2	118.0	124.2	113.9	147.4	165.4	190.6
percentage	5.9	10.9	12.1	9.9	13.1	12.5	11.5	13.9	13.0	12.8

Sources: ISSER (1992, 1994, 1995 and 1996).

concessions before being logged ('normally' is used to account for illegal logging activities). Off-reserves logging is essentially a salvage felling regime, with minimum girth limits being the only control. In general, the Forestry Department is able to exert little control over exploitation of forest products outside reserves. With respect to the productive forest reserves, concessions are divided into compartments of about 129.60 ha within each felling series (Forestry Dept). Pre-harvesting stock mapping of each compartment is undertaken prior to yield selection. Entry permits are issued to concessioners to enter the forest reserves to fell trees offered from the yield so that exploitation is purported to be in accordance with the principle of good silviculture and on a sustained yield basis (Forestry Dept).

The exploitation policy is quick removal of 'overmature' trees over a certain period of time. This period is based on the average 'time of passage' of the most desirable species across a 20 cm diameter class interval for trees above 50 cm diameter at base height, i.e. the time taken to grow from the class interval below the felling limit into the exploitable size class. For example, to grow from 50 to 70 cm diameter, odum requires 41 years, whereas wawa takes 29 years and dahoma 17 years. This period was 15 years in 1970 and was changed to 25 years. Since 1989 it has been changed to a 40-year period (ITTO, 1993). The reason for this new period of time is to enable a sustained yield management regime which will provide sufficient time for the residual forest to recover and regenerate satisfactorily after harvesting. It is also to ensure security of tenure, which it is hoped will create an awareness among concessionaires of the benefits to be derived from long-term sustained management of the forest resource. Whether or not this 40-year period is being followed is very difficult to verify.

6.4   THE DIVERSITY OF EXPLOITED TIMBER TREES AND THE EXPORT BAN

Total production of logs is shown in Table 6.6. It shows an increasing and decreasing trend which is more responsive to economic trends than to other policies such as the log export ban. Table 6.6 shows that bans have very little effect on total log production. The 1979 ban (Appendix 6.5) culminated in a fall in total log production but the falling trends started in the early 1970s, the beginning of the economic crisis. One can see that after 1983 total log production began to increase again in spite of the 1979 ban. This was in response to the incentives in the structural adjustment of the industry. The 1988 ban did not have any effect on

Table 6.6   Industrial output of wood and wood products

Year	Log production (1000 m³)	Log exports (1000 m³)	Percentage of logs exported	Local consumption of logs (1000 m³)	Mill production (1000 m³)	Sawn timber exports (1000 m³)	Other mill exports (1000 m³)	Total mill exports (1000 m³)
1965	1921	560	29.15	1361				
1970	1920	472	24.58	1448				
1973	2050	1007	49.12	1043	446	235	41	276
1974	1420	472	33.24	948	526	215	23	238
1975	1680	602	35.83	1078	485	174	20	194
1976	1590	531	33.40	1059	476	149	18	167
1977	1420	454	31.97	966	434	73	12	85
1978	1100	312	28.36	788	354	77	15	92
1979	880	198	22.50	682	326	78	13	91
1980	660	105	15.91	555	277	69	14	83
1 981	420	154	36.67	366	146	53	11	64
1982	420	53	12.62	367	190	40	7	47
1983	445	61	13.71	384	173	45	1 1	56
1984	510	70	13.73	440	198	56	14	70
1985	626	130	20.77	496	223	76	16	92
1986	803	196	24.41	607	322	84	17	101
1987	1027	298	29.02	729	380	162	25	187
1988	1137	339	29.82	798	439	170	28	198
1989	996	201	20.18	795	437	154	21	175
1990	1290	200	15.50	1092	550	202	26	228
1991	1229	218	17.74	1014	578	183	27	210
1992	1318	181	13.73	1144	600	232	38	270
1993	1682	520	30.92	1186	600	240	48	288
1994	1682	614	36.50	1110	530	259	51	310
1995	1194	150	12.56	1113	580	286	67	353

Source: TEDB (1996). Forestry Department (several years), annual report of the Forestry Department of Ghana, Ministry of Lands and Natural Resources, Accra.

total log production, and not even the 1993 ban on wawa, which forms a major proportion of total log production (Table 6.7), reflected much in the 1994 level, although it did show up in the 1995 level. It is noted that the total log production in 1993 was higher than any level after 1974, and this after the 1979 and 1988 bans. It portrays the amount of waste in the processing sector, because similar levels of logs are being produced, but exports have reduced drastically (given that most of the banned species are major exports (Table 6.8) and the major species extracted (Table 6.7). Mill production has not increased to match the levels of log production which now find their way to the processing market. This

Table 6.7　　*Production levels of major timber species from reserved forest (1000 m³), 1965–94*

Species	1965	%	1973	%	1978	%	1984	%	1988	%	1994	%
Scarlet Red Star												
Utile	63.3	10.4	88.7	5.15	97.5	12.1	30.7	8.32	23.6	5.81	9.8	1.61
Sapele	87.3	14.4	157.3	9.14	103.6	12.8	29.6	8.03	30.2	7.44	7.3	1.2
Makore	15.5	2.5	46.05	2.68	24.8	3.1	10.6	2.88	13.9	3.42	10.7	1.8
Mahogany	58.5	9.7	133.9	7.78	117.6	14.6	42.4	11.5	43.7	10.8	23.1	3.8
Candollei	6.1	1.01	8.75	0.51	6.2	0.76	2.3	0.62	5.1	1.26	0.87	0.14
Odum	20.3	3.35	78.4	4.55	41.5	5.14	26.3	7.14	55.9	13.7	17.7	2.91
Afromosia	55.5	9.17	599.0	34.8	41.4	5.14	12.9	3.5	5.3	1.3	0.14	0.00
Emire	11.92	1.97	19.6	1.13	11.4	1.14	8.5	2.31	5.7	1.4	190.0	31.2
Edinam	18.5	3.05	69.0	4.01	44.5	5.51	14.6	3.96	19.8	4.88	11.8	1.94
Black Hyedua	2.2	0.36	11.0	0.63	0.98	0.12	3.5	0.94	8.3	2.0	4.2	0.69
Subtotal	339.1	55.92	1211.7	70.39	489.5	60.6	181.2	49.2	211.5	52.1	275.6	45.2
Wawa	246.5	40.8	430.9	25.03	216.8	25.8	82.1	22.2	99.1	24.4	71.4	11.7
Normal Red Star												
Walnut	1.61	0.27	6.94	0.4	4.6	0.57	1.6	0.43	3.0	0.74	2.0	0.33
Niangon	5.14	0.85	1.82	0.11	0.93	0.12	1.8	0.49	3.7	0.91	8.2	1.35
Papao	0.03	0.00	4.08	0.23	0.06	0.01	1.1	0.29	4.7	1.18	1.41	0.23
Kyere			2.07	0.12	13.3	1.65	6.9	1.87	14.3	3.5	8.1	1.33
Guarea	1.98	0.33	5.98	0.34	3.7	0.46	2.2	0.6	5.3	1.31	2.3	0.38
Mansonia	3.67	0.61	20.8	1.21	17.2	2.1	5.4	1.46	5.7	1.4	2.8	0.46
Asanfina			0.077	0.00	2.1	0.26	6.3	1.71	11.1	2.73	4.1	0.67
Subtotal	12.42	2.06	41.77	2.43	41.9	5.18	25.3	6.86	47.8	11.7	28.91	4.75
Pink- Red Star												
Danta	0.678	0.112	3.5	0.2	5.7	0.71	6.5	1.76	8.4	2.07	3.4	0.55
Otie			1.02	0.06	0.03	0.01	1.2	0.33	7.1	1.75	6.1	1.0
Ofram	0.03	0.01	0.60	0.03	5.0	0.62	3.6	0.97	2.1	0.52	10.8	1.77
Dahoma	8.2	1.36	6.8	0.4	9.5	1.18	8.1	2.2	11.7	2.88	13.0	2.13
Kyekyen	0.961	0.16	7.13	0.41	4.6	0.57	2.3	0.62	6.5	1.6	23.3	0.03
Ceiba	0.005	0.00	2.6	0.12	0.71	0.09	0.34	0.09	1.5	0.37	0.15	0.65
Avodire	0.528	0.09	1.76	0.1	0.7	0.09	2.9	0.78	NA		3.9	0.64
Subtotal	10.41	1.72	23.4	1.32	26.24	3.25	24.94	6.77	37.3	9.19	60.65	9.94
Total (all species)	604.8		1721.1		807.3		368.6		406		609.1	

Notes: Data from total forest area are not available. Totals do not add up to 100% because other species not mentioned are excluded.

Source: ITTO (1993); Forestry Department (several years), annual report of the Forestry Department of Ghana, Ministry of Lands and Natural Resources, Accra.

shows the extent of the impact of the local processing sector on forests and biodiversity loss in Ghana.

From the 1940s to the 1970s, eight timber species constituted the entire export trade: white mahogany (*Khaya anthotheca*); African mahogany

Table 6.8   Log exports of major timber species (1000 m³), 1965–88

Species	1965	%	1973	%	1979	%	1983	%	1988	%
Scarlet Red Star										
Utile	48.5	11.0	79.1	9.2	20.0	9.7	0.11	1.1	–	–
Sapele	44.3	10.0	70.0	8.2	12.6	6.1	–	–	–	–
Makore	3.2	7.3	40.0	4.7	7.7	3.7	0.01	0.1	–	–
Mahogany	37.4	8.5	69.5	8.1	12.9	6.2	0.034	0.62	–	–
Candollei	0.41	0.9	10.8	1.3	20.3	1.0	–	–	–	–
Odum			0.06	0.1	–	–	–	–	–	–
Afromosia	7.5	1.7								
Emire	2.2	0.5	13.1	1.5	6.3	3.1	2.7	7.62	22.2	6.5
Edinam	12.8	2.9	43.8	5.1	8.4	4.1	–	–	–	–
Wawa	220.3	46.2	465.6	54.4	106.3	51.3	69.9	74.5	147.8	43.62
Normal Red Star										
Walnut	1.8	0.4	2.5	0.3	0.4	0.2	–	–	2.04	0.68
Niangon	16.7	3.7	2.5	0.3	1.5	0.7			–	–
Papao			0.19	–	–	–	–	–	–	–
Kyere									31.9	9.4
Guarea	2.0	0.5	3.7	0.4	2.6	1.2	0.15	0.39	3.8	1.13
Mansonia	16.0	3.6	12.1	1.4	1.2	0.6	–	–	–	–
Pink–Red Star										
Danta	0.1	–	4.2	0.5	3.7	1.8	0.07	0.06	21.5	6.33
Otie			0.93	0.1	–	–	–	–	–	–
Ofram	0.049	–	1.5	0.2	2.5	1.2	–	–	7.1	2.09
Dahoma			0.38	0.1	0.33	0.2	–	–	–	–
Kyekyen	7.9	1.8	5.7	0.7	1.1	0.5	–	–	10.6	3.12
Ceiba										
Avodire	0.32	–	0.8	0.1	0.43	0.2	–	–	–	–

Source: ITTO (1993). Forestry Department (several years), annual report of the Forestry Department of Ghana, Ministry of Lands and Natural Resources, Accra.

(*K. ivorensis*); edinam (*Entandrophragma angolense*); sapele (*E. cylindricum*); utile (*E. utile*); afromosia (*Pericopsis elata*); makore (*Tieghemella heckelii*); all *Scarlet Red Star* species, and wawa (*Triplochiton scleroxylon*). Today, of the approximately 126 forest tree species which grow to timber size, 50 are considered merchantable, 23 of which are commercially important for logs, sawn timber or for processing into veneers and plywoods, or furniture (Francois, 1987). Of these, ten species accounted for 79 per cent of the total volume extracted in 1991 (FPIB data), with wawa alone constituting 41 per cent in 1965 (Table 6.7).

Data available shows that the proportion of timber harvested from unreserved areas increased greatly from 1991 (ITTO, 1993). This has been attributed to the increasing controls implemented by the Forestry Department inside reserves. This reinforces the impression that outside reserve areas act as 'buffers' to variations in on-reserve harvests. But as shown earlier, given the rate of official and unofficial extraction, this 'buffer' will not last for long. Very soon most of these species will be extinct in the off-reserves and the reserves will be the only source of supply.

Exporters of logs have officially responded to the export ban. Between 1965 and 1973 log exports saw an increasing trend. The period 1974–78 saw a sharp decline in log exports (Table 6.6) in response to the economic crisis. With the export ban of 1979 there was a drastic fall in total log exports from 1979 to 1982, which can also be attributed to the economic crisis, because after that period export levels began to increase in response to policies in the structural adjustment programme. However, with respect to the banned species, exports officially gradually tend to zero, though with some species like Walnut, Danta and Ofram they tend to increase again (Table 6.8). In the same way exports of the 1988 banned species also gradually fell to zero. The 1993 export ban on Wawa, a very important species in total exports, did not have much effect on total exports (Table 6.6). It is very difficult to explain the fall in 1995 since it was not expected. However, it was possible that stringent measures were put in place to enforce the bans. This is, however, difficult to substantiate since data on different species exported after 1989 are not available. The conclusion is that the export ban works on exports (Table 6.8). The concern is that the overall production of these banned species did not fall drastically. It has merely been diverted into the less-efficient domestic processing market, defeating the objectives of sustainable use of the species and conservation of the biodiversity of the forest resources. The export ban may not be a solution to conserving biodiversity since the domestic market is able to absorb the production in spite of its inefficiency.

Average world prices for logs have tended to fall (Table 6.9). However, in spite of this it is still attractive to export in the structural adjustment period because of the exchange rate realignment, which makes the domestic value of exports relatively attractive. Indeed, it has become more profitable to export logs in the Structural Adjustment Programme period, although the export ban has helped to reduce the impact on the forest biodiversity, at least with regard to the *Scarlet Red*, *Normal Red* and *Pink Red Star* species.

International prices of processed timber have tended to rise (Table 6.9). And with the attractive exchange rate and other sector-specific incentives, it is very profitable to export processed timber. With the export ban, the banned species have become relatively cheap locally. Given that there is no control as to how much can be sold in the local

Table 6.9   *Average unit price (US$/m³) of wood and wood products,*
            1985–95

Year	Logs	Lumber	Veneers	Plywood	Other wood products
1985	70	198	221	238	427
1986	127	221	285	194	598
1987	116	235	332	276	631
1988	130	260	409	271	682
1989	117	280	591	296	795
1990	150	373	758	369	974
1991	131	292	629	409	819
1992	131	305	694	465	994
1993	111	300	607	358	932
1994	113	382	663	384	811
1995	96	392	772	387	906

Source: TEDB (1996).

market, and given inefficiencies in domestic processing (estimated wastage of 30–50 per cent), it follows that such incentives may lead to overuse of forest resources, especially of banned species. This has implications for forests and biodiversity loss. The conclusion is that incentives provided under the SAP, especially with regard to the timber processing sector may encourage the misuse of the forest resource since there is no regulation on the domestic use of 'endangered' timber species. As much as the government wants to promote domestic processing of timber it should help improve efficiency in processing and there should be some control on the domestic use of 'endangered' species if one of the objectives of the export ban (conserving the resource) is to be achieved. Processing 'other' timber species will also help to achieve the above stated objective of the log export ban.

6.5   AGRICULTURE IN GHANA: COCOA AND MAIZE

The production of food and cash crops is an additional and major cause of forest loss. Studies have shown that maize, unlike other cereals, is grown in the cocoa-producing areas, mainly in the high forest zone. It competes with cocoa for land use, making maize and cocoa substitutes in the demand for forest land. Therefore, their relative price determines the decision to convert forest land to cocoa or maize land. However, where one of the crops is already planted then we have what may be called a one-way substitution, that is from cocoa land to maize land and not vice versa. This is because maize land tends not to have enough nutrients for conversion to cocoa land especially if the land has been cropped for some time. It follows that if the price of cocoa falls relative to maize then farmers might convert their cocoa land into growing maize, even though they may also decide to abandon the cocoa farms. Konings (1986) argues, although without quantitative evidence, that during the economic crisis cocoa farmers increasingly shifted their efforts from cocoa production to food crops, especially maize.

Agriculture is the largest and most important sector in the economy of Ghana. National economic development has been closely linked with the performance of the sector (Ministry of Agriculture, 1991), and it is expected to continue to play a major role in the short and medium term. The agricultural sector's importance is by virtue of its contribution to several important economic variables. It contributes the highest proportion to the Gross Domestic Product (GDP). In the past decade its contribution to GDP averaged about 52 per cent. Before that period the figure was about 60–70 per cent. However, since 1987, the proportion has declined gradually to 38 per cent in 1995 and was projected to fall to about 36.9 per cent in 1996 (ISSER, 1996).

Agriculture accounts for the highest proportion of the economically active population (EAP) mainly as farmers, farm labourers and other workers in agricultural related activities. The proportion of EAP in agriculture declined from about 56 per cent in 1980 to about 48 per cent in 1991 and further to 47 per cent in 1995. However, the absolute number of the EAP in agriculture has tended to increase. For example, from about 2.3 million in 1980 to about 2.8 million in 1991 and 2.95 million in 1995. An increase of about 1.6 per cent per annum (FAO, 1991; ISSER, 1996, 1997). Under the Structural Adjustment Programme, the sector is expected to play a very important role in terms of employment generation given the rate of redundancy in the public sector, and the rate of population growth, which is about 2.6–3 per cent per annum.

Agriculture, particularly cocoa, contributes substantially to government revenue in the form of duties paid on exports. This contribution has also declined steadily. In 1979 the contribution to government revenue from cocoa tax alone was about 35 per cent but declined to 10 per cent in 1992 (ISSER, 1993). The main reason for this fall was the increase in the producer price of cocoa paid to farmers (refer to Chapter 8) to rekindle their interest in cocoa production after it fell to its lowest level in more than three decades in 1983.

Until 1992, agriculture accounted for the highest proportion of total foreign exchange earned by the country with cocoa the highest contributor. The contribution of cocoa alone was about 60 per cent in the 1970s. This dropped to 40 per cent in 1990 and further to 25.8 per cent in 1994. The decline has been attributed to two main factors; a decline in the world market price of cocoa and a low level of cocoa production. The world market price which was about $2369 per tonne in the 1983/84 season, declined in a fluctuating fashion to about $1295 in the 1989/90 season, a decline of about 45 per cent in six years (ISSER, 1993). The production of cocoa also declined steadily from about 400 000 tonnes in the 1975/6 season to about 158 000 in the 1983/4 season. Production levels however increased to about 300 000 tonnes in the 1990s. The dwindling amount of foreign exchange earned by the country's few traditional export commodities brought into sharp focus the need to expand the export base. In the light of this, since 1986, the government has promoted non-traditional commodities for export. The performances of such crops have, however, been unstable. In 1989, 61 non-traditional agricultural commodities were exported. The number dropped to 50 in 1990, though their volume increased. The foreign exchange earned by non-traditional agricultural commodities in total non-traditional exports dropped from about 76 per cent in 1986 to 17.2 per cent in 1995 (ISSER, 1996; 1992). The implication is that, in terms of foreign exchange earnings, cocoa export is and will still be very important to the economy.

The suitable agricultural lands are distributed in all the six agroecological zones of the country, namely, the high rainforest, the semi-deciduous forest, the forest–savanna transition, the Guinea savanna, the Sudan savanna and the coastal savanna. The weather, soil and other environmental conditions allow some crops to be more successfully cultivated in some agroecological zones than others. For example, cereals (maize, rice and sorghum) and yam in the Northern Guinea and Sudan savanna and the transitional zones, while tree crops, plantain, cocoyam and cassava do much better in the high rain and the semi-deciduous forest zones.

About 13.6 million hectares, representing 57 per cent of the country's land area, are classified as suitable for agriculture purposes, of which about one-third was cultivated in 1990. Thus from the overall availability standpoint, there is not yet a shortage of land for agricultural production purposes in the country (Ministry of Agriculture, 1991). The problem is the movement of some crops into marginal lands or less suitable climatic area. Expansion of agricultural land is expected to proceed at a rate of about 2.5 per cent per annum even though the policy is to increase agricultural output through enhancing productivity. The expansion of land area is expected to be the driving force in the production of tree crops, like cocoa, until the appropriate enabling environment has been established to promote intensification of production (Ministry of Agriculture, 1990). The view of the Cocoa Board and Cocoa Services Department (CSD) is that almost all the suitable land for cocoa has been used up, and what is left is either too acidic, wet or rocky, or not accessible (due to tenure security). In other words, cocoa has nowhere to go, except into reserve forest areas or back to old areas which may not be very fertile.

The productivity of land and labour in agriculture is very low due largely to the extensive use of traditional technology and methods of cultivation. Shifting cultivation and bush fallow have remained the dominant systems for natural restoration of soil fertility. Many of the fields are prepared by slashing and burning the vegetation *in situ* (zero tillage), destroying the forest in its wake. This is especially the case with respect to food crops like maize. For cash crops like cocoa, because of the importance of shade, some trees are left to serve that purpose (see Appendix 6.4). However, most of the forest is still destroyed. Mixed cropping predominates the crop layout in the fields, particularly where production is mainly for subsistence. The use of modern inputs such as fertilizers, pesticides or improved seed is not yet widespread and simple cutlass, knives and hoes are the dominant tools for cultivation and harvesting.

Farming activities are highly labour intensive, with the bulk of the labour supplied by the farm households. The use of institutional credit is very low. The predominantly small-scale producers are mostly illiterate, aged and above all women. Available data on output (Table 6.10), area cultivated (harvested) (Table 6.11) and yield per hectare (Table 6.12) indicate that output increases have been attributed more to land expansion than to increases in land productivity (ISSER, 1996). This has implications for forest loss and biodiversity. It must be noted that the data does not differentiate between new forest land converted, fallow land or old farmlands cropped. For example, from Table 6.11, land cultivated under cereals increased from 853 ha in 1990 to 1297 ha in 1995, an increase of 444 ha (34 per cent), and from 1127 ha in 1987, an increase of 170 ha (13 per cent). Whichever figure one prefers, it still shows that an increase in cultivated land implies forest conversion.

Table 6.10   Output of major crops, 1970–95 (1000 metric tons)

Commodity	1970/74	1975/79	1980/82	1983	1984/86	1987/89	1990/92	1993/95
Cereals								
Maize	452	304	317	141	509	638	739	987
Rice	62	69	48	27	75	84	121	180
Millet	127	134	129	114	123	182	107	191
Sorghum	171	152	151	106	163	200	212	337
Roots and tubers								
Cassava	2836	2198	2534	1376	3339	3115	4694	6203
Yam	791	569	454	354	790	1222	1947	2182
Cocoyam	1210	777	859	613	1580	1109	1105	1257
Plantain	1809	993	843	755	1224	1106	1020	1478
Cash crops								
Cocoa	405	309	221	159	207	256	277	282
Cotton	1805	6741	573	115	2321	6145	10851	NA
Tobacco	2005	1358	560	657	1218	1560	1960[a]	NA
Oil Palm	760	727	897	889	706[b]	397[c]	429[d]	NA

Notes
[a]1990/91 average; [b]1984/85 average; [c]1989 only; [d]1990 only.
NA 'Not available.

Source: Policy Planning, Monitoring and Evaluation Department (PPMED), Ministry of Agriculture, Accra; ISSER (1996).

Table 6.11   Cultivated area of major food crops, 1987–95

	Area cultivated (1000 ha)								
	1987	1988	1989	1990	1991	1992	1993	1994	1995
Cereals	1127	1046	1149	853	1177	1204	1228	1200	1297
Maize	548	540	567	465	610	607	637	629	669
Rice	72	52	72	49	95	80	77	81	100
Millet	235	228	224	124	209	210	204	191	193
Sorghum	272	226	286	215	263	307	310	299	335
Roots and tubers	790	663	839	584	967	972	911	853	832
Cassava	390	354	455	323	535	552	532	520	551
Yam	204	168	217	119	229	224	206	154	176
Cocoyam	196	141	207	142	203	196	173	179	205
Plantain	170	119	164	129	174	157	164	184	212

Source: ISSER (1992, 1994, 1996).

Table 6.12   Yield per hectare of major food crops, 1987–95

					Yield (metric tons per ha)				
	1987	1988	1989	1990	1991	1992	1993	1994	1995
Cereals	0.9	1.1	1.0	1.0	1.1	1.1	1.4	1.4	1.4
Maize	1.1	1.1	1.3	1.2	1.5	1.2	1.5	1.5	1.6
Rice	1.1	2.1	0.9	1.7	1.3	1.7	2.0	2.0	2.2
Millet	0.7	0.8	0.7	0.6	0.5	0.6	1.0	0.9	1.1
Sorghum	0.8	0.8	0.8	0.6	0.9	0.8	1.1	1.1	1.1
Roots and tubers	6.2	8.5	6.9	7.5	NA	NA	NA	NA	NA
Cassava	7.0	9.3	8.0	8.4	10.7	10.3	11.2	11.6	12.0
Yam	5.8	7.1	5.9	7.4	11.5	10.4	13.2	11.0	12.0
Cocoyam	5.2	7.9	5.7	5.7	6.4	6.1	7.1	6.4	6.7
Plantain	6.3	10.1	6.3	6.2	6.8	6.9	8.1	8.0	7.9

Source: ISSER (1992, 1994, 1996).

APPENDIX 6.1   STAR CATEGORIES FOR TREE SPECIES IN GHANA

Hawthorne and Abu Juarn (1993) assigned a star category to species of trees in Ghana based on their rarity in Ghana and internationally, with subsidiary consideration of the ecology and taxonomy of the species. Species were rated Black Star, Gold Star, Blue Star or Green Star in order of decreasing conservation priority. Fairly common or widespread species that are heavily exploited or show great economic potentials are rated as Red Star species. The star ratings have the meanings, and have been assigned the weights outlined in the table.

The weight column shows the relative value (outside brackets) of each species in building up a standard spot conservation score, which is referred to as a Genetic Heat Index (GHI). Forests with high GHI are thus those rich in species which are internationally rare. For the calculation of the GHI, the various shades of Red Star are not treated differently – they all score one unit. However, the degree of exploitation of these species – Scarlet Red and Normal Red Star species particularly –

is likely to undermine their status as commodities of high financial and utilitarian merit, by undermining their population structure and by degrading the genetic quality. These species are therefore of conservational concern for reasons different from those applying to Black to Blue Star species. The richness of the forest in Red Star species is expressed as an Economic Index (EI) analogous to GHI. The weights employed are in approximate proportions to the degree of exploitation relative to the standing crop in 1989. Forests with high EI are thus those rich in species threatened in Ghana by over exploitation. For a full discussion of the methods for and implications of calculating these indices refer to Hawthorne and Abu Juam (1993).

Star	No.	Weight for GHI (and EI)	Comment
Black	52	27 (0)	Urgent attention to conservation of population needed. Rare internationally, and at least uncommon in Ghana. Ghana must take particular care of these species.
Gold	208	9 (0)	Fairly rare internationally and/or locally. Ghana has some inescapable responsibility for maintaining these species.
Blue	414	3 (0)	Widespread internationally but rare in Ghana, or vice versa. It may be in Ghana's interest to pay attention to protecting some of these species.
Scarlet Red	14	1 (3)	Common, but under serious pressure from heavy exploitation. Exploitation needs to be curtailed if usage is to be sustainable. Protection on all scales vital.
Normal Red	40	1 (2)	Common, but under pressure from exploitation. Need careful control and some tree by tree and area protection.
Pink Red	19	1 (1)	Common and moderately exploited. Also non-abundant species of high potential value.
Green	1044	0 (0)	No particular conservation concern.
Others		0 (0)	Filtered out. Non-forest species, or excluded from the analysis for other reasons.

Source: Extracted from Hawthorne and Abu Juam (1993).

APPENDIX 6.2   STANDING VOLUME OF MAIN TIMBER SPECIES IN GHANA

Species	Standing vol > felling limit	Standing vol < felling limit	Years from 1993					
			0	10	20(R)	30(R)	60(R)	>100(R)
Scarlet Red Star								
Utile	382800	162400	16758	12449	8140	8140	8140	8140
Sapele	672800	440800	46077	36787	27496	27496	0	0
Makore	75400	69600	22472	15816	9160	0	0	0
Mahogany	904800	614800	85833	62156	38479	38479	38479	0
Candollei	92800	69600	8758	6072	3385	0	0	0
Odum	1484800	696000	142152	88697	35242	35242	35242	35242
Afromosia	23200	81200	7063	4883	0	0	0	0
Emire	777200	58000	20691	12785	4879	0	0	0
Edinam	487200	336400	39403	28230	17057	17057	0	0
Black Hyedua	174000	324800	8990	6448	3906	3906	3906	0
Subtotal	5753600	2853600	398197	274323	147744	130320	85767	43382
Wawa	8212800	5974000	499602	323817	148032	148032	148032	148032
Normal Red Star								
Walnut	429200	139200	5877	5346	4814	4814	0	0
Niangon	232000	185600	11897	8651	5405	5405	0	0
Papao	464000	243600	12063	6794	1524	1524	0	0
Kyere	417600	591600	42090	25116	8141	8141	0	0
Guarea	510400	429200	11445	9332	7219	7219	7219	7219
Mansonia	406000	696000	2625	2396	2167	2167	2167	2167
Asanfina	510400	464000	25570	17575	9580	9580	0	0
Subtotal	2969600	2749200	111567	75210	38850	38850	9386	9386
Pink-Red Star								
Danta	951200	1635600	8589	7431	6273	6273	6273	6273
Otie	1879200	1624000	20704	28950	37195	37195	37195	37195
Ofram.	4872000	1078800	23286	30742	38198	38198	38198	38198
Dahoma	2180800	1867600	29213	25137	21060	21060	21060	21060
Kyekyen	3967200	742400	12990	14920	16850	16850	16850	16850
Ceiba	8758000	1252800	37855	52673	67490	67490	67490	67490
Avodire	406000	916400	4192(R)	4192 (R)	4192	4192	4192	4192
Subtotal	23014400	9117600	136829	164045	191258	191258	191258	191258
Other Sp.	51504000	15091600	85518	125180	164842	164842	164842	164842
Total	91454400	35786000	1231713	962575	690726	673302	599285	556900

Notes

R = logs from reserve forest only. Note from the table, given a 'business as usual scenario', by 2023 the reserve forest will be the only source of log supply. This implies increased pressure from both log extraction and farming on the forest reserves.

Source: ITTO (1993).

APPENDIX 6.3   FOREST INVENTORY CLASSIFICATION OF GHANA'S HIGH FOREST TREE SPECIES

Latin name	Local name	Alternative name

Class 1 (Species registered as having been exported from Ghana 1973–1988)

Latin name	Local name	Alternative name
Afzelia bellalafricana	**Papao**	**Apa, Apal, Afzelia**
Albizia ferruginea	Awiemfosamina	
Albizia zygia	Okoro	Atanza
Alstonia boonei	Sinuro	
Anphinas pterocarpoides	Yaya	Lati
Aningeria spp.	**Asamfena**	**Asamfona**
Anopyxis klaineana	Kokote	
Antiaris toxicaria	**Kyenkyen**	**Ako**
Atrocaryon nicraster	Aprokuma	
Berlinia spp.	Kwatafompaboa	Tetekon, Limbali
Bombax brevicuspe	Onyinakoben	West African Bombax
Bombax buonopozense	Akonkodie	Akata
Canarium schwinfurthii	Bediwomua	Aile
Ceiba pentandra	**Onyina**	**Fromoger**
Celtis mildbraediilzenkeri	Esa	Ohia, Akosika, Chia
Chrysophllum/giganteun /subnundun/albidun	Akasaa	Adasema, Akatio
Copaifera salikounda	Entedua	Bubinga
Cordia nilleniilplatyhyrsa	Tweneboa	
Cylicodiscus gabunensis	Denyao	Okan
Cynometra ananta	Ananta	
Daniellia ogealthurifera	**Hyedua**	**Sopi, Faro, Gun/Niger Copal**
Dialium aubrevillei	Duabankye	
Diopyros sanza-ninika	Sanza-mulika	Kusibiri, African Ebony, Flintark
Distenonanthus benthanianus	Bonsamdua	Avan, Movingui
Entandophragma angolense	**Edinam**	**Gedunohor, Tiana**
Entandophragma cylindricum	**Penkwa**	**Sapele**
Entandophragma utile	**Efoobrodedwo**	**Utile, Sipo**
Entandophragma candollei	**Penkwa-akoa**	**Onu, Kossipo, Ceda-kokote**
Erythophleun spp.	Potrodom	Odon, Missanda, talli
Guarea cedrata	**Kwabohoro**	**Scented Guarea, Bosse**
Guarea thompsonii	Kwadwuma	Black Guarea, Bosse
Guibotia ehie	Anokye-hyedua	Black Hyedua, Anazakoue, Ovangol
Heretiera utilis	**Nyankom**	**Niangon**
Khaya anthothecalgrandifoliola	Krumben	African Mahogany, Akajou, Boules
Khaya ivorensis	Dubini	African Mahogany
Klainedoza gabonensis	Kroma	
Lophira alata	Kaku	Ekki, Azobe
Lovoa trichilioides	**Dubinibiri**	**African Walnut**
Manea africana	Bompagya	Pegya
Mansonia altissina	**Oprono**	**Mansonia, bete**
Melicia excelsalregia	**Odum**	**Iroko, Chlorophora**
Mitragyna ciliatalstipulosa	Subaha	Abura, Bahai
Nauclea diderrichii	Kusia	Opepe, Bilinga
Nesogordonia papaverifera	**Danta**	**Kotibe**

Latin name	Local name	Alternative name
Parkia bicolor	Asoma	
Pericopsis elata	**Kokrodua**	**Afromosia, Asanela**
Petersianthus macrocarpus	Esia	
Piptadeniastrum africanum	**Dahoma**	**Dabema**
Pterygota macrocarpa	**Kyereye**	**Kote**
Pycnanthus angolensis	**Otie**	**Illomba**
Sterculia rhinopetala	Wawabima	
Strombosia glaucescens	Afema	
Terminalia ivorensis	**Emire**	**Idigbo, Framire**
Terminalia superba	**Ofram**	**Afara**
Tieghemella heckelii	**Baku**	**Makore, Bakure**
Triplochiton scleroxylon	**Wawa**	**Obeche, Sanba, Ayous**
Turraeanthus africanus	**Apapaye**	**Avodire**

Class 2 – Species attaining 70 cm dbh (diameter at breast height) and occurring at a frequency of more than 1 km² and not presently exported.

Afrosersalisia afzelii	Bakunini
Albizia adianthifolia	Pampena
Albizia glaberrina	Okora-Akoa
Aningeria spp.	Asamfena
Balanites wilsoniana	Krobodua
Blighia spp.	Akye
Bussea occidentalis	Kotorepre
Calpocalyx brevibracteatus	Atrotre
Celtis adolfi-friderici	Esakosua
Celtis wightii	Prempresa
Chidlwia sanguinea	Ababima
Chrysophyllum perpulchrun	Atabene
Chrysophyllum pruniforme	Duatadwe
Cleistopholis pateas	Ngonenkyene
Cola gigantea	Watapuo
Corynanthe pachyceras	Pampenama
Coula edulis	Bodwue
Dacryodes klaineana	Adwea
Duboscia viridiflora	Akokoragyehini
Erthoxylum anaii	Pepeanini
Ficus spp. (non-stranglers)	Domini
Gibertiodendron spp.	Tetekon
Hannoa klaineana	Folie
Hezalobus crispiflorus	Duabaha
Holoptela grandis	Nakwa
Honalium letestui	Esononankoroma
Honalium stipulaceum/dewev	Owebiribi
Irvingia gabonensis	Abesebuo
Lannea welwitschii	Kumanini
Lonchocarpus sericeus	Sante
Maranthes spp.	Afam, etc.
Margaritaria discoidea	Pepea
Morus nesozygia	Wonton

Latin name	Local name	Alternative name
Monodora nyristica	Wedeaba	
Ongokea gore	Bodwe	
Pachypodanthium staudtii	Kumdwie	
Panda oleosa	Kokroboba	
Parinari exelsa	Afam	
Parkia filicoidea	Asoma-nua	
Pentaclethra macropylla	Ataa	
Phyllocosnus africanus	Akokorabeditoa	
Protomegabaria stapfiana	Agyahere	
Pseudospondias nicrocarpa	Katawani	
Pteleopsis hylodendron	Kwae-kane	
Picinodendron heudelotii	Wama	
Scottellia klaineana	Tiabutuo	
Sterculia oblongo	Ohaa	
Sterculia tragacantha	Sofo	
Stereospernum acuninatissinum	Esono-tokwakofuo	
Tabernaeanontana spp.	Obanawa	
Talbotiella gentii	Takorowanua	
Treculia africana	Brebretim	
Trichilia prieuriana	Kakadikuro	
Trichillia tesananii	Tanuronini	
Trilepisium madagascariene	Okure	
Uapaca guineensis	Kontan	
Xylia evansii	Abobabema	
Zanthoxylum spp.	Oyaa/Okuo	

Class 3 – All other species

Note: Names of species in bold type are the 'Scarlet Red', 'Normal Red' or 'Pink Red Species', some of which are endangered.

Source: ITTO (1993).

APPENDIX 6.4　'GOOD TREES' AND 'BAD TREES' ON COCOA FARMS – INDICATIONS FROM AN IIED VILLAGE FORESTRY STUDY

WE	ME	MS–NW	MS–SE	DS
Most commonly mentioned 'good trees'				
Emire	Odum	Otie	Nyamedua	Onyina
Onyina	Mahogany	Mahogany	Kakapenpen	Odum
Ofram	Onyina	Odum	Mahogany	Mahogany
Mahogany	Emire	Wawa	Tanduro	Orange
Odoma	Orange	Odoma	Odum	Avocado
Quite commonly mentioned 'good trees'				
Baku	Oil palm	Wamma	Esa	Kakapenpen
Odum	Avocado	Onyina	Kokonisuo	Odoma
Nyankyerene	Ofram		Onyina	Otie
Kakapenpen	Nyankyerene		Wamma	Wamma
Pampena	Kakapenpen		Hyedua	Ofram
	Foto		Emire	Mango
	Pepdiewu		Sapele	Foto
	Sese		Odoma	Kokonisuo
	Raphia palm		Nyankerene	Nyamedua
	Sapele		Wawa	Nyankyerene
Most commonly mentioned 'bad trees'				
Dahoma	Wawa	Nyankyerene	Wawa	Nyamedua
Odoma	Esa	Foto	Watapuo	Nyankyerene
Quite commonly mentioned 'bad trees'				
Kroma	Onyina	Dahoma	Wawa	Nyankorna
Denya	Emire	Odoma	Ntediedupo	Kakapenpen
Emire	Funtum	Kyenkyen	Foto	

Notes

The top two-thirds in each list were the most mentioned.

WE = Wet evergreen forest zone; ME = Moist evergreen forest zone, MS-NW = Moist semi-deciduous (north west subtype) forest zone; MS-SE = Moist semi-deciduous (south-east subtype) forest zone; DS = Dry semi-deciduous forest zone (after Hall and Swaine 1981).

Source: ITTO (1993).

APPENDIX 6.5   LOG EXPORT BANS

Species classification	1979	1988	1993
Scarlet Red Star	Sapele	Emire	
	Utile		
	Mahogany		
	Candollei		
	Makore		
	Afromosia		
	Odum		
	Edinam		
	Black Hyedua		
	Wawa		Wawa
Normal Red Star	Niagon	Asanfina	Walnut
	Subaha	Mansonia	
Pink-Red Star	Avodire	Ofram	Danta
Other	Teak	Black Ebony	

Source: Ministry of Lands and Forestry.

NOTES

1. Biodiversity, according to Article 2 of the Convention on Biological Diversity, is 'the variability among living organisms from all sources including inter alia, marine and other aquatic ecosystems and the ecological complexes of which they are part, this includes diversity within species, between species (defined by their genes) and of the ecosystems' (Glowka et al., 1994). The Global Biodiversity Assessment (UNEP, 1995) also defines biodiversity as 'the total diversity and variability among living things and of the systems of which they are part, which covers the total range of variation in and variability among systems and organisms, at the regional, landscape, ecosystem and habitat level, at the various organism levels down to species, population and genes and the complex sets of structural and functional relationships within and between these different levels of organizations, including human action, and their origins and evolution in space'.

2. An ecosystem means 'a dynamic complex of plants, animals and micro-organism communities and their non-living environment interacting as a functional unit' (Glowka et al., 1994). The interaction between and among components of an ecosystem, for example, foodwebs, and with light, water, air, minerals and nutrients are the bases of an ecosystem functioning, which taken together with the functions of others provide services upon which life on earth depends. Some of them include maintaining the balance of the atmospheric gases, recycling nutrients, regulating climates, maintaining hydrological cycles and creating soil (Ehrlich, 1988).

3. Sustainable use in this context means the use of the components of biodiversity in a way and at a rate that does not lead to the long-term decline of biodiversity, thereby maintaining its potential to meet the needs and aspirations of the present and future

generations (Glowka et al., 1994). 'Sustainable use' has its parallel in 'sustainable development' defined as meeting the needs of the present generation without compromising the needs of the future generations (1987 World Commission on Environment and Development, also known as the Brundtland Commission).

4. Conservation is not defined by the Convention on Biological Diversity, however it was recognized that sustainable use of living resources and the ecosystems of which they are part is a prerequisite for biological conservation.

5. This is the consequence of market failure. Market failure occurs if markets fail to reflect biodiversity values. This may result from the presence of open access resource exploitation and public environmental goods, externalities (for example, non-marketed environmental services), incomplete markets, uncertainty, the distribution of income and assets, and imperfect competition. This market failure leads to a distortion of economic incentives, such that the full value of the forest is not taken into account in forest land use decisions. As a result excessive deforestation occurs (Barbier et al., 1995).

6. The Guinea-Congolean is the area White (1983) termed as 'Low Africa' because the land is largely below 600 metres, except where ancient, mostly Precambrian, rocks such as the Guinea Highlands, the Jos Plateau and the Cameroon Highlands rise above 100 metres. The soils are often very deep attaining 20 metres or more before the bedrock is reached. The vegetation they support is more dependent on the climate than on the original parent material. Thus in areas where rainfall is highest (evergreen forest) the soils are more leached and more acidic, lighter in colour and poorer in nutrients than where rainfall is more moderate (semi-deciduous forests). Gentry (1992), has pointed out that high diversity forest are concentrated in the lowlands areas with high and relatively even rainfall. Endemism is only partly correlated with diversity and is concentrated into isolated patches of unusual habitats. Differences in soils are reflected in vegetation, the most obvious being the swamp forest, especially where there is impeded drainage. Even though the temperatures are high, the climatic conditions are relatively stable and not of greatest importance in determining the distribution of forest types. Walter et al. (1960) cites the Guinea-Congolean Region as usually having a mean monthly temperature represented by an almost horizontal line indicating little variation throughout the year. However, extreme values are often more important than average values as far as plants are concerned. Thus, where temperatures at the ground inside forest, might have a diurnal range of about 7°C, those in the nearby clearing may vary nearly twice as much. There is a high variation of rainfall, which is the most important variable with regard to plant life. Rainforests need a minimum of about 2000 mm per annum to persist but semi-deciduous forests can get by on upwards of 1250 mm per annum. The distribution of rainfall throughout the year and lengths of the dry season may be more critical in their effect on vegetation. Thus, even where the total rainfall is low, as in the Accra Plains in Ghana, a two-peak distribution of annual rainfall permits the development of a dry type of forest in parts. The occurence of drought years is also likely to be important. In West Africa, apart from the areas to the North and the South of the equator, where there is a two-peak type of rainfall, by far the greatest part of the Guinea-Congo region has a humid-equatorial diurnal (day/nights temperatures variations greater than mean monthly variations) climate with rain more or less throughout the year except for a short dry season (Peters, 1990). The floristic and vegetation patterns are very complex. Of the 2.8 million km² or so of Guinea-Congolean lowland forest, 80 per cent of the 8000 or so species of vascular plants it contains are found nowhere else (White, 1983). These species are by no means homogenously distributed (White, 1979; Denys, 1980, Jacobs, 1988). Although the Guinea-Congo region represents a simple (albeit subdivisible) florist ariel or phytoclorion, it contains within itself many natural vegetation types including evergreen, rain, forest, semi-deciduous (or semi-green) forest, freshwater swamp forest, mangroves and coastal vegetation, and various types of Savannah. Much of these have, however, been altered or degraded and are no longer natural. Even the forest reserves are not necessarily natural forests and include areas of coppical firewood plantation or stands of quick-growing exotics such

as Gmelina. Comparing the tropical rainforests of America and Indo-Malaysia with the African (Guinea-Congolean), Richards (1973) concluded that Africa is the 'odd man' out because of the (1) comparative poverty of African flora, wide distribution of African plants and poor representation of certain groups such as palms, orchids and tree plants of the family Lauracae. White (1983), however, realized that it is important to stress that this conclusion is relative to the fact that over 8000 species of vascular plants can be found in the Guinea-Congolean region; (2) relatively poorly endowed with some life forms such as Lianes and Epiphytes; (3) uniqueness of African forest due to the absence of uniform high rainfall, humidity and temperature and the presence of a regular dry season – a distinct dry season often over two months; and because (4) the impact of human beings on vegetation has been longer and more sustained in Africa than elsewhere, so much so that the presence of any truly primeval or so-called virgin forest is very questionable, except for mangroves.

7. The *taungya* system is a system of forest plantation in which farmers plant seedlings and tend trees in return for being allowed to cultivate crops for the first few years between the seedlings in the plantation.

8. Farming systems in the high forest zone involve land rotation with bush-fallow. Cocoa cultivation and, to a much lesser extent, oil palm, coffee and coconut production, have brought much of the land under permanent agriculture but a mixed cropping system involving spatial rotation is still the norm. Within this system, depending on the relative availability of forest resources outside the farm, the farmer keeps certain trees and forest plants on the farm for the products they produce or their cultural significance. For example, cocoa, which is the dominant cash crop in the forest zone requires considerable shade tree cover and cocoa land is characterized by a density of trees over about 20 cm diameter at breast height of 15–80 per hectare (Falconer, 1990) (refer to ITTO, 1993, Appendix 4, Tables 1 and 2 for types of trees on sampled farmlands in Ghana). It has been observed, however, that the new hybrid cocoa requires less shade from trees and therefore less trees. Food crop farms also require very few trees. This implies that the greater the use of new hybrid cocoa seeds and the greater the number of food crop farms, the greater the loss of forest and biodiversity.

9. Scarlet Red Star are species that are classified as under immediate threat of extinction (refer to Appendix 6.1 and 6.2 for type of tree species in this category).

10. Normal Red Star are species whose current rates of exploitation may present a significant danger of genetic erosion over 10 years, beginning in 1994 (refer to Appendix 6.1 and 6.2).

11. Pink-Red Star are species of trees significantly exploited but not sufficiently under threat at present (refer to Appendix 6.1 and 6.2).

REFERENCES

Abbiw, D. (1990), *Useful Plants of Ghana: West African Uses of Wild and Cultivated Plants*, London: Intermediate Technology Publications.

Alexandre, D.Y. (1978), 'Le rôle disséminateur des éléphants en forêt de Taï, Côte d'Ivoire', *La Terre at la Vie*, **32**, 47–72.

Apumasah, J.B. (1992), 'Plantation programme under the forest resources management project', in A.A. Asiamah, O.K. Adade and M. Poku-Marboah (eds), *Forest Resources Management Project: Proceedings of Regional Seminars 26 May–10 June 1992*, sponsored by ODA and the Forestry Department of Ghana.

Asabere, P.K. (1987), 'Attempts at sustained yield management in the tropical high forest of Ghana', in F. Mergen and J.R. Vincent (eds), *Natural Management of Tropical Moist Forest*, Princeton, NJ: Yale University Press.

Asenso-Okyere, F.A. Asante and O. Gyekye (1993), 'Policies and strategies for rural poverty alleviation in Ghana', Technical Publication No. 57, ISSER, University of Ghana.

Baidoo, J.F. (1970), 'The selection system as practiced in Ghana', *Community Forestry Review*, **49**, 159–65.

Baidoo, J.F. (1976), 'Yield regulation in the high forest in Ghana', *Ghana Forestry Journal*, **2**, 22–7.

Barbier, E.B., J.C. Burgess and A. Markandya (1991), 'The economics of tropical deforestation', *Ambio*, **20**, 55–8.

Barbier, E.B., J.C. Burgess and C. Folke (1995), *Paradise Lost? The Ecological Economics of Biodiversity*, London: Earthscan.

Brown, K. and D. Pearce (eds) (1994), *The Causes of Tropical Deforestation*, London: University College London Press.

Burgess, P.F. (1971), 'The effect of logging on hill depterocarp forest', *Malaysia Nature Journal*, **24**, 231–7.

Chachu, R. (1989), 'Allowable cut from the forest', in J. Wong (ed.), *Ghana Forest Inventory Project Seminar Proceedings 29-30 March 1989*, Accra: Ghana Forestry Department and ODA.

Denys, E. (1980), 'A tentative phytogeographical division of tropical Africa based on a mathematical analysis of distribution maps', *Bulletin du jardin botanique national Belgique*, **50**, 465–504.

Ehrlich, P.R. (1988), 'The Loss of Diversity', in E.O. Wilson (ed.), *Biodiversity*, Washington, DC: National Academy Press.

Falconer, J. (1990), 'Major significance of "minor" forest products: the local use and value of forests in the West African humid forest zone', *Community Forestry Note 6*, Rome: FAO.

FAO (1988), *An Interim Report on the State of the Forest Resources in the Developing Countries*, Rome: FAO.

FAO (1991), *Production Yearbook*, Vol. 45, Rome: FAO.

FAO (1995), *State of the World's Forests, 1995*, Rome: FAO.

FAO/UNEP (1981), *Tropical Forest Resources Assessment Project. Forest Resources of Tropical Africa, Part II: Country Briefs*, Rome: FAO.

Foggie, A. (1957), 'Forestry problems in the closed forest zone of Chana', *Journal of West Africa Science Association*, **3**, 141–7.

Foggie, A. (1962), 'The role of forestry in the agricultural economy', in J.B. Wills (ed.), *Agricultural and Land Use in Ghana*, London:Oxford University Press.

Foggie, A. and B. Piaseck (1962), 'Timber, fuel and minor forest produce', in J.B. Wills (ed.), *Agriculture and Land Use in Ghana*, London: Oxford University Press.

Forestry Department (1962–1990), *Annual Report of the Forestry Department*, Accra.

Francois, J.H. (1987), 'Timber resources: demands and management approaches', *National Conference on Resource Conservation for Ghana's Sustainable Development: Volume 2 – Conference Papers*, Accra: Environmental Protection Council/Forestry Commission/European Economic Community, pp. 151–5.

Friends of the Earth (1992), *Plunder of Ghana's Rainforest for Illegal Profit. Vol. 2: Research Report*, London: Friends of the Earth.

Frimpong-Mensah, K. (1989), 'Ghana Forest inventory project seminar proceeding's 29–30 March 1989', In: J. Wong, (ed.) *Requirements of the Timber Industry*, Accra: Ghana Forestry Department and the Overseas Development Administration (ODA).

General Wood, (1993), 'Technical and financial audit of the Ghana timber industry', Vol. 1-6. Prepared for the Ministry of Lands and Forestry, Ghana. General Woods and Veneer Consultants International Ltd. Quebec (unpublished).

Gentry, A.H. (1992), 'Tropical forest biodiversity: distribution patterns and their conservational significance', *Oikos*, **63**, 19–28.

Glowka, L., F. Burhenne-Guilmin, H. Synge, A. J. McNeely and L. Gündling (1994), 'A guide to the convention on biological diversity', Environmental Policy and Law Paper No. 30, IUCN.

Hall, J.B. (1957), 'Conservation of forests in Ghana', *Universitas*, **8**, Accra, University of Ghana, 33–42.

Hall, J.B. and M.D. Swaine (1981), 'Distribution and ecology of vascular plants in tropical rainforest: forest vegetation in Ghana', *Geobotany*, **1**, The Hague.

Hawthorne, W.D. (1989), 'The flora and vegetation of Ghana's forests', in *Ghana Forestry Inventory Project Seminar Proceedings*, pp. 8–14, Accra: Forestry Department.

Hawthorne, W.D. (1990), 'Field guide to the forest trees of Ghana', Ghana Forestry Series 1, Natural Resources Institute, Ghana.

Hawthorne, W.D. (1991), 'Fire damage and forest regeneration in Ghana', Forestry inventory and management project. Forestry Department (unpublished).

Hawthorne, W.D. and M. Abu Juam (1993), 'Forest protection in Ghana: with particular reference to vegetation and plant species', Forest inventory and management project, Kumasi, ODA and Forestry Department.

ICBP/IUCN (1985), 'Threatened birds of Africa and related islands', *The ICBP/IUCN Red Data Book, Part 1*, Cambridge: ICBP/IUCN.

IIED (1988), 'Natural forest management for sustained timber production; Africa part II, country reports', a draft report prepared by the International Institute for Environment and Development for the International Tropical Timber Organization, October 1988.

ISSER (1992), 'The state of the Ghanaian economy in 1991', ISSER, University of Ghana. Legon.

ISSER (1993), 'The state of the Ghanaian economy in 1992', ISSER, University of Ghana. Legon.

ISSER (1994), 'The state of the Ghanaian economy in 1993', ISSER, University of Ghana. Legon.

ISSER (1995), 'The state of the Ghanaian economy in 1994', ISSER, University of Ghana, Legon.

ISSER (1996), 'The state of the Ghanaian economy in 1995', ISSER, University of Ghana, Legon.

ISSER (1997), 'The state of the Ghanaian economy in 1996', ISSER, University of Ghana, Legon.

ITTO (1993), 'Study of incentives for the sustainable management of the tropical high forest of Ghana', a report prepared by IIED and the Forestry Department of Ghana for the ITTO (unpublished).

IUCN (1988a), 'Ghana, conservation of biological diversity', briefing paper prepared by the International Union for the Conservation of Nature and Natural Resources Tropical Forest Programme, February, Cambridge.

IUCN (1988b), *1988 IUCN Red List of Threatened Animals*, Cambridge: The IUCN Conservation Monitoring Centre.

IUCN (1992) *The Conservation Atlas of Tropical Forests: Africa*, World Conservation Union, London: Macmillan.

Jacobs, M. (1988), *The Tropical Rain Forest: A First Encounter,* London: Springer-Verlag.

Jones, N. (1970), 'Forest tree improvement in Ghana', *Commonwealth Forestry Review.*

Kaimowitz, D. and A. Angelsen (1997), 'A users guide to economic models of deforestation', draft, Bogor, Indonesia: Center for International Forestry Research (CIFOR).

Keeling, W. (1991), 'Ghana aims for a fitter forestry sector', *Financial Times,* 6 June.

Kingdom, J. (1990), *Island Africa: The Evolution of Africa's Rare Animals and Plants,* London: Collins.

Konings, P. (1986), *The State and Rural Class Formation in Ghana: A Comparative Analysis,* London: Routledge.

Malingreau, J.P., G. Stephens and L. Fellows (1985), 'Remote sensing of forest fires: Kalimantan and North Borneo in 1982–1983', *Ambio,* **14,** 314–21.

Martin, C. (1990), *The Rainforests of West Africa: Ecology, Threats and Conservation,* Basel: Birkhäuser Verlag.

Martin, C. (1991), *The Rainforests of West Africa,* Ghana: Elsevier Publishers.

Mensah-Ntiamoa, A.Y. (1989), 'Pre-feasibility study on wildlife potentials in the Kakum and Asin-Attandoso Forest Reserves – Central Region – Ghana', Accra: Department of Game and Wildlife (unpublished).

Ministry of Agriculture (1990), *Ghana Medium Term Agricultural Development Programme (MTADP): An Agenda for Sustained Agricultural Growth and Development.* Accra: PPMED, Ministry of Agriculture.

Ministry of Agriculture (1991), 'Agriculture in Ghana: facts and figures', Policy Planning, Monitoring and Evaluation Department (PPMED), Ministry of Agriculture, Accra.

Nash, S. (ed.) (1990), 'Project: green', Final Report, Cambridge University.

Norton, A. (1991), 'Participatory forest management of non-reserved forest in Ghana: Report on a consultancy mission', Centre for Development Studies, Swansea (unpublished).

Nsenkylre, E.O. (1992), 'Ghana – progress towards the year 2000. Sustainable management of tropical forests' (unpublished).

Oldfield, S. (1988), *Rare Tropical Timbers,* Gland and Cambridge: World Conservation Union.

Oldfield, S. (1991), 'Pre-project study on the conservation status of tropical timbers in trade', Final report, prepared for the International Tropical Timber Organization by the World Conservation Monitoring Centre, February, Cambridge.

Olsen, D.K. and S. Curtin (1984), 'The role of economic timber species in the ecology of black and white colobus and dana monkeys in Bia National Park, Ghana', *International Journal of Primatology.*

Pennist, E. (1994), 'Biodiversity helps keep ecosystem healthy', *Science News,* **145** (84).

Peters, C.R. (1990), 'African wild plants with rootstocks reported to be eaten raw: the monocotyledons, part 1', proceedings, 12th Plenary Meeting AETFAT. *Mitteilungen aus den Institut für allgemeine Botanik in Hamburg,* **23,** 935–52.

Plumtre, R., L. Jayaneti, A. Fraser, T. Fawcett, G. Elliot and M. Gane (1991), 'Incentives in producer and consumer countries to promote sustainable development of tropical forests', pre-project report for the International Tropical

Timber Organization, prepared by the Oxford Forestry Institute in association with the Timber Research and Development Association, Oxford.

Repetto, R. (1988), *The Forests for the Trees? Government Policies and the Misuse of Forest Resources*, Washington DC: World Resources Institute.

Richards, M. (1995), *Role of Demand Side Incentives in Fine Grained Protection: A Case Study of Ghana's Tropical High Forests*, London: ODA.

Richards, P.W. (1973), 'Africa, the "Odd man out"', in B.J. Meggers, E.S. Ayensu and D. Duckworth (eds), *Tropical Forest Ecosystems in Africa and South America: A Comparative Review*, Washington, DC: Smithsonian Institution Press.

TEDB (1996), 'The Ghana timber industry: basic information, facts and figures', Timber Exports Development Board, Ghana (unpublished).

Uhl, C. and J.B. Kauffman (1990), 'Deforestation, fire susceptibility and potential tree responses to fire in the Eastern Amazon', *Ecology*, **71**, 437–49.

UNEP (1995), *Global Biodiversity Assessment*, Cambridge: Cambridge University Press.

Walter, H. et al. (1960), *Klimadiagram – Wetlands*, Jena: Gustav Fishcher.

White, F. (1979), 'The Guinea-Congolian region and its relationship to other phytochoria', *Bulletin du jardin botanique nationale Belgique*, **49**, 11–55.

White, F. (1983), *The Vegetation of Africa*, New York: AETFAT/UNSO.

Wildlife Conservation Monitoring Centre (WCMC) (1992), *Global Biodiversity: Status of the Earth's Living Resources*, London: Chapman and Hall.

Wong, J. (1989), *Ghana Forest Inventory Project Seminar Proceedings*, 29-30 March 1989, Accra: Ghana Forestry Department and the ODA.

World Bank (1987a), *Ghana Policies and Issues of Structural Adjustment*, Washington DC: World Bank.

World Bank (1987b), 'Ghana forestry sector review', Annexes, Washington DC: World Bank.

World Bank (1988), 'Ghana Forest Resource Management Project', Working Papers 1–6, Washington DC: World Bank.

World Bank (1989), *World Development Report 1993*, Oxford: Oxford University Press.

7. The Structural Adjustment Programme and deforestation in Ghana

James K. Benhin and Edward B. Barbier

7.1 INTRODUCTION

This chapter reviews the nature of the Structural Adjustment Programme in Ghana, its purpose and the form it took. It also reviews the policies undertaken under the programme with specific reference to the agricultural and timber and other forestry policies and their implications for deforestation and biodiversity loss in Ghana. The rest of the chapter includes an overview of the Programme; agricultural policies; timber and forestry policies; policies affecting deforestation and policies addressing deforestation and biodiversity loss. We first present a short review of the nature of Structural Adjustment Programmes (SAPs), and then look at the specific form of SAP in Ghana.

Structural Adjustment Programmes are one type of macroeconomic adjustment programme that countries, especially developing countries, are undertaking to move out from their economic decline or what is generally termed 'economic crisis'. The other type of macroeconomic adjustment programmes is the Economic Recovery Programme (ERP). ERPs or stabilization policies are short term in nature while SAPs are more long term. In recent times however there is very little difference made between the two, since invariably both have been undertaken hand in hand towards the same long-term goal of economic growth. In the discussion that follows very little difference is made between the two and in some cases macroeconomic adjustment will be synonymous with the Programmes.

According to Khan and Knight (1981) the essence of macroeconomic adjustment programmes is to eliminate supply–demand imbalances which have caused serious distortions and exhaustion of external financial resources. The source of these distortions has mainly been uneconomic prices and overvalued currencies which encouraged trading and speculation at the expense of productive activities such as agriculture and manufacturing. The main policies, according to them, that are needed to correct such distortions are embedded in the ERP and the SAP. These include:

1. Demand management policies to influence domestic absorption;
2. Exchange rate policies to influence the composition of domestic absorption and the production of tradable and non-tradables;
3. External financing policies to influence capital flows;
4. Structural policies to influence current and potential output.

Demand management policies are mainly policies to restrain domestic demand. The two main tools used, are fiscal and monetary policies (Dell, 1982; and Diaz-Alejandro, 1984). Fiscal policies are mainly restrictive in nature, which include curtailing public spending, at the same time as raising revenues. This is to help reduce domestic demand in order to eliminate supply–demand imbalances (Barro, 1974; Khan, 1987). The main tool used under monetary policy is the interest rate. This is based on the assumption that interest rates are the transmission mechanism between monetary policies and aggregate demand (Frenklen and Johnson, 1976). Therefore, by manipulating interest rates it will help reduce the supply–demand imbalances.

The objectives of exchange rate policies are to improve upon the international competitiveness of a country and to redirect the economy's productive activities from non-tradables to tradables. The main tool used is devaluation. The policy is simultaneously expenditure-reducing and expenditure-switching (Johnson, 1958). The demand and supply effects of devaluation work to reduce excess demand and the current account deficits. This depends, however, among other things, on the relative price elasticities of imports and exports, on the shares of tradables and non-tradables in total production, and on other policies adopted at the same time. Getting the right real exchange rate is also very important.

The basis of external financing polices is the belief that, because developing countries face scarcity of capital, they should be net foreign borrowers. The main lesson of this 'growth with debt' literature is that a country can and should borrow abroad as long as the capital produces a return to cover the cost of borrowing. In that case, the borrower will be increasing capacity and expanding with the aid of net foreign savings. In a sum, a country should depend on an external loan if the real interest rate on new loans is less than or equal to the expected growth in the volume of exports.

As compared to demand management, structural policies lay emphasis on growth rather than control of domestic demand and immediate improvement in the current account. Moreover, such policies may take a long time to show results since they usually require a significant rise in investment in the more efficient sectors combined with the release of capital and labour from the weak sectors to the strong sectors. Structural policies can be put into two main categories:

1. Policies to improve efficiency and resource allocation;
2. Policies to expand productive capacity of the economy.

Economic efficiency aims at increasing output from a given stock of resource allocation without reducing consumption. This includes measures to reduce distortions that cause a differential between price and marginal cost. Such distortions arise from price controls, imperfect competition, taxes, subsidies and trade restrictions. Removing these distortions is, however, rife with certain practical difficulties. These include reduced mobility of capital and labour between sectors which may result in unemployment. A careful study of the controls and the reasons for imposing them is needed before their removal. Due consideration also has to be given to the political realities of taking such a step. Moreover, given several significant distortions, removing some may not lead to efficiency.

Productive capacity in this context may be defined as the maximum amount of output that a country is physically capable of producing given the fullest and the most efficient use of its available resources, both human and natural. The rate at which an economy's capacity can be expanded depends among other things on the split between consumption and investment, and the nature and quality of the capital stock being added. Both of these help increase supply and reduce the supply–demand imbalances in the economy.

It is realized that, given that economic crisis has been caused by supply–demand imbalances, these policies under the Programme are aimed at either addressing the supply factors, and/or demand factors in order to address the problem. The above policies have generally been prescribed by the International Monetary Fund (IMF) and the International Bank for Reconstruction and Development (IBRI) – World Bank), to countries like Ghana, who needed such reforms.

Why the Ghanaian Economy Needed Reform

Despite earlier prosperity based on cocoa and timber exports, gold production and a relatively large reservoir of skilled labour, Ghana's economic fortunes deteriorated steadily from the late 1960s onwards. The pace of decline accelerated rapidly in the 1970s. Alternate bouts of liberalization and the enforcement of controls were compounded by fluctuations in trade earnings from the traditional exports (Ewusi, 1987). Agriculture performance in particular weakened dramatically with low producer prices and chronically inefficient systems for inputs delivery and credit. Disastrous economic policies led to an annual decline in the Gross Domestic Product (GDP) of about 0.5 per cent per annum, a fall in real per capita income of over 30 per cent and a decline in real export earnings of over 50 per cent between 1970 and 1982. The economic policies pursued during the period were characterized by maintenance of overvalued exchange rates, declining real producer prices of export commodities, low public utility prices which covered only a fraction of utility costs, negative real interest rates, greater reliance on administrative allocative mechanisms than on relative prices, overextension of the parastatal sector especially state monopolies and the prevalence of sellers' markets that provided little inducement for productivity advances. The real effective exchange rate for example was allowed to appreciate by 816 per cent by 1981 from a relatively undisturbed rate in 1973. Interest rates were, on average, negative in real terms by 30 per cent while budgetary deficits in the range of 10–122 per cent of GDP were tolerated year after year. The tax–GDP ratio declined to 5 per cent which was one-fourth the average for similar countries in Africa. In fact, a study (see World Bank, 1983) ranking developing countries according to the nature and intensity of distortions (in exchange rate, interest rate, inflation, acceleration of inflation, and energy prices) prevailing, during the 1970–80 decade found Ghana with a top score of 2.9 out of a maximum distortion index of 3.0. The consequences of these distortions for output and exports were disastrous.

Agriculture declined at a rate of 0.3 per cent per annum between 1970 and 1980 and this was made still worse by the severe drought of 1982/83 (World Bank, 1985). Cocoa production, which constituted about 60 per cent of total exports, fell from a level of 400 000 tons in 1975 to 179 000 tons in 1982, a drop of about 55 per cent. Between 1975 and 1983 the output of timber and timber products, which accounted for 9 per cent of exports in the mid-1970s, fell by 57 per cent. In the same period, output in the mineral sector, which accounted for 12 per cent of exports in 1974–78, also fell. The overall production of gold, diamonds, manganese and bauxite fell by 55 per cent (Ewusi, 1989). Accompanying these relapses in all basic indicators of economic performance were high levels of public budget deficits, a dwindling tax base and unrestrained growth in the money supply which led to a high level of inflation of about 123 per cent in 1983. Exchange rate overvaluation also undermined the competitiveness of traditional exports while at the same time stimulating the import of food items. It was asserted that around that period cocoa farmers cut down their cocoa trees because they were uneconomic. The overvaluation of the currency also gave raise to high dealings in the parallel market which was a disincentive to manufacturing activities. Thus, both export crop performance as well as the production of food crops fell back, placing further strain on the overextended public budget. The poor performance of agriculture was more than matched by developments in other sectors. The earlier attempts at industrialization and import substitution were also submerged by the tide of economic decline. From having generated nearly 20 per cent of GDP in the early 1970s, industry and manufacturing share fell to less than 10 per cent by 1983. Among other consequences, this meant that agriculture became even more central to the economy.

Other exogenous variables that further affected Ghana's economic performances were the fall in the world prices of her major exports and the rise in oil prices in 1973–74, and 1978–79, both of which worsened the terms of trade and led to a drop in foreign exchange earnings. Moreover, assistance from the international community was extremely low. For example, in 1982 Ghana received an average of $12.6 in aid per capita compared with an average of $26.1 in Sub-Saharan Africa. The shortage of foreign exchange led to a fall in import volume, large balance of payments deficits and subsequent drawing down of reserves.

Despite the substantial public deficits and falling overall economic performance, public employment continued to grow at around 14 per cent per annum in the period 1975–82, leading to chronic overstaffing and inappropriate composition of manpower in government and public agencies, one of the main causes being the high level of nepotism. The largest parastatal – the Cocoa Marketing Board (CMB) – appeared to have accounted for more than 10 per cent of wage employment (for institutions with over ten workers) by the early 1980s (Ewusi, 1987).

The crisis affected real incomes, government expenditure and service coverage, and therefore the standard of living of the populace. Real incomes fell in both urban and rural areas. By 1980, despite increases in nominal incomes, real minimum wages had fallen by 15 per cent from the level of 1974. In the rural areas incomes fell because of the fall in cash crop production and the low real producer prices. For example the producer price for cocoa was just about 30 per cent of the 1970 price in real terms. Poverty levels were between 30 and 35 per cent and between 60 and 65 per cent in the urban and rural areas respectively (Cornia et al., 1988).

Given this backdrop of high economic decline and the concomitant effects on the standard of living, the way out was to revitalize the economy. The only way to achieve this was to rely on high foreign capital inflow and therefore the need to depend on the IMF, the World Bank and other international financial institutions. The precondition for these capital inflows was the Structural Adjustment Programme.

7.2 THE ECONOMIC REFORM STRATEGY IN GHANA

Since April 1983, Ghana has undertaken a series of comprehensive macroeconomic and structural adjustment reforms aimed at reversing the economic decline, increasing the capacity of the economy to adjust to both external and internal shocks and generating sustainable growth and development. This was in response to the recognition of the cost of the crisis and the realization that the crisis could not be halted without a massive infusion of foreign exchange. The reforms are generally in the IMF and International Bank for Reconstruction and Development (IBRD – World Bank) direction, summarized under the phases of the Economic Recovery Programme (ERP) and the Structural Adjustment Programme (SAP) (see Appendix 7.1 for credit facilities undertaken). The ERP composed mainly of stabilization policies involving fiscal, monetary and exchange rate adjustment. The SAP, basically growth-oriented, includes resource mobilization, public sector and institutional reforms, and market liberalization. As stated elsewhere, the distinction between the objectives of the ERP and SAP is not very rigid since both aim at growth. The discussion that follows therefore makes no distinction between the two and their phases.

Macroeconomic policies embarked upon sought to realign relative prices, liberalize markets, introduce fiscal discipline and rehabilitate the country's social and economic infrastructure. These macroeconomic measures are supplemented by sectoral and institutional reforms aimed at encouraging savings and investment and introducing efficiency and equity (ISSER, 1992). The reform strategy pursued since 1983 can be grouped into three main components: price interventions, public expenditure management (budgetary reforms) and institutional restructuring. The measures associated with each component are listed in Appendix 7.2 (Ewusi, 1987).

In implementing the document, however, there have been some shifts in emphasis over the years. Initially, much emphasis was placed on increasing the productive capacity of the export sector and rehabilitating industries that generated high revenues for the government. After a disappointing outcome, attention was directed to removing bottlenecks in the infrastructure especially the transportation sector. Emphasis then again shifted to attaining food sufficiency which led to an agricultural policy for the period 1984–86. Later, there was the need for the growth of the economy to spill over to other sectors. Resources were therefore mobilized, at a donor's meeting in London in 1986, for the industrial sector. Five major policies implemented are identified for discussion. These are exchange rate, fiscal management and the divestiture programme, monetary/financial policies and trade liberalization.

Exchange rate adjustment Despite the devaluations in the 1970s, the Cedi was still overvalued. Its repercussions on the foreign exchange earning ability of the economy and developments of the industrial sector were far-reaching. It led to structural distortions in the economy, encouraging trading and speculation at the expense of production and productivity. The overvalued currency together with the high inflation level led to a declining real producer price of export commodities which was a disincentive to exporters, such as cocoa farmers (Quansah, 1987).

Against this background, a logical solution to the country's economic woes was a drastic adjustment in the exchange rate of the Cedi. Review of the exchange rate system began in April 1983 with the introduction of a scheme of bonuses on foreign exchange earnings and surcharges on foreign exchange use. And in line with the dictates of the underlying economic trends several adjustments were made in January 1986, and the rate was adjusted to 490/US$1 (Ewusi, 1987). In September 1986 a two-tier exchange rate system was adopted, known as Window I and II. To further liberalize the market, in 1988, privately owned 'forex bureaus' were allowed to participate in the foreign exchange market to determine their own sale and purchase prices (Ewusi, 1987; Sowa, 1990). Simultaneously, the exchange rate was unified in the context of the interbank market. The interbank market allows participating banks and forex bureaus to purchase foreign exchange from the Bank of Ghana for resale to customers. Weekly foreign exchange rates determined by market forces are published by the Bank of Ghana. This serves as the basis for determining the cost of foreign currencies of the commercial banks and rates for official transactions.

Fiscal management The objective of the policy of fiscal restriction was to restore fiscal balance and through that control the level of inflation. Instruments used to address the problem were government expenditure reducing and improvements in tax collection. Later during the adjustment programme, fiscal policy measures were designed to create incentives for the private sector (for example reduction in corporate taxes and tax reliefs, as in the timber processing sector) and to rehabilitate physical and social infrastructures.

In an attempt to reduce government expenditure several cost-sharing and cost-recovery measures have been introduced in most public departments and services. These measures have included redeployment, retrenchment of several thousands of workers on government payrolls and the removal of subsidies on agricultural inputs and other goods.

Government has also intensified efforts at revenue collection. The tax net has been widened with improved means of collecting taxes. It is estimated that between 1985 and 1987, government made savings of about 0.3 per cent of GDP in respect of budgetary transfers to state enterprises (Sowa, 1990) because of the divestiture programme.

Monetary/financial policies Monetary and financial policies introduced in the country have both stabilization and resource allocation objectives. On the one hand, the policies sought to control money supply so as to control inflation, while financial restructuring was expected to mobilize domestic resources, a precondition for generating investment and hence economic growth. However, monetary control through credit ceilings, the interest rate and open market operations affect both inflation and domestic resource mobilization and investment.

The policy package adopted has included selective credit controls which were eventually removed in 1991 (Nyanteng, 1993), retirement of government debts to the banks, financial sector restructuring and the establishment of the stock exchange market all aimed at mobilizing resources.

Trade liberalization Price controls on most commodities have been eliminated. Interest rates are also free from Bank of Ghana controls. These measures allow the market to efficiently determine the allocation of resources in the country. Several restrictions on payments and transfers with regard to international transactions have also been removed. For example, exporters are now allowed to retain some percentage of their earnings in external accounts as an incentive for increased exports.

These policies have brought about some economic benefits to the economy. These have included growth in output, foreign trade and balance of payments improvements, a better fiscal performance and reduced inflation rate. Sowa (1990, 1993) has examined some of these economic impacts of the adjustment programme in Ghana. The overall results, though positive compared to the economic crisis period, show that Ghana has a long way to go to reach an acceptable standard of living. These policies have both direct and indirect, intended and unintended impacts on the forest through the use made of the resource.

Attention is now turned to a discussion of the specific adjustment policies that affected the agriculture sector, timber and timber products, the forest and their concomitant effects on the environment.

Before tackling specific policies under SAP, it is first important to give a general overview of agricultural policies before the SAP as background to why a policy change was necessary. Ghana's pre-independence agricultural policy was geared towards the production of export crops, especially cocoa, in which the country had a comparative advantage. Ghana became the largest producer of cocoa during this period.

After independence, agricultural policy shifted from the concerns of small-scale farming to mechanized large-scale agriculture. The State Farms Corporation was formed to undertake large-scale mechanized farming and the Food Distribution Corporation was established to undertake the distribution of food throughout the country. A Cattle Development Board was also set up to produce meat on a large scale for consumption and to supply a meat factory in the Upper Region of the country. The poor performance of the agricultural sector during the period from 1960 to 1966 was a testimony to the inappropriateness of such policies of that period (Asenso-Okyere et al., 1993).

From 1966 to 1981, various policies were pursued in the agricultural sector. Notable among them was a policy of food-sufficiency with the launching of the Operation Feed Yourself and Operation Feed Your Industries programmes. These programmes spearheaded a campaign to increase food production and the production of agricultural raw materials needed for domestic industries. Attempts were made to increase the production of small-scale farmers by increasing the acreage available to them. While these efforts met with some success, many of the gains in food production corresponded with a dramatic decline in cocoa production. Cocoa output dropped by 41 per cent from about 462000 tonnes in 1972 to 271000 in 1978. The still dismal performance of the sector, an important factor for the economic crisis, showed the ineffectiveness of the policies.

When the SAP was launched in 1983 the need for agriculture to lead any sustained overall economic growth was recognized (as it was in the period before that) given the already important role that agriculture plays in the economy of Ghana. Emphasis was therefore placed on the sector. Incentives for the production of food, industrial raw materials and export commodities were restored. The government also embarked upon improvements in the infrastructure to aid such incentives in order to reduce the high transport cost involved in agricultural commodities marketing.

The focus of agricultural development in the 1990s as contained in the Medium Term Agricultural Development Programme (MTADP) (Ministry of Agriculture, 1990) included the following:

(i)   Pursuing a strong domestic and foreign demand-driven production goals;
(ii)   Enhancing productivity partly to reduce unemployment in agricultural production activities;
(iii) Improving production competitiveness;

(iv) Promoting an effective linkage between agriculture and industry in order to ensure that they supply the inputs needed by each other;

(v) Promoting agricultural growth based on regional comparative advantage and resource endowment;

(vi) Enhancing food security by way of adequate nutritionally balanced diets at affordable prices;

(vii) Increasing the foreign exchange earnings base by diversifying into non-traditional export crops;

(viii) Increasing the production of import substitutes;

(ix) Ensuring sound ecological management (environmental protection); and

(x) Alleviating rural poverty.

A further aim of the MTADP was for sustained annual growth in agricultural GDP of about 4 per cent. This was, however, and from 1990–94 was 1.1 per cent, though it picked up to 4.2 per cent in 1995 (CEPA, 1996; ISSER, 1996). These objectives are explicitly and implicitly similar to the objectives set out after independence until 1983 (Nyateng, 1993) except for export crop diversification and environmental protection.

Since the MTADP, other major developments have taken place, most of which have their basis in the MTADP. In October 1993, a Five-year National Agricultural Research Project was launched with the objective to restructure Ghana's agricultural research services (ISSER, 1993). In 1994, the Agricultural Sector Investment Project (ASIP) was also established to provide financial support for community or group investment in infrastructure in rural areas. It is aimed at providing some of the needed incentives for increased agricultural production and thereby enhance incomes and reduce rural poverty (ISSER, 1993; ISSER, 1995). In 1995, the National Agricultural Research Strategic Plan (NARSP) was also unveiled. This sets out a strategy for the National Agricultural Research System (NARS) for the decade beginning January 1995. The broad objectives of the strategic plan are to ensure that agriculture research priorities in Ghana are consistent with National Agricultural Policy, address farmers' needs and ensure sustainable use of the resources of the country (ISSER, 1996). In the same year there was implementation of the National Agricultural Extension Project (NAEP) which aims at evolving unified and efficient agricultural extension services in Ghana, based on a Training and Visit (TV) approach to agricultural extension.

Given the failure of the MTADP, in 1995 there was an initiative by the Ministry of Food and Agriculture to evolve a new agriculture sector strategy to replace it. For, in spite of the achievements of the MTADP, the general performance of the sector was still unfavourable with the sector's growth rate tumbling to 1.2 per cent in 1994 against an objective of 4 per cent. Moreover, farmers were complaining about the high prices of inputs, bottlenecks in the marketing system, unavailability and high cost of credit and the low profitability of production on the farm. There was also the underutilization of farm inputs, notably fertilizers and other agrochemicals and it was clear that the projected growth rate in agriculture envisaged under the MTADP could not be achieved or sustained. The committee set up to plan the new strategy recommended, among other measures, the re-introduction of input subsidies (about 20 per cent for a start) on fertilizer, and the need to address post-production issues with respect to transportation, storage, processing, market structure, grading and standardization. Other recommendations relate to technology development and dissemination, infrastructure including roads, power and water, resource management and environmental issues. The implication of these recommendations is that there was more to be done in the sector to enable the full potential of the sector to be realized.

We now turn attention to specific incentives under the Structural Adjustment Programme and their implications for the forest in Ghana.

7.3 AGRICULTURAL POLICIES AND THE STRUCTURAL ADJUSTMENT PROGRAMME

Both short- and medium-term policies and strategies have been formulated and implemented. The major short-term policies and strategies centre around the following: (i) improving producer incentives through output pricing; (ii) increasing the quantity and reliability of inputs supply; (iii) rehabilitation of road and transport infrastructure to enable produce to move to urban consuming centres. In the medium term, policies and strategies aimed at (i) improving the consistency between macro and sectoral policies through measures that improve resource use efficiency; (ii) strengthening the capacity of the public sector to support agricultural development; (iii) revitalizing agricultural research and extension services; (iv) increasing the level and efficiency of rural financial intermediation in order to increase the role of the private sector in agricultural development, small farmers and small rural entrepreneurs; and (v) increasing the productivity and incomes of majority of farmers through selective intervention in key areas such as small scale irrigation, output diversification and increased artisinal production and marketing (ISSER, 1992). The objective here as stated by the SAP was to remove supply–demand imbalances in the agricultural sector by providing the necessary incentives through the policies to encourage farmers to expand production. These policies and how they were implemented can be further grouped under the following (see Appendix 7.3 for some more details);

1. Improving agricultural productivity;
2. Reducing the risk and uncertainty factors associated with production and post-harvest activities;
3. Enhancing production incentives;
4. Providing the required support infrastructure.

Each of these policies is discussed below.

Improving Agricultural Productivity

Prior to the SAP, low productivity in both land and labour was reflected in the yields per hectare of almost all crops produced. In the 1990s under the SAP, productivity was expected to improve at a rate of 1.5 per cent per annum. (Ministry of Agriculture, 1990). The yields per hectare of the major crops grown in the country are shown in Table 7.1. In general, there has been some improvement, however, many of the crops have yet to reach their achievable levels. For example, maize was far below its achievable level of 5 metric tons per hectare. This has implications for the forest. If yields improve, it will reduce the rate of conversion of forest land. However, this depends on the source of this increased yield, whether from the increased application of modern technology, such as

Table 7.1   Average yields (metric tons) per hectare of major crops, 1987–90 (A1), 1991–95(A2)

Crop	Actual			Achievable		Percentage	
	A1	A2	B	Africa	World	A1/B	A2/B
Cereals							
Maize	1.2	1.45	5.0	1.6	3.7	24	29
Rice	1.2	1.80	3.0	2.0	3.5	40	60
Millet	0.7	0.78	2.0	0.7	0.8	35	39
Sorghum	0.75	1.00	2.5	0.8	1.3	30	40
Roots and tubers							
Cassava	8.2	11.6	29.0	7.7	9.9	37	40
Yam	6.6	11.6	10.0	9.1	9.0	66	116
Plantain	7.2	7.50	10.0	19.0	25.0	72	75

Source: Calculated from data from PPMED, Ministry of Agriculture, Accra.

the use of fertilizers, or from the nutrients from new converted forest land. The latter seems to be the case. Considering the general picture, output levels of maize between 1993–95 increased by 7.06 per cent (Table 7.4), yield increased by 6.25 per cent (Table 7.5), area increased by 4.68 per cent (Table 7.6). It is very easy to say that the increase in production has been due to more use of inputs like fertilizer and not forest land. However, it will be seen very soon that fertilizer consumption fell over that same period (Table 7.3), so that the increased productivity must be from nutrients from new forest lands. This simple analysis has serious implications for forest and biodiversity. With respect to cocoa, Ghana has, since the 1978/9 crop year, ranked third after Côte d'Ivoire and Brazil in world cocoa production mainly due to the relatively low yield per hectare (Table 7.2), and between 1990–1993 fluctuated between fourth and second position (ISSER, 1996).

Table 7.2   Average yields per hectare of cocoa in major producing countries, 1989–97

Country	Average yield (kg/ha)		
	1989–91	1992–94	1995–97
Ghana	3933	4051	4212
Nigeria	3583	3523	3566
Cameroon	3062	2931	3541
Côte d'Ivoire	5418	5514	5650
Brazil	5369	4622	4003
Malaysia	8204	6489	5788
Indonesia	8783	8729	9834

Source: FAO (1998), FAOSTATS database.

While several factors can be cited as contributing to the low level of land and labour productivity in agriculture, it is largely attributed to the type, quality and quantity of inputs used, the extension network and inadequate moisture for plant growth. Consequently, policy measures have emphasized improvement in the supply and distribution of improved input using the private sector, restructuring, retraining and equipping the public extension service, establishing small-scale and farmer-managed irrigation facilities, strengthening research capabilities and other productivity-enhancing factors.

To improve productivity a decade of research was undertaken into maize breeds by the Crop Research Institute (CRI) with funding from the

Ghana Grains Development Project (GGDP). By 1991, the research had produced about six high-yielding open pollinated maize varieties suitable for various growing environments. All the varieties have yields better than local varieties under all types of management conditions; however, the differences in yield are greatest under good management including fertilizer use, adequate plant stand and good weed control (ISSER, 1996; ISSER, 1993). However with the removal of subsidies on fertilizer and other inputs it is unlikely that the use of these inputs will increase significantly. In achieving any appreciable increase in maize production, for example, this implies the use of more land, that is, forest land.

Two significant developments have occurred in agricultural extension since 1986. Sasakawa Global 2000 (SG2000), a non-governmental organization has, since 1986, with the support of the Ministry of Agriculture, been actively involved in spreading new technologies in farming through its demonstration plots and supervised credits to small-scale farmers. The other significant development is the creation of a Department of Agricultural Extension Services (DAES) in the Ministry of Agriculture in 1987, which unified all extension bodies under one umbrella. This has brought about some improvements in agricultural extension services.

Production Risks and Uncertainties

Production risks and uncertainties are caused mainly by weather conditions, particularly rainfall and drought, not discounting factors such as timely availability of inputs including labour. The rainfall is quite unreliable with respect to onset, duration, intensity, amount, and so on. The rainfall pattern is partly the cause of the considerable seasonal fluctuations in crop output as reflected in the yield per hectare. The dependence on rainfall also limits the cultivation of crops (except maize in the forest and transitional agro-ecological zones) to only once per year, during the main rainy season (150–220 days). The cultivation of a second maize crop in the minor rainy season is usually less reliable. Given sufficient moisture, maize, rice, vegetables and some other crops can be cultivated at least twice a year.

One policy instrument to address the moisture problem has been to develop irrigation facilities throughout the country. A total of about 7500 hectares or about 0.2 per cent of the total land area cultivated in 1990 was irrigated. Most of the irrigation facilities have been large scale. There are problems with effective utilization and maintenance. There is now a shift in the irrigation development strategy towards small- to medium-scale schemes which can be operated by farmers. In spite of this in 1994 only 8000 ha, still about 0.2 per cent of the total cultivated land was irrigated. This also implies that the moisture in new forest lands used for cultivation has to be increasingly relied upon for additional agricultural production.

Post-harvest Risks and Uncertainties

Post-harvest risks and uncertainties are associated with the nature of storage, transport, market outlet and prices. The first two are discussed below while the last two are discussed under the subsection on production incentives.

Storage   A reduction of 30–50 per cent in the level of losses, it is asserted, will significantly reduce Ghana's dependence on food imports needed annually to meet consumption demand (Nyanteng, 1993). The storage losses of all food crops (including cereals, roots, tubers and plantain) were estimated to be between 15 and 30 per cent in the period before 1990 (Ministry of Agriculture, 1990). This is because of the inefficient traditional structures used by farmers. To solve the problem the government prioritized the development of a number of large-scale and modern facilities for grain (cereals and legumes) storage of 70 000 mt capacity. The problem with this was where they were sited which created additional transportation costs for farmers, and therefore low utilization of the facility. The Sasakawa Global 2000 (SG2000) is also helping small-scale farmers to develop cost-effective and vastly improved on-farm storage facilities.

A scheme for the small-scale farmer, the Cooperative Inventory Credit scheme with the Agricultural Development Bank, was started in 1989 to help farmers reduce post-harvest losses arising from falling prices immediately after harvest, due to poor storage facilities. Under the scheme, loans are given to farmers, using their stored produce, under the supervision of the scheme, as collateral. When the produce is sold later by the farmers themselves at a time when the market prices are high, they are able to pay back the loans with interest and still make a profit. However, the scheme has been affected by cheaper imports and unchecked infestation of stored produce (ISSER, 1993).

Transportation   The risks here relate to (i) poor road conditions which sometimes render some roads impassable, particularly during rainy seasons, (ii) availability of transport, and (iii) breakdown of vehicles in the process of moving commodities. The SAP therefore emphasized the need for a feeder road development. Maintenance of rural roads was to be among the top priorities of the District assemblies in the short and medium term. It is hoped that improving rural road networks and other road networks leading to major marketing centres will provide considerable incentive (through increased farm gate prices) for the production of marketable surpluses.

As part of the policy to improve the transportation system, the importation of commercial vehicles has been duty free since 1986. This led to an increase in the proportion of goods vehicles. The current situation, however, is that the bulk of the vehicles on the road are those that carry passengers (most imported goods vehicles have been converted to passenger vehicles), defeating the objective of the policy. The prime reason for this is that rural roads are still not sufficiently improved to attract vehicles to transport foodstuffs from such areas.

Production incentives Several incentive measures have been applied to agriculture in order to promote general or specific commodity development. The incentive measures have included:

(i)   Input price subsidy and input supply;
(ii) Institutional credit;
(iii) Output market outlets;
(iv) Guaranteed producer prices;
(v)   Producer bonus.

Input price subsidy and input supply In Ghana, the prices of all inputs and services handled by the government and quasi-government agencies were directly subsidized until the end of 1990. The subsidized inputs included fertilizers, improved seeds, production credit as well as insecticides, spraying machines and other hand tools used in cocoa cultivation. Indirect subsidies were in the form of reduced or zero tariffs on all agricultural inputs including heavy machinery such as tractors and combine harvesters imported for direct use or distribution by the private sector. It is claimed, however, that these subsidies led to a lot of waste. A story was told of how bags of fertilizer were placed in a flooded part of a road to allow a vehicle to pass over: an illustration of the extent to which subsidies lead to waste in developing countries. The subsidies also increased the financial burden of the government.

With the full removal of subsidies (over a five-year period, 1985–1990), privatization in the production, import and distribution of essential inputs, notably fertilizers, seed, insecticides and small hand tools and motorized equipment used in cocoa cultivation, was fully implemented in 1990. The objective of the policy reform was to establish a competitive private market that will ensure availability and timely supply of such input at the farm gate. It was envisaged that the competition would induce efficiency in distribution, lower costs and increase benefits to farmers in the form of lower prices.

The problem with the policy is the inability of the private sector to readily respond to the reforms and fully take over the distribution of these inputs, causing the prices of some of these inputs to increase beyond the reach of farmers.

Another problem is that output price has not increased as much as input prices (Jebuni et al., 1990). The resulting decreases in output–input price ratios will theoretically reduces the use of the purchased input. Available data shows that even though the imports of both fertilizer and insecticides (important inputs in maize and cocoa production, respectively) have increased the consumption of fertilizer has not increased (ISSER, 1993; ISSER, 1996). The consumption of fertilizer in 1992 was said to be lowest between the years 1988 and 1992 (Table 7.3). This has led to a decreasing rate of increase in the importation of fertilizer (imports were zero in 1991, immediately after the full removal of subsidies). This shows that even though the supply of fertilizer has improved, the prices, with the removal of subsidies and the realignment of the exchange rate, have not encouraged increased usage. Table 7.4 shows that fertilizer prices continued to increase substantially in 1994. The price increase ranged

Table 7.3   Fertilizer imports, total supply and consumption (metric tons), 1988–95

Year	Imported	Stocks	Total supply	Consumption
1988	39 575	8613	NA	30 962
1989	65 239	41 195	73 852	32 657
1990	43 750	75 936	106 545	30 609
1991	0	31 000	75 936	44 936
1992	30 900	36 000	6 100	25 000
1993	19 600	NA	NA	NA
1994	24 040	NA	NA	NA
1995	33 340	NA	NA	NA
Five year average				
1990/94	24 568	NA	NA	NA
1985/89	38 595	NA	NA	NA

Note: NA = Not available.

Sources: Crop Services Department, Ministry of Agriculture. ISSER (1993, 1996).

Table 7.4   Prices of important fertilizers, 1982–95 (Cedis/50 kg)

Year	Ammonium	15-15-15/20-20-20	Muriate of potash	Super-phosphate
1982	25	30	25	NA
1983	45	58	45	NA
1984	295	440	295	NA
1985	295	440	295	NA
1986	400	700	490	NA
1987	820	1380	1270	840
1988	1600	2300	2100	840
1989	2350	3350	3250	840
1990	3100	4200	3800	3000
1991	3100	4200	3800	3000
1992	6400	4200	10000	3000
1993	7800	NA	12000	3000
1994	8800	NA	14000	5000
1995	8000	NA	12500	14500

Note: NA = Not available.

Sources: Crop Services Department, Ministry of Food and Agriculture, Accra. ISSER (1993, 1996).

from 12.8 per cent to 82 per cent. In 1995, given the problem of usage, some fertilizer prices were reduced by 4 per cent to 35 per cent (for example, ammonium sulphate by 9 per cent) but still others increased by between 190 and 317 per cent. These prices have been disproportionate to the increase in the price of food crops such as maize. The price of insecticides increased by 77 per cent between 1990 and 1991, remained stable until the 1992/93 season, and then was reduced by 42 per cent in 1993/94, and remained stable in 1994/95. The objective was to increase usage to give increased cocoa production, given the high dependence of the economy on cocoa proceeds. These price trends led to consumption of insecticides falling by 81 per cent between 1988/89 and 1992/93), and increasing by 84 and 87 per cent in 1993/94 and 1994/95, respectively, when the price was reduced by 42 per cent (ISSER, 1996).

It has been observed in the Upper Eastern Region of Ghana that where prices and market outlets have been adequate, farmers have willingly paid higher prices for inputs. This means that farmers can afford to pay for inputs if they receive adequate prices for their outputs. This mismatch between output and input price has been due to the low response of the private sector in input production and distribution which was expected to reduce prices at the farm gate. Another cause is the import liberalization policy which has led to tough competition from imported goods which are relatively cheaper.

The irony is that both the increase in fertilizer prices and the reduction in the use of insecticides may lead to more use of forest land. Fertilizer is needed to improve the nutrients in the soil for increased production; given current prices and the fall in consumption, an alternative is the nutrient from new forest land. Insecticides are important in the early years of cocoa planting, not for the improvement in soil quality. This means a fall in its price, given increases in cocoa prices, may make farmers demand more land for cocoa farming. This land is basically forest land, since cocoa farming needs the shade provided by a limited forest in its early growing stage. Both imply the removal of some forest. This is a typical case of conflict in policies leading to policy failure with respect to the forest and biodiversity in Ghana.

Agricultural credit The availability of production credit is a constraint, to a large extent, on the adoption and extensive use of modem agricultural inputs in Ghana, particularly among small-scale farmers. Small-scale farmers obtain production credit from both formal and informal financial markets but mainly from the latter. Informal credits are provided by friends, relatives, traders, private money lenders and private groups through schemes such as '*susu*'. These are mainly short-term loans which are used predominantly for consumption rather than for production. The interest rates are quite high due partly to the high risks of granting the loans without adequate collateral and the high rates of default in repayment. The policy to provide formal credit to small-scale farmers in particular and for agricultural development in general eventually resulted in the establishment of the Agricultural Development Bank (ADB). Besides the ADB, the commercial banks were obliged, as a matter of policy, to lend not less than 25 per cent of their loanable funds to the agricultural sector and also at subsidized interest rates (Nyanteng, 1993). However, these policies were not adhered to since it was not easy to penalize banks when they failed to obey the directive. The policy was therefore not effective.

These policies were abolished in 1990. Subsequently, agricultural interest rates have been raised to the same levels as the interest rates charged for the non-agricultural use of loans. One disadvantage, however, is that, given the high risk in agricultural production, high rates of default in repayment and the high cost of administering loans to many small-scale farmers, the agricultural sector does not receive adequate loans from the banks. Table 7.5

*Table 7.5   Commercial and secondary bank loans and advances to the
agricultural sector, 1975–93 (million Cedis)*

Year	Commercial banks		Secondary banks	
	Amount	Percentage of total	Amount	Percentage of total
1975	33	8.3	72	37.8
1980	45	9.6	267	34.4
1984	2155	31.9	624	29.7
1985	2897	22.9	2311	23.7
1990	6161	15.8	6484	16.1
1991	5804	13.6	8625	13.0
1992	6988	11.1	7728	8.7
1993	7575	9.6	9682	7.5

Sources: Ghana Statistical Service, Quarterly Digest of Statistics (June 1983, June 1985,
June 1990, March 1994). Accra. ISSER (1996).

shows that even though total advances to the agricultural sector in the SAP
period have increased, the proportion has fallen. In 1989, the proportion
was only about half the level in 1984, and was even less in subsequent
years. Credit unavailability plus high prices of inputs implies inability to
purchase needed inputs for improved production; this, in turn, promotes a
reliance on the free input provided by the forest for increased production.

Market outlets The unavailability of ready marketing outlets for agricultural output is a major disincentive to produce marketable surpluses in
the sector, resulting in part of the produce going rotten at the
production points. As part of the solution, the Ghana Food Distribution
Corporation (GFDC) was established in 1947 to trade in farm goods
alongside the private sector. However, the GFDC has been able to handle
only 10 per cent of the marketable surplus. Under the SAP, the government is encouraging private business to become involved in agricultural
marketing. This has led to reforms in the Cocoa Board (Cocobod) system
(in the distribution of inputs, purchase and export of cocoa beans), grain
marketing and crop marketing.

In the Cocobod system there has been the divestiture of subsidiaries
such as plantations and a chemical formulation plant and feeder roads. The
monopoly of the Produce Buying Company (PBC) over cocoa haulage has
also been eliminated and the operations of the cocoa extension services
have been streamlined. These measures have exerted considerable impact

on the level of Cocobod's operating costs, lowering them by about one-third since 1987, and thereby enabling the producer price, as a proportion of the FOB price, to rise over the period. The domestic and external marketing of coffee and sheanuts have also been liberalized. The aim is to abolish the monopsony of PBC by introducing private buying.

Competition is expected to induce each marketing intermediary to control costs or go out of business.

In grain marketing, the domestic buying of grains by the GFDC for price support purposes was abolished in the 1990 crop season. Government is also encouraging the building of efficient medium-size grain storage, putting a halt to the expansion of inefficient large-size storage facilities by the GFDC. All these measures are aimed at reducing the role of the government-funded GFDC in grain marketing. Similar liberalization in marketing has been introduced in other agricultural goods including cotton and palm oil.

Producer price The producer prices of some agricultural products have received government support for several decades. Prices were set for traditional crops as well as some industrial crops and guaranteed minimum prices (GMP) were set for some food crops, notably maize and rice, which together accounted for about 5 per cent of agricultural GDP. The producer price intervention policy was intended to ensure that the producers received fair prices and adequate incentives for increased production. The implication was that the open markets failed to pay fair prices for farm products. As part of the general policy under SAP of non-interference and privatization of economic activities, the GMP and the raw materials price intervention policies were abolished in 1990. The prices of all food crops are now determined in the open markets and prices of raw materials are determined through negotiations between producers and buyers. However, farmers can still benefit from a GMP which can provide a basis for production decisions, determining expected revenue, ability to repay loans, and so on (Nyanteng, 1993). With respect to cocoa, the exchange rate policy has enabled the government to review upwards the producer price from 12000 Cedis per metric tonne in the 1983/84 crop season to 258 000 Cedis in 1992/93, and again to 1.2 million Cedis in the 1996/97 crop season. Sijim (1993) noted however, that the price has yet to reach the 1970s levels in real terms. With the government reducing the role of the Cocobod, it is expected that further costs will be saved to enable further increases in the producer price. Increased output prices are expected to encourage the use of modern technology in farming activities thereby indirectly reducing the reliance on the forest for nutrients.

Producer bonus to cocoa farmers The strategy of paying a bonus to cocoa farmers as extra income has been implemented in the country since the 1972/73 crop year. It was stopped briefly and reintroduced in the second half of the 1980s and has been very prominent under the SAP. In fact, it is not a bonus as such but a pricing strategy. It was the policy of the government to pay farmers about 50 per cent of the world market price. As the world market price could not be determined with accuracy at the time of fixing the producer price at the beginning of the buying season, farmers sometimes received a price lower than 50 per cent of the world market price. They were therefore paid the difference in the form of price compensation. The price compensation scheme has been misinterpreted and farmers now demand it each year as a bonus payment. The amount of the bonus is determined by the world market price and the tonnage of cocoa produced. To operate the bonus scheme, a cocoa 'price' Compensation Account was set up in 1986. A positive difference between the actual and anticipated world market price goes into that account which is shared between producers (60 per cent) and government (40 per cent). Alderman (1991) has argued that the system of paying bonuses, being in amount and timing, does not produce the same incentive effect as an increase in the producer price announced at the beginning of the season, unless the amount of the bonus is fully anticipated. However, since the bonus forms only a very small proportion of the producers' price, it is unlikely to add much to the incentive if added to the producer price initially.

Recognition, awards and statutory holiday Farmers in the country are accorded recognition through a national farmers' day which is celebrated throughout the country on 1 December each year. During the celebrations, outstanding farmers are awarded prizes at district, regional and national levels. There is also the agricultural show which is held once a year at a different time.

In 1992, the government declared the farmers' day a statutory public holiday in further recognition of the farmers' contribution to the country's economic development. The recognition and awards are expected to provide incentives for hard work and increased production to the benefit of the nation as a whole. Even though it is difficult to measure the impact of this policy on farmers' production, it is generally believed that the public holiday benefits the public and some private employees more than the farmers (farmers attend to their farms anyway). There is therefore a high social cost attached to the holiday – paying salaries and wages as normal for no work done.

The review has shown that agriculture is an important sector in the economy of Ghana. The development of the country depends very much on improvements on the sector. However, the sector is faced with many constraints in production and marketing. Some of these are what the SAP intended to help remove. It is also realized that increases in output before the SAP was due to land expansion and not productivity, given the type of technology used. Under the SAP, despite some improvements in the sector due to the policies implemented, the removal of input subsidies, and the inability of the private sector to respond to the government's privatization exercise, has led to a fall in the output–input ratio. Given that the farmers cannot afford the increased input prices, given their scarcity, it is expected that increases in output during the SAP may be more due to land expansion than to productivity improvements. The use of more land, which is basically by clearing and burning, has negative implications for forest and biodiversity in Ghana.

7.4   FORESTRY POLICIES AND THE STRUCTURAL ADJUSTMENT PROGRAMME

The forestry sector has mainly been influenced by supply-side policies of control or regulation of the supply of timber to concessionaires through an annual allowable cut, girth size limits and control of harvesting practices. As far back as 1906, legislation was enacted to control the felling of commercial tree species, followed by the creation of the Forestry Department in 1908. The demarcation and reservation of forest estates were largely completed by 1939 and a Forest Policy was adopted in 1948. The policy mainly emphasized the sustained supply of forest produce for the wood industry and promoted the exploitation and eventual demise of unreserved forests.

Subsequent years up to the 1970s and early 1980s, saw the growth and decline of the wood industry and its contribution to the economy, as already seen in preceding chapters. One important policy in that period was the 1979 export ban on 14 species of log (see Appendix 6.5 of Chapter 6). The objective was to control the extraction of the species in addition to helping the domestic processing market. In spite of this policy, Ghana saw the decline of both the export and processing sector, especially in the late 1970s and early 1980s in response to the economic crisis of that period. Factors such as poor exchange rates were disincentives to the sector. Low credits and lack of foreign investment, especially to the processing sector, were a hindrance to adopting improved technology in the sector. In a nutshell, the sector epitomized the decline of the economy. In spite of the low cost of extraction (low royalties), it was still not attractive to extract, process and export timber and timber products. These problems are what the SAP has attempted to solve to revitalize the sector.

Under the Structural Adjustment Programmes, policies have also aimed at reducing the extraction of some species and encouraging the extraction of less known species through control and regulations in extraction. In this direction some additional species of timber have been banned from exports. And to improve upon the marketing of timber and timber products, the Ghana Timber Marketing Board (GTMB) was disbanded to make way for the Timber Export Development Board (TEDB) and the Forest Products Inspection Bureau (FPIB). The former is responsible for providing price guidelines and export markets, while the latter oversees all contracts, monitors quality standards and grades lumber and timber products. Other activities of the latter include the administration of regulations and procedures for exports. A new policy, the Forest and Wildlife Policy was promulgated in 1994 to replace the 1948 Policy (IIED, 1996). Species of timber on the export list have been encouraged by realignment of the exchange rate and the retention of a certain amount of foreign earnings for the importation of equipment. Another area of emphasis is the domestic processing market. In addition to the exchange rates, credit facilities have been advanced to the sector with corporate tax reliefs. The Ghana Investment Promotion Centre Act, 1994 (Act 478) for example, makes provision for the automatic award of investment incentives and benefits without prior approval requirements.

Exchange rate policies and the forestry sector The objective of foreign exchange realignment is to increase the return in local currency for exporters of timber and timber products. All things being equal, if earnings increase the log export and processing export market pick up. This is proven by the performance in both exports over the period of adjustment. An advantage of increased earnings is the ability to import the necessary inputs, leading to greater efficiency and reduced forest loss. One disadvantage, however, is that it may lead to more exports of logs rather than domestic processing, since it is easier and cheaper to export logs. It is in this light that other specific policies have been applied.

Timber and timber products exporters are allowed to retain 20 per cent of their foreign exchange earnings for the main purpose of importing needed equipment for improved efficiency in both the extraction and processing (the removal of import licensing also has the same objective) sector. This policy is expected to help reduce inefficiencies and therefore preserve the forest. To fully support this objective, the Investment Act,

1994 (Act 478) provides that imported plant, machinery, equipment and parts thereof are zero-rated for customs import duty. And provision has also been made for any special equipment not zero-rated to be granted exemption from customs import duty and related charges upon application by the investor to the Ghana Investment Promotion Centre (GIPC). The problem, however, is that there is no way to check whether such retained foreign earnings are being used for the purpose designed.

Credit facilities Under the Export Rehabilitation Project, the government contracted a number of loans/credits facilities from IDA, ECGD, ODA, CIDA and DANIDA for the sector. Appiah (1990) reported that between 1983 and 1986, some US$58 million from IDA and bilateral agencies was invested in 'sawmill improvement' while a further $70 million went into logging equipment. In total about $140 million was contracted for the sector between 1983 and 1986 (Friends of the Earth, 1992). The Ghana Investment Centre also revealed that some $265 million was made available to the industry between 1986 and 1989 (Richards, 1995). At the end of 1988, under a Five-year Forest Resource Management Project (FRMP) the IDA provided $39.4 million to the sector. The objective, among others, was to stabilize forestry production and export earnings, promote conservation and tree planting so as to counteract fuelwood shortages and ecological deterioration, and strengthen forestry sector institutions. However, with much emphasis on the rehabilitation and expansion of exports, scant consideration was given to forest conservation (Friends of the Earth, 1992). The incentive from these credits was an increased use of the forest resource.

Tax relief Income tax incentives provided under the reforms include:

1. Locational incentives, which provide for 25 per cent rebate for industries located in the regional capitals, Accra or Tema, the two main industrial centres, and 50 per cent rebate for industries located outside regional capitals;
2. Corporate tax rebate which provides for 35 per cent rebate for all timber products except for non-traditional timber products for export, which is 8 per cent;
3. Capital allowance, which provides for a depreciation rate of 50 per cent per annum for 2 years, for plant and machinery, and 20 per cent for 5 years for buildings.

Richards (1995) has observed that owing to these generous rebate allowances, if a company exported 25 per cent or more of their produce by value, they ended up paying an effective 5–10 per cent corporation tax, as opposed to the nominal rate of 35 per cent. Such tax reliefs are an attraction for more firms to enter the industry; however, if they are inefficient misuse of the forest resource is high as has been described in previous sections.

Impacts on Deforestation

As stated elsewhere, forest loss has been caused by the interaction of different complex factors. These include, social, cultural, political and economic, referred to as proximate and underlying factors. The proximate factors have been discussed in Section 7.2. This section focus on the underlying factors both with respect to timber and timber products and agriculture, some of which have unintended effects on the forest in Ghana.

The first has to do with the allocation of concessions. The customary and common law 'ownership' of timber trees lies with the *stools* but the government exercises control of their exploitation. The concession allocation policy requires very little or no input by *stools* and local authorities. Chiefs do however receive some unofficial payments from concessionaires, in cash or building materials. These 'gifts' are generally very small and most of the time are kept by the chief for his personal use. To the farmer the forest is valued more highly as a land bank than as forest. The farmer, both native and migrant, have few rights to timber trees on the land they work, save the right to use some for individual 'domestic' purposes. Farmers have no right to sell timber trees on their land, although in some places such 'sales' take place. They also do not receive any portion of royalties (except in rare cases at the discretion of the relevant chief) and have no legal rights to be informed of or to refuse felling of trees by timber concession holders. Furthermore, destruction to tree crops and farms is often sustained when timber trees are felled, with little or no compensation generally received. Farmers are therefore keen to remove such trees because they feel their crops will do better without them, given the negative effects of maintaining the trees. Thus there is a net disincentive to plant, protect and nurture timber trees in that the costs to the farmer may include the 'bad' qualities of pest harbouring and competition with crops, but also the eventual damage to crops from felling. These may far outweigh the benefits from tree products, 'good' qualities of shade, soil and microclimate functions and eventual compensation for felling damage (López, 1995).

Weak institutions, conflicting and inadequate policy, and fiscal and financial effects have been cited as the underlying causes of forest loss and degradation in Ghana. The primacy of agriculture, particularly the continued attractiveness of cocoa cultivation is due to these underlying factors. The acreage of cocoa is directly influenced by the producer price, which in turn is affected by three major factors: (a) the export price for Ghana's cocoa is reportedly falling, but with steadily increasing world demand most analysts predict moderately rising cocoa prices; (b) the overvalued exchange rate effectively acted as a tax on cocoa producers in the past, but is no longer a problem since Ghana moved to a more flexible exchange rate; (c) the proportion of the export price passed on to the producer by the government in recent years has been about 30–40 per cent. It is the policy of the government to gradually increase this. So with increasing profitability of cocoa farming projected into the foreseeable future, the pressure on forests off-reserves (ITTO, 1993) and even reserves will remain steady and may even be increased.

The unstable market-determined price of maize, due to poor storage facilities, low credit facilities to the sector for the adoption of improved technology, and increases in fertilizer prices (though there has been increased improved varieties of maize, fertilizer is needed for good performance) is a disincentive to control forest conversion, since it becomes cheaper for the maize farmer to rely on the nutrients from the converted forest for increased production in order to maintain his income level. On the other hand, the increased producer price of cocoa, improved varieties and falling prices of pesticides are also incentives to convert more forest given the nature of cocoa production.

In the timber industry, exchange rate policies, foreign exchange retention, credit facilities to the sector together with the export ban, which implies increased exports of timber and timber products, may lead to more forest loss. The last two policies are to help reduce the impact of the first two policies on forests in Ghana, however, given the inefficiencies in domestic processing, it implies more use of forest resources. Attempts at increasing the cost of using the forest resources through increased royalties have not been effective since charges are still relatively very low. This is a conflict in policies which might lead to more forest use in the activities of the three commodities, leading to forest and biodiversity loss.

Rapid population growth in Ghana, and migration in particular to areas in the west of the high forest zone, has until now been accommodated by the extension of agriculture into the unreserved forest and the progressive shortening of the fallow cycle. As population density increases and land becomes more scarce, its value should rise and farmers should then find it cost-effective to intensify production. However, in Ghana there are limited alternatives of proven worth available to the farmer in terms of improved inputs, access to credit and reliability of markets, to help in production intensification to avert the negative impact of rapid population growth on forest loss.

7.5 POLICIES ADDRESSING DEFORESTATION AND FOREST DEGRADATION

Both supply and demand-side policies have been used to address deforestation in Ghana. Some of the policies are intended for the purpose. Others are unintended, but may have an indirect effect on reducing forest loss in Ghana. Supply-side policies, which mainly have to do with the forestry sector, as stated earlier, refer to the control or regulation of the supply of timber to the concessionaires, for example through an annual allowable cut, girth size limits and control of harvesting practices. Another policy on the supply side is to encourage tree planting. Demand-side policies can both be direct and indirect. With respect to agriculture, such policies include credit facilities, improved fertilizer supply and increased output prices. In the timber industry, they include forest fees and trade restrictions.

Supply-side Policies

A national tree planting programme, attuned to planting areas outside forest reserves, was launched in 1984. Targeted areas for planting include farms, watersheds, dams and dugouts. Others are the precincts of educational institutions, parks, avenues and approaches to towns and villages. Here the Forestry Department plays a lead role by educating the public and providing free seeds and seedlings. The public is advised on what to plant, how and when to obtain it, where to plant it and how to plant and manage it to maturity.

Measures have been taken in the harvesting of timber for sustaining the forest resource. Some of these are discussed. Growth modelling, for example, has been introduced to assist the forester in arriving at a more accurate yield production. This is to help determine mortality, growth and yield. The objective is to help reduce overexploitation. And to consolidate and simplify management, forest reserves have been grouped into Forest Management Units (FMU). Each FMU is about $500 \, km^2$ and lies within one forest type. It is the FMU which forms the basic unit from which sustained yield management is practised.

All tree species have since 1989 been reclassified into three new groups (Class I, II and III) to reflect the potential of the forest resource. The reclassification provides for the utilization of a broader species base. Harvesting of the forest using a much wider species base is expected to provide an environment which is more favourable to maintaining the biodiversity of the forest ecosystem.

Determination of the felling limits of all commercial species is also based on their frequency, distribution within diameter classes and natural size within the forest. Any species whose distribution is not normal or whose occurrence is less than two stems per km^2 cannot be harvested without a special permit. This approach helps to conserve those species that have been heavily exploited in the past or naturally occur at a very low frequency.

A 100 per cent pre-felling stock survey of all Class I trees above 50 cm diameter at breast height is carried out to produce a two-dimensional map of species location and diameter class. The map is then translated into a three-dimensional representation of the forest using different sized wood screws for the various diameter classes of individual tree species (small sizes for lower diameter classes). The three-dimensional perspective of the distribution and size of the commercial species helps in the selection of trees which form the yield, leaving a better distribution of seed trees for regeneration.

At the present level, yield is regulated by using a formula which takes into consideration (i) the abundance of individual species both above and immediately below the felling limit, (ii) a 40 per cent retention of trees above their felling limit and (iii) a 20 per cent mortality of trees during the 40-year felling cycle. The yield is then evenly distributed throughout the compartment in an effort to minimize the effect of logging on the forest environment and to effect favourable regeneration of the harvested species. Thus, the formula, simply prescribes a yield which has a bias towards species abundance.

In sensitive areas such as the dry semi-deciduous fire zone which forms the interface between the savannah and the high forest, the percentage retention of trees over the felling limit is increased to 60 per cent in an effort to reduce the opening of the canopy and therefore the prevention of savannization. This also has the effect of indirectly reducing the incidence of fire and encouraging regeneration.

A logging manual (Forestry Department, 1992) has been introduced and promulgated to ensure sound harvesting techniques which minimize damage to the residual forest and reduce wood waste during extraction. The manual makes provision for the following: full protection of trees on slopes greater than 30 per cent, high altitude plateaux, riparian strips, sacred groves, and areas of scientific or archeological importance; restricted felling on slopes less than 30 per cent and flat land; approved harvesting equipment.

To streamline management and control over timber harvesting, a maximum number of concessions (4) have been provided for each Forest Management Unit. In addition, the lease period for a concession has been increased from 25 to 40 years to coincide with the felling cycle.

Security of tenure ensures an awareness, among concessionaires, of the benefits to be derived from long-term sustained management of the forest resource. Continuous assessment of performance determines whether a concessionaire can continue harvesting.

For the effective control and monitoring of the yield from forest reserves, all felled trees are individually marked on the butt end and stump with a reserve code; the compartment number; stock number; the concessionaire's property mark; a locality mark; the concessionaire's log number; species names; and diameter and volume. The coding system has the added advantage of identifying trees harvested from managed forests. A single authority, the Concessions Unit, established within the Forestry Department now has responsibility for concession management. It includes membership of all organizations related to the forest and timber. The Concession Unit seeks the views of District Councils, land owners and local communities before granting concessions.

Demand-side Policies

In the agricultural sector, the provision of credit facilities, improved seedlings, improved extension services and increased market prices are intended to make it possible for less reliance on the forest resource for increased production. For example, the provision of credit improves the farmer's ability to purchase inputs. Improved research and extension services and seedlings increase productivity. Improved storage facilities help reduce post-harvest losses. Reduced post-harvest losses will improve the market price of maize, and increases in the producer price of cocoa will increase the relative returns and therefore the ability to purchase and adopt environmentally friendly input and reduce the demand for forest land for increased production.

In the timber industry, the provision of credit facilities, low corporate taxes, exchange rates and foreign exchange retention help improve efficiency in the processing market and, together with the export ban, help to reduce the overuse of tree species. Attention is now being turned to direct demand-side policies such as forest fees and trade restrictions like the export ban on timber species.

Forest fees Forest fees in Ghana include taxation of the stumpage value of the timber, as in the case of royalties and concession rent; payments for services, as in the case of export levies; and penalties for transgressing forest management regulations. Table 7.6 shows official forest fees according to the institution responsible for levying them: 1993 fee levels are in US dollar equivalents and estimated collection levels cover the period

Table 7.6   Forest fees and collection levels

Institution/fee	1993 level	Average revenues 1989–1991 ($1000)	($/m³)
Forestry Department (FD):			
Royalties[a]	Variable	2539	2.03
Concession rent[a]	$0.16/ha p.a.	10	0.01
Compensation payments	Variable	1	0.00
Fines, penalties	Many 1000%	2	0.00
Property mark	royalty	42	0.04
Taungya fees	$80/concession p.a.	0	0.00
Minor forest products	Variable	20	0.02
Concession preparation fee[b]	Variable		
Silvicultural fees	$806 (once only) Discontinued	12	0.01
Forest Products Inspection Bureau (FPIB):			
Export registration fee	$48 p.a.	24	0.02
Retailer registration fee[c]	$8 p.a.		
Log measurement certificate	$0.32 per log	39	0.03
FPIB and Timber Export Development Board (TEDB):			
Export levy	3% FOB	2768	2.36
Export Promotion Council (EPC):			
Registration fee	$48 p.a.	70	0.06
Ghana Chamber of Commerce:			
Export document fees[d]	$8/cargo		
Ghana Shippers Council:			
Registration fee[d]	$194 p.a.		
Total forest fees		5526	4.58

Notes
[a] On reserve payments to FD, off reserve payments to Land Commission. Royalties include payments by non-concessionaires for major forest products (timber).
[b] Only introduced in 1992, therefore no revenue was collected over the 1989–1991 period.
[c] Fees collected included under Export Registration Fee.
[d] Collection 1989–1991 included Export Promotion Council fee (this was an estimate of the combined revenue collection of these other regulatory bodies).

Source: Richards (1995).

1989–1991 (Richards, 1995). The third column of Table 7.6 shows that an average of about US$5.5 million per annum was collected over the period 1989–1991, and the final column shows that this amounted to US$4.72/m^3 of officially harvested roundwood, about 3 per cent of its unit export value. The only two significant fees were royalties and the export levies, which between them accounted for about 95 per cent of the total.

Log royalties are the main instruments of forest taxation in Ghana and are set by the Ministry of Lands and Forestry (MLF). Royalties are charged on a standing timber per tree basis (although there are plans to move to a volume-extracted basis, which has the advantage of increased revenues). Royalties from the reserves were collected by the Forestry Department (FD), and from off-reserves by the Lands Commission. While the latter institution has retained revenue collection rights outside the reserves, it has lacked the mandate and capacity to manage the forest. Because of this problem, in 1994 it was decided to extend FD's responsibility to the area outside forest reserves.

Richards (1995) shows that even though royalties as a percentage of Ghana's mean FOB log export price from 1986 to 1992 gives a high estimate of the royalty percentage (since the mean FOB log prices exclude higher value species on which there is a log export ban), there is a clear pattern in which the percentage rises whenever royalties are raised (1986, 1989 and 1992), and falls sharply between owing to inflation. He also showed that, with respect to specific species, although real royalties rose in 1992, royalty levels of even the most valuable species were only 3–4 per cent of FOB values in 1992, and even though they rose to 5 per cent in 1993 they fell back to 3–4 per cent in 1994.

Low log royalties encourage resource depletion, wastage and inefficiency in the forest industry, besides failing to contribute adequately to government revenue and to the cost of managing the resource. A new royalty structure introduced in 1989 provides for an increase in fees in real terms, a greater increase in fees for overuse than for neglected species, and adjusting royalty fees more easily and more frequently. The fees are renewed annually and are adjusted to reflect changes in the FOB values, exchange rates, and local costs of cutting, transportation and processing timber. This is expected to reduce waste and conserve the resource.

In addition to the low level of royalties, not all that are levied are collected (Richards, 1995). Downstream royalty collection methods (introduced in 1992) and abuse by concessionaires of the log marketing system, have contributed to low collection rates. Richards (1995) estimates the average collection to be between one-half and two-thirds of royalties due, although it is probably well below 50 per cent if illegal extraction is included (annual illegal extraction is estimated to be in excess of 200000 m^3).

A further major problem of the collection system both on and off reserves has been delayed payments by concessionaires, so that inflation erodes the real value. According to the FD Concession Unit, outstanding royalties at September 1992 amounted to about 3.1 billion Cedis (then some US$6.7 million) (Richards, 1995).

In terms of exports, a 3 per cent *ad valorem* export tax is levied on all timber products. This is shared between the Forest Products Inspection Bureau (FPIB) and the Timber Export Development Board (TEDB). The two are responsible for the control of the trade and market promotion respectively. Of this, 2 per cent was received in local currency and 1 per cent in foreign exchange. However, only about 60 per cent of the latter was actually received due to problems with defaulting exporters. The export levy raised an estimated annual average of $2.36/m^3$, over half of forest revenue. In 1993, export levies of 15–50 per cent were announced for air dried lumber, and 20–40 per cent for logs of species not subject to the continuing log export ban. While this awaited ratification in mid-1994, export levies were completely removed for secondary and tertiary products such as doors, moulding and furniture.

Table 7.6 shows that other forest fees raised only about 5 per cent of the total forest fees. Concession rents have been set at a low and uniform rate in the absence of bidding. Fines have been set too low to act as a deterrent (though they were increased to 1000% of the royalty level in 1992, this still comes to only about one-third of the FOB log value of the tree in 1993) to the abuse of the forest regulations, and have rarely been applied since this involves taking the concessionaires to court, involving further costs. Various small registration payments levied by the FPIB and other downstream institutions have, in some cases, irritated the industry.

Low forest fees send out a signal that the resource is in abundant supply and the cost of exploitation is relatively low and therefore more profitable to investment in the extraction industry. This has resulted in excess demand for concessions and the proliferation of informal payments which attempt to either legally or illegally secure the unearned rent.

Low royalties, especially when charged downstream, have also encouraged wastage in the forest. This increases the demand pressure on the resource. Wastage by loggers has been estimated to be as high as 50 per cent (Grut, 1989; World Bank, 1988). There is also evidence that concessionaires leave logs in the forest because they cannot conveniently be transported or because a market cannot be found. The downstream log identification and royalty collection system encouraged this. If identification and royalty collection were done in-forest, this would reduce this waste.

Forest pricing has also provided no incentive to farmers or local communities to plant or protect trees in a system in which their access to and benefits from the resource are severely limited by law. Rural communities rarely see any benefit from the distribution of royalties, in particularly the lack of transparency in the system has reduced their interest in the forest, except as a source of land for farming.

Low forest fees have also reduced the capacity of the Forestry Department to protect and manage the resource, for example through control of illegal exploitation and logging wastage. It has increased its dependence on central government and external financing. Even though the Forestry Department is responsible for the sustainable management of the forest, it lacks the essential resources to carry out its responsibilities.

Regarding the resource itself, even though it is very difficult to separate out the impact of forest fees from other effects, but it can be said that the low fees have allowed market forces to determine the rate of resource exploitation, and given the problem of market failure with regard to environmental resources, one expects overexploitation of the forest resource. In addition to the 1979 log export ban, there was a further ban on six species in 1988 (see Appendix 6.5 of Chapter 6), with the environmental objective given prominence. According to Richards (1995), the fact that only one of the species concerned was in the 'Scarlet Red Star' species category implies that there were non-environmental objectives behind the ban. In 1993, the export of wawa logs was banned: this was also presented primarily as an environmental measure. For species not already on the banned list export levies of between 20 and 40 per cent were planned to be introduced in 1994.

It was expected that the ban will reduce the demand for the banned species and reduce forest loss. However, for the concessionaire who does not also process the timber, the effect is to lessen his interest in the species, which will tend to increase wastage. It may also lead to smuggling to neighbouring countries without export bans, defeating the very objective of preserving the forest resource (Richards, 1995).

Domestic prices of these species are also depressed. Ahadome (1991) reported that domestic prices of banned species were only one-fifth of their FOB values. The FBIP also reported a three-fold fall in the price of wawa logs with the implementation of the ban (Richards, 1995). The ban therefore acts as a subsidy to the processing industry: cheap logs have encouraged inefficiency and overcapacity, thereby increasing demand pressure on the resource. General Woods (1993) observed that the Ghanaian lumber industry had grown to about double that required for processing a sustainable annual allowable cut. It has been observed earlier that even though exports of such species have reduced, production levels have not, defeating the very objective of preserving these species.

APPENDIX 7.1 GHANA'S POLICY-BASED LOANS, 1983–91

Year	Loan type	Amount
IMF		(SDR Millions)
1983–84	Standby	238.50
1984–86	Standby	180.00*
1986–87	Standby	81.80*
1987–90	Extended Fund Facility	245.40*
1987–90	Structural Adjustment Facility (SAF)	129.86*
1988–91	Enhanced SAF (ESAF)	368.10
Total committed 1983–1991		1243.66
World Bank		(US$ Millions)
1983	Reconstruction Import I	40.0
1984	Export Rehabilitation	76.0
1985	Reconstruction Import II	87.0
1986	Health and Education	15.0
1986	Industrial Sector	53.5
1987	Education Sector	34.5
1987	Structural Adjustment I	129.6
1987	Agricultural Services	17.0
1987	Institutional Support	10.5
1988	PAMSCAD	10.6
1988	Financial Sector Adjustment	100.0
1988	Public Enterprise Assistance	10.5
1988	Cocoa Rehabilitation	40.0
1989	Structural Adjustment II	120.0
Total committed 1983–1989		744.2

Note: *Programme abrogated before the end of the period.

Source: Sowa (1990).

APPENDIX 7.2   COMPONENTS OF THE ADJUSTMENT PROGRAMME IN GHANA

1. Prices interventions
   (i)   Exchange rate adjustment with price and trade liberalization;
   (ii) Increasing the role of market mechanism with relaxations and elimination of price controls and output levies;
   (iii) Reduction of subsidies (commonly on food, agricultural inputs and energy).

2. Public expenditure management (budgetary reforms)
   (i)   Reduction of government deficits through
         (a) Increasing public revenues and improving the buoyancy of the tax system;
         (b) Improvement on the performance of public enterprises;
         (c) Rationalization of staffing in the public sector;
   (ii) Increased effectiveness of public investment and medium term planning through
         (a) More support for recurrent expenditures, leading to better capacity utilization of existing industries;
         (b) Increased public allocations to agriculture with strict privatization of investment projects;
         (c) Raising of public enterprise charges and reduction of subsidized services;
         (d) Improved management systems and controls;
         (e) Introduction of new charges, example user charges for water, veterinary services.

3. Institutional restructuring
   (i)   Rationalization of parastatals, particularly Marketing Boards, involving manpower reductions and a reduced set of functions;
   (ii) Increased competition in the provision of services with privatization of input supply;
   (iii) Reduction or elimination of Area Development Programmes and the concentration on building-up the Ministry of Agriculture;
   (iv) Selective decentralization of the operation of government institutions;
   (v)   Substantial technical assistance to government institutions.

Source: Ewusi (1987).

APPENDIX 7.3   SELECTED AGRICULTURAL POLICY DECISIONS SINCE 1983

1983

- Agricultural Commodity Pricing Committee (ACPC) established as a permanent committee on pricing of some 20 scheduled commodities. Due to some changes in government pricing policies, ACPC now acts as a regulatory body that reviews price agreements between processing companies and grower associations.
- Cocoa producer price increased by 67 per cent.
- Oil palm fruits producer price increased by 47 per cent.

1984

- Government intervention in the pricing of oil palm was abolished. The price of fresh fruit is determined by the major processors of oil palm products based on cost-plus accounting, deduction of processing and transport costs and 25 per cent profit margin to the processor. The wholesale prices of oil palm and kernels are also set by the processors and the major consumers.

1985

- Cocoa Price Compensation account established.

1986

- Ghana Seed Company abolished.
- Ghana Cotton Company formed.
- Cocoa producer price raised by 65 per cent for the 1986/87 minor season.
- 500 Cedis/mt was paid as cocoa producer bonus for 1986/87.

1987

- Cocoa producer price raised by 15 per cent effective 1987/88 minor season.
- Cocoa Board reduced staff by 12 000 in order to reduce its operational cost.
- 10 000 Cedis/mt was paid as cocoa producer bonus for 1987/88.

1988

- Subsidy on fertilizer reduced to 40 per cent; Privatization of input distribution introduced at the retail level.

1989

- Subsidy on fertilizer reduced to 15 per cent.

1990

- Subsidy on fertilizer removed.
- Guaranteed minimum price policy abolished.
- Ghana Cotton Company monopsony over cotton buying as well as its monopoly of cotton ginning were abolished.
- Government intervention in cotton producer price was abolished. The price is negotiated between the Cotton Producers Association and the cotton buyers.
- Restrictions on cotton exports lifted.
- Deputy Regional Secretaries for agriculture appointed.

1991

- Special import tax and super sales tax of 100 per cent abolished.
- Unification of responsibility for sector-wide policy formulation and monitoring under an interministerial body while retaining programme implementation under existing institutions in line with the government's objective of decentralization.

1992

- Privatization of fertilizer imports and wholesale trade introduced. Government continues to control fertilizer distribution margins.
- Competition was introduced in the internal buying of cocoa by allowing private buyers alongside the Produce Buying Company of the Cocoa Board.
- All extension activities in the country were centralized under the Ministry of Agriculture's Department of Extension.
- Regional Agricultural Management Committees formed with the following functions: (i) to give support to the districts in identification and formulation of agricultural projects; (ii) to give technical support for project implementation; (iii) to coordinate the district

budget requests and to facilitate the financial management process; and (iv) to monitor and evaluate project and programme implementation.

- Statutory holiday on national farmers' day announced.
- Cocoa producer price increased to 258,000 Cedis/mt in June.

1993

- Private buyers issued with licence to purchase cocoa beginning in the minor season of the 1992/93 crop year.
- Ministry of Agriculture begins to progressively increase the total expenditure for which authority is delegated to the Regions and Districts.
- Cocoa producer price increased to 308 000 Cedis/mt in June.

REFERENCES

Ahadome, E.C. (1991), 'Forestry taxation system in Ghana', Accra: Forestry Commission (unpublished).

Alderman, H. (1991), 'Downturn and economic recovery in Ghana: Impact on the poor', *Monograph*, **10**, Ithaca: Cornell Food Nutrition Program.

Appiah, S.K. (1990), 'Status report on Ghana timber industry', in *Further Processing of Tropical Timber in Africa: Report on a Seminar on the Promotion of Further Processing of Tropical Hardwood Timber*, Accra, 13–16 February 1990, Timber Export Development Board and International Tropical Timber Organization.

Asenso-Okyere, F.A. Asante and O. Gyekye (1993), 'Policies and strategies for rural poverty alleviation in Ghana', Technical Publication No. 57, ISSER, University of Ghana.

Barro, R.J. (1974), 'Are government bonds net wealth?', *Journal of Political Economy*, December, 1095–117.

Centre for Policy Analysis (CEPA) (1996), *Macroeconomic Review and Outlook*. Accra: Tanels Ltd.

Cornia, A.G., R. Jolly and F. Stewart (eds) (1988), *Adjustment with a Human Face, Vol II: Ten Country Case Studies*, London: Oxford University Press.

Dell, S. (1982), 'Stabilization: the political economy of overkill', *World Development*, August, 597–612, Washington, DC: World Bank.

Diaz-Alejandro, C. (1984), 'IMF conditionality: what kind?' *PIDE Tidings*, January–February, 7–9.

Ewusi, K. (1987), *Structural Adjustment and Stabilization Policies in Developing Countries: A Case Study of Ghana's Experience in 1983–1986*, Tema: Ghana Publishing Corporation.

Ewusi, K. (1989), 'The impact of the structural adjustment programme on the agricultural sector in Ghana', ISSER, University of Ghana, Legon.

Forestry Department (1992), *Logging Manual for Forest Management in Ghana*, Accra: Forestry Department.

Frenklen, J.A. and H.G. Johnson (1976), 'The monetary approach to the balance of payments', *Journal of International Economics*, February, 65–74.

Friends of the Earth (1992), *Plunder of Ghana's Rainforest for Illegal Profit. Vol. 2: Research Report*, London: Friends of the Earth.

General Woods (1993), 'Technical and financial audit of the Ghana timber industry', Vol. 1–6. Prepared for the Ministry of Lands and Forestry, Ghana, General Woods and Veneers Consultants International Ltd. Quebec (unpublished).

Grut, M. (1989), 'Economics of managing the African rainforest', Paper presented at the 13th Commonwealth Forestry Conference, New Zealand.

IIED (1996), 'Incentives for sustainable forest management. A study in Ghana', IIED Forestry and Land Use Series, No. 6.

ISSER (1992), 'The state of the Ghanaian economy in 1991', ISSER, University of Ghana, Legon.

ISSER (1993), 'The state of the Ghanaian economy in 1992', ISSER, University of Ghana, Legon.

ISSER (1995), *The State of the Ghanainan Economy in 1994*, ISSER, University of Ghana, Legon.

ISSER (1996), 'The state of the Ghanaian economy in 1995', ISSER, University of Ghana, Legon.

ITTO (1993), 'Study of incentives for the sustainable management of the tropical high forest of Ghana', A report prepared by IIED and the Forestry Department of Ghana for the ITTO (unpublished).

Jebuni, C.D., S. Asumang-Brempong and K.Y. Fosu (1990), 'Ghana: economic recovery programme and agriculture', USAID/Ghana, Accra.

Johnson, H.G. (1958), 'Towards a general theory of the balance of payments', in *International Trade and Economic Growth*, London: Allen and Unwin.

Khan, M.S. (1987), 'Macroeconomic adjustment in developing countries: a policy perspective, *The World Bank Research Observer*, 2(1), 23–42.

Khan, M.S. and M.D. Knight (1981), 'Stabilization programs in developing countries: a formal framework'. *Staff Papers*, **28**, 1–53, Washington, DC: International Monetary Fund.

López, R. (1995), 'Environmental externalities in traditional agriculture and the impact of trade liberalization: The case of Ghana', University of Maryland, College Park (unpublished).

Ministry of Agriculture (1990), 'Ghana medium term agricultural development programme (MTADP): an agenda for sustained agricultural growth and development', PPMED, Accra.

Nyanteng, V.K. (ed.) (1993), 'Policies and options for Ghanaian economic development', ISSER, University of Ghana, Lagon.

Quansah, A. (1987), *Economic Panorama: Notes on Ghana Recovery Programme*, Accra: Nsamkow Press.

Richards, M. (1995), *Role of Demand Side Incentives in Fine Grained Protection: A Case Study of Ghana's Tropical High Forest*, London: ODA.

Sijim, J. (1993), *Food Security and Policy Interventions in Ghana*, Rotterdam: Erasmus University.

Sowa, N.K. (1990), 'The social and economic consequences of the Structural Adjustment Programme in Ghana', University of Ghana, Legon (unpublished).

Sowa, N.K. (1993), 'Ghana', in A. Adepoju (ed.), *The Impact of Structural Adjustment on the Population of Africa: The Implication for Education, Health and Employment*, Oxford: James Currey Publishers.

World Bank (1983), *World Development Report, 1983*, London: Oxford University Press.
World Bank (1985), *Ghana Agricultural Sector Review*, Washington DC: World Bank.
World Bank (1988a), 'Ghana forest resource management project', Working Papers 1–6, unpublished.
World Bank (1988b), 'Ghana forestry sector review, Annexes', Washington DC: World Bank.

8. Estimating the biodiversity effects of structural adjustment in Ghana

James K. Benhin and Edward B. Barbier

8.1 INTRODUCTION

A dynamic optimal control problem approach is used to derive the optimal conversion and exploitation of the stock of forest land to cocoa and maize production, and timber extraction along the optimal time path (Ehui and Hertal, 1989; Ehui et al., 1990; Deacon, 1995; López, 1995). The objective is to derive a relationship for forest land conversion to cocoa and maize land, and the exploitation of timber; that is the demand for the stock of forest land as an input for the production of cocoa, maize and timber. Following Barbier and Burgess (1997) we introduce additional relevant macroecononic variables that influence these demands. A species–forest relationship is also developed, which is later used to explain the link between policy and price changes on one hand and forest and biodiversity loss on the other.

The following model assumes three sectors: cocoa production, maize production and timber extraction. The production function for each sector is assumed to be a single-valued continuous function with continuous first- and second-order partial derivatives, and also to be increasing and strictly concave.

The production functions for the cocoa, maize and timber sectors are defined as

$$C(t) = C(L^c(t), X^c(t)) \tag{8.1}$$

$$M(t) = M(L^m(t), X^m(t)) \tag{8.2}$$

$$H(t) = H(F(t), X^h(t)) \tag{8.3}$$

Where $C(t)$ is the output of cocoa in each time period, t, $L^c(t)$ is the total land input used in cocoa production, measured in hectares, and $X^c(t)$ represent other inputs used in cocoa production. $M(t)$ is the output of maize in number of bags in each time period t, $L^m(t)$ is the total land input used in maize production and $X^m(t)$ represents other inputs used in maize production. The production of timber, $H(t)$, is assumed to depend on the stock of forest land in each time $F(t)$, and other inputs used in timber extraction, $X^h(t)$.

The net benefits from cocoa, maize and timber production, in each time t, are defined respectively, by the difference between the total revenue and the total cost:

$$P^c(t)[C(L^c(t), X^c(t))] - W^c(t)X^c(t) \tag{8.4}$$

$$P^m(t)[M(L^m(t), X^m(t))] - W^m(t)X^m(t) \tag{8.5}$$

$$P^h(t)[H(F(t), X^h(t))] - W^h(t)X^h(t) \tag{8.6}$$

where $P^i(t)$, $i = c$, m, h is the per unit output price for each respective sector, and $W^i(t)$, $i = c$, m, h is the per unit input price. The output and input prices are assumed to be exogenously determined.

The net benefits in each of the three sectors are the incentives to use more of the stock of forest land. As the net benefits increase, either through output price increasing and/or input price falling, it becomes more profitable to use more of the stock of forest land for the three activities.

One important observation can be made from these simplified net benefit functions for the three sectors. The cost of the stock forest land, either in terms of conversion to cocoa or maize land or exploited for timber, is not considered in the output decisions of the three sectors. This is because the market is not able to capture these costs due to market and policy failures. Later, we introduce these costs through 'shadow prices' for converted and existing forested land. It may be argued that in some cases a cocoa or maize farmer may make some payments to the owner of the land in the form of either crop or cash. But it must be noted that these payments are not payments for the stock of forest land converted to agricultural land but for the right to farm the land. Where the land belongs to the farmer, such payments are not accounted for in markets. In general, therefore, there is no market price for land as such, and any existing price is not an adequate reflection of the costs of this input.

It is further assumed that the stock of forest land provides other environmental benefits, $B(F(t))$, apart from its use for timber production. These include maintaining local climates, watershed protection, non-timber products and the preservation of natural habitats:

$$B(F(t)), \ B_F > 0 \text{ and } B_{FF} < 0 \qquad (8.7)$$

However, the total stock of forest land, F, is not static but is linked to agricultural land expansion and timber production. Changes or increase in land under cocoa production dL^c/dt and maize production dL^m/dt are due to the conversion of forest land to cocoa land, $l^c(t)$ and to maize land, $l^m(t)$, respectively:

$$\dot{L}^c = l^c(t) \qquad (8.8)$$

$$\dot{L}^m = l^m(t) \qquad (8.9)$$

Equations (8.8) and (8.9), imply that changes in the stock of forest land over time are a result of the conversion of the stock of forest land to cocoa land (l^c) and maize land (l^m). Such conversion of forest land is assumed to be irreversible.

It is also assumed that timber extraction leads to a fixed amount of stock of forest land loss, given by a timber-related conversion factor, α. However, forest land extracted for timber can be regenerated by an amount given by k. Therefore extraction of timber in any time t leads to the stock of forest land changing by $-(k-\alpha)H(F(t), X^h(t))$. The change in the stock of forest land, $\dot{F}$, or the amount of deforestation, D, is defined by

$$\dot{F} = -D(t) = -l^c(t) - l^m(t) - (\alpha - K)H(F(t), X^h(t)) \qquad (8.10)$$

8.2 THE MAXIMIZATION PROBLEM

Given these assumptions, the objective of society is to maximize the stream of net benefits (8.4)–(8.7) from the uses of the stock of forest land, subject to (8.8), (8.9) and (8.10). That is

$$\text{Max}\Pi(t) = \int_0^\infty e^{-\delta t}[B(F(t)) + P^c(t)(C(L^c(t), X^c(t)) - W^c(t)X^c(t)$$
$$+ P^m(t)(M(L^m(t), X^m(t)) - W^m(t)X^m(t) \qquad (8.11)$$
$$+ P^h(t)H(F(t), X^h(t)) - W^h(t) X^h(t)]dt$$

$$F(0) = F_0, \ L^c(0) = L^c_0, \ L^m(0) = L^m_0 \qquad (8.12)$$

$$\dot{L}^c = \ell^c(t) \qquad (8.13)$$

$$\dot{F} = -D(t) = -\ell^c(t) - \ell^m(t) - (\alpha - K)H(F(t), X^h(t)) \qquad (8.14)$$

$$\ell^c(t), \ \ell^m(t), \ H(t) \geq 0 \qquad (8.15)$$

$$\dot{L}^m = \ell^m(t) \qquad (8.16)$$

where
Π = present value of net benefits;
δ = social discount rate.

The control variables in the model are X^c, X^m, X^h, l^c, and l^m. The state variables are F, L^c, and L^m.

Optimality Conditions

The current value Hamiltonian for the above optimal control problem is[1]

$$H(X^c, X^m, X^h, \ell^c, \ell^c, L^c, L^m, F, \lambda, \psi, \mu) = [B(F) + (P^c C(L^c, X^c)$$

$$- W^c X^c) + (P^m M(L^m, X^m) - W^m X^m) + (P^h H(F, X^h) - W^h X^h)] \qquad (8.17)$$

$$- \lambda((\alpha - k)H(F, X^h) - \ell^c - \ell^m) - \psi \, \ell^c - \mu \ell^m$$

where λ, is the co-state variable or shadow price of the forest, and ψ and μ are also the co-state variable for forest land converted to cocoa and maize land, respectively. The current value Hamiltonian (8.17) can be interpreted as the total increase in the value of the stock of forest land. The group in the first term $[B(F) + (P^c C(L^c, X^c) - W^c X^c) + (P^m M(L^m, X^m) - W^m X^m) + (P^h H(F, X^h) - W^h X^h)]$ is the flow of net returns at instant t. The second term, $\lambda((\alpha - k)H(X^h, F) - \ell^c - \ell^m)$, is the increase in the value of the stock of forest land at instant t. The third term, $\psi \ell^c$, is the increase in the value of cocoa land, while the fourth term, $\mu \ell^m$, is the increase in the value of maize land.

Assuming an interior solution, the first-order conditions for maximizing (8.17) are equations (8.8), (8.9) and (8.10) plus

$$\frac{\partial H}{\partial X^c} = P^c C_x(X^c, L^c) - W^c = 0 \tag{8.18}$$
$$\Rightarrow P^c C_x (X^c, L^c) = W^c$$

$$\frac{\partial H}{\partial X^m} = P^m M_x(X^m, L^m) - W^m = 0 \tag{8.19}$$
$$\Rightarrow P^c M_x (X^m, L^m) = W^m$$

$$\frac{\partial H}{\partial X^h} = P^h H_x(X^h, F) - W^h - \lambda(\alpha - k)H_x(X^h, F) = 0 \tag{8.20}$$
$$\Rightarrow P^h H_x (X^h, F) = W^h + \lambda(\alpha - k)H_x(X^h, F)$$

$$\frac{\partial H}{\partial \ell^c} = \lambda - \psi = 0 \tag{8.21}$$

$$\frac{\partial H}{\partial \ell^m} = \lambda - \mu = 0 \tag{8.22}$$

$$-\frac{\partial H}{\partial F} = \dot{\lambda} - \delta\lambda = -B_F(F) - P^h H_F(F, X^h) + \lambda(\alpha - k)H_F(F, X^h) \tag{8.23}$$
$$\Rightarrow \dot{\lambda} + B_F(F) + P^h H_F(F, X^h) = \delta\lambda + \lambda(\alpha - k)H_F(F, X^h)$$

$$-\frac{\partial H}{\partial L^c} = \dot{\psi} - \delta\psi = -P^c C_L(X^c, L^c) \tag{8.24}$$
$$\Rightarrow \dot{\psi} + P^c C_L (X^c, L^c) = \delta\psi$$

$$-\frac{\partial H}{\partial L^m} = \dot{\mu} - \delta\mu = -P^m M_L(X^m, L^m) \tag{8.25}$$
$$\Rightarrow \dot{\mu} + P^m M_L (X^m, L^m) = \delta\mu$$

$$\lim_{t \to \infty} e^{\delta t} \lambda(t)F(t) = 0 \tag{8.26}$$

$$\lim_{t \to \infty} e^{\delta t} \mu(t)L^m(t) = 0 \tag{8.27}$$

$$\lim_{t \to \infty} e^{\delta t} \psi(t)L^c(t) = 0 \tag{8.28}$$

Equations (8.18) and (8.19) indicate that, at any point along the optimal path, the value of marginal products of inputs used in cocoa and maize productions are equal to their respective input prices. However, equation (8.20) is a little bit different. For timber, on the optimal path, the sum of the private cost of production, W^h, and the social cost of timber related deforestation, $\lambda(\alpha-k)H_x(X^h, F)$, should be equal to the value of the marginal product of input, $P^h H_x(X^h, F)$.

It can be inferred from (8.20) that

$$\lambda = \frac{P^h H_x(X^h, F) - W^h}{(\alpha - k)H_x(X^h, F)} \tag{8.20'}$$

Equation (8.20') has an interesting interpretation: on the optimal path, the shadow price of forest land, λ, must equal the ratio of the net marginal returns of timber operation to net timber-related deforestation. Alternatively, the cost of the net timber-related deforestation, $\lambda(\alpha-k)H_x(X^h, F)$, must equal the net marginal returns to timber operations, $P^h H_x(X^h, F) - W^h$. Equations (8.21) and (8.22) govern the optimal state of the stock of forest land conversion to cocoa and maize. In each case the marginal value of the stock of forest land converted, ψ and μ, should be equal to the cost or shadow price of forest land, λ.

Equation (8.23) indicates that the stock of forest land should be employed in timber production and other environmental purposes up to the point where the benefits are equal to its social cost. The left-hand side of the equation represents the benefits. It has three parts: the direct value of the stock of forest in terms of environmental benefits, $B_F(F)$, the value of the stock of forest land as in timber extracted, $P^h H_F(F, X^h)$, and a capital gains term, $\dot{\lambda}$. The right-hand side are the costs. It includes the social cost of the net timber-related deforestation, $\lambda((\alpha-k)H_F(F, X^h))$, and an interest charge, $\delta\lambda$, for the use of the forest as a capital.

Similarly, equation (8.24) implies that the land under cocoa production, which is the stock of forest land converted into cocoa land, should be employed up to the point where benefits from the converted forest land are equal to its social cost. The left-hand side of the equation is the benefits. It includes the value of the marginal product of the converted stock of forest, $P^c C_L(X^c, L^c)$ and a capital gains term, $\dot{\psi}$. The right-hand side is similar to equation (8.23). It measures the cost of employing the services of per unit stock forest land, $\delta\psi$.

Equation (8.25) also indicates that the stock of forest land should be converted to maize land for maize production up to the point where the benefits also equal to its social costs. The left-hand side are the benefits which include the value of the marginal product of converted forest land, $P^m M_L(X^m, L^m)$ and a capital gains term, $\dot{\mu}$. The right-hand side also measures the cost of employing the services of per unit stock forest land as maize land, $\delta\mu$. Finally, equations (8.26) to (8.28) are the transversality conditions.

From equations (8.21) and (8.22)

$$\lambda = \psi = \mu \tag{8.29}$$

which implies that, along the optimal path, the shadow price of forest land must be equal across all uses. The implication is that the forest land has the same opportunity cost for any use to which it is put. It follows also from equation (8.29) that the following equation holds:

$$\dot{\lambda} = \dot{\psi} = \dot{\mu} \qquad (8.30)$$

Combining equations (8.29), (8.30), (8.23), (8.24), and (8.25), we have

$$B_F(F) + (P^h + \lambda(\alpha - k)) \, H_F(X^h, F)$$
$$= P^c C_L(X^c, L^c) = P^m M_L(X^m, L^m) \qquad (8.31)$$

Equation (8.31) indicates that along the optimal path, the stock of forest land should be allocated up to the point where the marginal returns are equal across all uses – forest land, cocoa land and maize land.

Specification of the Demand for the Stock of Forest Land Equations

Equation (8.31) is similar to a result obtained by Barbier and Burgess (1997). Following their approach, a useful interpretation of (8.31) is that the opportunity cost, or price of using the stock of forest land for one land use, is the forgone benefits of other uses. Thus each land use has a price, which can be denoted by $V^i(t)$, $i = h, c, m$. By utilizing $V(t)$ for each land use in (8.31), and substituting for λ, we obtain (see Appendix 8.1)

$$B_F + (P^h H_F) + \frac{P^h H_x(X^h, F) - W^h}{H_x(X^h, F)} H_F(X^h, F) = V(t) \qquad (8.32)$$
$$\Rightarrow V^h(F, X^h, W^h) = V^h(t)$$

$$P^c C_L(X^c L^c) = V(t) \Rightarrow V^c(L^c, X^c, P^c) = V^c(t) \qquad (8.33)$$

$$P^m M_L(X^m, L^m) = V(t) \Rightarrow V^m(L^m, X^m, P^m) = V^m(t) \qquad (8.34)$$

In equation (8.32) the opportunity cost or price of maintaining an additional stock of forest land for environmental benefits plus timber production is the forgone benefits from converting the stock of forest land to either cocoa land or maize land. As this price, $V^h(t)$, increases (which means it will be more beneficial to convert to either of these two uses), less and less stock of forest land is maintained. This implies that there is a negative relationship between this opportunity and maintaining more stock of forest land. In (8.33), the opportunity cost or price of converting an additional stock of forest land to cocoa land is either the forgone benefits from maintaining the given stock of forest land or conversion to maize land. Similarly, as this price $V^c(t)$ increases, the quantity demanded for cocoa land converted from the stock of forest land falls. In the same vein, in equation (8.34), the opportunity cost or price of converting an additional stock of forest land to maize land is the forgone benefit from either maintaining the given forest stock or converting it to cocoa land. As this price $V^m(t)$ increases, less stock of forest land will be converted to maize land (Barbier and Burgess, 1997).

These three equations (8.32–8.34) therefore form the optimal demand for the stock of forest land for timber production, for cocoa land and maize land. However, some of the key arguments of the equations are endogenous. For example, from (8.18) to (8.20), it follows that X^c and L^c are a function of P^c and W^c; X^m and L^m are a function of P^m and W^m; and X^h and F are a function of P^h, W^h and λ. Recall also that $\lambda(t)$, which is the marginal value of forest land, is essentially endogenous, and depends on the optimal solution of the value function, $\Pi(t)$. That is, at any time t,

$$\lambda(t) = \frac{\partial \Pi(t)}{\partial F} = \max \int_t^\infty [B_F(F) + P^h H_F(F, X^h)]\, e^{-\delta t}\, dt \qquad (8.35)$$

It follows that $\lambda(t) = \partial \Pi(t)\partial F$ is a function of X^h and F, and in turn, from (8.20') the latter are both a function of P^h and W^h respectively (see also equation (8.20)).

Consequently, substituting for the endogenous terms in (8.32)–(8.34) and utilizing the fact that $V^h = V^c = V^m$, then the optimal stock of timber production, cocoa land and maize land in the model is determined by the following reduced form system of equations, which are determined by the price parameters of the model.

$$H_t = h(P^h_t, P^c_t, P^m_t, W^h_t, W^c_t, W^m_t) \qquad (8.36)$$

$$L^c_t = c(P^h_t, P^c_t, P^m_t, W^h_t, W^c_t, W^m_t) \qquad (8.37)$$

$$L^m_t = m(P^h_t, P^c_t, P^m_t, W^h_t, W^c_t, W^m_t) \qquad (8.38)$$

The final equation in our system is equation (8.10) determining an optimal forest loss or deforestation. Using discrete notation ($\dot{F} = F_t - F_{t-1}$) 1, we write this equation as

$$-(F_t - F_{t-1}) = (L^c_t - L^c_{t-1}) + (L^m_t - L^m_{t-1}) + (k - \alpha)H_t$$
$$= f(\ell^c_t, \ell^m_t, H_t) \qquad (8.39)$$

Biodiversity Loss Equation

This subsection attempts to derive a relationship between forest land, cocoa land and maize land on one hand and biodiversity on the other hand. The relationship is then used to estimate the levels of biodiversity in Ghana between 1965 and 1995, and to investigate the impact of the Structural Adjustment Programme on biodiversity in Ghana.

Following Reid (1992) and others,[2] a relationship between the number of species, S_F, and the area of forest is assumed:

$$S_F(t) = F^{\alpha 1}(t) \tag{8.40}$$

where:

$S_F(t) =$ a species index representing the number of species in a given forest area in time t. The greater the index the higher the level of biodiversity;

$\alpha =$ a parameter reflecting the elasticity or responsiveness of the species–forest area relationship.

It is further assumed, based on Chapter 6, that farms, especially cocoa farms, may contain some tree species.[3]

We therefore have a species–farmland relationship, of cocoa and maize land, given as

$$S_L(t) = (L^c(t))^{\alpha 2} + (L^m(t))^{\alpha 3} \tag{8.41}$$

where:

$S_L(t) =$ a species index representing the number of species in a given area of farmland in time t;

$\alpha_2 =$ a parameter reflecting the strength of the species–cocoa land area relationship;

$\alpha_3 =$ a parameter reflecting the strength of the species–maize land area relationship.

Combining (8.40) and (8.41), the aggregate total species–area relationship is given as

$$S(t) = S_F(t) + S_L(t) = F^{\alpha 1}(t) + (L^c(t))^{\alpha 2} + (L^m(t))^{\alpha 3} \tag{8.42}$$

We assume $\alpha_1 > \alpha_2 > \alpha_3$. As the majority of trees have to be removed to make way for cocoa farming, one expects more species to be in a given forest area than on cocoa land ($\alpha_1 > \alpha_2$). However, because cocoa needs more shade than maize to grow, and maize needs more cleared land, one can expect more tree species on cocoa farms than on maize farms ($\alpha_2 > \alpha_3$).

From equation (8.42) the total level of biodiversity in each time period can be estimated by substituting values for F, L^c, L^m. Given that $\alpha_1 > \alpha_2 > \alpha_3$, one would expect the total level of biodiversity in Ghana to decrease as the proportion of total land held as forest land falls over time. An increase in the proportion of farm land allocated to maize production would also cause $S(t)$ to decrease.

The problem is that the parameters α_1, α_2 and α_3 for Ghana are currently unknown. But since α_1 has been estimated to be in the range $0.16 \leq \alpha_1 \leq 0.39$ (WCMC, 1992), based on this, we can estimate values for α_2, α_3 assuming percentage forest areas for cocoa farmland and maize farmland, respectively. We assume that cocoa land may contain about 25 per cent forest cover, while maize land may contain 5 per cent forest cover.[4] Given that the estimate for α_1 implies a 100 per cent forest cover, the corresponding estimates for α_2 and α_3 are $0.04 \leq \alpha_2 \leq 0.098$, and $0.008 \leq \alpha_3 \leq 0.0195$. The estimated lower and upper boundary values of α_1, α_2 and α_3, and the index of biodiversity levels, $S(t)$, are summarized in Table 8.1, where $S_l(t)$ and $S_u(t)$ give estimates for the lower and upper boundary levels, respectively, for each year's biodiversity.

Table 8.1　Lower and upper boundaries of biodiversity indexes

	Lower boundary (l)	Upper boundary (u)
α_1	$\alpha_{1l} = 0.16$	$\alpha_{1u} = 0.39$
α_2	$\alpha_{2l} = 0.04$	$\alpha_{2u} = 0.098$
α_3	$\alpha_{3l} = 0.008$	$\alpha_{3u} = 0.0195$
$S(t)$	$S_l(t) = F^{\alpha_1 l}(t) + (L^c(t))^{\alpha_2 l}$ $+ (L^m(t))^{\alpha_3 l}$	$S_u(t) = F^{\alpha_1 u}(t) + (L^c(t))^{\alpha_2 u}$ $+ (L^c(t))^{\alpha_3 u}$

Given equations (8.36), (8.37), (8.38), (8.39) and (8.42), it can be inferred that price changes that affect L^c, L^m, H and F will affect species level S and therefore biodiversity loss. It also follows that policy changes like the Structural Adjustment Programme, which influences price will also influence biodiversity loss in Ghana.

In this section we have developed a dynamic model of forest land use in Ghana and have used this model to derive demand equations for optimal timber harvesting, cocoa land and maize land that are a function of the price parameters of the model (equations (8.36) to (8.38)). We have also developed an equation to estimate biodiversity level in Ghana. As deforestation in the model is a function of the change in land use and timber production, equation (8.39) will also by definition be a function of the price parameters of the model. In the next section, we attempt to estimate the reduced form demand equations (8.36) to (8.38) and deforestation equation (8.39). We also attempt to estimate biodiversity loss in Ghana using equation (8.42). These estimated equations are then used to explain the influence of the structural adjustment on these relationships.

8.3   EMPIRICAL ANALYSIS

In this section three main hypotheses are tested. First, the key hypothesis of the theoretical model of the previous section is that increasing cocoa and maize land expansion and greater timber extraction have been the principal proximate causes of deforestation in Ghana in recent decades. Thus prices and other economic factors (basically incentives) determining the expansion of these activities are the underlying causes of deforestation in Ghana. Secondly, by affecting the prices and economic factors determining the expansion of cocoa and maize land, as well as timber production, the introduction of the Structural Adjustment Programme (SAP) in the early 1980s may have also influenced deforestation significantly. Thirdly, as the fundamental species–area relationship suggests that the number of species declines with forest habitat area, the same underlying factors determine biodiversity loss and so will the SAP policies which may have influenced these underlying causes.

The hypothesized relationship between deforestation in Ghana and its proximate and underlying causes are examined through estimating for the 1965–95 period equations (8.36)–(8.39) derived from the theoretical model of section 8.4. The possible influence of structural adjustment on these relationships is analysed through employing a piecewise regression to distinguish the influences of the post from the pre-adjustment period. To examine the third hypothesis, a species index is constructed for Ghana by estimating equation (8.42) based on the various land uses over the period. This index, together with the estimated equations (8.36)–(8.39), are then used to examine the impact of the adjustment on biodiversity loss.

In the rest of the section a description of the estimation procedure is undertaken. The results of the estimated timber production (8.36), cocoa land (8.37), maize land (8.38) and forest loss (8.39) equations are also discussed. The section concludes with an estimation of a species-index for Ghana and assessment of the impact of the adjustment on this index and biodiversity loss.

Estimation Procedure

Equations (8.36)–(8.39), as with any other demand functions, and also inferred from the literature, are also affected by income (per capita GDP, Y_p) and the population (population density, *popd*).[5] Secondary data collected from the Ministry of Agriculture, the Forestry Department of Ghana and the Food and Agriculture Organization (FAO) were used in the estimations (*see* Appendix 8.2 for the definitions and data sources of each of the variables). The equations to be estimated for timber production, cocoa land, maize land and forest loss, respectively, are as follows:

$$H_t = \beta_{01} + \beta_{i1}(P_t^h + P_t^c + P_{t-1}^m + W_t^h + W_t^c + W_t^m + Y_{p_t} + popd_t) + \mu_{1t} \quad (8.43)$$

$$L_t^c = \beta_{02} + \beta_{i2}(P_t^h + P_t^c + P_{t-1}^m + W_t^h + W_t^c + W_t^m + Y_{p_t} + popd_t) + \mu_{2t} \quad (8.44)$$

$$L_t^m = \beta_{03} + \beta_{i3}(P_t^h + P_t^c + P_{t-1}^m + W_t^h + W_t^c + W_t^m + Y_{p_t} + popd_t) + \mu_{3t} \quad (8.45)$$

$$-(F_t - F_{t-1}) = \beta_{04} + \beta_{i4}((L_t^c - L_{t-1}^c) + (L_t^m - L_{t-1}^m) + H_t) + \mu_{4t} \quad (8.46)$$

Where, L_t^c is the demand for cocoa land measured by total hectares of land under cocoa production in time t; L_t^m is also the demand for maize land measured by the total hectares of land under maize production at time t, and H_t is the demand for the stock of forest land for timber production measured by total production of industrial roundwood in time t; F_t is the total closed forest area, measured in square kilometres (km²); P_t^h is the current year's average price of industrial roundwood; P_t^c is the current year's producer price of cocoa; P_{t-1}^m is the price of a 100 kg bag of maize lagged one year. Current year's prices are used for timber and cocoa, because timber prices are based on current year's contracted price and cocoa prices are government determined. However, for maize, farmers do not know how much they will receive for their produce, since the eventual price depends on how much is produced in the current year. Therefore, decisions on maize land in the current year depend more on what prices were in the previous year. W^h is the cost of logging, W^c is the price of insecticides and W^m is the price of ammonium sulphate. These input prices are used because they are either the most important inputs or are a good representation of all other inputs in each of the sectors. The population density *popd* is the population per given land area, and Y_p is the per capita GDP. Price variables and the per capita GDP are in 1990 constant values (Appendix 8.2).

Equations (8.43)–(8.46) forms a recursive system and so ordinary least squares (OLS) is a reasonable procedure for the time series analysis. The first step in the estimation procedure was to determine whether there is any significant difference in the functional forms (linear and log–log) of the estimated equations. This was done by the use of the Mackinon, White and Davidson (MWD) test (Gujarati, 1995). The next step was to determine whether the piecewise regression allowing for the influence of structural adjustment is preferred to the continuous regression of the entire 1965–95 period. First, the data were separated into pre (1965–82) and post-adjustment (1983–95) periods. Estimations were done for the two separate periods and a Chow test was used to determine whether there is any significant difference in the regressors of the two periods. Where the results showed a significant difference, a SAP dummy variable (*DS*) was included in the model for the estimation of the piecewise regression.[6]

The MWD test shows that the linear functional form was preferred to the log–log functional form in all the four equations. Moreover, the piecewise regression was preferred in the forest loss, cocoa land and maize land equations but not for the timber production equation. The following discusses each of the estimated equations, starting with forest loss (8.46), then cocoa land (8.44), maize land (8.45) and finally timber production (8.43).

Forest Loss Results

A Chow test performed on equation (8.46) confirmed a significant difference between the pre and post adjustment periods. The following linear piecewise estimation of forest loss in Ghana was undertaken.

$$-(F_t - F_{t-1}) = \beta_{04} + \beta_{14}(L_t^c - L_{t-1}^c) + \beta_{24}H_t + \beta_{34}D1$$
$$+ \beta_{44}(L_t^{c*} - L_{t-1}^{c*})DS + \beta_{54}(H_t^*)DS + \mu_{4t} \qquad (8.47)$$

where:
$L_t^{c*} - L_{t-1}^{c*} = (L_t^c - L_{t-1}^c) - (L_{t0}^c - L_{t0-1}^c); \; t_0 = 1983$
$H_t^* = H_t - H_{t0}; \; t_0 = 1983$
DS = dummy for the structural adjustment period; $DS = \begin{cases} 1 \text{ if } t > \text{year 1983} \\ 0 \text{ if } t \leq \text{year 1983} \end{cases}$
$D1$ = dummy for 1968.

$D1$ is a dummy to capture the increase in total forest area in 1968, due to the re-demarcation of more forest lands as reserve forests.

The estimated results and the computed marginal values and elasticities of the pre and post-adjustment period are presented in Table 8.2. The change in the maize land ($L_t^m - L_{t-1}^m$) variable was dropped because it was not statistically significant and did not have the right sign. Its inclusion also did not improve upon the significance of the whole model.

Table 8.2   Forest loss: linear piecewise regression results

Estimated results		Pre-adjustment		Post-adjustment	
Coefficients	*t*-values	Marginal values	Estimated elasticities[1]	Marginal values	Estimated elasticities[1]
β_{04} 53.753	0.275	β_{04} 53.753		β_{04} 53.753	
β_{14} 0.948	2.231**	β_{14} 0.948	–0.157	$\beta_{14} + \beta_{44}$ –0.345	–0.191
β_{24} 0.212	1.783*	β_{24} 0.212	1.069	$\beta_{24} + \beta_{54}$ –0.121	–2.39
β_{34} –606.021	–2.368**	β_{34} –606.021		β_{34} –606.021	
β_{44} –1.294	–1.936*				
β_{54} –0.333	–1.667				

Notes
Dependent variable $-(F_t - F_{t-1})$ change in total closed forest area in 1000 km².
R-squared = 0.493; F = 4.671; D-Watson = 2.24; No. of observations = 30
The dependent variable is positive, therefore a positive coefficient means increasing levels of the explanatory variable leads to increasing levels of forest loss whereas a negative coefficient means increasing levels of the explanatory variable leads to falling levels of forest loss.
[1] Elasticities were calculated by using average means in the respective periods.
** Statistically significant at 5 per cent level
 * Statistically significant at 10 per cent level

The dummy variable for 1968, *D*1 is negative and very significant as expected. This indicates that the re-demarcation of new forest reserves led to increased total closed forest area and helped reduce the total amount of forest loss.

In the pre-adjustment period there was a positive relationship between the change in harvested cocoa land expansion and forest loss. A 1000 ha increase in change in cocoa land led to a 0.95 km² increase in closed forest area loss. Total timber production also led to an increase in forest loss. A 1000 CUM increase in total industrial roundwood production led to about 0.2 km² increase in closed forest area loss. The hypothesis that cocoa land expansion and timber production are important proximate factors in forest loss in Ghana is supported by the model in the pre-adjustment period.

These results support the hypothesis that, in the post-adjustment period, timber production but not cocoa land expansion is an important proximate factor determining forest loss in Ghana. Policies with respect to cocoa in the adjustment period may have helped reduce the impact of cocoa land expansion on forest loss. It is also possible that the negative influence of cocoa land expansion on forest loss in the post-adjustment period may be explained by the increased rehabilitation of old cocoa lands which were destroyed in the 1982/83 bushfires. However, timber-related policies have not had a very significant impact in reducing the effects of timber production on deforestation.

There is a significant difference in the impacts of forest loss due to a change in cocoa land in the pre and post-adjustment period. Table 8.2 shows that in the post-adjustment period, cocoa land expansion reduces the rate of forest loss. A 1000 ha increase in harvested cocoa land expansion leads to a reduction in forest loss by $0.35 \, km^2$. The elasticity shows that a 1 per cent increase in cocoa land expansion leads to the rate of forest loss or the rate of deforestation falling by about 0.2 per cent. There is, however, no significant difference between the impact of industrial roundwood production in the pre- and post-adjustment period. Even though the estimated marginal value is negative, with the elasticity portraying that a 1 per cent increase in industrial roundwood leads to a 2.4 per cent fall in the rate of forest loss or the rate of deforestation, the post-adjustment dummy coefficient (β_{54}) is not very significant. It can therefore be stated that timber production still has a negative impact on the forest in Ghana. However, to some extent, this impact has reduced, as shown by the near significance of the post-adjustment dummy coefficient.

A factor explaining this regression result is that industrial roundwood production might have captured much of the effects of changes in both cocoa and maize land on deforestation. It has been noted that logging increases the expansion of agricultural activity in the tropical forest area by providing access to previously inaccessible areas. Amelung and Diehl (1992) stated that more than 70 per cent of the primary forest areas brought under cultivation are first degraded by commercial logging. Furthermore, according to the FAO, deforestation rates due to agricultural conversion are eight times greater in logged-over forests than undisturbed forests (Sun, 1995). Barbier (1994) also reports that in many African countries, around half of the area that is initially logged is subsequently deforested, while there is little if any deforestation of previously unlogged forest lands.

The second explanation is that cocoa and especially maize farmers may be shifting production from existing land to either new forest land or fallow land, or to old cocoa farms in the case of maize. Thus when the total harvested area of cocoa or maize land is estimated, it might appear to be constant, but the proportion of the total harvested land from forest areas may be higher or lower. The fact is that it is difficult to estimate how much of the newly harvested area in each period is from converted forest land.

To summarize, the regression results do not support the hypothesis that expansion in maize land is a significant proximate cause of forest loss, either in the pre or post-adjustment period. Cocoa land expansion was a significant proximate cause in the pre but not in the post-adjustment period. However, industrial roundwood production is a significant proximate factor in both periods, though less so in the post-adjustment period. The next step in the analysis is to look at how output and input prices in the agricultural and forestry sectors during the pre and post-adjustment periods have influenced these proximate factors.

Harvested Cocoa Land

A Chow test performed on equation (8.44) confirmed a significant difference between the pre and post-adjustment period. The following linear piecewise equation was therefore estimated for harvested cocoa land:

$$L^c = \beta_{02} + \beta_{12}P^c + \beta_{22}W^c + \beta_{32}Y_p + \beta_{42}D2$$
$$+ \beta_{52}(P^{c*})DS + \beta_{62}(W^{c*})DS + \mu_{2t} \qquad (8.48)$$

where:

$D2$ = dummy for year 1983–86; $D2 = 1$ for $t = 1983–1986$. $D2 = 0$ for all other years

$P^{c*} = P_t^c - P_{t0}^c;\ t_0 = 1983$

$W^{c*} = W_t^c - W_{t0}^c;\ t_0 = 1983$.

The estimated results, and the computed marginal values and elasticities for the pre and post-adjustment period are presented in Table 8.3.

Other price variables P^m, P^h, W^m, W^h, and the population density (*popd*), were not significant and therefore were dropped. The inference is that, from the point of view of the cocoa farmer, maize production is not

Table 8.3　Harvested cocoa land

Estimated results			Pre-adjustment		Post-adjustment	
				Estimated		Estimated
Coefficients	*t*-values		Marginal values	elasticities	Marginal values	elasticities
β_{02}　−11.514	−0.033	β_{02}	−11.514		β_{02}　−11.514	
β_{12}　11.959**	−2.196	β_{12}	−11.959	−0.22	$\beta_{12} + \beta_{52}$　−3.834	−0.089
β_{22}　12.752**	3.655	β_{22}	12.752	0.15	$\beta_{22} + \beta_{62}$　−1.351	−0.022
β_{32}　9.046**	3.375	β_{32}	9.046	1.07	β_{32}　9.046	1.22
β_{42}　−143.596	−1.905	β_{42}	−143.596		β_{42}　−143.596	
β_{52}　8.125	−1.328					
β_{62}　−14.103**	−2.943					

Notes
Dependent variable = L^c (harvested cocoa land in 1000 ha)
R-squared = 0.824; F=18.737; D-Watson = 2.16; No. of observations = 31.
**Statistically significant at 5 per cent level
*Statistically significant at 10 per cent level.

an alternative in land use decision-making, and thus maize output and input prices (P^m and W^m) are not relevant to the cocoa farmer. The insignificance of timber output and input prices was expected, as the cocoa farmer has no influence on the allocative decisions of the forest area for timber production. The insignificance of population density (*popd*) suggests that population changes have very little or no impact on cocoa land expansion.

The $D2$ variable represents a dummy for the period 1983–86, a period when there was a drastic fall in cocoa land as a result of major bushfires in 1982/83. This variable is negative and significant (Table 8.3), attesting to the fact that bushfires had a significant effect on reduced cocoa and in the years immediately following the fires. Real per capita income (Y_p) has a positive influence on cocoa land. A 1 per cent increase in real per capita income leads to 1.07 per cent and 1.22 per cent increase in harvested cocoa land in the pre and post-adjustment periods, respectively (Table 8.3).

The producer price of cocoa in the pre-adjustment period had a negative effect on cocoa land. A 1 per cent increase in the producer price of cocoa led to a 0.22 per cent fall in cocoa land (Table 8.3). One possible explanation for this result is that because the government fixes the producer price of cocoa, when farmers know that the price of cocoa is to be fixed at a lower level, they may not invest in rehabilitating existing cocoa farms but instead open up new areas for production. When the price of cocoa is fixed at a high level, it is worthwhile for farmers to rehabilitate existing farms so less land is opened up. Because the producer price of cocoa was consistently low in the pre-adjustment period, and given farmers' expectations of further falling prices, at each price they tended to open up new land rather then rehabilitate existing farms. This was in order to both reduce the cost of production and maintain some level of income.

The post-adjustment period also shows a negative relationship between cocoa price and cocoa land expansion, although this outcome must be treated with caution because the post-adjustment period price dummy (β_{52}) is not highly significant. With consistent increases in the producer price of cocoa during the post-adjustment period, farmers expect further higher prices and therefore may have some incentive to rehabilitate and invest in existing farms rather than open up new lands. The conclusion is that the post-adjustment period has reduced the impact of the producer price of cocoa on cocoa land expansion through higher prices.

The regression results also show a significant positive relation between the price of insecticides and the demand for cocoa land in the pre-adjustment period (Table 8.3). This means that in that period, insecticide inputs were a substitute for cocoa land in cocoa production. A 1 per cent increase in the price of insecticides led to a 0.15 per cent increase in cocoa land. Although there was a high subsidy on insecticides in the pre-adjust-ment period, given the low producer price of cocoa, many cocoa farmers could not afford to buy the input. Moreover, insecticides were very scarce because of the lack of foreign exchange to import them. Therefore, the alternative to using more insecticides to increase productivity was to rely on opening up new lands for production.

The impact of the price of insecticides on cocoa land changed signifi-cantly in the post-adjustment period. Insecticides and cocoa land now appear to be complements in cocoa production. A 1 per cent increase in the price of insecticides leads to 0.022 per cent fall in cocoa land. Given the increasing producer price of cocoa, farmers now have the incentive to rehabilitate existing farms. The use of insecticides becomes a significant factor in that effort and so is its price. Although all subsidies on inputs were removed in the post-adjustment period, because of the expected increases in the producer price of cocoa, farmers found it relatively cheap to rehabilitate existing farms by using insecticides rather than opening up new lands. Moreover, the increased availability of the input has helped its more widespread use on cocoa farms. We conclude that the adjustment policies, through both the producer price of cocoa and the price (and availability) of insecticides, has encouraged farmers to invest in existing lands rather than opening up new lands.

Harvested Maize Land

A Chow test on equation (8.45) confirmed a significant difference between the pre and post-adjustment period. The following linear piece-wise equation was therefore estimated for the harvested maize land:

$$L^m = \beta_{03} + \beta_{13}P^m_{t-1} + \beta_{23}W^m + \beta_{33}\,popd + \beta_{43}\,D2$$

$$+ \beta_{53}\,(P^{m*}_{t-1})DS + \beta_{63}\,(W^{m*})DS + \mu_{3t} \tag{8.49}$$

where:

$$P^m_{t-1} = \text{real price of maize lagged one year}$$

$$P^{m*}_{t-1} = P^m_{t-1} - P^m_{t0-1}\,;\,t_0 = 1983$$

$$W^{m*} = W^m_t - W^m_{t0}\,;\,t_0 = 1983$$

The estimated results, and the computed marginal values and elasticities for the pre and post-adjustment period are presented in Table 8.4. Other price variables P^c, P^h, W^c, W^h, and the real per capita GDP (Y_p) were not significant and therefore were dropped. As expected, cocoa prices are not relevant because it is not easy to convert maize land to cocoa land. This requires high capital investment to restore soil fertility depleted after maize farming, which most farmers cannot afford. Moreover, the majority of trees which initially may be needed to support cocoa cropping would have been cleared under maize farming. The insignificance of timber output and input prices was also expected, as the maize farmer has no influence on the allocation decisions of the forest for timber production. The level of income also appears to have very little influence on the demand for maize land.

The $D2$ variable was initially included to test the hypothesis that, given the drastic fall in cocoa land in the 1983–86 period, farmers may have diverted to food crop production such as maize. However, as this variable was not significant, this hypothesis of a substitutional shift from cocoa production into maize farming was rejected.

As expected, the population density (*popd*) variable is positive and significant. A 1 per cent increase in the population density will lead to about 1.2 per cent increase in harvested maize land in both the pre and post-adjustment periods (Table 8.4). This suggests that population increases in Ghana lead to increasing demand for maize and therefore maize land. This is not surprising given the importance of maize as a food crop in Ghana.

The coefficient of the lagged real price of maize was positive but insignificant in the pre-adjustment period (Table 8.4), indicating that the

Table 8.4   Harvested maize land

| Estimated results | | | Pre-adjustment | | Post-adjustment | |
Coefficients	*t*-values		Marginal values	Estimated elasticities	Marginal values	Estimated elasticities
β_{03} −219.931	−1.115	β_{03}	−219.931		β_{03} −219.931	
β_{13} 0.286	0.695	β_{13}	0.286	0.112	$\beta_{13}+\beta_{53}$ 1.3	0.23
β_{23} 8.125**	2.244	β_{23}	8.125	0.263	$\beta_{23}+\beta_{63}$ −1.135	−0.052
β_{33} 10.867**	3.083	β_{33}	10.867	1.22	β_{33} 10.867	1.23
β_{43} 36.587	0.761	β_{43}	36.587		β_{43} 36.587	
β_{53} 1.014**	2.052					
β_{63} −9.260*	−1.868					

Notes
Dependent variable = L^m (harvested maize land in 1000 ha).
R-squared = 0.827; F = 18.324; D-Watson = 1.252; No. of observations = 30.
**Statistically significant at 5 per cent level.
*Statistically significant at 10 per cent level.

price of maize was not an important factor in maize farmers' demands for land during this period. This is expected, as the relatively low and stagnant guaranteed price paid to farmers in the pre-adjustment era offered little incentive for farmers to expand production. Moreover, the poor storage facilities and the government's inability to purchase all maize produce at the guaranteed price meant that any excess supply of maize had to be disposed of at a relatively low price in the open market. This reduced the effect of maize prices in determining the area of maize cropping.

In the post-adjustment period the lagged real maize price variable was positive and significant, indicating that a 1 per cent increase in the lagged price of maize led to about 0.23 per cent increase in the demand for maize land in the current year (Table 8.4). With the removal of guaranteed or controlled prices under the adjustment programme, the price of maize became more market-determined, and thus a significant consideration in maize land decision-making in this era. As the lagged price of maize increases, farmers expect it to stay the same or even increase in the current year, and they therefore increase their demand for all inputs, including maize land, in order to increase production.

The price of ammonium sulphate had a positive and significant influence on maize land in the pre-adjustment period. A 1 per cent increase in the price of ammonium sulphate led to a 0.26 per cent increase in the demand for maize land (Table 8.4). This suggests that ammonium sulphate and maize land were substitute inputs in maize production. Given the relative low prices of maize, maize farmers could not afford to purchase other farm inputs like fertilizer and therefore tended to substitute land or converted forest land for fertilizer in production.

In the post-adjustment period, the impact of the price of ammonium sulphate on maize land was significantly negative, suggesting complementarity between these two inputs in maize production. A 1 per cent increase in the price of ammonium sulphate leads to a 0.05 per cent fall in the demand for maize land. The high dependence of maize farmers on land for production is therefore expected to fall, given that the price of ammonium sulphate has increased in the post-adjustment period following the removal of subsidies on farm inputs, including ammonium sulphate. Even though input prices have increased, the increased availability of the fertilizer to farmers and the relative higher market-determined output price of maize, as compared to the pre-adjustment period, has meant that maize farmers have had to rely on fertilizer use rather than land conversion for any increased maize production. The reduction in unreserved forest area in the post-adjustment period may have also decreased the availability of new land for maize production. Finally, although maize production in the post-adjustment period has increased, the consumption of fertilizer, including ammonium sulphate, has risen less than expected (ISSER, 1996). The pressure on the forest from maize production is therefore still a potential threat.

Industrial Roundwood Production

The Chow test did not show any significant difference between the pre and post-adjustment period regressors for equation (8.43). This was confirmed by the insignificance of the relevant variable in the piecewise regression. Therefore, the following linear regression without the adjustment coefficient dummy best describes industrial roundwood production in Ghana between 1965 and 1995:

$$H = \beta_{01} + \beta_{11} \frac{P^h}{W^h} + \beta_{12} Y_P + \mu_{1t} \qquad (8.50)$$

The estimated coefficients and elasticities are presented in Table 8.5. The ratio of the real average price of industrial roundwood exports and the real nominal logging cost of timber per cubic metre (CUM), P^h/W^h, were found to be more significant in explaining the timber model. Other price variables (for cocoa and maize) were also not significant in explaining timber production, as explained previously. Population density (*popd*) was also insignificant in explaining the demand for timber production in Ghana. The coefficient of the real per capita GDP (Y_p) is positive and significant. An increase in income leads to a large increase in the demand for industrial roundwood. If real per capita GDP increases by 1 per cent, total industrial roundwood production increases by 1.6 per cent.

The regression results show that relative price of outputs to inputs has a positive impact on timber production. A 1 per cent increase in the relative price of timber leads to a 0.16 per cent increase in timber production (Table 8.5).

To summarize, this subsection has examined the influence of agricultural and timber prices on the demand for harvested maize and cocoa land and on wood production in Ghana, distinguishing where appropriate the pre-adjustment and post-adjustment periods. The impacts of agricultural land conversion and timber on forest loss in Ghana before and after the implementation of the SAP in 1983 were also examined. In the next stage of the analysis, we use the regression results to determine the impacts of price changes in the pre as opposed to the post-adjustment periods on deforestation in Ghana.

Table 8.5   Total industrial roundwood production

Estimated results = Pre-adjustment = Post-adjustment

Coefficients		t-values	Estimated elasticities
β_{01}	−1126.063	−2.525	
β_{11}	123.689**	2.163	0.155
β_{23}	16.002**	4.933	1.606

Notes
Dependent variable = H (total industrial roundwood in 000 CUM)
R-squared = 0.639; F = 24.773; D-Watson = 1.228; No. of observations = 30.
**Statistically significant at 5 per cent level.

8.4   PRICE IMPACTS ON FOREST LOSS

Using the results from Tables 8.2–8.5, elasticities are computed to examine the relative impacts of output and input prices of cocoa, maize and timber, on forest loss in the pre and post-adjustment periods (see Appendix 8.3 for procedure). The estimated price elasticities of forest loss are presented in Table 8.6. From Table 8.6, in the pre-adjustment period, a 10 per cent rise in the rate of change in the producer price of cocoa led to a 0.03 per cent increase in forest loss, while the same level of increase in the post-adjustment period leads to 0.12 per cent rise in forest loss. Thus, in Ghana, increasing cocoa prices lead to increasing rates of deforestation. However, because of the rapid rise in producer prices in the

Table 8.6   Change in output and input price elasticity of forest loss

Variable	Estimated elasticities[1]			
	Pre-adjustment		Post-adjustment	
Cocoa price (P^c)	I	0.02752	II	0.12251
Price of insecticides (W^c)	III	−0.4329	IV	−0.00447
Ratio of timber price and cost of logging (P^h/W^h)	V	2.3	VI	1.3

Notes
Each period's price averages were used in the elasticity estimations, except for the ratio of timber price and cost of logging where the whole period averages were used.
[1]See Appendix 8.3 for the computational procedure.
A 10 per cent increase in change in output and input prices is assumed.

post-adjustment period, the rate of impact is greater in the post-adjustment period than the pre-adjustment period. These results suggest that policies that lead to increasing prices for cocoa in Ghana will tend to induce farmers to convert more forest to cocoa land.

Although our earlier results from the cocoa analysis suggest that farmers have tended to invest in existing cocoa lands because of expectations of higher prices (Table 8.3), the estimate of the change in cocoa price elasticity of forest loss indicates that there is still some cocoa price effect on forest loss. In response to rising cocoa prices, cocoa farmers are not fully shifting from the conversion of forests to investing in existing cocoa land.

$$I = \beta_{14} \cdot \beta_{12} \cdot \frac{\overline{\hat{P}^c}}{\hat{F}} \qquad II = (\beta_{14} + \beta_{44}) \cdot (\beta_{12} + \beta_{52}) \frac{\hat{P}^c}{\hat{F}} \qquad III = \beta_{14} \cdot \beta_{22} \cdot \frac{\overline{\hat{W}^c}}{\hat{F}}$$

$$IV = (\beta_{14} + \beta_{44}) \cdot (\beta_{22} + \beta_{62}) \cdot \frac{\hat{W}_c}{\hat{F}} \qquad V = \beta_{24} \cdot \beta_{11} \cdot \frac{\overline{P}_h / \overline{W}_h}{\hat{F}}$$

$$VI = (\beta_{24} + \beta_{54}) \cdot \beta_{11} \cdot \frac{\overline{P}_h / \overline{W}_h}{\hat{F}}$$

With respect to timber, the relationship between its relative output–input prices in the pre and post-adjustment periods are not significantly different even though a 10 per cent increase in the relative output–input price of industrial roundwood will lead to a 2.3 per cent and 1.3 per cent increase in the rate of forest loss in the pre and post-adjustment period, respectively. This is because β_{54} used for the post-adjustment period elasticity estimate is less significant (refer to Table 8.2). However, the results show that policies that increase the relative returns to timber production in Ghana could be contributing to additional forest loss. Alternatively, greater rent capture by the government through increased stumpage royalties may reduce timber-related deforestation.

There is a negative relationship between the change in the price of insecticide used in cocoa production and forest loss in Ghana (Table 8.6). However, there is a significant difference between the impact of the price of insecticides on the rate of forest loss in the pre- and post-adjustment periods. A 10 per cent increase in the price of insecticides during the pre-adjustment period led to a 0.4 per cent fall in the rate of forest loss, while the same level of increase in the price of insecticides in the post-adjustment period led to a 0.004 per cent fall in the rate of forest loss. The relationship is strong in the pre-adjustment period because of the high level of subsidies. The post-adjustment period has reduced the extent of the relationship between the change in the price of insecticides and forest loss because of the removal of subsidies, which raised the overall input price. Comparing the estimates for the two periods one can conclude that if the price of insecticides continues to increase drastically over time, there may be a positive relationship between increasing insecticide prices and forest loss. The conclusion is that there should be a limit to which the price of insecticides is increased to achieve both the objectives of the SAP and at the same time help reduce forest loss in Ghana.

Overall, relative timber output–input prices appear to have the greatest impact on forest loss in Ghana in both the pre and post-adjustment period. The adjustment policies have had little influence on the impact of timber prices on forest loss in Ghana. In contrast, the SAP has affected the influence of cocoa and insecticide prices. There is evidence to suggest that in the post-adjustment period high and rising cocoa prices are inducing farmers to convert forest land. Although rising insecticide prices may offset this effect their impact is relatively marginal in comparison.

Biodiversity Loss

The upper boundary species–area relationship in Table 8.1 is used to estimate biodiversity levels[7] (S) in Ghana between 1965 and 1995, using the actual levels of closed forest area, (F), harvested cocoa land, (L^c) and harvested maize land (L^m) recorded over the period. This allows us to make comparisons between the pre and post-adjustment biodiversity levels. To further investigate the impact of the structural adjustment on biodiversity, estimations from the recursive model in Tables 8.2–8.5 are used. The pre-adjustment estimations for forest land, cocoa land and maize land equations, are employed to derive estimates for closed forest area, $(\hat{F}_1)$, harvested cocoa land $(\hat{L}^c_1)$, and harvested maize land, $(\hat{L}^m_1)$, for the post-adjustment period. These estimates are in turn employed to estimate biodiversity levels, $(\hat{S}_1)$, for the post-adjustment period. Comparison is then made between these derived estimated biodiversity levels, $(\hat{S}_1)$, and their corresponding actual levels (S). The results are presented in Tables 8.7 and 8.8 and Figures 8.1 and 8.2.

The results show that biodiversity levels have fallen over the period 1965–1995 (Table 8.7 and Figure 8.1). This falling trend was, however, steeper in the pre-adjustment period than the post-adjustment period, suggesting that biodiversity loss was more rapid in the earlier period. The explanation is that, as shown earlier in the estimated recursive model, there is relatively more incentive to invest in existing lands, as in cocoa

Table 8.7   *Estimated biodiversity levels in Ghana, 1965–95*

	Pre-adjustment period				Post-adjustment period			
	1965	1970	1975	1980	1983	1985	1990	1995
F	23278	21357	19432	18090	17504	17298	17086	16862
L^c	1830	1451	1400	1200	800	900	1050	1350
L^m	173	452	320	440	400	579	465	669
S	53.672	51.979	50.199	48.880	48.217	48.039	47.848	47.676

Note: $S = F^{(0.35)} + (L^c)^{(0.087)} + (L^m)^{(0.0175)}$

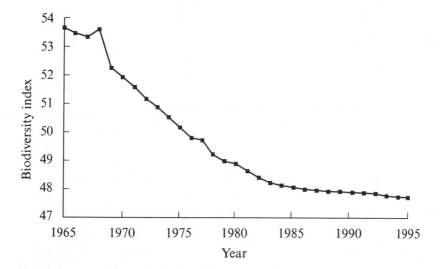

Note: Biodiversity index = S from Table 8.7.

Figure 8.1   *Estimated biodiversity levels for Ghana, 1965–95*

land, and use more insecticides and fertilizer, as in cocoa land and maize land, to increase production rather than rely on forest conversion. These incentives relate to higher prices for cocoa and maize, and the availability of inputs. Other incentives include high yielding variety seeds. The conclusion is that the structural adjustment has provided a conducive environment for less reliance on the forest for production and therefore the conservation of higher levels of biodiversity, or reduced rates of biodiversity loss.

*Table 8.8   Estimated biodiversity levels in the post-adjustment period
based on the imposed pre-adjustment relationship*

	Year			
	1983	1985	1990	1995
$\hat{F}_1$ 5	17643	17582	16408	14834
$\hat{L}_1^c$ 6	779	501	614	961
L_1^m 7	413	515	523	638
$\hat{S}_1$ 8	48.352	48.214	47.056	45.443
S_9	48.217	48.039	47.848	47.676

Note: $\hat{S}_1 = \hat{F}_1^{(0.39)} + (\hat{L}_1^c)^{(0.098)} + (\hat{L}_1^m)^{(0.0195)}$

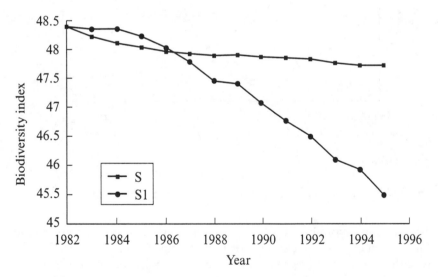

Notes
S = S = estimated biodiversity levels in the post-adjustment period.
S1 = $\hat{S}_1$ = estimated biodiversity levels with the imposed pre-adjustment period relationships.

Figure 8.2   Biodiversity levels in the post-adjustment period

The above outcome is confirmed in Table 8.8 and Figure 8.2. If the pre-adjustment species–area relationship continued in the post-adjustment period, the trend levels of biodiversity ($\hat{S}_1$) would have been lower than the actual levels in the post-adjustment period, (S) (or the rate of biodiversity loss would have been higher). The conclusion is that the structural adjustment may have helped reduce the rate of biodiversity loss in Ghana.

8.5 CONCLUSIONS

The chapters in Part II have investigated the impacts on forest and biodiversity loss of the Structural Adjustment Programme introduced in Ghana in 1983, directly through the proximate causes of agricultural land expansion and timber production and indirectly through output and input prices for cocoa, maize and timber. A piecewise linear estimation procedure which separated the pre-adjustment period from the post-adjustment period influences was used to estimate a recursive model consisting of forest loss as well as cocoa land, maize land and timber production equations as a function of input and output prices developed from an optimal control problem. A species-index for Ghana was also estimated using a species–forest area relationship. This index together with the recursive model estimates were employed to assess the impact of the Structural Adjustment Programme on biodiversity loss.

The empirical results do not support the hypothesis that maize land expansion is a proximate cause of forest loss, either in the pre or the post-adjustment period. Cocoa land expansion and timber extraction are significant factors, but their impacts on forest loss are reduced in the post-adjustment period. The inference is that the Structural Adjustment Programme has significantly reduced the impacts of cocoa land expansion and to a lesser extent, timber extraction on forest loss. Expansion in cocoa land in the post-adjustment period led to a reduced rate of forest loss as compared to the pre-adjustment period. This is attributable to some increased investment in existing cocoa land, probably as a result of an increased producer price for cocoa, the availability of needed inputs, and other efforts aimed at rehabilitating existing cocoa farms.

The price impact analysis of forest loss indicates that the ratio of timber output–input price has a relatively higher impact on forest loss than cocoa output and input prices. However, an increase in the producer price of cocoa has a greater impact on forest loss in the post-adjustment period than in the pre-adjustment period. A rising price for cocoa may therefore lead to increasing forest loss in the post-adjustment period. In comparison, an increasing trend in the price of insecticides reduces forest loss but the rate of reduction is far greater in the pre-adjustment period than in the post-adjustment period. The reason for this is the complete removal of subsidies in the latter period. There may be a limit to which the price of insecticides can be increased if it is to be a tool of reducing the rate of forest loss. Beyond this limit, any increases will lead to increasing rates of forest loss as farmers expand production by converting forest to cocoa land.

The species-index estimates for Ghana also indicate that the rate of biodiversity loss has reduced in the post-adjustment period. In fact, if the pre-adjustment relationships between the proximate and underlying causes of forest loss on one hand and biodiversity loss on the other, had existed in the post-adjustment period, the rate of biodiversity loss would have been very much higher. The inference is that policies relating to prices and other incentives have reduced the rate of cocoa and maize land expansion and improved upon timber extraction. These effects may have reduced the rate of biodiversity loss.

In conclusion, we have demonstrated that cocoa and maize policies undertaken under the Structural Adjustment Programme since 1983 have influenced the demand for maize and cocoa land and thus forest land and biodiversity loss. Although we found little significant impact of the SAP on the timber sector and harvesting trends, we found that the relative returns to timber production have an important impact on the rate of deforestation and biodiversity loss in Ghana. Specifically, higher agricultural and timber prices, even when subsidies on inputs are removed, may have helped reduce demand for forested land and therefore have helped to conserve biodiversity.

APPENDIX 8.1   FOREST LAND USES AND THE OPPORTUNITY COST OF FOREST LAND

Given that on the optimal time path (from (8.29) and (8.30) in main text)

$$\lambda = \psi = \psi \Rightarrow \dot{\lambda} = \dot{\psi} = \dot{\mu} \qquad (A8.1)$$

which implies that

$$\dot{\lambda} - \delta\lambda = \dot{\psi} - \delta\psi = \dot{\mu} - \delta\mu$$

and

$$B_F(F) + (P^h - \lambda(\alpha - k)\,H_F(X^h, F) = P^c\,C_L(X^c, L^c) = P^m\,M_L(X^m, L^m) \qquad (A8.2)$$

substituting (8.20) in main text into the first term in (8.31) we have

$$B_F + \left(p^h + \left(\frac{P^h\,H_x(X^h, F) - W^h}{(\alpha - k)H_x(X^h, F)}\right)(\alpha - k)\right)H_F(F, X^h)$$

or

$$B_F + P^h H_F(F, X^h) + \left(\frac{P^h\,H_x(X^h, F) - W^h}{(\alpha - k)H_x(X^h, F)}\right)H_F(F, X^h) \qquad (A8.3)$$

The first term in expression (A8.3) is the marginal benefit of the forest itself. The second term is the marginal value of the forest used as an input in timber production, while the last term represents the net marginal value of other inputs used in timber production.

If $V(t)$ is the opportunity cost or 'price' of maintaining the forest land for timber production and other benefits, it implies that on the optimal path, (A8.3) equals $V(t)$ in (A8.4)

$$B_F + P^h H_F(F, X^h) + \left(\frac{P^h\,H_x(X^h, F) - W^h}{H_x(X^h, F)}\right)H_F(F, X^h) = V(t) \qquad (A8.4)$$

Given that prices are assumed constant, as the left-hand side of equation (A8.4) increases, more forest land will be maintained until the marginal productivity of the stock of forest land maintained falls, and the equilibrium is re-established. And if $V(t)$ falls or increases, more forest land will be maintained or converted, respectively. It is important to note that if the marginal productivity of maintaining additional forest land is constant, then what changes the equations, and therefore leads to more stock of forest land being maintained or converted, are prices of outputs and inputs (this also applies to (A8.5) and (A8.6)). Therefore prices become important factors in determining whether to maintain the stock of forest land or not.

Given (8.31) it follows that

$$P^c\, C_L\, (X^c, L^c) = V(t) \tag{A8.5}$$

that is, if prices are constant, then the left-hand side is dependent on the marginal productivity of the additional stock of forest land converted to cocoa land ($C_L\, (X^c, L^c)$). It follows that if ($C_L\, (X^c, L^c)) > V(t)$ more forest land will be converted to cocoa land until ($C_L\, (X^c, L^c)$) falls to equal $V(t)$; and if ($C_L\, (X^c, L^c) < V(t)$ less forest land will be converted to cocoa land until ($C_L\, (X^c, L^c)$) increases to equal $V(t)$;

On the other hand, if ($C_L\, (X^c, L^c) < V(t)$, it implies that the opportunity cost of converting additional forest land to cocoa land is relatively higher and therefore less will be converted, and if ($C_L\, (X^c, L^c)) > V(t)$, it implies the opportunity cost is relatively lower and more forest land will be converted. This explains the negative relationship between $V(t)$ and the demand for cocoa land. Similarly

$$P^m M_L\, (X^m, L^m) = V(t) \tag{A8.6}$$

as $V(t)$ increases or falls, demand for maize land will also fall or increase, showing a negative relationship between the demand for maize land and the price. Given that on the optimal path, (A8.4), (A8.5) and (A8.6) are equal, and the fact that $V(t)$ is not easily estimated, what determines each demand equation is their respective output and input prices and the output and input prices of the last alternative uses for the stock of forest land as shown in equations (8.36)–(8.38).

APPENDIX 8.2   DEFINITIONS AND SOURCES OF DATA FOR THE ANALYSIS

Definition and data sources

F Total closed forest area (national level, 1000 km^2). Total closed forest area, for 1965–91, collected from the Forestry Department, Accra; estimations for 1992–95 using a rate of change of –1.3% as given by the FAO (State of the World's Forest, 1997).

L^c Cocoa land area harvested (national level, 1000 ha). Data from the Ghana Cocoa Board, Accra, and FAOSTAT database, FAO.

L^m Maize land area harvested (national level, 1000 ha). Data from Policy Planning. Monitoring and Evaluation Department (PPMED), Ministry of Agriculture, Accra, and FAOSTAT database, FAO.

H Industrial roundwood production (national level, 1000 CUM). Data from the Forest Products Inspection Bureau (FPIB), Timber Exports Development Board (TEDB), and Forestry Department, Accra.

P^c Real producer price of cocoa (national level, constant 1990 prices, 1000 Cedis/tonne). Producer price of cocoa data from the Ghana Cocoa Board, Accra.

P^m Real average price of maize (national level, constant 1990 prices, 1000 Cedis/100 kg). Maize price data from PPMED, Accra.

P^h Real average price of exported industrial roundwood (constant 1990 prices, 1000 Cedis/CUM). Average price of exported industrial roundwood data from RIB and TEDB.

W^c Real price of insecticides (national level, 1000 Cedis/litre). Price of insecticides data for 1965–81, derived from Stryker et al. (1990); 1982–1995 from ISSER (1993 and 1996).

Wm Real price of ammonium sulphate (national level, 1000 Cedis/litre). Price of ammonium sulphate data for 1965–81, derived from Stryker, et al. (1990); 1982–1995 from ISSER (1993 and 1996).

W^h Real average logging costs (national level, 1000 cedis/CUM). Data from RIB and TEDB. Estimations done for 1991–95 using the annual national rate of inflation.

Y_P Real per capita GDP (national level, GDP in constant 1990 values/population). GDP and population (millions) data derived from the IMF's International Financial Statistics.

popd Population density (national level, population/total land area (1000 ha)). Total land area data from FAOSTAT database, FAO.

Note: The consumer price index (CPI) for 1990 was used to estimate the real prices.

APPENDIX 8.3   APPROACH TO ESTIMATING OUTPUT AND INPUT ELASTICITIES OF FOREST LOSS

(Each equation is modified to compute for the post-adjustment elasticities.)
The change in cocoa land elasticity of forest loss from (8.46) is given by

$$e_{\hat{F}, \hat{L}^c} = \frac{\partial \hat{F}}{\partial \hat{L}} \cdot \frac{\overline{\hat{L}^c}}{\overline{\hat{F}}} \Rightarrow \beta_{14} \cdot \frac{\overline{\hat{L}^c}}{\overline{\hat{F}}} \tag{A8.7}$$

where:

$$\hat{F} = F_t - F_{t-1}; \quad \hat{L}^c = \hat{L}^c_t - \hat{L}^c_{t-1}$$

$$\overline{\hat{F}} = \text{mean of } \hat{F}; \quad \overline{\hat{L}^c} = \text{mean of } L^c$$

The cocoa price elasticity of the demand for cocoa land from (8.44) is given by

$$e_{L^c, P^c} = \frac{\partial L^c}{\partial P^c} \cdot \frac{\overline{P^c}}{\overline{L^c}} \Rightarrow \beta_{12} \cdot \frac{\overline{P^c}}{\overline{L^c}} \tag{A8.8}$$

where;

$$\overline{L^c} = \text{mean of } L^c; \quad \overline{P^c} = \text{mean of } P^c$$

If we assume that

$$\hat{L}^c = \hat{L}^c_t - L^c_{t-1} = \beta_{12} (P^c_t - P^c_{t-1}) = \beta_{12} \hat{P}^c \Rightarrow \frac{\partial \hat{L}^c}{\partial \hat{P}^c} = \beta_{12} \tag{A8.9}$$

then using (A8.7), (A8.8) and (A8.9) implies that the *change in cocoa price elasticity of forest loss* (given 8.48) will be given by

$$e_{\hat{F}, \hat{P}^c} = e_{\hat{F}, \hat{L}^c} \cdot e_{\hat{L}, \hat{P}^c} = \left(\frac{\partial \hat{F}}{\partial \hat{L}^c} \cdot \frac{\overline{\hat{L}^c}}{\overline{\hat{F}}} \right) \left(\frac{\partial \hat{L}^c}{\partial \hat{P}^c} \cdot \frac{\overline{\hat{P}^c}}{\overline{\hat{L}^c}} \right) \tag{A8.10}$$

$$= \beta_{14} \cdot \beta_{12} \cdot \left(\frac{\overline{\hat{P}^c}}{\overline{\hat{F}}} \right)$$

similarly the *change in maize price elasticity of forest loss* (given 8.46 and 8.49) will be given by

$$
e_{\hat{F},\,\hat{P}m} = e_{\hat{F},\,\hat{L}m} \cdot e_{\hat{L}\hat{P}m} = \left(\frac{\partial \hat{F}}{\partial \hat{L}^m} \cdot \frac{\overline{\hat{L}^m}}{\overline{\hat{F}}} \right)\left(\frac{\partial \hat{L}^m}{\partial \hat{P}^m} \cdot \frac{\overline{\hat{P}^m}}{\overline{\hat{L}}} \right)
$$

$$
= \beta_{ij} \cdot \beta_{13} \left(\frac{\overline{\hat{P}^m}}{\overline{\hat{F}}} \right) \tag{A8.11}
$$

and the change in *cocoa input (insecticides) price elasticity of forest loss* (given 8.47 and 8.48) will be given by

$$
e_{\hat{F},\,\hat{W}c} = e_{\hat{F},\,\hat{L}c} \cdot e_{\hat{L}c\,\hat{W}m} = \left(\frac{\partial \hat{F}}{\partial \hat{L}^c} \cdot \frac{\overline{\hat{L}^c}}{\overline{\hat{F}}} \right)\left(\frac{\partial \hat{L}^c}{\partial \hat{W}^c} \cdot \frac{\overline{\hat{P}^c}}{\overline{\hat{L}^c}} \right)
$$

$$
= \beta_{14} \cdot \beta_{22} \left(\frac{\overline{\hat{W}^c}}{\overline{\hat{F}}} \right) \tag{A8.12}
$$

and the *change in maize input (ammonium sulphate) price elasticity of forest loss* (given 8.46 and 8.49) will be given by

$$
e_{\hat{F},\,\hat{W}m} = e_{\hat{F},\,\hat{L}m} \cdot e_{\hat{L}m\hat{W}m} = \left(\frac{\partial \hat{F}}{\partial \hat{L}^m} \cdot \frac{\overline{\hat{L}^m}}{\overline{\hat{F}}} \right)\left(\frac{\partial \hat{L}^m}{\partial \hat{W}^m} \cdot \frac{\overline{\hat{P}^c}}{\overline{\hat{L}^m}} \right)
$$

$$
= \beta_{ij} \cdot \beta_{23} \left(\frac{\overline{\hat{W}^m}}{\overline{\hat{F}}} \right) \tag{A8.13}
$$

and the *change in relative timber output–input price elasticity of forest loss* (given 8.47 and 8.50) will be given by

$$
e_{\hat{F},\,} \frac{P^h}{W^h} = e_{\hat{F},H} \cdot e_{H}, \frac{P^h}{W^h} = \left(\frac{\partial \hat{F}}{\partial H} \cdot \frac{\overline{H}}{\overline{\hat{F}}} \right)\left(\frac{\partial H}{\partial P^h/W^h} \cdot \frac{\overline{P^h/W^h}}{\overline{H}} \right)
$$

$$
= \beta_{24} \cdot \beta_{11} \left(\frac{\overline{P^h/W^h}}{\overline{\hat{F}}} \right) \tag{A8.14}
$$

where:

$\hat{\overline{P^c}}$ = mean of the change in cocoa price

$\hat{\overline{P^m}}$ = mean of the change in maize price

$\hat{\overline{W^c}}$ = mean of the change in cocoa input price

$\hat{\overline{W^m}}$ = mean of the change in maize input price

$\dfrac{\overline{P^h}}{\overline{W^c}}$ = the mean of the relative timber output – input price.

But given equation (8.47) this implies that (A8.11) = (A8.13) = 0.

NOTES

1. From this point onwards notation is simplified by omitting the argument of time-dependent variables and partial derivatives are represented by subscripts.
2. Connor and McCoy (1979), MacArthur and Wilson (1967), May (1975), Reid and Miller (1989) and Simberloff (1986).
3. This also follows the criticism by Lugo, Parrotta and Brown (1993) that the simple species–forest area relationship fails to take account of land use after forest clearing and assumes that land is biotically sterile after forest clearance. The implication is that other land uses after forest clearance may contain some species.
4. This is based on the fact that cocoa can successfully grow on land which supports closed tropical rain forest (Manu and Tetteh, 1987). These forests consist of patches of permanent forests, temporary forest (both of which provide shade) and mangroves. Maize land may also contain some mangroves.
5. Some of these studies include Angelsen et al. (1996), Barbier and Burgess (1995, 1997), Burgess (1993), Capistrano (1994), Reis and Margulis (1991), Sankhayan (1996) and Southgate (1991).
6. The assumption under a piecewise linear model is that the true model is continuous, with a structural break. In this study, the structural break occurred in 1983 when the Structural Adjustment Programme was introduced in Ghana. Our piecewise equations therefore consist of two segments, where the first and second segments represent the pre and post-adjustment periods, respectively.
7. The lower boundary estimates will follow a similar trend to the upper boundary. Since we are interested in the trend, the choice of either of the boundaries in the estimation will not make much difference.

REFERENCES

Amelung, T. and M. Diehl (1991), 'Deforestation of tropical rainforests: economic causes and impact on development', Kieler Studien 241, Tubingen, Mohr, Germany.

Angelsen, A. et al. (1996), 'Causes of deforestation: an econometric study from Tanzania', mimeo.

Barbier, E.B. (1994), 'The environmental effect of the forestry sector', in *The Environmental Effects of Trade*, Paris: Organization for Economic Cooperation and Development (OECD).

Barbier, E.B. and J.C. Burgess (1995), 'Economic analysis of deforestation in Mexico', Department of Environmental Economics and Environmental Management (EEEM), University of York.

Barbier, E.B. and J.C. Burgess (1997), 'The economics of tropical forest land use options', *Land Economics*, 73(2), 174–95.

Burgess, J.C. (1993), 'Timber production, timber trade and tropical deforestation', *Ambio*, 2, 136–43.

Capistrano, A.D. (1994), 'Tropical forest depletion and the changing macroeconomy', in K. Brown and D.W. Pearce (eds), *The Causes of Tropical Deforestation*, London: University College London Press.

Connor, E.F. and E.D. McCoy (1979), 'The statistics and biology of the species–area relationship', *American Naturalist*, 13, 791–833.

Deacon, R.T. (1995), 'Assessing the relationship between government policy and deforestation', *Journal of Environmental Economics and Management*, 28,1–8.

Ehui, E.K. and T.W. Hertel (1989), 'Deforestation and agricultural productivity in the Côte d'Ivoire', *American Journal of Agricultural Economics*, 71(3), 701–11.

Ehui, E.K., T.W. Hertel and P.V. Preckel (1990), 'Forest resource depletion, soil dynamics and agricultural productivity in the tropics', *Journal of Environmental Economics and Management*, 18, 136–54.

Gujarati, D.N. (1995), *Basic Econometrics* (3rd edn), New York: McGraw-Hill.

ISSER (1996), 'The state of the Ghanaian economy in 1995', ISSER, University of Ghana, Legon.

López, R. (1995), 'Environmental externalities in traditional agriculture and the impact of trade liberalization: the case of Ghana', University of Maryland, College Park (unpublished).

MacArthur, R.H. and E.O. Wilson (1967), '*The Theory of Island Biogeography*: *Monographs in Population Biology 1*, Princeton: Princeton University Press.

Manu, M. and E.K. Tetteh (1987), 'A guide to cocoa cultivation', Cocoa Research Institute of Ghana, Ghana Cocoa Board, Accra.

May, R.M. (1975), 'Patterns of species abundance and diversity', in M.L. Cody and J.M. Diamond (eds), *Ecology and Evolution of Communities*, Cambridge, MA: Belknap Press.

Reid, W.V. (1992), 'How many species will there be?', in T.C. Whitmore and J.A. Sayer (eds), *Tropical Deforestation and Species Extinction*, London: Chapman and Hall.

Reid, W.V. and K.R. Miller (1989), *Keeping Options Alive: The Scientific Basis for Conserving Biodiversity*, Washington, DC: World Resources Institute.

Sankhayan, P.L. (1996), 'Effects of structural adjustment programmes on cropping pattern and environment: A study in the southern highlands of Tanzania', in 'Structural adjustment policies and environmental degradation in Tanzania, Zambia and Ethiopia', Preliminary Seminar Report, 9–10 January, Agricultural University of Norway.

Simberloff, D. (1986), 'Are we on the verge of a mass extinction in tropical rain forests?', in D.K. Elliot (ed.), *Dynamics of Extinction*, New York: John Wiley.

Southgate, D. (1991), 'Tropical deforestation and agriculture development in Latin America', *LEEC Discussion Paper*, 9–01, London: London Environmental Economic Centre.

Stryker, D.J. et al. (1990), 'Trade, exchange rate and agricultural pricing policies in Ghana', World Bank Comparative Studies, Washington, DC: World Bank.

Sun, C. (1995), 'Tropical deforestation and the economics of timber concession design', Department of Agricultural Economics, University of Illinois at Urbana-Champaign, Urbana, doctoral dissertation proposal.

WCMC (World Conservation and Monitoring Centre) (1992), *Global Biodiversity: Status of the Earth's Living Resources*, London: Chapman and Hall.

9. Policies for biodiversity conservation in Sub-Saharan Africa

Charles Perrings and Jon Lovett

9.1 INTRODUCTION

The first policy question to be resolved is whether the problem of biodiversity loss may be addressed without undertaking specific, targeted initiatives. It was remarked in Chapter 1 that economists have identified a relation between per capita income and certain measures of environmental quality that is similar to the familiar Kuznets relation between per capita income and income inequality. If selected indicators of environmental damage are mapped into per capita income, the graph has the shape of an inverted U. As per capita income rises environmental damage first rises and then falls. It was also observed that Panayotou (1995) and Antle and Heidebrink (1995) found the same general relation between deforestation rates – one of the proximate causes of biodiversity loss – and per capita income. The inference drawn from this relation is that economic growth may eventually take care of one of the main causes of biodiversity loss. That is, policies which are growth promoting may have the incidental effect of eventually eliminating an important driver of biodiversity loss.

The consensus view in both the natural and economic sciences is more cautious than this. Economic growth is not thought to be sufficient to assure environmental improvement. In all cases, environmental improvement has followed specific institutional reforms, environmental legislation and market-based incentives designed to internalize harmful external effects. It has also been limited to cases where societies have a direct incentive to internalize the environmental costs of their own activity. The inverted U relation has been shown for pollutants involving a fairly localized and short-term costs (such as dark matter, sulphur particulates and so on), but not for pollutants with longer-term and more dispersed costs (Barbier, 1997). Where the environmental costs of economic activity have been borne by the poor, by future generations, or by people in other countries, the incentive to address environmental questions has been much weaker. The inverted U relation is evidence that environmental improvements have occurred in some cases. It is not evident either that they will occur in all cases, or that they will occur in time to avert many important and irreversible environmental implications of economic growth (Arrow et al., 1995).

This is not to say that economic growth and growth-promoting policies have a neutral effect on biodiversity. Nor is it to say that the economic climate has no consequences for targeted policies: it does. Indeed, these are explored in the next section. But it does say that the problem of biodiversity conservation should be addressed through specific targeted actions.

A common thread running through this volume is that the problem of biodiversity loss stems from the fact that biological resources are used without due regard for the interests of other members of society. Individual users are able to ignore the wider consequences of their actions. This has partly to do with the public-good nature of biodiversity, partly to do with the structure of property rights in resources, and partly to do with the effect of the policy regime. Users are 'authorized' by current policies, administrative structures and property rights to ignore the environmental consequences of their decisions. There are two main challenges to policymakers in this problem. The first, the challenge of Article 8 of the Convention, is to find the right composition and level of public investment in biodiversity protection. The second, the challenge of Article 11 of the Convention, is to establish an incentive structure that will conserve resources for which markets either do not exist or are incomplete by providing users with the right signals.

Parts I and II confirm that the main drivers of biodiversity loss in Sub-Saharan Africa are the growth in demand induced by population expansion and economic growth (population and consumption growth); the lack of markets for many of the environmental consequences of economic activity (externality and market failure); the adverse effects of inappropriate economic and social policies (public goods and policy failure); and a distribution of assets that often leaves people with little choice but to overexploit the natural resources they use (poverty). These drivers are not independent of each other.

The main recommendations that flow from the studies reported in Parts I and II all involve highly specific and localized instruments. Before drawing these together, however, it is important to appreciate the limitations of the economic and policy environment within which policymakers in Sub-Saharan Africa have to work. In very few cases do they have much room for manoeuvre either to undertake public investments or to impose additional costs on resource users. If policy recommendations are to be helpful they need to respect these limitations.

9.2   THE ECONOMIC POLICY ENVIRONMENT

Liberalization of Domestic and International Markets

The policy environment within which governments are being asked to develop conservation strategies has two main planks: liberalization of domestic and international markets and privatization of publicly-owned natural resources. Both are designed to promote economic efficiency and growth. Both have quite pronounced environmental effects. The conventional wisdom on liberalization of domestic and international markets is that it has broadly beneficial environmental consequences. Munasinghe and Cruz (1995) argue that the removal of market price distortions, such as agricultural or energy subsidies, both improves the efficiency of economic activity and reduces the impact of that activity on the environment. They note that improving the security of land tenure by assigning private property or use rights promotes investment in land conservation and environmental stewardship. Moreover, greater macroeconomic stability encourages investment, and persuades resource users to take a longer-term view of their decisions. Liberalization creates new economic opportunities. To the extent that this reduces poverty, it also reduces pressure on scarce but open-access environmental resources.

The liberalization of agricultural markets may be expected to have implications for both the level and stability of prices. It is generally expected that average producer prices will rise, but given that most administered prices were designed to stabilize incomes, it may also be expected that producer prices will become more variable. The presumption is that administered prices impose welfare losses that significantly outweigh any welfare gains from stabilization. This may be true, but it is an empirical question that has not been satisfactorily addressed. Certainly, the empirical evidence is that liberalization has occurred alongside a marked increase in price risk. The coefficient of variation of detrended prices for the major food products rose sharply between the mid-1960s and the mid-1980s. In addition, these prices became positively correlated (they began to move together) so reducing the value both of diversification within agriculture, and of export-earning stabilization schemes (Hazell, 1987).

The implications of trade liberalization for the price level ought to be easier to identify. During the 1980s, the average price of food crops was held below the expected world price in the interests of controlling consumer costs and urban wages (Markandya, 1995). There was an anti-agricultural bias in policy reflected in the distortion of tradable input and output prices due to the monopsonistic pricing of outputs, monopolistic pricing of inputs, and the income-depressing effects of taxes and tariffs. It follows that liberalization of agricultural markets ought to have resulted in a rise in producer prices.

The environmental effects of liberalization are, however, ambiguous at best. On the positive side, trade liberalization may stimulate environmental protection by lowering costs (Anderson and Blackhurst, 1992). It may also facilitate the diffusion of environmental protection technologies. But there are costs as well as benefits to expanding trade. If it stimulates demand for the products of environmentally damaging activities, then it follows that it will increase environmental damage. If the value of that damage exceeds the gains from the increased level of activity, there may be a net welfare loss (Anderson and Blackhurst, 1992). The change in developing country share in world production and trade in the smoke-stack industries is, for example, largely a result of the liberalization of national and international markets. The costs of the associated pollution need to be set against the benefits of the increased level of activity.

A complicating factor is the changes that have simultaneously taken place in the world trade regime. The Uruguay Round of the GATT in fact led to a worsening of the trade balance of net food importers and countries that have historically enjoyed preferential access to the EU under the Lomé Convention (mainly in Sub-Saharan Africa). During the period 1983–93 the World Bank estimates that per capita consumption and GDP declined at, respectively, 1.8 and 0.8 per cent per year in Sub-Saharan Africa (World Bank, 1994). The Uruguay Round is expected to raise international food prices which could cause this trend to continue. Indeed, Sub-Saharan Africa is the one region where the poor are expected to increase both numerically and as a proportion of the population (World Bank, 1994). Under the 'Brundtland hypothesis', countries locked in to products for which the terms of trade decline will tend to increase exports of those products just to maintain foreign exchange earnings (Pearce and Warford, 1993). Consistent with this hypothesis, the response to falling real primary commodity prices in Sub-Saharan Africa has not been a reduction in primary commodity production, but an increase in the volume of exports.

Structural Adjustment Programmes

A second complicating factor is that where liberalization and privatization were introduced as components of a structural adjustment programme targeted at improving the internal and external balances of the economy, these effects have been magnified. During the 1980s, many agricultural markets in Sub-Saharan Africa were reformed, and a number of policies that had limited trade were removed – often under structural adjustment programmes agreed with the World Bank and the International Monetary Fund. Between 1979 and 1987, twenty-two Sub-Saharan African countries received structural adjustment loans by the World Bank. In most cases (around 70 per cent) these were associated adjustments of agricultural input and output prices, together with reform of agricultural institutions. In 50 per cent of the cases the loans were also associated with reform of trade policy and public expenditure in agriculture (Pearce and Warford, 1993; Sebastian and Alicbusan, 1989). The central elements of structural adjustment loans in the period were, then, the alignment of domestic prices with world prices through the elimination of distortionary taxes, subsidies and administered pricing practices; the reduction of public expenditure; deregulation of industry; the imposition of wage restraints; institutional reforms; trade liberalization; and the privatization of state-owned assets. Even more significant were the changes that occurred in exchange rate policies. Between 1984 and 1988 average real effective exchange rates in Sub-Saharan African economies were virtually halved, so reducing the disincentive to agricultural production posed by overvalued exchange rates.

Only comparatively recently have the environmental impacts of structural adjustment programmes begun to be analysed (Cruz and Repetto, 1992; Panayotou and Hupé, 1995). As with economic liberalization, it was held that structural adjustment would have no net negative environmental effects providing that there existed a functioning set of markets, infrastructure and natural resources (Sebastian and Alicbusan, 1989). Indeed, Warford et al. (1994) argued that structural adjustment programmes were not just necessary but perhaps sufficient conditions for environmentally sustainable development. Others have been much less confident, arguing that structural adjustment programmes may have negative environmental effects, but should not be directly concerned with the environment—being too blunt an instrument to address environmental effects (Panayotou and Hupé, 1995).

Despite such changes, however, the evidence for the predicted impact of trade liberalization on either income or investment in conservation measures in the agricultural sector is weak. Overall, per capita income in the region declined at an average annual rate of 1.2 per cent in the period 1980–1991, while gross domestic investment fell over the same period by

3.3 per cent, and external debt as a percentage of GNP rose from 28.6 to 107.9 per cent (World Bank, 1994). Additional effects included reductions in the budgets of agencies protecting the environment and a reduction of credit to small rural investors leading to lower on-farm investment.

Part II of this volume offers one of the most detailed studies yet undertaken of the impacts of structural adjustment in Ghana. Working through the effect of changes in relative input and output prices confronting resource users in agriculture and forestry, it finds that structural adjustment in this case led to the intensification of agricultural production. Benhin and Barbier argue that it did not lead to deforestation, and to the extent that biodiversity loss is a function of deforestation, it did not lead to any increase in biodiversity loss.

The Debt Problem

An important part of the difficult policy environment in Sub-Saharan Africa is the combination of low income, primary product dependence and indebtedness. Per capita income and the external indebtedness of these countries have both been deteriorating over much of the last two decades. In part this has been a consequence of their dependence on primary commodity production – primary commodity prices having to follow a downward secular trend. The barter terms of trade of countries in Sub-Saharan Africa show a marked decline over the last two decades (Figure 9.1).

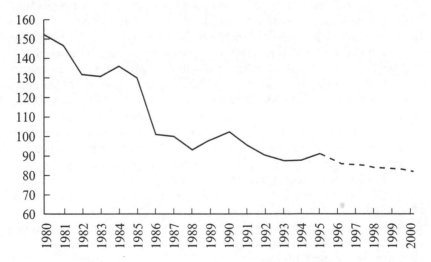

Source: World Bank (1996).

Figure 9.1   Barter terms of trade in Sub-Saharan Africa, 1980–2000

This has been partially offset by the increasing volume of exports. During the same period the economies of Sub-Saharan Africa have become increasingly extraverted. Exports of goods and non-factor services increased from 21 to 28 per cent of GNP between 1970 and 1991 (World Bank, 1994). It is, however, noticeable that during the 1980s the income terms of trade also declined (Pearce and Warford, 1993). That is, consistent with the Brundtland hypothesis, the volume of agricultural exports rose during the period but still lost ground in terms of purchasing power. The environmental implications of this are at present unclear. Most of the increase in agricultural output is argued to have derived from increased yield rather than increased land allocation. The recorded change in land allocation to crop production in arid and semi-arid areas is certainly much smaller than the recorded increase in the volume of output. Similarly, the recorded change in land allocated to pasture is trivial compared to the recorded change in herd sizes. So there is evidence of intensification of land use. But data on agricultural inputs does not suggest that increased yield reflects a significant change in agricultural technology in the arid and semi-arid areas, with the possible exception of draft power. Without detailed analysis of agricultural performance in particular areas it is not possible to say very much more than this, but the general impression is that increased agricultural output and exports have been achieved by putting the existing agroecosystems under greater pressure without change to agricultural technology.

Both price responsiveness and the propensity to adopt new technologies are more tightly constrained by institutional factors in Sub-Saharan Africa than elsewhere (Junankar, 1989). Moreover, since a substantial proportion of goods and services are not traded, farmers are less sensitive to price changes than elsewhere (Beynon, 1989). In addition, constraints on the supply of basic natural resources and rural credit limit the capacity of those who do participate in the market to respond to price incentives. Raising the return on productive assets will not help if people do not have access to those assets. Moreover, even where farmers do have access to productive assets, the lack of physical and financial infrastructure has limited their capacity to respond to changes in real returns on those assets (Addison and Demery, 1989).

The coincidence between indebtedness, trade liberalization and export dependence in primary products is now quite striking. Most low income exporters of primary products in the region are now classified by the World Bank as 'severely indebted' (see Table 9.1). This is a major constraint on their ability to introduce any environmental policies that threaten exports. Between 1980 and 1991, Debt:GDP and Debt:Export ratios increased more than threefold. A slight easing of the terms on

Table 9.1   Sub-Saharan African countries by income and indebtedness

	Low income			Middle income		
	Severely indebted	Moderately indebted	Less indebted	Severely indebted	Moderately indebted	Less indebted
Exporters of primary products	Burundi Congo Equ'l Guinea Ethiopia Ghana Guinea-Bissau Liberia Madagascar Mauritania Niger Nigeria São Tomé Somalia Tanzania Uganda Zambia	Guinea Malawi Rwanda Togo	Chad Zimbabwe	Angola Congo Côte d'Ivoire	Gabon	Botswana Namibia Reunion Swaziland
Exporters of services, and diversified exporters	Kenya Mali Mozambique Sierra Leone Sudan	Benin CAR Comoros Gambia	Burkina Faso Lesotho		Cameroon Senegal	Cape Verde Djibouti Mauritius Seychelles South Africa

Source: World Bank (1994).

which debt was held has meant that Debt Service:Export ratio increased by a smaller amount, but this was still a very significant additional burden given the weakness of the economies of Sub-Saharan Africa. A large part of the explanation for the trend in indebtedness in this period is to be found in movements in primary commodity prices.

Given the effects of both liberalization and structural adjustment, there is a growing body of opinion that each should be accompanied by a set of environmental policies designed to minimize the environmental damage they cause. For example, if policy reform stimulates demand for timber without ensuring that stumpage fees reflect the social opportunity cost of the resource, it will increase rather than reduce environmental damage. The same is true for other sectors. If liberalization stimulates industrial growth without addressing the pollution impacts of that growth, it will have negative environmental effects. Indeed, it is now thought that environmental policies should be an integral part of the programme. The questions to be answered are what policies, and with what targets?

9.3 PROTECTED AREAS, CONSERVATION AND DEVELOPMENT

To put the requirements of Article 8 into the context of the arguments of earlier chapters, the problem of biodiversity conservation requires more than just 'getting the prices right'. It is important to provide resource users with the right economic incentives – to internalize the external costs of the use of biological resources – and this is discussed in Section 9.4. But while this may improve the efficiency with which biological resources are allocated it cannot, in general, protect key biodiversity thresholds. It is also important to bound economic activity in a way that minimizes the risk of irreversible damage to the ecosystems on which human activity depends.

Conventionally, this is achieved through the establishment of protected areas. This implies a 'habitat' rather than a 'species' approach to conservation. The interactions among species typically makes it necessary to protect a number of species to ensure the protection of any one. So even if species are not valued for their own sake, they may be protected because of their role in supporting other species. By the same reasoning, ecological services may be protected because they are by-products of habitat. Panayotou and Ashton (1992) cite watershed protection, carbon sequestration, harvesting of non-timber forest products, and recreational and scientific use as joint products of habitat conservation. Nevertheless, while protecting wild flora and fauna through nature or wildlife reserves, national parks, zoos, arboreta or botanical gardens is an important short-term step where such resources are threatened with immediate extinction, it does not address the general problem of biodiversity loss. The goal of biodiversity conservation should not be to safeguard all wild resources in a limited set of wildlife reserves. It should be to protect critical biodiversity thresholds everywhere.

Most conservation strategies, both nationally and internationally, begin and end with the designation of protected areas. Protected areas have become entrenched as the main mechanism for conservation of all biological resources. Indeed, this has now been translated into universal goals. The 1992 Caracas Action Plan of the World Parks Congress set a goal of protecting at least 10 per cent of the world's major biomes. At present most developing countries protect less than half that amount (see Table 9.2), but the fact the designation of protected areas is still the primary vehicle for addressing the biodiversity problem. The view of biodiversity described in Parts I and II suggests that this may not be appropriate.

Table 9.2   Protected areas in developing countries

	Number	Area (1000 ha)	Proportion of land area (%)
Africa	704	138893	4.6
Asia	2181	121161	4.4
North & Central America	1752	263250	11.7
South America	667	114596	6.4
Europe	2177	45533	9.3
Former USSR	218	24330	1.1
Oceania	920	84505	9.9

Source: World Resources Institute (1994).

The preservation of wild resources through designation of protected areas at Caracas levels may be appropriate in some cases. But designation of protected areas can also be both inefficient and inequitable. The establishment of protected areas may, for example, lead to loss of traditional access rights and employment opportunities. In such cases it may lead to increasing rather than decreasing pressure on the resource as users resort to illegal harvesting and encroachment (McNeely, 1993). Indeed, this remains a problem in the Marsabit Forest Reserve in Kenya (see Chapter 4).

In Sub-Saharan Africa the designation of protected areas has been popular for another reason: that they are necessary adjuncts to the development of tourism. Early studies of the value of biodiversity were dominated by estimates of the willingness of ecotourists to pay to visit protected areas (Tobias and Mendelsohn, 1991; Munasinghe, 1993; Brown and Henry, 1993; Kramer et al., 1994). These studies showed that protected areas can yield a very high rate of return as tourist resources in certain conditions. This is reflected in the greater than average proportion of land set aside as protected in Eastern, Central and Southern African countries where large mammals are to be found (Table 9.3).

Table 9.3   Protected areas in selected Sub-Saharan African countries

	Proportion of land area protected (%)
Botswana	17.6
Kenya	6.0
Malawi	8.9
Namibia	12.6
Tanzania	13.8
Uganda	7.9
Zambia	8.5
Zimbabwe	7.9

Source: World Resources Institute (1994).

The study of Nyae Nyae in Namibia (Chapter 5) reflects the tourist value of wildlife in the comparison it offers between the yield on livestock and mixed wildlife/livestock land uses. This is also a factor in recent proposals for making biodiversity the focus of development options over a substantial part of Mozambique, South Africa, Zimbabwe, Botswana, Namibia and Angola (Walker, 1998). These proposals make the point that wildlife are better adapted than livestock to environmental conditions in the semi-arid savannas of Southern Africa, and call for the removal of structural biases in favour of irrigated and rain-fed arable agriculture or livestock. Chapter 5 offers one way of assessing the relative advantages of wildlife and livestock options.

A word of caution here is that the value of wildlife for tourism needs to be assessed alongside its value for supporting the provision a number of ecological services over a range of environmental conditions. For example, wildlife that are most valuable for recreational hunting and tourism are not necessarily the most valuable for watershed protection. In other words, the value of biodiversity in assuring ecosystem resilience cannot always be approximated by its value for tourism. In addition, the benefits of tourism are typically less equitably distributed than the benefits of watershed or soil protection. That is, local communities may derive fewer benefits from biodiversity conservation for the promotion of tourism than from biodiversity conservation for the protection of agriculture (Perrings et al., 1995).

The important point is that setting aside land necessarily has local opportunity costs – in terms of forgone local benefits from alternative land uses. Perrings et al. (1995) argue that biodiversity conservation in many developing countries has been complicated by the fact that the local benefits of conservation are less than local opportunity costs. The local population can do better by exploiting biological resources than by conserving them. The key to conservation whether inside or outside of formal protected areas is to construct economic and financial incentives to capture and internalize the benefits of conservation to local populations. Where incentives for land conversion are strong among local communities, it has been argued that the designation of protected areas is unlikely to succeed without environmentally sound intensification of crop and livestock production in areas away from agricultural frontiers (Southgate and Clark, 1993).

Partly as a response to this, the still-popular Integrated Conservation and Development Projects (ICDPs) attempt to combine the creation of employment and development opportunities with the designation of protected areas (Wells and Brandon, 1993). In particular, the use of buffer zones around park boundaries as sites for joint conservation and development, and the encouragement of local participation in protected area management, are both designed to secure local support for protected areas. The ICDP record in respect of both conservation, development and local participation has been disappointing. ICDPs have not generally resolved the basic problems caused by the loss of traditional access rights to the protected areas proper. But the principle upon which ICDPs are founded – that there should be a measure of environmental protection in areas designated for development – is a sound one.

By extension, biodiversity conservation is as much an issue in agriculture, forestry and fisheries as it is in designated parks. Indeed, the studies of fisheries in Lake Malawi, flood plain agriculture in Nigeria and treecrops in Ghana reported in Parts I and II focus on the biodiversity problem in these systems. The importance of biodiversity in maintaining productivity in managed ecosystems was discussed in some detail in Chapter 1. These specific studies have shown (a) the direct economic significance of the diversity of harvested fish or arable crops, (b) the way in which incentive structures have impacted on harvest and crop diversity, and (c) the indirect effect of changes in the crop mix on biodiversity elsewhere in the system. Protected areas are largely irrelevant in these cases, as they are for most of the region, but biodiversity still matters.

Moreover, biodiversity in these areas is a problem for policy precisely because it is subject to both market and policy failure. The deletion of particular species in Lake Malawi, for example, is a reflection of the structure of property rights, the regulatory regime and market conditions. Analogous problems currently exist in the East African Lakes: Edward, George (Kazoora, 1998), and Victoria (Ikiara, 1998; Muramira, 1998). Similarly, interference in the hydrology of wetlands in the Hadejia-Nguru wetlands of Nigeria, which has had implications for both domesticated crops and wild species, reflects the public-good nature of the flood resource (Chapter 2). Equivalent issues arise in wetlands in East Africa (Nabbumba, Tumislime and Ndyaberema, 1998).

While the creation of an appropriate incentive structure, in the sense of Article 11 of the Convention on Biological Diversity, is important in all of these cases, so is the establishment of a regulatory regime that protects the biodiversity thresholds by limiting economic activities. In the case of fisheries it is obvious that aggregate allowable catches that are 'blind' to the species mix cannot protect against the deletion of particular species through overfishing. What are required are species-denominated allowable catches together with supporting restrictions on gear and harvest times. Similar observations hold for the protection of other managed ecosystems.

9.4 PATTERNS OF SPECIES DIVERSITY AND THE LEVEL OF BIODIVERSITY PROTECTION

The distribution of plant species in Africa south of the Sahara is far from random (Lovett and Friis, 1996) with some areas much more species rich than others. A number of broad theories have been advanced to explain global variation in diversity, for example variation in history, energy, climate and productivity (Ricklefs and Schulter, 1993), but on a local or regional scale there are few convincing ecological and evolutionary explanations of the pattern of species distribution (Harper et al., 1997). Nevertheless, it is clear that this distribution matters. Experimental studies of the functionality of plant species diversity have shown that more diverse communities are more productive and resilient (Naeem et al., 1995; Tilman and Downing, 1994). If these experimental studies can be translated to natural systems, then management options that reduce diversity will also decrease productivity and resilience. Indeed, this is a recurrent theme of the work reported in Parts I and II. But the precise effect of management interventions will depend on the ability of the plant species that comprise an ecosystem to tolerate a management regime. It may be possible to predict the amplitude of ecological fluctuations a species can survive from its distribution pattern. Hence the aggregate distributions of species in a particular vegetation community may be used to identify the appropriate level of protection (or, conversely, the appropriate level of usage) in any one part of that range.

For Africa south of the Sahara there are three main hypotheses that can be used to explain variations in species richness. The first is a straightforward explanation based on habitat heterogeneity: the more variable the habitat the greater the number of species it can support. The second is that 'hotspots' of species richness are due to species becoming extinct in areas outside of climatic refugia during periods of extreme climate change, in other words events extrinsic to the refugium determine richness (Hamilton, 1976). The third is that certain places have particular intrinsic properties that promote speciation and the accumulation of species (Fjeldså and Lovett, 1997). The latter two hypotheses are not mutually exclusive, but the primary underlying cause of species richness may have important implications for how vegetation communities react to management. Geographical range of a species is considered to be correlated with its ability to cope with environmental fluctuations (Stevens, 1992). Geographically rare species will be less tolerant of a variety of ecological conditions than widespread species. If richness is due to large numbers of restricted range species, then the vegetation can be predicted to be less resilient than if the species are widespread.

This may be illustrated by reference to the distribution of four different plant types: the herbaceous genus *Impatiens;* the shrubby and herbaceous genus *Crotalaria*; the herbaceous geophyte *Watsonia*; and the genus of forest trees, *Tabernaemontana*. For each of these plant types we show two plots: a species richness plot (which indicates the density of species per grid cell), and a range-size rarity plot (which indicates the range size of species in each grid cell). The first indicates areas of high or low species richness: the darker the plot the higher the level of species richness. The second indicates areas of high or low range size: the darker the plot the higher the level of endemism. We emphasize that these plant types have not been selected for their economic importance or their functionality, merely for the fact that they illustrate the principles upon which regional approaches to biodiversity protection should be founded.

The herbaceous genus *Impatiens* shows a peak of richness in Gabon, with a general area of high species richness on the Atlantic coast of west-central Africa and other areas of richness in far western Africa, highlands of the Albertine rift, mountains of eastern tropical Africa and south-eastern Africa. It has much the same centre of endemism or range-size rarity (Figure 9.2). The shrubby and herbaceous genus *Crotalaria*, on the other hand, shows a peak at the southern end of Lake Tanganyika with high richness in the uplands of south-western Africa, north-eastern Africa and the central African plateau. But the centre of endemism or range size rarity shifts to the mountains of south-western Angola (Figure 9.3). The genus of forest trees, *Tabernaemontana*, has a peak of richness in Cameroon with patches of richness in western, central and eastern Africa. Again, its centre of endemism is different (although some caution needs to be exercised in this case as the data set is comparatively small) (Figure 9.4). The herbaceous geophyte *Watsonia* has a peak of both species richness and endemism in the south western cape and is more or less confined to Southern Africa (Figure 9.5).

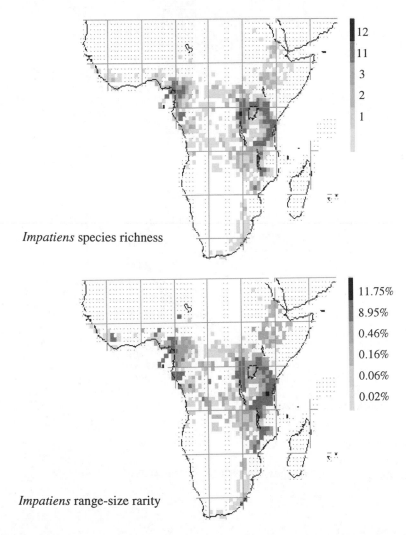

Impatiens species richness

Impatiens range-size rarity

Source: See text.

Figure 9.2   Species richness and range-size rarity plots: Impatiens

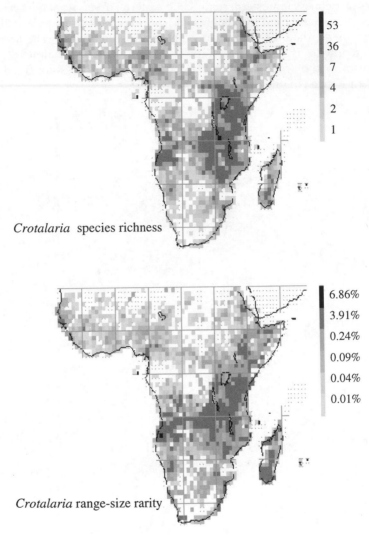

Crotalaria species richness

Crotalaria range-size rarity

Source: See text.

Figure 9.3 *Species richness and range-size rarity plots*: Crotalaria

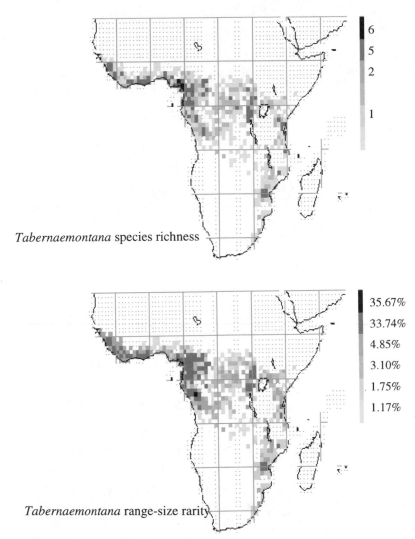

Source: See text.

Figure 9.4 Species richness and range-size rarity plots: Tabernaemontana

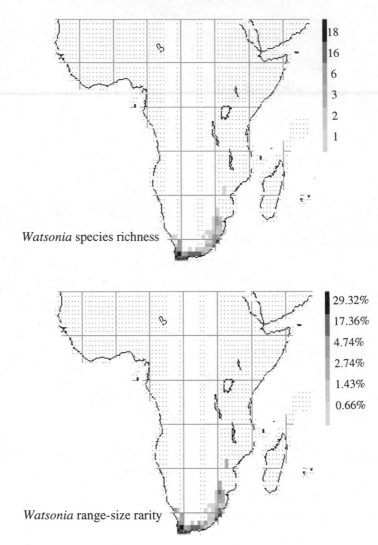

Source: See text.

Figure 9.5   Species richness and range-size rarity plots: Watsonia

The fact that centres of endemism or range-size rarity can be in different locations from centres of species richness for particular plant groups is important in developing appropriate levels of biodiversity protection. For example, ecologically dynamic habitats that are in a state of flux may support a high species richness as there will be a mosaic of vegetation types resulting from a variety of disturbance regimes. In most cases species richness is correlated with habitat heterogeneity, particularly in mountains where vegetation communities change rapidly with elevation (Lovett, 1996, 1998), but may be associated with variation in soils and landscape, or rainfall patterns (Goldblatt, 1989). These need not coincide with centres of endemism where the vegetation is composed of rare species with small geographical ranges. Species of restricted distribution in centres of endemism would not generally be expected to be resilient to anthropogenic stress or shocks as they are quite specific in their ecological requirements. Modification of environmental conditions in such circumstances may make the site unsuitable for endemics. This is not necessarily the case with centres of species richness if they are composed of widespread ecologically tolerant species. In these centres vegetation is made up of species that may be tolerant of the environmental fluctuations resulting from management. Indeed, this is precisely the point made in Chapters 1 and 5 about the effect of management on the grass sward in semi-arid rangelands.

In vegetation composed of widespread ecologically tolerant species, resource users may alter environmental conditions without unduly adverse effects. Where species diversity is of functional significance in terms of enhancing resilience and productivity (Naeem et al., 1995; Tilman and Downing, 1994) resource users will still have a direct incentive to maintain a certain level of biodiversity, but management need not by itself drive species to extinction.

However, where species diversity is composed of restricted range endemics which cannot tolerate disturbance – as has been argued to be the case in 'biodiversity hotspots' (Myers, 1988, 1990) – then any management-induced change in environmental conditions may well result in species extinctions. This has the following implications for biodiversity protection that run counter to the sovereignty principle in the Convention on Biological Diversity. It suggests that an appropriate strategy for biodiversity conservation in any one location should take the general pattern of distribution of species into account in determining the right level of protection in that location. Any policy of biodiversity protection should be sensitive to the patterns of distribution of species: and that wherever species preservation is a goal of policy, the level of protection should become tighter the more restricted is the range of species concerned. But we emphasize that there is a continuum of protection requirements. A crude combination of fully protected no-go areas on the one hand, and complete *laissez-faire* on the other, is simply not appropriate.

9.5   INCENTIVES FOR BIODIVERSITY CONSERVATION

There are four main elements in a policy for biodiversity conservation: a regulatory regime to protect key species, habitats and ecological services – including a system of protected areas; an appropriate set of property rights in natural resources (along with their supporting institutions); a compensation mechanism; and a supporting structure of incentives and disincentives to induce the desired response. Examples of the last three include recognition of customary access rights to common property biological resources and appropriate compensation where these are removed; establishment of secure land tenure/use rights; removal of subsidies that encourage land conversion; the development of mechanisms to transfer the benefits of wildlife use to local communities; establishment of access to credit/real assets, technology and markets to open up alternative economic opportunities; and the provision of alternative employment opportunities (Perrings et al., 1995). In other words, a policy for the conservation of biodiversity should aim to protect important ecological thresholds. It should bring the private and social cost of biological resources into line, and it should give resource users the means to respond to the social cost of resource use in a way that is consistent with social interests. It is not sufficient that resource users be charged the true value of environmental resources. They should also be enabled to respond appropriately. This section considers the implications of the research reported in Parts I and II for the incentives structures called for in Article 11 of the Convention on Biological Diversity.

We begin with the 'supporting structure of incentives and disincentives to induce the desired response'. Any change in the relative private cost of a resource has two effects: a substitution effect and an income effect. The substitution effect will always induce a substitution in favour of the resource whose relative price has decreased and against a resource whose relative price has increased. But the income effect may move in either direction. An increase in the price of a resource reduces the real income of the user. In most cases this will induce a fall in demand for the resource. However, for a large class of resources (inferior goods) the reduction in real income induces an increase demand for the resource. In the extreme case of Giffin goods the income effect outweighs the substitution effect, and an increase in the price of the good induces people to buy more of that good. The Giffin good is evidence of a form of poverty trap. Where income effects come close to dominating substitution effects, as is likely for many marginal environmental resources, it is important to ensure that resource users are not caught in such a poverty trap.

The evidence from developing countries remains patchy. There are few reliable estimates of the income and price elasticity of demand for environmental resources in those countries on which to base environmental policy. But such evidence as does exist suggests that resource users may not always be price-responsive. The study reported in Part II estimates supply responses to the changes in relative prices associated with structural adjustment in Ghana. While none of the responses reported are perverse, they are more sluggish than might be expected. In fact, long-run aggregate agricultural supply elasticities in many countries turn out to be low, and in some cases are even negative (Rao, 1989; Markandya, 1991).

Since the removal of agricultural subsidies elsewhere has often been claimed to be environmentally beneficial this is significant. A reduction in input subsidies will reduce the profitability of agriculture and so farmer income. If farmers increase output to compensate for the reduction in their income, the environmental consequences of the price change may be perverse. It follows that getting prices right may be a necessary condition for the efficient allocation of environmental resources, but is not sufficient. Because the income effects of price changes tend to be more pronounced at lower incomes, it is more important to consider the income effects of changing relative prices in developing than developed countries.

Although market-based incentives for biodiversity conservation do have considerable potential in developing countries, there are not many good working examples (OECD, 1992). Nonetheless, market-based incentives are used to manage a range of biodiversity-related environmental problems in developing countries. Some of the instruments in current use in developing countries are summarized in Table 9.4. The main options are tradable harvesting quota; taxes, subsidies and charges; penalties; financial incentives; liability and insurance; and environmental bonds and deposit refund systems.

Table 9.4   A typology of market-based incentives for environmental protection

	Property rights and market creation	Taxes and charges	Penalties	Financial incentives	Liability systems	Bonds and deposit–refund systems
Lakes and seas	fishing licences; tradable quota		fines; gear and boat seizures for breach of fishing regulations			oil spill bonds
Forests	logging concessions; forest management concessions; communal rights; concession bidding	taxes; royalties		reforestation incentives	natural resource liability	reforestation bonds; forest management bonds
Wildlife	hunting licences	access and park fees; hunting licences	poaching penalties			
Bio-diversity	patents; prospecting rights; transferable development rights	park fees; scientific tourism charges		debt-for-nature swaps	natural resource liability	

Source: Adapted from Panayotou (1994).

Tradable quotas allow individual resource users to trade use rights within the limits imposed by the quota. They offer a potentially efficient allocation mechanism behind an environmentally protective barrier. Formally, there are few working examples of tradable quotas in Sub-Saharan Africa, although there is obvious potential in marine and freshwater fisheries, and in the harvesting of other wild living resources. Informally, however, *de facto* tradable permit systems for resource use already exist in many parts of Sub-Saharan Africa. The extraction of fuelwood/water from Marsabit forest reserve described in Chapter 4 is a case in point. A recent study of fisheries on Lake George in Uganda has revealed a quite well-developed informal market in fishing rights (Kazoora, 1998). In some cases single permits are used by many different people, each of whom extracts resources up to the limit allowed by the permit. In such cases the permit limit is meaningless. Much could be done to improve both the efficiency of resource use and the effectiveness of permit systems if these informal markets in permits were regularized and permit limits enforced.

In similar vein, Panayotou (1994) has recommended a system of Transferable Development Right (TDR) for the conservation of biodiversity. The proposal is for developing countries to set aside habitats for biodiversity conservation, each being divided into a number of TDRs. Each TDR would state the location, condition, diversity, and a degree of protection of the habitat and any rights that are attached. Rights may include scientific research or genetic prospecting. The price would have to exceed the local opportunity cost for the community having ownership of the land to be interested. The mechanism provides a vehicle for the beneficiaries of conservation to pay the local opportunity cost. Debt-for-nature swaps may be seen as one application of the TDR principle, but without the efficiency that tradability offers.

Environmental taxes, subsidies and charges have been much more widely used in developing countries than tradable permits, and are also an effective way of confronting resource users with the social costs of their actions. The main problem with existing taxes, subsidies and charges is, however, that they do not reflect the social opportunity cost of the activity to which they apply. Reference has been made to the incentives offered by stumpage fees/royalties in forestry that bear little relation to the social opportunity cost of deforestation. Other examples include water extraction charges, hunting and fishing permit fees, destumping subsidies, land clearing subsidies, fuelwood permits. In some cases, fees and charges were established at a time when the resources to which they apply were not scarce, and have not subsequently been adjusted.

In others, they have been negotiated through the political process without reference to the state of the resource. In Botswana, for example, the set of agricultural subsidies, fees and charges has been inextricably linked with the system of rural drought relief (Perrings, 1996).

Another class of incentives, environmental bonds and deposit–refund systems, are a means of guaranteeing performance in cases where there is no effective means of supervision. Deposit–refund systems have been used for a considerable period of time and in a wide range of countries. Environmental bonds have a shorter history, but are now common in the management of the restoration of sites disturbed by mining or forestry. Both provide *ex ante* compensation for environmental risks that are difficult either to monitor or to control. Bonds can provide incentives to minimize the environmental damage caused by forestry; to restore damaged forest ecosystems; and can be used to compensate local communities if the system is not restored. Although common in logging concessions in Malaysia and other Southeast Asian countries, forest restoration bonds have not yet been employed much in Sub-Saharan Africa.

In general, deforestation occurs because the local benefits of conservation (in terms of the supply of fuelwood and construction timber, water and non-timber forest products) are low relative to the local opportunity cost of conservation (in terms of the provision of both timber and land for arable or pastoral production). Conservation requires an incentive structure that favours forest conservation and sustainable management. To be effective such an incentive structure should enhance the local benefits and lower the opportunity costs of conservation. The former implies the introduction of mechanisms to capture the value of conservation for local users. The latter implies the removal of subsidies on forest conversion, the provision of alternative employment opportunities, and the enhancement of agricultural productivity in existing croplands and rangelands.

One example of an instrument that enhances the benefits of conservation is the watershed protection charge. Although local communities do derive benefits from watershed protection, the main beneficiaries are often downstream users who benefit from both flood protection and water supplies. Those beneficiaries do not, however, pay for the watershed services provided by national parks or protected forests. In turn, local users have no incentive to conserve forests. The watershed value of forests may, however, be captured through water and hydropower pricing that includes a watershed protection charge. A working example of this is the Dunoga Bone Combined Irrigation and National Park System in Sulawaesi, Indonesia (Heywood, 1995). A second example addresses the problem of encroachment on protected areas discussed in Chapter 4.

This example – now common in developing countries – uses the expertise of local users hiring them as forest guards and tour guides (Heywood, 1995).

An instrument which raises the costs of conversion, and which should be readily adaptable to Sub-Saharan African conditions, is the differential land use tax. Forest uses (or any land uses) are classified according to the environmental damage they involve. Conservation of natural forest might be classified as environmentally benign, while conversion of forests for industrial production might be classified as environmentally destructive. Land that is converted from one use to another attracts an additional charge if the land use is more damaging, or a refund if the land use is less damaging.

In addition to these instruments, a range of instruments have been designed to capturing some of the global benefits of conservation. These include, for example, forest compacts and carbon offsets. Compacts are agreements between developed and developing countries to conserve forests for their role in carbon sequestration. Carbon offsets are simply a particular kind of forest compact involving joint implementation of a commitment to reduce CO_2 emissions. They may involve a developing country commitment to forest conservation on the one side, and credit for carbon saved or sequestered on the other side. The potential benefits stem from differential costs of CO_2 reductions in developed and developing countries. Such instruments may be induced by developed country commitments under the Convention on Biological Diversity, but they are beyond the scope of this study (see Pearce, 1994; Pearce and Brown, 1994; Brown, Adger and Turner, 1993).

9.6   INCENTIVES AND THE DISTRIBUTION OF INCOME

Finally, we return to the complex problem of the association between income, environmental policy and performance, responsiveness to incentives, and enforceability of protective regulations. It has already been observed that although Panayotou (1995) reported a Kuznets relation between deforestation and per capita income in a sub-sample of tropical countries, the relation is a very weak one. Using the same data set as Panayotou, Perrings and Ansuategi (1998) we show that there is no evidence for a Kuznets relation when the whole sample is considered. Although there is some limited support for a Kuznets relation between deforestation and three measures of performance – income, consumption and the human development index – when only tropical countries are considered, none of the models has much explanatory power. To test the Brundtland assertion about the link between poverty and biodiversity loss, the same study considers the relation between deforestation and a poverty index: IFAD's Integrated Poverty Index (M). The IPI is based on Sen's composite poverty index (Sen, 1976), and is calculated by combining a head count index of poverty, the income gap ratio, life expectancy at birth, and the annual rate of growth of per capita GNP.[1] The results are summarized in Table 9.5.

Table 9.5   Relationship between deforestation and welfare

A Per capita income

Variable	1 (a)	1 (b)
constant	−12.143	−11.713
	(−2.775)	(−2.727)
	(**−4.193**)	(**−4.223**)
INCOME	3.4554	2.8363
	(2.967)	(2.388)
	(**4.408**)	(**3.810**)
INCOME^2	−0.22903	−0.17854
	(−2.980)	(−2.234)
	(**4.354**)	(**−3.538**)
RUPOP		0.33465
		(1.887)
		(**1.466**)
Turning Point	1888.52	2815.90
Adjusted R^2	0.09	0. 13
F	4.44	4.27
B-P chi-squared	10.5324[2]	8.80976[3]
N	65	65

B Consumption

Variable	2(a)	2(b)
constant	−13.133	−12.677
	(−2.759)	(−2.718)
	(**−3.886**)	(**−4.223**)
CONSUMPTION	3.7966	3.1137
	(2.940)	(2.370)
	(**4.071**)	(**−2.205**)
CONSUMPTION^2	−0.25720	−0.19939
	(−2.955)	(−2.205)
	(**−4.026**)	(**−3.398**)

Table 9.5 continued

RUPOP		0.35359	
		(1.899)	
		(1.525)	
Turning Point	1604.61	2482.67	
Adjusted R²	0.09	0.12	
F	4.37	4.25	
B-P chi-squared	8.32347[2]	6.86583[3]	
N	6.2	62	
C Poverty			
Variable	3(a)	3(b)	3 (c)
constant	0.76108	0.55193	–0.57263
	(4.624)	(1.789)	(–0.626))
	(3.876)	**(2.011)**	**(–0.790)**
IPI	–0.00013595	0.010088	0.011776
	(–0.047)	(0.726)	(0.859)
	(–0.041)	**(0.789)**	**(0.915)**
IPI²		–0.00010221	–0.000095617
		(–0.733)	(–0.696)
		(–0.733)	**(–0.707)**
RUPOP			0.25224
			(1.708)
			(1.348)
Adjusted R²	–0.019(ERR)	–0. 02 (ERR)	0.007
F		4.09	5.38
B-P chi-squared	1.58669[1]	3.89546[2]	7.57929[3]
N	62	62	62

Notes
All variables are in logs.
t-statistics in parentheses, White's heteroscedasticity-corrected.
t-ratio in bold.

Source: Perrings and Ansuategi (1998).

There is little evidence in support of the hypothesis that biodiversity loss, at least, is driven by poverty in the developing world and by overconsumption in the developed world if environmental degradation is proxied by indicators of the type used in the EKC literature. It is worth recalling (a) that the results have been developed for single equation models based on cross-sectional data that assume away any feedbacks between environment and economy; and (b) that in no case is the indicator of environmental quality related to the assimilative or carrying capacity of the ecosystem concerned. To the extent that the results of this work do tell us anything, however, they tell us that the problem of habitat loss will not be resolved by growth-promoting policies.

Measures of economic performance are important, but for a different reason. They influence both the amount of information that policy-makers and resource users can command, and their response to information. Resource users are generally more concerned about the short-term environmental impacts of economic activity in their own neighbourhood than they are about long-term impacts occurring at geographically distant locations. There is empirical evidence that the measure of their concern for the wellbeing of future generations or those who live far away – the rate at which they discount future and distant costs – is a function of per capita income. The rate at which people discount the wider and future environmental costs of their actions appears to fall with income. Poverty induces people to behave as if they are myopic, while affluence allows people the luxury of 'caring' more about both future generations and distant members of the present generation (Holden, Shiferaw and Wik, 1998).

One implication of this has already been noted. It is that there is a real risk that market-based incentives may not work or may work in the 'wrong' direction. Another is that policymakers confronted with evidence that economic activities impose environmental costs on future generations may choose not to introduce corrective measures. Indeed, this is the main threat to the implementation of the Convention on Biological Diversity in many Sub-Saharan African countries. For highly indebted countries in which economic reform/structural adjustment is squeezing both public expenditure and private real disposable income, the prospects for the introduction of new biodiversity conservation measures that impose short-term costs on resource users are not good. But this should not imply inaction. Wherever it can be shown that biodiversity yields capturable local benefits it will be optimal to invest resources in its conservation. The studies in this volume have sought to identify what the direct and indirect local benefits of biodiversity conservation are in specific systems. These are admittedly only a sample of the managed ecosystems currently exploited in the region – freshwater fisheries, wetlands, forests and rangelands – but they are not unrepresentative.

The main points here are both that it is important that the structure of incentives reflects the real value of biological and other resources, and that users should be enabled to respond to changing incentive structures. Given that the non-existence of markets is a major cause of the divergence between the private and social cost of species deletion, and since the non-existence of markets reflects the incompleteness of property rights, an important component of an effective incentive structure is the allocation of property rights. This is particularly appropriate where the problem is one of local depletion as a consequence of some unidirectional externality. Though biodiversity in general is in the nature of a public good, the individuals and populations within a species are both exclusive and rival in consumption. Similarly, though many aspects of the biosphere are in the nature of a public good, many ecosystems and ecosystem services are similarly exclusive and rival in consumption. If it is possible to generate markets in these, it may be possible to remove the discrepancy between private and social cost – bearing in mind that the word 'market' can mean something much more general than the locus of price-based transactions. It includes, for example, all those institutions which facilitate negotiation between stakeholders (Dasgupta, 1991; Dasgupta and Mäler, 1991).

The effectiveness of such markets often depends on the distributional impact of changes in property rights. Property rights should not be allocated in such a way that they make it impossible for resource users to respond positively to signals about the scarcity of biological resources. Similarly, the indirect threat to biodiversity of high levels of indebtedness in the low income countries is what lies behind various proposals to reduce the debt burden of those countries, including the proposals to swap debt for 'nature'.

From a policy perspective, the distribution of the benefits of biodiversity conservation as between individual users of biological resources, nation states, regional groupings and the international community determines how effectively the problem may be addressed. The central argument of the studies reported in Parts I and II is that the main costs of biodiversity loss lie in the loss of ecosystem resilience and productivity. This implies that the main benefits of conservation will accrue to local users. This point is important. If the largest part of the social benefits of biodiversity conservation are local, not only is the problem easier to address at a national level, but the relative value of the transfers needed to induce international cooperation is reduced. The optimal policy response is a local one.

APPENDIX 9.1   DATA ON SUB-SAHARAN AFRICAN COUNTRIES USED TO EVALUATE THE LINK BETWEEN POVERTY AND DEFORESTATION

Country	INC	HDI	DEF	IPI	CONS	POPG	AG SHARE	RUPOP	EXP SHA
Angola	840	0.143	0.7	0.596		2.70	13.0	71.7	
Benin	1043	0.113	1.3	0.622	1022	3.00	37.0	62.3	20
Botswana	3419	0.552	0.5	0.434	2153	3.71	3.0	72.5	64
Burkina Faso	618	0.074	0.7	0.871	593	2.66	32.0	91.0	11
Burundi	625	0.167	0.6	0.805	618	2.91	56.0	94.5	8
Cameroon	1646	0.31	0.6	0.304	1349	3.27	27.0	58.8	21
Cape Verde	1769	0.479		0.360	1645	2.65	14.4	71.4	17
C.African Rep.	768	0.159	0.4	0.878	783	2.77	42.0	53.3	17
Chad	559	0.088	0.7	0.563	642	2.47	38.0	70.5	25
Comoros	721	0.269		0.472	764	3.45	35.8	72.2	41
Congo	2362	0.372	0.2	0.695	1653	3.16	13.0	59.5	49
Côte D'Ivore	1324	0.286	1	0.236	1138	3.78	47.0	59.6	37
Djibouti	1000	0.104		0.613	1040	2.88	4.0	19.3	47
Eq. Guinea	700	0.164		0.666	742	2.42	58.7	71.3	28
Ethiopia	369	0.172	0.3	0.643	346	2.67	41	87.1	13
Gabon	4147	0.503	0.6	0.166	2612	3.47	9.0	54.4	56
Gambia	913	0.086	0.8	0.826	830	2.89	34.1	76.8	68
Ghana	1016	0.311	1.4	0.524	914	3.15	48.0	67	21
Guinea	501	0.045	1.2	0.672	395	2.86	28.0	74.4	30
Guinea-Bissau	841	0.09	0.8	0.753	933	1.99	47.0	80.2	8
Kenya	1058	0.369	0.6	0.515	856	3.58	29.0	76.4	25
Lesotho	1743	0.431	0	0.497	2457	2.85	24.0	79.8	14
Liberia	857	0.222		0.212	702	3.16	37.0	54.1	43
Madagascar	704	0.327	0.8	0.499	647	3.18	33.0	76.2	15
Malawi	640	0.168	1.4	0.827	576	3.52	33.0	88.2	24
Mali	572	0.082	0.8	0.462	514	3.04	46.0	80.8	18
Mauritania	1057	0.140	0	0.766	1035	2.73	26.0	53.2	47
Mauritius	5750	0.794	0.2	0.087	4485	1.17	12.0	59.5	67
Mozambique	1072	0.154	0.8	0.675	1200	2.65	65.0	73.2	16
Namibia	1400	0.289	0.3		1190	3.19	11.0	72.2	55
Niger	645	0.080	0.4	0.348	632	3.14	36.0	80.5	16
Nigeria	1215	0.246	0.7	0.490	850	3.30	36.0	64.8	39
Rwanda	657	0.186	0.2	0.857	630	3.41	38.0	92.3	9
Senegal	1248	0.182	0.7	0.659	1135	2.78	21.0	61.6	26
Seychelles	4191	0.761		0.085	3688	0.60	6.0	43.0	48
Sierra Leone	1086	0.065	0.6	0.633	1031	2.49	32.0	67.8	17

Country	INC	HDI	DEF	IPI	CONS	POPG	AG SHARE	RUPOP	EXP SHA
Somalia	836	0.087		0.685	652	3.26	65.0	63.6	10
South Africa	4865	0.673	−0.8		3648	2.22	5.0	40.5	26
Sudan	949	0.152		0.807	930	2.88	36.0	78	8
Swaziland	2384	0.458		0.444	2026	3.44	23.2	66.9	90
Tanzania	572	0.270	1.2	0.592	600	3.66	59.0	67.2	18
Togo	734	0.218	1.5	0.288	653	3.07	33.0	74.3	41
Uganda	524	0.194	1	0.802	529	3.67	67.0	89.6	7
Zaire (Congo)	367	0.262		0.802	322	3.14	30.0	60.5	25
Zambia	744	0.314	1.1	0.791	617	3.75	17.0	50.1	32
Zimbabwe	1484	0.398	1.7	0.543	1172	3.16	13.0	72.4	32

Notes

Values for income (INC) are real GDP per capita (PPP$)1990 reported in the UNDP's Human Development Report 1993. Values for the Human Development Index (HDI) are from the same source. Annual deforestation rates during the 1980s (DEF) refers to the permanent conversion of forestland to other uses. Estimates of forest area are derived from country statistics assembled by the FAO and the UNECE. The data are reported in the Human Development Report 1997. Values for consumption (CONS) are obtained by multiplying income by the share of consumption (both private and public consumption) in GDP. Data on the share of consumption are from the World Tables 1992. These data refer to 1990. For some countries these are for the closest year to 1990. Values for the Integrated Poverty Index (IPI) are from Jazairy et al. (1992). Data on population growth (POPG) are from the UN population statistics. Data on agricultural share of GDP (AGSHARE) are from the World Bank's World Tables 1992. Data on rural population as percentage of total population (RUPOP) are obtained from the Human Development Report 1994. Data on the export of goods and non-factor services' share of GDP (EXPSHA) are obtained from the World Bank's World Tables 1992.

NOTE

1. The head count index is simply the percentage of the population below the poverty line. The income gap ratio is the difference between the highest per capita GNP in the sample and the per capita GNP of the country concerned, expressed as a percentage of the former. Life expectancy at birth is included as a proxy for income distribution below the poverty line. Using this measure it is possible to classify countries into three broad groups. An IPI of 40 or less indicates severe poverty; an IPI between 40 and 20 indicates moderate poverty; while an IPI of less than 20 indicates little poverty. The IPI used here was developed on the basis of data for a number of different years, but notionally describes the situation in 1988.

REFERENCES

Addison, A. and L. Demery (1989), 'The economics of rural poverty alleviation', in S. Commander (ed.), *Structural Adjustment and Agriculture: Theory and Practice in Africa and Latin America*, London: ODI, pp. 71–89.

Anderson, K. and R. Blackhurst (1992), 'Trade, the environment and public policy', in K. Anderson and R. Blackhurst, *The Greening of World Trade Issues*, Hemel Hempstead: Harvester Wheatsheaf, pp. 3–22.

Arrow, K.J., B. Bolin, R. Costanza, P. Dasgupta, C. Folke, C.S. Holling, B.-O. Jansson, S. Levin, K.-G. Mäler, C. Perrings and D. Pimentel (1995), 'Economic growth, carrying capacity, and the environment', *Science* **268**, 520–21.

Barbier, E.B. (1997), 'Introduction to the Environmental Kuznets Curve special issue', *Environment and Development Economics*, **2**(4), 357–67.

Beynon, J.G. (1989). 'Pricism v. structuralism in Sub-Saharan African agriculture', *Journal of Agricultural Economics*, **40**(3), 323–35.

Brown, G.M. and W. Henry (1993), 'The economic value of elephants', in E.B. Barbier (ed.), *Economics and Ecology: New Frontiers and Sustainable Development*, London: Chapman and Hall.

Brown, K., W.N. Adger and R.K. Turner (1993), 'Global environmental change and mechanisms for north–south resource transfers', *Journal of International Development*, **5**, 571–89.

Cruz, W. and R. Repetto (1992), *The Environmental Effects of Stabilization and Structural Adjustment Programs: The Philippines Case*, Washington DC: World Resources Institute.

Dasgupta, P. (1991), 'The environment as a commodity', in P. Blasi and S. Zamagni (eds), *Man-Environment and Development: Towards a Global Approach*. Rome: Nova Spes International Foundation Press, pp. 149–80.

Dasgupta, P. and K.-G. Mäler (1991), 'The environment and emerging development issues', in *Proceedings of the World Bank Annual Conference on Development Economics, 1990*, Washington DC: World Bank, pp. 101–31.

Fjeldså, J. and J.C. Lovett (1997), 'Geographical patterns of phylogenetic relicts and phylogenetically subordinate species in African forest biota'. *Biodiversity and Conservation*, **6**, 325–46.

Goldblatt, P. (1989), 'The genus Watsonia', Kirstenbosch: National Botanic Gardens.

Hamilton, A.C. (1976), 'The significance of patterns of distribution shown by forest plants and animals in tropical Africa for the reconstruction of Upper Pleistocene palaeoenvironments: a review', *Palaeoecology of Africa, the Surounding Islands and Antarctica*, **9**, 63–97.

Harper, J.L., J. Silvertown and M. Franco (1997), *Preface to Plant Life Histories: Ecology, Phylogeny and Evolution*, Cambridge: Cambridge University Press.

Hazell, P.B.R. (1987), 'Economic policy for diversification', in T.J. Davis and I.A. Schirmer (eds) *Sustainability Issues in Agricultural Development: Proceedings of the Seventh Agriculture Sector Symposium*, Washington DC: World Bank.

Heywood, V. (ed.) (1995), *Global Biodiversity Assessment*, Cambridge: Cambridge University Press.

Holden, S.T, B. Shiferaw and M. Wik (1998), 'Poverty, market imperfections and time preferences: of relevance for environmental policy?', *Environment and Development Economics*, **3**(1), 105–30.

Ikiara, M. (1998), 'Production technology and natural sustainability: the case of Kenya's Lake Victoria fisheries', mimeo, School of Environmental Studies, Moi University, Kenya.

Jazairy, I, M. Almagir and T. Panuccio (1992), *The State of World Rural Poverty*, London: IT Publications for IFAD.

Junankar, P.N. (1989), 'The response of peasant farmers to price incentives: the use and misuse of profit functions', *Journal of Development Studies*, **25**(2), 169–82.

Kazoora, C. (1998), 'The contribution of the undervaluation of the licensing system to the degradation of Lake George', mimeo, Sustainable Development Centre, Kampala.

Kramer, R.A., N. Sharma, P. Shyamsunder and M. Munasinghe (1994), 'Cost and compensation issues in protecting tropical rainforests: case study of Madagascar', Environment Department Working Paper, World Bank.

Lovett, J.C. (1996), 'Elevational and latitudinal changes in tree associations and diversity in the Eastern Arc mountains of Tanzania', *Journal of Tropical Ecology*, **12**(5), 629–50.

Lovett, J.C. (1998), 'Continuous change in Tanzanian moist forest tree communities with elevation', *Journal of Tropical Ecology*, **14**.

Lovett, J.C. and I. Friis (1996), 'Some patterns of endemism in the tropical north east and eastern African woody flora', in L.J.G. van der Maesen, X.M van der Burgt and J.M van Medenbach de Rooy (eds), *The Biodiversity of African Plants*, Proceedings XIVth AETFAT Congress, 22–27 August 1994, Wageningen, The Netherlands. Dordrecht: Kluwer Academic Publishers, pp. 582–601.

Markandya, A (1991), 'Technology, environment and employment: a survey'. World Employment Programme Research Working Paper, WEP 2-22/WP.216, International Labour Office, Geneva.

Markandya, A. (1995), 'Technology, environment and employment in Third World agriculture', in I. Ahmed and J.A. Doelman, *Beyond Rio: The Environmental Crisis and Sustainable Livelihoods in the Third World*, London: Macmillan, pp. 69–94.

McNeely, J. (1993), 'Economic incentives for conserving biodiversity – lessons for Africa', *Ambio*, **22**(2-3), 144–50.

Munasinghe, M. (1993). 'Environmental economics and biodiversity management in developing countries', *Ambio*, **22**(2–3), 126–35.

Munasinghe, M. and W. Cruz (1995), 'Economy-wide policies and the environment', World Bank Environment Paper 10, Washington, DC: World Bank.

Muramira, T.E. (1998), 'The impact of market liberalisation on the Lake Victoria fishery', mimeo, East African Development Bank, Nairobi.

Myers, N. (1988), 'Threatened biotas: "hot spots" in tropical forests', *The Environmentalist*, **8**, 187–208.

Myers, N. (1990), 'The biodiversity challenge: expanded hot-spots analysis', *The Environmentalist*, **10**, 243–56.

Nabbumba, R., M. Tumusiime and R. Ndyaberema (1998), 'Economic valuation of wetland resources in Uganda', mimeo, Economic Policy Research Centre, Makerere University, Kampala.

Naeem, S., L.J. Thompson, S.P. Lawler, J.H. Lawton and R.M. Woodfin (1995), 'Empirical evidence that declining species diversity may alter the performance of terrestrial ecosystems', *Philosophical Transactions of the Royal Society of London, Series B*, **347**, 249–62.

OECD (1992), *Economic Instruments for Environmental Management in Developing Countries*, Paris: OECD.

Panayotou, T. (1994), *Economic Instruments for Environmental Management and Sustainable Development*, Cambridge MA: Harvard Institute for International Development.

Panayotou, T. (1995), 'Environmental degradation at different stages of economic development', in I. Ahmed and J.A. Doelman (eds), *Beyond Rio: The Environmental Crisis and Sustainable Livelihoods in the Third World*, London: Macmillan, pp.13–36.

Panayotou, T. and P. Ashton (1992), *Not By Timber Alone*: *Economics and Ecology for Sustaining Tropical Forests*, Washington, DC: Island Press.

Panayotou, T. and K. Hupé (1995), *Environmental Impacts of Structural Adjustment Programs*: *Synthesis and Recommendations*, Cambridge MA: HIID.

Pearce, D.W. and K. Brown (1994), 'Saving the world's tropical forests', in K. Brown and D.W. Pearce (eds) *The Causes of Tropical Deforestation*. London, UCL Press, pp. 2–26.

Pearce, D.W. and J. Warford (1993), *World Without End*, Oxford: Oxford University Press.

Perrings, C. (1996), *Sustainable Development and Poverty Alleviation in Sub-Saharan Africa*: *The Case of Botswana*, London: Macmillan.

Perrings, C., K.-G. Mäler, C. Folke, C.S. Holling and B.-O. Jansson (eds) (1995), *Biological Diversity*: *Economic and Ecological Issues*, Cambridge: Cambridge University Press.

Perrings, C. and A. Ansuategi (1998), 'Sustainability, growth and development', paper presented to the ESRC Development Economics Study Group Workshop, University of Strathclyde, 20 March 1998.

Rao, J.M. (1989), 'Agricultural supply response: a survey', *Agricultural Economics*, **3**(1), 1–22.

Ricklefs, R.E. and D. Schulter (eds) (1993), *Species Diversity in Ecological Communities*, Chicago: University of Chicago Press.

Sebastian, I. and A. Alicbusan (1989), 'Sustainable development: issues in adjustment lending policy', Environment Department Divisional Paper 1989–6, World Bank, Washington DC.

Sen, A. (1976), 'Poverty: an ordinal approach to measurement', *Econometrica* **44**(2), 219–41.

Southgate, D. and H.L. Clark (1993), 'Can conservation projects save biodiversity in South America?' *Ambio*, **22**(2-3), 163–6.

Stevens, G.C. (1992), 'The elevational gradient in altitudinal range: an extension of Rapoport's latitudinal rule to altitude', *American Naturalist*, **140**, 893–911.

Tilman, D. and J.A. Downing (1994), 'Biodiversity and stability in grasslands', *Nature*, **367**, 363–5.

Tobias, D. and R. Mendelshon (1991), 'Valuing ecotourism in a tropical rainforest reserve', *Ambio*, **20**(2), 91–3.

Walker, B.H. (1998), *Environment and Development Economics*, in press.

Warford, J., A. Schwab, W. Cruz and S Hansen (1994), 'The evolution of environmental concerns in adjustment lending: a review', Environment Working Paper 65, Washington, DC: World Bank.

Wells, M.P. and K.E. Brandon (1993), 'The principles and practices of buffer zones and local participation in biodiversity conservation', *Ambio*, **22**(2–3), 157–72.

World Bank (1994), *Global Economic Prospects and the Developing Countries*, Washington DC: World Bank.

World Bank (1996), *Global Economic Prospects and the Developing Countries*, Washington, DC: World Bank.

World Resources Institute (WRI), (1994), *World Resources 1994–1995: People and the Environment*, The World Resources Institute in collaboration with the United Nations Environment Programme and the United Nations Development Programme, Oxford: Oxford University Press.

Index